THE ECONOMIC SUPERPOWERS
AND THE ENVIRONMENT

THE ECONOMIC SUPERPOWERS AND THE ENVIRONMENT
THE UNITED STATES, THE SOVIET UNION, AND JAPAN

Donald R. Kelley
MISSISSIPPI STATE UNIVERSITY

Kenneth R. Stunkel
MONMOUTH COLLEGE, NEW JERSEY

Richard R. Wescott
MONMOUTH COLLEGE, NEW JERSEY

W. H. Freeman and Company
SAN FRANCISCO

Library of Congress Cataloging in Publication Data

Kelley, Donald R.
  The economic superpowers and the environment.

  Bibliography: p.
  1. Environmental policy—United States.
2. Environmental policy—Russia.
3. Environmental policy—Japan.   I. Stunkel,
Kenneth R., joint author.   II. Wescott,
Richard R., Joint author.   III. Title.
HC110.E5K45   363.6   76—1003
ISBN 0-7167-0720-9
ISBN 0-7167-0721-7 pbk.

Printed in the United States of America

CONTENTS

PREFACE

This book's objectives and limitations are best explained in advance. Rather than have our readers search fruitlessly for what has not been done, we wish for them to know from the outset what we have and have not attempted to accomplish.

Three specific countries have been chosen for analysis. Among the world's nations they are clearly the leading producers, consumers, and polluters. Moreover, their political, economic, and social institutions exhibit important differences. We take it as fact that the nation-state is a basic unit of political organization. For better or worse, national sovereignties constitute the framework within which solutions to the environmental crisis must be found, barring the sudden and improbable emergence of effective world government. Thus we have attempted to provide some insight into the cogency and promise of existing value patterns and institutional structures to halt and reverse environmental deterioration in the United States, the Soviet Union, and Japan, the three indisputable economic giants of the modern world. Their performance and example, we believe, are crucial to the outlook and behavior of other nations, whether developed or developing.

Our unit of analysis, then, is the state and not entire regions. It might be illuminating to do comparative regional studies of Western Europe, East Asia, and Latin America, but we have not chosen that option. Some readers will lament the omission of Western Europe from this study. We can only respond that inclusion of Western Europe would have altered and frustrated our original purpose.

We have aimed not only to elucidate specific environmental problems and policies in the three countries, but to do so in a broad cultural, historical, political, and economic context. Serious engagement with the texture of reality demands wide rather than narrow focus when investigating a phenomenon so complex as the environmental crisis. Our analysis ranges over a spacious field of topics. No doubt all of them could be explored more deeply and documented copiously, but a line must be drawn somewhere. Hence the authors bear final responsibility for emphases, choice of topics, and selection of data that might legitimately invite dispute. In many respects the book is a pioneer study, so it goes without saying that in other hands a different study would have emerged.

The reader will note variations in the quantity and quality of data from one country section to the next. Such disparities reflect the uneven quality of sources and available knowledge. With respect to the Soviet Union, an obsession with secrecy has blocked access to certain types of information. Wherever possible the authors have tried to converge in their presentation of evidence, but irregularities are unavoidable. On the other hand, much care has been taken to use the latest factual material. Obviously many topics in this book deal with problems that are dynamic rather than static. Thus in some respects a situation may be getting better than we depict it, while in other instances it may be getting worse. Events tend to run ahead of knowledge in the environmental crisis, but changes are unlikely to be so dramatic in the near future as to invalidate our general observations and conclusions.

This book is not a thoroughly integrated comparative study—an impression that might be suggested falsely by a quick glance at the table of contents. At best it may be described as a quasi-comparative treatment of the three superpowers. A precise characterization might be: three detailed national profiles developed within a common topical framework. The profile of each country could be read separately, but our intention is that all three be studied together, and the book has been organized to facilitate and encourage that end. Readers are urged to make their own comparisons throughout. The authors have reserved the last chapter for their own explicit comparisons.

A word about the authorship of the book's three major divisions: The American part was contributed by Richard Wescott, the Soviet part by Donald Kelley, and the part on Japan by Kenneth Stunkel. The introduction and the conclusion were more or less collective efforts, though Stunkel wrote the former and Kelley the latter.

D. R. K.

K. R. S.

R. R. W.

June 1975

ACKNOWLEDGEMENTS

Many people have been connected directly or indirectly with the completion of this book. The authors extend grateful thanks to all. Some, however, must be singled out for special comment. Paul Ehrlich initially brought the project to the attention of W. H. Freeman and Company. Dennis Pirages, then political science editor, put the book under contract when it was little more than an idea and a prospectus. Subsequently he made valuable suggestions in the early stages of research and writing. Full and useful critiques of the first draft were provided by James Morrison of the University of Florida and Nobutake Ike of Stanford University. Portions of the manuscript benefited from the suggestions of Lester Milbrath and Frederick Inscho.

Donald Kelley profited from the comments of Cynthia Enloe of Clark University and the research assistance of Sally Kelley. He also owes thanks to W. A. D. Jackson and John M. Kramer for their assistance in securing certain materials for the Soviet section.

Kenneth Stunkel is indebted to Kenichi Baba and Kazu Kato of the International Affairs Division, Japan Environment Agency, for providing indispensable materials, arranging numerous interviews, and cooperating with the author in a hundred small ways. Mr. Kato was especially kind to volunteer his services as an interpreter for many interviews. Jun Ui of Tokyo University was both encouraging and a source of valuable information on both pollution and citizen's movements. The library staffs of Princeton University, Michigan State University, the Japan Documentation Center, Columbia University, and the Oriental Division of the Library of Congress were most helpful.

Sally Kelley, Mary Carol Stunkel, and Carol Wescott provided encouragement and assistance throughout the project. Special thanks are due to Sally and Mary Carol for many hours of typing and proofreading.

Kenneth Stunkel and Richard Wescott wish to acknowledge modest financial assistance from the Grant-in-Aid Committee for Creativity, Monmouth College.

INTRODUCTION

The substance of this study is a comparative analysis of three powerful nations—the United States, the Soviet Union, and Japan—in the context of their interaction with the environment. As leading producers, consumers, and polluters among the world's nations, these superpowers are conspicuous agents of environmental deterioration. How they conduct themselves in the near future is likely to have profound consequences not only for their own citizens but for all of mankind. Their perception of environmental imperatives may well make the difference between a planet with healthy life-support systems and sufficient resources for all and one universally impoverished by a crippled biosphere.*

---

*The "biosphere" is a tenuous region of the earth capable of generating and sustaining life. It extends roughly from the bottom of the deepest oceanic trench to a few miles above the surface of our planet. The term "ecosphere" suggests much the same life-sustaining film of atmosphere, water, and soil, but it includes the organisms that inhabit it and emphasizes the dependent interrelationships of its components and the physical-chemical-biological cycles by which it is activated and preserved. The ecosphere consists of myriad ecosystems, or local associations of plant and animal life adjusted to particular environmental conditions. An ecosystem is essentially a system for the production, distribution, and utilization of energy. The global ecosphere itself may be regarded as a massive organic mechanism which channels and balances the energy flows of ecosystems.

Although the environmental crisis is the background of this inquiry, it is not part of our objective to demonstrate the existence of such a crisis, or to argue *in extenso* that people and nations must begin to define their relations to the world and to one another in the ecological frame of reference. Those tasks have been accomplished elsewhere with detail, clarity, and force. We take for granted that anyone who wishes to understand the prospects of mankind in the second half of the twentieth century will have to acknowledge ecological imperatives. In this section we shall discuss briefly the main outlines of the environmental crisis. Thereafter we shall be concerned with illuminating the respective roles of three national cultures in that crisis.

THE ENVIRONMENTAL CRISIS

It is now established beyond a reasonable doubt that humans and their activities are disrupting the life-support systems of the planet at a serious rate. Indeed, there is compelling evidence that certain kinds of damage are too well advanced to justify complacency. Troubled scientists have warned that uncritical, unrestrained population growth, massive pollution, and uncontrolled energy consumption could result in calamities on a global scale: disastrous climatic changes, the annihilation of oceanic life, widespread famine and disease, and the breakdown of chemical-biological cycles essential to the maintenance of life itself. Among the experts there is disagreement about the length of time required for present trends to end in catastrophe, but there is little disagreement about the inevitable results. Recently thirty-three distinguished British scientists endorsed "A Blueprint for Survival" which calls for a "steady state" in production, consumption, and human numbers in order to prevent disintegration of the global ecosystem. A now famous computer simulation of what might be the consequences of continued pollution, economic expansion, and population growth *(The Limits to Growth,* [Meadows et al., 1972], researched by an interdisciplinary group at the Massachusetts Institute of Technology) concludes that "the limits of growth on this planet will be reached sometime within the next hundred years." Even if burgeoning populations and pollution were brought under control, according to the study, industrial growth alone would entail self-destruction within a few generations. Richard Falk recently headed the American wing of an international research team whose purpose was to examine mankind's prospects in the balance of this century. His conclusion, in part, states that

> the planet and mankind are in grave danger of irreversible catastrophe. . . .
> There are four interconnected threats to the planet—wars of mass destruc-
> tion, overpopulation, pollution, and the depletion of resources. They have

a cumulative effect. A problem in one area renders it more difficult to solve the problems in any other area. . . .

Another detailed M.I.T. study, *Man's Impact on the Global Environment* (Wilson and Matthews, 1970), points out that earlier in our history, the prevailing values assigned an overriding priority to the primary effects of applied science and technology: the goods and services produced. The secondary side effects, including pollution, were largely ignored. Paul and Anne Ehrlich, in their comprehensive *Population, Resources, Environment* (1972), chart the growing environmental threat, emphasizing that "the preservation of the diversity of life and the ecological systems of the earth are absolutely essential for the survival of man."

Testimony of this sort could be multiplied indefinitely from respected and scientifically impeccable sources. Prudent people should not discount or ignore these signals of planetary distress just because all the facts are not in (*all* the facts are never in) or because there are disputes among the experts about the severity of the crisis and its precise nature. Belief in the imminent extinction of the human species is not a necessary condition for confessing that dangerous events unprecedented in human history are now occurring on this planet.

Implied in all expressions of concern about biosphere deterioration is the ecological frame of reference. The premises underlying that frame of reference can be summarized briefly. First, all life on earth is a result of evolution. The entire global ecosystem (as well as local systems) has been fashioned and balanced by evolutionary processes in vast periods of geological time. Second, various components of the ecosphere (the atmosphere, water, soil, plant and animal life, as well as human life) are interdependent and sustained in delicate equilibrium. Third, the ecosphere, with its unimaginably complex interrelationships, is finite and susceptible to degradation. When its components and intricate cycles are degraded below a certain level (which knowledge at this stage cannot determine precisely), higher forms of life would no longer be viable, and below a still lower level, all life would perish. Fourth, the ecosphere is unique. No imaginable technology could recreate it in the event of collapse. Cessation of photosynthesis (the basic source of energy for all living things) or of fundamental chemical-biological cycles (carbon, nitrogen, phosphorous) would be irreversible. Consider the analogy of an extinct animal species: once a species has vanished, mankind is not in a position to reconstitute what nature required billenia to produce.

This ecological frame of reference, now invested with dramatic force by the environmental crisis, has added a new dimension to our understanding of our present circumstances and future prospects. Familiar, traditional, and still dominant frames of reference—political, social, economic, ideological, and religious—by which most human beings orient themselves are not structured to grasp the implications of degraded ecosystems. A shift to the ecological perspective calls for nothing less than a fundamental reorientation of human attitudes and behavior.

The "environmental crisis" itself may be understood as follows:

1.   It is global in scope. Industrial and domestic pollutants circulate throughout the atmosphere and hydrosphere of the planet. Some half million substances previously alien to the ecosphere are now discharged into it at the rate of millions of tons a year, and thousands of new chemicals are being devised annually. Toxic heavy metals like mercury are concentrated in oceanic food chains, and pesticides such as DDT are now found in most life forms, including polar bears and penguins in Antarctica. Smog has been detected over desolate stretches of ocean and in the polar regions. Contributors to *Man's Impact on the Global Environment* identify no less than eleven potent sources of global pollution which directly threaten the stability of the ecosphere (they are carbon dioxide, sulfur dioxide, nitrogen oxide, chlorinated hydrocarbon biocides, other hydrocarbons, particulate matter, toxic metals such as lead, mercury, and cadmium, oil, radionuclides, heat, and nutrients). Modern industrial states are extracting fossil fuels from the earth's crust in the billions of tons and releasing wastes resulting from their combustion into the ecosphere. Although the environmental crisis is more intense on the local level, where people are experiencing massive fish kills, dead or dying bodies of water, unhealthy air, declining soil fertility, and the like, it is the emergence of global symptoms, however imponderable at the moment, which should give pause to reasonable persons.

2.   Interferences with environmental balance on a global scale by a single species has no precedent in the history of the planet. Those who dismiss ecologists as apocalyptists in modern dress fail to understand that very little in our previous experience has prepared us to recognize or deal with deterioration of the global ecosphere. Physical, chemical, and biological processes that make the earth hospitable to life evolved and matured long before the emergence of *Homo sapiens*. During virtually all of mankind's relatively short history, the environment and its elaborate processes have been taken for granted without being comprehended. Human works and thoughts have proliferated largely outside of and prior to the ecological frame of reference. In the past there have been crises of disease, famine, war, social revolution, and rapid cultural change; civilizations and peoples have risen and fallen. Never, however, has there been a crisis of the global environment. Present difficulties are a direct result of human history. In the long perspective of his evolution as a culture-bearing animal with special endowments, man has drifted across the millennia on a collision course with

nature. In the past six hundred thousand to one million years human beings were never sufficiently numerous nor possessed of enough power to undermine the ecosphere. Ecological ignorance, insensitivity, and destructiveness were manifested on the local level, although the perimeter of "local" impact has expanded steadily with the march of centuries. As hunters and gatherers numbering less than five million persons in 10,000 B.C., we seem to have pursued many animal species to extinction. As agriculturists numbering more than a billion by 1850, we decimated forests, eroded soil, created deserts, fouled local waters, and continued to press on surrounding animal life. As producers and consumers of industrial goods, and as users of new energy sources, numbering four billion in 1974, we have entered a radical new phase of our discordant relationship with nature, one in which we have all the means necessary to undo the environment on a global scale. A multitude of severe local disruptions are running together to threaten one universal disruption. Thus the "crisis" of the environment in the second half of the twentieth century is utterly *sui generis*.

3.   The range and intensity of environmental problems appear to be expanding in ever smaller increments of time. Human numbers have increased from five hundred million in 1650 A.D. to four billion in 1974, doubling three times in a bit more than three hundred years, where better than six hundred thousand years were required to bring world population to the 1650 mark of five hundred million. The present population of the globe is expected to double again in a mere thirty-five years to more than seven billion, and reach fourteen billion by the year 2014, barring a population "crash" due to famine and disease or stringent population controls. The consumption of nonrenewable resources is increasing at an exponential rate. It is likely that in fifty years the level of industrial output throughout the world will have grown by a factor of five, again assuming that resources and energy hold out.* This enormous expansion of population and economic activity in so short a time can be expected to impose a staggering burden on the ecosphere solely as a result of energy consumption and the generation of pollutants.† In addition, there will be heavier pressure on the land to augment food production, more insistent exploitation of forests, fisheries, and mineral resources, less opportunity for other forms of life to exist unmolested, and heightened chances of significant imbalances in the chemical-biological cycles of nature.

---

*Where certain resources are plentiful, the question is whether there will be time, will, and investment capital to make them available. Demand is far ahead of supply (in the sense of what is available for use) and is likely to stay that way without restraints in population growth and consumption.

†Those who exult in the prospect of exploiting still vast reserves of fossil fuels in the earth's crust seldom ponder the consequences of releasing such a vast amount of waste and heat into the ecosphere in a brief period of time.

4.   The causes of the crisis are complex, therefore the solutions are also likely to be complex. Societies and governments have devoted comparatively little money or time to the understanding of environmental problems. Knowledge is full enough to assert that a crisis exists, and to predict the consequences which probably will ensue should present trends continue unabated. But knowledge is not adequate to pin down explicitly how grave present conditions are, or to say precisely when a point of no return will be reached in a given sector of the environment, for example, the collapse of oceanic food chains as a result of pesticide impact on photosynthesis in phytoplankton, or rapid climatic changes as a result of rising carbon dioxide and particulate levels in the atmosphere. Amassing such knowledge in a reasonable period of time will not be easy, even if financial and political support are forthcoming. Moreover, the nonscientist has difficulty coming to terms with what is already known in the environmental field. Instead of a set of discrete events which can be isolated from one another and manipulated individually, the citizen, politician, business man, or bureaucrat finds himself confronted with a dynamic system of interrelated events constantly shifting from one moment to the next. René Dubos has said, "all environmental problems are so tangled and at the same time so diffused that they cannot be effectively dealt with by the linear methods of the prestigious hard sciences." In general, the previous experience and interests of people have not prepared them to cope with an organic, systems approach to nature in which everything must be perceived as being related to everything else.

5.   Closely associated with all of these problems is a negative time factor. The longer proposed solutions are delayed, the more difficult they become. Both the magnitude of the problems themselves and the social costs involved in solving them seem to grow exponentially as time passes. Added to this dilemma is the lack of certainty as to when critical points of no return will be reached. We admit that fragile ecosystems can be pressed only to finite limits before damage becomes irreversible, but in reality we have little indication of when the point of imminent collapse will be reached.

Without further elaboration, the foregoing comprises our provisional understanding of the environmental crisis, which becomes intelligible only when discussed within the ecological frame of reference. That frame of reference points to biological realities of a finite, vulnerable, irreplaceable ecosphere whose equilibrium cannot be unbalanced with impunity, and informs us that rational management of the earth's resources must be guided by a sense of limits. In the wake of uncontrolled consumption and waste, individuals, societies, and nations cannot expect nature to make all the adjustments. It remains to be said that few persons on the planet comprehend or accept the ecological frame of reference. Pollution is viewed frequently as a mere inconvenience which one may or may not wish to tolerate. It is thought to be a matter of individual taste and values and not of survival. Only a handful of human beings see their needs, demands, and activities in the context of balanced life-support systems. Most people continue to look upon the earth and its resources as a bounty to be exploited without end, and upon man as an invincible solitary phenomenon standing apart from nature and its laws.

An ecological perspective on man's place in nature has yet to be given precedence over the special interests of political, social, and religious factions. In recent global conferences on population, food, and a law of the sea, relevant problems were largely ignored as various national groups squabbled and maneuvered in narrow, self-defeating gambits to achieve small political and ideological advantages. At the very moment in history when all the world's people are growing profoundly interdependent and require among themselves the closest cooperation, national sovereignties are multiplying and have congealed into hostile blocs.

When one is caught up in the ecological frame of reference, however, traditional problems and concerns are seen in a new light and take on fresh dimensions. As Robert Heilbroner (a rare economist who has begun to think ecologically) has remarked, "who cares, in the perspective of ultimate environmental safety, if institutions of present-day capitalism and socialism disappear?" The conventional preoccupations of economists may seem anachronistic. Elaborate analyses of how existing economic systems function, of interest rates, market conditions, and fluctuations of gross national product may suggest a farmer counting chickens in a henhouse about to burn down. Economists on the whole have not heeded Barry Commoner's admonition in *The Closing Circle* (1971): "the lesson of the environmental crisis is . . . [that] if we are to continue to survive, ecological considerations must guide economic ones." With a few notable exceptions, the most distinguished economists have not attempted to formulate economic practices and institutions that might harmonize with the environment. In the political arena it is doubtful whether the security of nations and the well-being of peoples can be assured solely through diplomatic maneuvering and balance-of-power strategies without national and international institutions designed to preserve a healthy ecosphere. Deterioration of the environment may well constitute the gravest danger to "national security" in this century. By failing to shift priorities in time, and by neglecting to alert their peoples to the need for ecologically responsible behavior, the world's statesmen are open to the charge of destructive negligence. Governments are not prepared to admit that ecological considerations must guide political ones. Yet one can question the sanctity of national sovereignty solely on the ground that nations cannot keep their pollution to themselves. The ecosphere is bigger and more important than any nation. The destruction of animal species, the poisoning of air and water on a sizable scale, and the obliteration of unique ecosystems are dangerous acts which transcend the mere internal affairs of a state.

The ecological frame of reference also cuts down to proper size the power and promise of technology. Widely viewed as a form of secular magic whose proven virtuosity can solve any problem, technology is the perpetual trump card of the optimists. But technology is a significant cause of the environmental crisis, and it is unrealistic to suppose that technology alone can heal its own ravages and reverse undesirable environmental trends. No imaginable technology can restore an extinct species, purify contaminated food chains, or create *de novo* the fundamental chemical-biological cycles of nature. Uncritical faith in anticipated or unknown technological solutions to environmental problems is a naive form of dependence on a single escape route. Moreover, piecemeal reliance on technology is just the opposite of the systems approach to nature in which everything must be seen as related to everything else. Too often the appeal to technological solutions is a substitute for individual prudence and national self-restraint. The secret hope is that people and nations will not be obliged to make sacrifices and that science will take up the slack, providing easy, mechanical answers to problems which are rooted in unwise, prodigal human behavior. The overriding problems of the modern world are human, not scientific. Although technology offers much in the way of immediate help, it is foolish to expect miracles if human societies cannot muster the will to accept the most elementary steps toward self-discipline and self-preservation. Technical solutions to many of the globe's problems exist but cannot be implemented without a willingness to invest money and brainpower, to take into account the environmental impact of technology, and to alter sociopolitical-religious patterns standing in the way of implementing those solutions. The implication is that disaster can overtake nations and peoples in the midst of highly sophisticated knowledge and technical power. The latter are useless without the will to use them.

ECONOMIC SUPERPOWERS AND THE ENVIRONMENT

The dominant form of political order on this planet is the nation-state system. That system, as well as the values, commitments, and attitudes associated with it, is *pre-ecological*, which is to say it came into existence to deal with needs and problems largely unrelated to the preservation of a stable ecosphere. It is by no means obvious that the environmental crisis can be resolved satisfactorily by a swarm of sovereign states in active competition with one another for resources and energy. How three of the largest economic powers are responding to the crisis may shed light on the capacity of pre-ecological institutions to make swift and effective adjustments to the new realities.

The United States, the Soviet Union, and Japan are major contributors to the environmental crisis, and the three have more in common than may be suggested by their diverse cultural backgrounds and ideological differences. First, they are growth-oriented, especially in the area of economic expansion. Second, they are already prodigious consumers of energy and expect to use substantially more in the next decade because of continued economic growth. Energy consumption may well be a definitive index of "modernization," for the ability to tap large quantities of energy implies automatically other features commonly associated with the modernized nation-state: industrialization, mechanized agriculture, high gross national product, sophisticated technology, efficient bureaucracies, a high literacy rate, and secularized, "progressive" beliefs about the desirability of material progress. Marion Levy has suggested that a capacity for high energy consumption and modernization should be regarded as synonymous: "In general the higher the multiplication of the applications of energy by tools the higher the level of modernization. The greater the ratio of energy from inanimate sources to that from animate sources the higher the level of modernization." With respect to this criterion, the three superpowers are among the world's most "modernized" states. Third, all three nations have an impact on both the local and global ecosystems far out of proportion to their population sizes. Indira Gandhi correctly observed at the Stockholm Conference "that when it comes to the depletion of natural resources and environmental pollution, the increase of one inhabitant in an affluent country, at his level of living, is equivalent to an increase of many Asians, Africans, or Latin Americans at their current material levels of living." The biologist Wayne Davis estimates that an American, in the course of his life, will consume at least twenty-five times more of the world's resources and generate twenty-five times more waste than an Indian or Chinese. Fourth, all three nations have aggressive nationalist traditions. They take pride in being "great nations" as measured by growth rates, economic influence, and military power (for the time being, Japan is an exception in the last instance, having channeled nationalist ambitions toward economic goals since 1945). Fifth, all three countries industrialized early, in the middle and late nineteenth or early twentieth centuries, long before the emergence of most nations in the underdeveloped world. In spite of wars, depressions, and other setbacks, this historical advantage has been maintained, enabling the three superpowers to capture a major share of global resources, world trade, and leverage in the world economy. Their respective social orders and nationalist aspirations have come to depend on benefits accruing from those advantages. A closer look at this picture is in order.

Of some 144 nation-states on the planet, the United States, the Soviet Union, and Japan preempt the bulk of nonrenewable resources. With fifteen to sixteen percent of the world's people, they harness more than sixty percent of the world's available energy each year and contribute a corresponding burden of pollutants to the environment. The United States alone, with only six percent of the world's population, devours some thirty-five percent of accessible energy and discharges an equivalent amount of waste into the atmosphere and the oceans. The combined gross national product (GNP)* of the three superpowers exceeds that of all other nations on earth together. In the ecological frame of reference, GNP is not just a measure of national wealth but of *impact on the environment* as well. Gargantuan GNP's signify utilization of energy and creation of waste on a colossal scale. American economists are confident that the United States will triple its present GNP of one trillion dollars in thirty years. Japanese economists argue enthusiastically that Japan will race ahead of the United States. Looking ahead a mere five years, the optimistic projection for 1980 (in U.S. dollars) is $1,900,000 million for the United States, $800,000 million for the Soviet Union, and $800,000 million for Japan. The only other area of significant economic expansion will be the European Economic Community, whose nations are expected to reach a combined GNP of $870,000 million, slightly more than the Soviet Union or Japan. To put these figures in some kind of useful perspective, consider that altogether some twenty-eight developed nations, aggregating roughly thirty percent of the world's people, presently consume better than eighty percent of the world's resources every year, leaving two thirds of humanity to manage the tasks of living with the remaining twenty percent. Obviously the superpowers are dramatically positioned in this scheme of things, in relation to both

---

*GNP is the total market value of a nation's output of goods and services in a given year. It is a crude, convenient, commonly used measure of productivity and economic growth. Unfortunately GNP has come to be equated with progress, national strength, and public well-being. The average citizen, many economists, and most politicians assume that a nation is better off in proportion as its GNP creeps or soars to higher levels. A static or falling GNP tends to be viewed with alarm; the economy is "stagnant," as the expression goes. However, GNP is not a measure of social and economic well-being, nor does it provide clues to the status of environmental quality. A high GNP may well be accompanied by poor housing, substandard medical care, high infant mortality, low per capita income, and a polluted, despoiled environment. Many goods and services included in the GNP are irrelevant to the quality of life. Thus a large defense budget nearly always drains energy and resources while contributing little to education, health, and economic security of most citizens. In the ecological frame of reference GNP is an indicator of how much energy a society consumes, and indirectly of how much waste it ejects into the ecosphere. In general, given the character of existing industrial technology, the larger the GNP the greater the environmental impact. GNP alone cannot tell us if energy is being used wisely in the interests of a better life in a sound environment.

developed and developing countries. They are, in truth, the industrial and economic lords of the contemporary world. If there is to be a meaningful and dramatic example of consumer discipline, energy conservation, and institutional adjustment to environmental realities, one that might guide and influence lesser nations, it will have to come from the big three. If the giants are unwilling to control their appetites and waste, and regulate their size, other nations will be less motivated to do so. At the same time, the poor of the world will be obliged to struggle through their short, painful lives without hope.

CHAPTER

1

THE CULTURAL AND ECONOMIC SETTING

HISTORICAL PERSPECTIVE

THE UNITED STATES

From the earliest decades of colonization to the twentieth century, Americans have celebrated and largely taken for granted the seemingly endless bounty of their land. In some three centuries they have shaped a nation of 3.6 million square miles through settlement, annexation, conquest, and purchase. It ranges from the Virgin Islands and Puerto Rico in the Caribbean across the southern half of North America westward to Hawaii and northward to Alaska, and thus illustrates a striking variety of climate and topographical patterns. Mountain ranges and plains alternate in the continental United States, broken up and drained by mighty rivers. In the north are those vast glacial basins known as the Great Lakes, a boon to industry and transportation. In the twentieth century, America's population, industry, and pollution crowded into the northeastern corner of the nation that extends southward from Boston to Washington, D.C., and thence westward through Pittsburgh and Cincinnati to Kansas City, and northward to the Great Lakes. This vast American domain was rich in forests, minerals, agricultural land, and majestic waterways, which were to be exploited with only a passing thought about limits or the effects of pollution.

Recent American awareness of environmental disruption is not without precedent. From the eighteenth century onward some notice was taken of clogged waterways used by sawmills and other fledgling industries, the disappearance of spawning grounds blocked by waterpower dams, the fouling of once pure streams by sewage, and urban air heavy with soot and fumes from domestic heating units and factories. By mid-nineteenth century, larger cities were already glutted with people, streets were soiled with refuse, and water supplies were frequent sources of disease.

In the eighteenth century there was occasional legislation to curtail isolated environmental damage, but no coherent policy or program emerged. Symptoms were dealt with piecemeal and weak enforcement vitiated what few laws there were. Environmental deterioration seemed inevitable, a distasteful but necessary concomitant of progress. The majority of Americans prior to the Civil War, immured as they were in rural settings, simply did not perceive the integrity of nature as a serious problem. They took what they wanted from the environment and seldom asked how it came to be there or how it might be replenished.

In the latter half of the nineteenth century, the pace of population growth, urbanization, and industrialization picked up, and was accompanied by worsening environmental conditions. Pollutants increased markedly in both quantity and type. The air, bodies of water, and open lands around cities functioned as cheap, convenient dumping sites for wastes. Now and then objections were raised and steps taken to protect such areas as Yellowstone Springs and the Adirondack Mountains. Although a few state governments formed commissions to promote efficient use of specific resources like forests and fish, most bluntly ignored the complaints and danger signals (Ekirch, 1973; Nash, 1973; Udall, 1963).

Not until the early twentieth century did a significant conservation movement develop before the prodding of professional resource managers like the forester Gifford Pinchot, and politicians like Theodore Roosevelt. The movement was a response to an evident dwindling of known mineral resources, the decimation of virgin forests, and a decline in the fish and game available to sportsmen. It was also an integral expression of the political movement known as progressivism, which stressed, among other things, the use of government power, guided by scientific knowledge and democratic principles, to solve national, social, and economic problems. The progressive conservationists pushed into existence a substantial body of legislation at state and national levels that aimed at the rational management of resources. For the most part, however, these laws had more form than substance, and in practice the exploitation of nature continued largely unchecked (Hays, 1959; Richardson, 1962; McConnell, 1954; Fleming, 1972).

By the 1920's progressivism had faded away, but its enthusiasm for scientific management and research remained active in the business community. Both the commitment to resource management research by industry and the allocation of funds to seek out untapped resources grew rapidly. Science and technology linked up more closely than before to devise means for their exploitation.

The amalgam of science, technology, and business interests not only fostered the continued growth of older industries, but also spawned new industries that fostered economic expansion at great environmental cost. The development of electric power raised manufacturing productivity and the material standard of living, but also polluted the air through the combustion of fossil fuels in huge amounts. The spread of automotive transportation entailed mobility and productivity, but exacted the price of long-term environmental costs, voracious energy consumption, and expropriation of land for roadways. The multifaceted petrochemical industry listed among its benefits better agricultural productivity from the use of chemical fertilizers and pesticides, but contributed heavily to air, water, and soil pollution. The aviation industry promoted mobility and cohesion within the nation and helped to end American isolation from the rest of the world, but promoted a new dimension of air and noise pollution, energy demands, and pressure on scarce land in urban areas for airports (Rosenberg, 1972).

American urbanization and industrialization continued to accelerate between World War I and the 1970's, with only a temporary slump in the depression era. Demand for iron, steel, coal, oil, gas, water, and food rocketed ahead during these years, stimulated particularly by the economic growth associated with World War II. By the 1970's the industrial might of the United States was an overpowering national and global reality. With six percent of the world's people, it consumes annually some thirty-five percent of the world's available resources, while generating proportionate burdens of harmful wastes. While Americans have been proud of their technical and industrial preeminence, it was only in the 1950's that persuasive environmental thinking began to remind them that being an economic superpower is a mixed blessing with profound ecological consequences (Commoner, 1971; Galbraith, 1958).

THE SOVIET UNION

The Soviet Union is a vast nation, covering one-sixth of the earth's land area and containing eight and one-half million square miles. Stretching six thousand miles from east to west, it encompasses eleven time zones.

Ranging three thousand miles north to south, it includes several climatic zones, from the frigidness of the European north and Siberia to the searing heat of central Asia and the subtropical Mediterranean climate of Georgia. In the most populous and industrially advanced sections of European Russia, the climate is typically continental, with wide-ranging extremes of summer heat and winter cold.

Three geographic zones are relevant here. The Eurasian plain, which includes European Russia and Western Siberia, is the nation's breadbasket and industrial heartland. It contains seventy percent of the population and accounts for eighty percent of industrial and agricultural production. The second and third regions—the Central Siberian Plateau and Highlands and Soviet central Asia—have become in recent years prominent investment targets for Soviet industrialists who wish to draw on their immense natural resources. While historically the industrial stepchildren of more developed European Russia, they are slated for rapid development in coming years (Lydolph, 1964).

Rapid industrial growth since the revolution brought in its wake all the woes of quick-paced and uncontrolled urbanization. From the ecological perspective, a twofold threat confronted the environment. The growing population density of urban industrial centers concentrated human waste and refuse to the point of overloading sewer and disposal systems, but the construction of new facilities was almost nonexistent in the early years because of capital scarcity. Water supply systems also proved inadequate even in better developed cities (Goldman, 1972b:88–101).

The second threat came from the new industries, which released an increasingly potent brew of pollutants. Little concerned with short-term consequences of their actions, political leaders and industrialists alike strove for top speed in the development of heavy industry and the extraction of needed resources from the earth. Scant funds were laid aside for pollution control or environmental restoration. Soviet officials have admitted that widespread deterioration of air quality began with the first five-year plan from 1929 to 1934. In 1926, several years before the advent of centralized planning, a million cubic meters of waste water were dumped into once pure streams and rivers; by the early 1950's this volume had increased twenty-seven times (Mote, 1971:59; Pryde, 1972:138). Despite the lengthening catalogue of harmful wastes, pollution was regarded as a local affair until the late 1950's and early 1960's, when the sheer magnitude of the problem compelled Soviet leaders to take belated measures (Goldman, 1972b:296). While limited in scope and poorly enforced, the enactment of these regulations signaled a new concern.

These formal regulations were by no means the first attempt to legislate environmental controls. The earliest conservation laws of tsarist times were limited to the protection of game animals in special preserves for the nobility. Peter the Great extended the principle of wildlife protection to forbid the hunting of species like sable, elk, and beaver. Forest preserves were also established, although Catherine the Great rescinded these regulations in 1782; nevertheless, the protection of wildlife continued. Early nineteenth-century industrialization led to uncontrolled exploitation of then unprotected forests until 1888, when cutting limitations were established (Pryde, 1972:9–13). But the damage had already been done; great timber stands were laid waste, which promoted in turn wide-scale erosion of fertile farmland.

Decrees for the protection of forests, park zones, and wildlife had been issued in the first years of Soviet rule, but compliance was the exception rather than the rule, for wild animals were killed for food and forests cut for fuel during the Civil War. A central office for the fishing industry was also created to protect spawning grounds, and a number of local wildlife preserves were set up under the auspices of the Agriculture Commissariat. Regulations were issued also to control the discharge of sewerage and to maintain the purity of domestic water supplies. The impact of these efforts was limited, however, in large part because of Civil War and its attending chaos.

During the 1920's, responsibility for the environment was vested in the Interdepartmental State Committee on Nature Preservation, which consisted of representatives from various government ministries. In 1933 this committee was abolished and replaced by a Committee on Natural Preserves and all other environmental problems. Late in the decade, executive authority was decentralized to similar committees formed at the union-republic level. Legislative output from 1920 to 1940 was sparse; a few regulations establishing sanitary zones around factories and protecting water supplies were enacted, but they were rarely enforced (Pryde, 1972:13–15).

The nation's first air-pollution law was passed in 1949, defining air quality standards and creating a Chief Administration of the Sanitary Epidemiological Service to monitor compliance. A major turning point in environmental legislation was reached between 1957 and 1964, when all fifteen union republics wrote comprehensive environmental laws. The 1960's and 1970's have witnessed an outpouring of environmental laws and regulations. While the impact of these enactments will be discussed at length in a subsequent chapter, a brief summary will suggest their variety. Soviety authorities in the 1960's penned additional measures to protect water resources, preserve Lake Baikal, regulate sewage and mine wastes, protect beaches, limit air pollution, conserve timber and wildlife, and forestall soil erosion. A new public health law of 1969 deals in part with environmental health, and a 1970 water resources law takes up all aspects of water pollution (Goldman,

1972b:293–299). Fresh attention has been focused on enforcement agencies and sterner penalties, and a central monitoring agency was established in 1973. While problems remain, especially in the area of enforcement, the last two decades have seen an environmental awakening for Soviet policy makers.

JAPAN

Japan is a fragile land markedly inhospitable to large numbers of people, sprawling urban centers, and massive industrialization. Her 142,726 square miles (about the size of California) comprise a long stream of islands, with most of the population crowded onto Honshu, the largest of them. About one fifth of the total land area is level ground, the remainder consisting of mountains and forests. Only about 16 percent of the land can be lived on comfortably or farmed profitably. Natural resources are neither plentiful nor diverse, except for timber and the rapidly diminishing bounty of the sea. In these beautiful but precarious islands, three percent of the world's people are now living on 0.3 percent of the world's total land mass.

Out of materially unpromising circumstances the Japanese have fashioned in the past hundred years one of the globe's mighty industrial states. This meteoric rise from an obscure, insular, agricultural status to the position of an economic colossus has exposed a new dimension of fragility. Japan is a land exceptionally vulnerable to the ravages of pollution. In recent years the phenomena of rapid industrialization, population growth, and urbanization have moved this inherent fragility into sharper focus.

The center of Japanese life and cultural history lies in a confined area along the southeastern side of the archipelago roughly between northern Kyushu and modern Tokyo. Only along this narrow strip are there large tracts of agricultural land, the most extensive being the Kantō Plain, between which access and communication are relatively easy. In this area one finds all of Japan's historic capitols, the six largest cities, the bulk of industrial and agricultural activity, and half the cities with more than one hundred thousand people. The industrial corridor running from Tokyo-Yokohama to Nagoya-Osaka-Kobe accounts for nearly three fourths of the nation's total production. Factories crowd into ports on the Pacific side where raw materials are shipped in, and add their effluent to the waste generated by huge urban populations. The outcome of these unique geographical circumstances, combined with Japan's pattern of historical development, is a degree of concentrated environmental devastation hard to observe elsewhere.

During the long sway of the Tokugawa Shogunate (1603–1868), there was undoubtedly some perceptible environmental impact due to the pressure of the population on arable land and water systems, but there is no evidence of serious disruption. Energy was supplied by water, wind, humans, and animals. Human waste was returned to the soil to help maintain its fertility. The Japanese relied chiefly on fish for protein, as they continue to do, and consequently made few demands on other forms of animal life. Houses were built of natural materials with a frequently sensitive and even exquisite regard for harmonization with natural surroundings.* The Tokugawa regime's practical and ideological bias against commerce, industry, trade, and finance was shored up by a borrowed philosophical system, Chinese Neo-Confucianism, whose principles rationalized agrarian economics, ethnocentrism, change within tradition, and the harmonious interaction of man with nature. The aim of Tokugawa leadership was to forestall political, social, and economic change in order to sustain indefinitely a hierarchical, feudal system that lasted in fact for better than two and a half centuries. It was a type of civilized order that did not lend itself readily to aggressive or dangerous confrontations with nature (Fairbank et al., 1965:180–194).

The relations of samurai warriors with their lords and the precarious life of most Japanese in rural villages shaped basic social values that continue to live and operate in modern Japan. In the first instance the paramount virtues were loyalty, devotion to duty, the fulfillment of defined obligations, and personal discipline. In the villages survival depended on group cooperation and the subordination of individual wills to the imperatives of collective welfare (hence the folk saying, "a protruding stake will be driven into the ground"). Group dynamics were regulated by a stress on conformity, seniority, and consensus. The structure and function of small groups in traditional Japan are linked with the pattern of human relations to be observed in the contemporary government office and business enterprise (Ike, 1973:30–32; Crawcour, 1974).

In spite of official government hostility, commerce and finance developed with remarkable speed in Tokugawa Japan. The agents of this forbidden change and "progress" were the canny townsmen (chōnin), excluded by custom and law from participation in the political and social life of the country. This ostensible disadvantage left them free to concentrate on business, yet they shared the group-oriented values of the samurai and the peasants. The townsmen were a nascent Japanese "middle class" which enriched itself at the expense of the ruling military aristocracy by monopolizing trade and exploring the possibilities of a money economy. While dealing in a profusion of luxuries, staple goods, and services to accomodate needs of the ruling elite, the townsmen themselves became formidable consumers. Thus at least one important segment of Japan's Old Regime

*The ideal was *shibui* (literally "astringent," or unostentatious).

was committed exclusively to economic growth and the gratification of rising expectations (Sansom, 1964:111–130).

The Meiji Restoration of 1868 abolished the feudal institutions of the past and inaugurated an intensive process of modernization. The period from 1868 to 1945 saw population growth, west coast urbanization, and economic development advance swiftly in conjunction with ever higher energy consumption and the first manifestations of environmental trouble. Population more than doubled in less than seventy-five years. Both light and heavy industries grew impressively, though textiles and shipping predominated. By 1918 Japan had become one of the world's formidable industrial powers.

Environmental pollution was a noticeable consequence of these trends. On the industrial front, textile plants, paper mills, and copper mines were the leading offenders. All three became heavy polluters of waterways by the end of the century, the most celebrated case being that of the Ashio Copper Mine on the Watarase River (Strong, 1972). Severe air pollution made its appearance. Heavy smoke from coal burning plagued Osaka, Tokyo, and Yahata. As cities grew the volume of sewage increased, but little was done to reduce its effect on water systems. Noise and bad odors multiplied wherever industry and large numbers of people came together. In the Tokyo commercial center known as Nihon-bashi, officials estimated that in 1927 some eighteen tons of soot were deposited on a one-square-kilometer area in one month (TMG, 1971:19–25).

Occasionally reform was in the air. Some ordinances were passed to regulate the proximity of factories to schools, hospitals, government buildings, and, of course, the Imperial Palace in Tokyo. However, the blunt truth is that legitimate grievances and complaints were seldom heeded. Industrialization and urbanization were symbols of national power and prestige. Pollution was merely an annoying side effect at worst and a mark of progress at best. Thus the government invariably defended and protected industrial and business interests. Cities were allowed to sprawl outward without planning, for the money was thought to be better spent on factories and armies. Whenever Japan was at war (as she was nearly a half dozen times between 1895 and 1945), dissatisfaction with environmental quality was regarded as unpatriotic.

After the Second World War the Japanese people recovered their identity and self-esteem in a prodigious feat of economic reconstruction (Kosaka, 1972). Once more the environment became an issue, but with a range of problems and threats difficult to grasp.

Cities have exploded upward and outward; factories have proliferated throughout the country, though chiefly in the Tokyo–Osaka corridor; energy consumption has soared; population has leaped ahead; and undreamed of environmental horrors have appeared. Referred to as "kogai"—public hazard or nuisance—by the Japanese, pollution has spread across the land. Few rivers or lakes are uncontaminated. Ports and bays, the Inland Sea, and most estuaries are laced with oil, filth, and effluent. Once teeming fisheries are impoverished enough to drive fishermen thousands of miles from home for a catch. Photochemical smog over Tokyo and other cities has a distinctive and unusually toxic composition. The Japanese have paid a high price for their status as an economic superpower, a price the magnitude of which has become evident only in the past decade (Ui, 1972; Iyer, 1972; Kobayashi, 1970).

ATTITUDES TOWARD NATURE AND IDEOLOGY

THE UNITED STATES

The dominant attitude of most Americans toward nature from the earliest years of settlement to the present has been a tendency to use it for the sake of material benefits. In remoter times this meant subduing the wilderness and clearing the land for crops. By the late eighteenth century the ideal environment was seen as a kind of pastoral landscape, celebrated by Jefferson and later depicted in Currier and Ives prints, in which people and animals mingled amicably in a neat setting of open cultivated fields, trees, and streams. This idealized landscape was to be covered with self-sufficient farms on which families would rationally use—but never exploit—the bounty of nature. This image remained strong in American thinking well into the twentieth century, even when it was belied by the steady development of large-scale commercial farming.

In the first half of the nineteenth century, writers, poets, and artists swayed by the Romantic movement presented an image of unspoiled nature that contrasted sharply with an emerging urban and industrial landscape. For them the forest glens, wild river gorges, and craggy mountains were inspirational sights capable of arousing subtle, powerful feelings toward nature and insight into God. Untamed nature was regarded as a spiritual tonic for the American character.

By the middle of the nineteenth century most of the nation's political and economic leaders favored rapid exploitation of the environment to speed up economic growth. Stable pastoral landscapes and the inspirational values of wilderness were of no interest to them. Progress, defined as economic growth, was to be measured by the virgin land brought under cultivation, the forests felled, and the minerals extracted from the earth. Industrial and municipal wastes were to be dumped in the easiest and cheapest sites. In the twentieth century, despite scattered warnings that such practices might kill the goose laying the golden eggs, America's political and business elite generally proclaimed economic growth as central to the quality of life (Ekirch, 1973; Nash, 1973; Udall, 1963; Huth, 1957; L. Marx, 1967).

The past decade has seen a subtle merging of the pastoral and industrial images of America. The celebration of nature *qua* nature has been the focus of renewed attention, a result of both new environmental awareness and a pressing desire to escape the din and congestion of inner cities and less than idyllic suburbs. The emerging point of view is a not yet clearly defined, or politically accepted, balance between the idea of nature preservation, which includes both conservation and pollution abatement, and the notion of using finite resources rationally for development. Oddly enough, this interpretation of man's place in nature is virtually identical with the original concept of "multiple use," which supposedly became national policy a century ago. Acceptance of the idea that man must use nature rationally, while insuring its survival through conservation, resource renewal, and recycling programs, has been furthered by the realization that pollution and unrestrained consumption of resources are pressing the environment near a point of no return. Many Americans have begun to grasp the fact that a world of finite resources cannot in the long run—and increasingly in the present—meet their insatiable demands (Commoner, 1963, 1971; Leopold, 1966; Carson, 1962; Mumford, 1970).

From an ideological perspective, Americans envision a society made up of individuals who are free and equal to make choices on matters, including political and economic issues, that affect their welfare. While it is generally agreed that society may place restraints on the individual through constitutional provisions and legislation, certain broad rights, such as life, liberty, and property, are specifically guaranteed by the Federal Constitution and most state constitutions. The emphasis on individual rights in American thinking has been central to much of the environmental trouble of recent years. Until very recently it was commonly understood that a person—even a "corporate person"—could do as he wished with his property, which included denuding it of trees, wastefully mining its resources, using or dumping harmful chemicals on it, or pouring sewage into streams running through it.

The concept of federalism, that is, the division of governmental power between the federal government and the states, also has contributed to environmental deterioration. The creation and enforcement of measures to protect the environment under the federal system traditionally have been the responsibility of state and local governments, which have resented the intrusion of federal authority, and of industrial and commercial interests, which have always found it easier to inhibit effective pollution control at the state and local levels.

A last feature of American ideological thinking that bears comment is a deeply rooted commitment to a modified form of mercantilism. The business community traditionally has taken an "aid me but do not regulate me" stance toward government intervention. Protective tariffs, tax incentives, land grants, and other legislation designed to promote economic growth have been accepted as proper forms of government activity, but the regulation of business has been viewed as unjustifiable interference with property rights. In the environmental context, government action that promoted environmentally destructive but economically profitable behavior was welcome, while government regulation of such behavior was attacked (Fine, 1964; Arieli, 1966; Curti, 1964).

It has become more apparent in the past few years that a traditional emphasis on individual freedom and rights, and on state or local control of environmental matters, has significantly helped to undermine the integrity of nature. The recent spate of environmental legislation suggests that Americans are more willing than before to tolerate government restriction of individual and corporate freedom to halt the spread of pollution.

THE SOVIET UNION

For Russia's nineteenth-century educated elite, attitudes toward nature were shaped by two conflicting philosophies. The so-called Westernizers glorified the development of industry and the quick-paced transformation of Russian society, arguing that Russia's only hope lay in copying the West. For them, nature was merely an object to be manipulated and exploited; when they thought of it at all, it was in instrumental terms related to the development of the nation's economic potential. At the opposite pole were the Slavophiles and their intellectual heirs, who saw the country's salvation in the reassertion of traditional Russian culture, which stressed both the organic harmony of society and man's unity with nature. Adding to this undercurrent of Slavophile thought were periodic back-to-nature movements which sprang up among dilettante intellectuals and the glorification of the peasant as the "true" Russian, which enjoyed brief popularity in the 1870's among disaffected students and social reformers. Literary figures such as Tolstoy also beckoned their readers to a simpler preindustrial comprehension of the world in which man and nature were united. However, despite environmental overtones, these contending viewpoints remained essentially *political;* industrialization and social change were lauded or condemned for their political rather than their environmental impact (Venturi, 1960; Seton-Watson, 1964). The only serious conservationist thought concerned with the preservation of nature for its own sake came from a handful of naturalists little involved in the political debate around them (Pryde, 1972:9–13).

The Russian peasant, on the other hand, saw nature in practical rather than in philosophical terms. Like any social class tied to the soil for its livelihood, the peasantry looked upon nature with a combination of reverence and grudging respect reserved for a reluctant provider and harsh taskmaster. The peasant's long-held desire to own the land he farmed came more from a wish for independence from the landowner than from any direct reverence for the soil. When the emancipation of 1861 failed to satisfy the needs of most peasants because of high redemption payments to former owners and widespread failure of individual farms, ties to the land were weakened. Uprooted and financially destroyed, large numbers of peasants simply migrated to expanding industrial centers (Seton-Watson, 1964:109–130; Robinson, 1949; Owen, 1937).

The revolution of 1917 resolved the intellectual debate of the previous century on the course of Russian development in favor of industrialization and the emulation of the economically advanced states of Western Europe, although it left unanswered for a decade the question of the pace of economic growth (see below). With Stalin's rise to power in the late 1920's, the nation charted a course of rapid industrialization that strengthened further an anthropocentric and manipulative attitude toward nature (Shapiro, 1971: Parts 2 and 3; Von Laue, 1964:139–219).

Soviet thinking on the relationship of man and nature reflects an anthropocentric view of the world. *Man* is the central focus of the universe and the *raison d'être* of society; it is for his interests that nature's resources are to be exploited. The unique contribution of Marxism to the effect that man plays a significant role in history as a member of a social class does not alter this basic orientation. Man, as represented by social classes, remains the key actor and the sole beneficiary of the unfolding dialectical process of social development. The emphasis placed on the social and material context of man's evolution tends to obscure the environmental factors not relating directly to social structure or economic processes.

Second, nature is viewed as subject to the domination of man, something to be "conquered" by means of engineering projects to divert rivers and irrigate deserts. Under Stalin's rule grandiose water-control projects became a mark of national achievement; their unintended environmental consequences, such as the disruption of watersheds and the flooding of agricultural land and mineral deposits, were overlooked by planners. While increased environmental awareness of the past decade has prompted reevaluation and occasional modification of some of these projects, the conviction that nature must be bent to human will remains strong (Goldman, 1972b:211–238).

Among most environmentalists, the notion persists that nature can be rationally exploited to permit nearly unlimited growth, although some economists now question the need for continued rapid expansion of the economy (Fyodorov, 1972:14; Oldak, 1970:11; VF, January 1973:48–60, February 1973:36–52, March 1973:51–73, April 1973:57–79). Environmental problems are seen as a temporary aberration that can be easily corrected without an extensive reordering of national priorities. Moreover, nature has until recently been regarded as an inexhaustible storehouse of raw materials ripe for development. Only in recent years have some timorously offered the argument that natural resources may be exhausted without some limits to growth in the future. The official outlook is best expressed in the optimistic dictum that man's ability to provide for his needs grows in rough proportion to his increasing numbers and technical sophistication. In other words, the problems of resource depletion, pollution, and over-population will be solved by improved technology; new food sources will be found and natural raw materials will be replaced by synthetics (Pryde, 1972:101–106; Fyodorov, 1972). Little thought is given to the environmental impact of such drastic technological solutions on animal and plant ecosystems other than those directly linked to man, to say nothing of the psychological and social traumas that would ensue.

With respect to ideology, traditional Marxism, despite its idyllic reference to the unity of man and nature, has done little to sensitize Soviet leaders to environmental problems. In the economic sphere, where ideological considerations have mandated nonscarcity prices for exhaustible raw materials, Marxism has done a positive disservice to the rational protection of the nation's limited natural resources (Kramer, 1973b; Goldman, 1972b:43–76).

In his early writing, Karl Marx held that the natural unity of man and nature had been corrupted by the capitalist economic system. By selling his labor to others, man had become alienated from the fruits thereof and hence from his natural state. The attainment of a communist society would mean the "accomplished union of man with nature" in which the alienation intrinsic to a system of exploited labor would vanish.

In his later writings, based primarily on an analysis of the industrial revolution, Marx stressed the importance of economic determinism at the expense of a broader focus on man's place in nature. His views on nature were not so much revised as they were merely ignored or deemphasized in the short-term interest of forging an interpretation of economic and social change in his own time (Marx, 1909, 1964; Mote, 1972; Bottomore, 1964; Lichtheim, 1965). Writing after Marx's death, Friedrich Engels returned to the theme of man and nature. He noted the environmental depredations of the industrial revolution, condemned them, and called for ecologically sound practices (Engels, 1964; Mote, 1972).

Like most Russian Marxists of the nineteenth century, Lenin was influenced chiefly by the economic content of Marx's work. With the restricted vision of a single-minded revolutionary, he borrowed selectively from the pages of the master and frequently reinterpreted them to suit his purposes. To the extent he took note of industrial slums and environmental decay, it was to point out that Russia had become an industrial state ready for revolution, a claim often disputed by more cautious reformers (Lenin, 1927; Mote, 1972; Meyer, 1965:19–106). After the Bolshevik seizure of power, environmental concerns receded even further from view during the early years of confusion and struggle. A single enactment about the felling of trees can be traced directly to Lenin (cited in Goldman, 1972b:17), although he routinely signed other environment-related legislation. Despite current attempts to picture him as actively aware of the problem in the 1920's, it seems likely that his attention was very superficial.

In stressing the role of a disciplined elite that would promote revolution in the name of a politically inert proletariat, Lenin introduced into Marxism an element of conscious voluntarism that fueled the disposition to regard nature as an object to be manipulated and dominated by man. The victory of his small revolutionary band against seemingly impossible odds planted the seeds of future schemes to alter the face of the land on a huge scale. With the vigor and self-assurance of men who had changed history and inaugurated a new society, Soviet leaders viewed the conquest of nature as another "battle" against formidable odds. Great water-management projects were "objectives" to be won—like the revolution—through discipline and labor. The intellectual arrogance that prompted Lenin and his followers to revise Marx modulated easily into ecological arrogance (Mote, 1972; Mead, 1951; Dicks, 1960; Bell, 1958; Gorer and Rickman; 1949; Kluckhohn, 1961; Inkeles and Bauer, 1959).

JAPAN

Traditional Japanese art, philosophy, literature, and religious belief attest a subtle awareness of human kinship with plants, animals, and even inanimate objects. The natural order was invested with three inseparable characteristics. In the first instance it was the benevolent source of life's necessities: food, water, wood for building, the sun for light and heat, the moon and stars to soften the darkness, and creatures for companionship. In the second instance it was the womb of the world, the primal ground of being and the ultimate source of life. In the third instance, it was the home of divinity, the mysterious, numinous dwelling place of spirits and gods. Given these features of nature, the proper attitude was one of gratitude, reverence, and awe (Bellah, 1957:1–30).

Three streams of religious and philosophical thought expressed and reinforced this organic view of man in nature. Shinto (The Way of the Gods), Japan's earliest indigenous religion, celebrated the wonder of the universe in song, dance, and colorful processions. Shrines were, and are, erected in places of memorable grandeur and beauty, and even unusually shaped rocks or ancient trees were objects of veneration (Campbell, 1962:474–479). The introduction of Buddhism from China revealed a new dimension of the man–nature relationship, for divinity was proclaimed to reside in the very fabric of the natural universe. The sect known as Zen was especially congenial to the Japanese, with its teaching of directness, simplicity, and the attainment of enlightenment through rapport with the given qualities of nature. In the Tokugawa era, Chinese Neo-Confucianism brought to Japan a mature philosophical conception of nature and man as complementary elements in a world structured for cooperation rather than conflict. Human purpose in relation to this world was to preserve equilibrium between its various and equally legitimate spheres (Earhart, 1964; Nakamura, 1964:350–406).

This intricate web of values, oriented toward the harmonious interaction of the human and natural realms, has been challenged by postwar industrialization, with its underlying drive to control and exploit nature, and by urbanization, which has weakened and obscured the rural background of Japanese empathy with the nonhuman universe. Modernization has stimulated an insatiable thirst for physical size and material consumption, in striking contrast to a traditional taste for the physically modest and unobtrusive, and for an austere life-style. Modern industrial Japan has contracted size-fever from the West, brazenly evidenced in the rush to achieve the largest GNP, the highest tonnage of steel production, the most gargantuan tankers, and the top per capita income. Nevertheless, the Japanese are fortunate in being surrounded by eloquent, often poignant reminders of an earlier, quieter scale of values. The many gardens, the temples, shrines, and tea houses in lovely settings, the still-to-be-seen beauty spots, the customs and festivals geared to the seasons—all of this lives on for the moment as a reproach to modern Japan's thoughtless assault on the environment (Watanabe, 1974).

During the long Tokugawa peace (1603–1868) the code and way of life known as Bushido (the Way of the Warrior) summed up as well as anything the Japanese consensus on common goals and "national ideology." Bushido originated as the value system of one social group, the Samurai, but later came to have a wider appeal and significance. Peasants and townsmen, as well as the military aristocracy, cleaved to the major ideals of Bushido: discipline, social solidarity, loyalty, obedience to superiors, attention to duty, and personal frugality. Order, stability, continuity, and the preservation of hierarchical distinctions were the objectives of government policy and social life.

In the Meiji era (1868–1912) Tokugawa class distinctions were abolished and ideology was restructured around the position of the emperor. But the old values were preserved and restated in the Imperial Rescript on Education (1890), which mandated civic and moral life based on moderation, benevolence, reciprocity, and the fulfillment of obligations to family and emperor as the paramount ends of life (Tsunoda, et al., 1958:646–647; Uyehara, 1910:89–106). In the 1930's this "national polity" *(kokutai)* was perverted to ultranationalistic ends by a military clique, with disastrous consequences for Japan. Since the end of World War II the nation has functioned without a coherent pattern of national ideals, save the new-found attachment to economic growth. It is, of course, misleading to think of the Japanese state as nothing more than a monolithic commercial enterprise, often caricatured disparagingly as "Japan, Inc." Nevertheless, there is much truth in the observation that economic growth has become the leading national purpose almost by default (Morley, 1970). In light of this fact, one can understand readily why the Japanese make a poor showing in international affairs, and why foreign policy is a largely day-to-day expedient, tied to economic goals with no larger vision of the nation's role and place on the world stage.

Japan's traditional pattern of social values has strong environmental implications because of its emphasis on the regulation of human relationships rather than on economic activity and material acquisition. Preservation of the social nexus and the interaction of people according to an elaborate code of behavior took precedence over the amassing of wealth or the production of goods. Political and social life counted for more than economic life and were perceived as more vital to the national interest. Production and consumption were subordinated to *noneconomic ends,* an ecologically significant point of view that has been lost in the commercialism of the postwar boom. A revival of these traditional values may be a key to Japan's future in this age of tightening limits. The social structure, if not national policy, still reflects historic patterns to a remarkable degree. *Giri* (obligation) and *ninjo* (human feeling) continue to regulate the lives of people in small groups despite the thickening veneer of western individualism. A nation whose citizens are preoccupied with status within the group is less dangerous to the environment than one in which limitless consumption of material goods is the ideal (Nakane, 1972:29–33). It remains to be seen if the Japanese can refashion their unique tradition with imagination and resourcefulness, and work out some other collective reason for existence than piling up a trillion dollar GNP.

ECONOMIC PATTERNS AND INSTITUTIONS

A striking fact to emerge from a comparative look at environmental problems in the United States, the Soviet Union, and Japan is that economic systems in the three cases make little difference in either the existence or the magnitude of those problems. Whether capitalist, communist, or on the middle ground of a "guided" or "regulated" economy, each of the three nations has experienced a similar pattern of environmental deterioration. Apparently the questions of capital ownership and industrial control are related only peripherally to the issue of effective environmental preservation. This is not to suggest, however, that economic factors are irrelevant, but rather that more particular concerns touching on industrial structure, the relations of industry and government, the operating style of individual factories, and the nature of incentive and evaluation systems are more germane to an explanation of relative sensitivity to environmental problems. It is to these aspects of economic life in the three nations that we now direct our attention.

THE UNITED STATES

The backbone of the American economy was agriculture from the early seventeenth through the middle of the nineteenth centuries. Before the turn of the nineteenth century, agricultural products such as tobacco and rice were being exported in quantity, and by the outbreak of the Revolutionary War the range of exported farm products had been much diversified. In the next hundred years the major farm exports were cotton and cereals, particularly wheat. The environmental impact of these agricultural activities was felt in the widespread clearing of land and the exhaustion of soils in the South to service huge tobacco and cotton markets. Land was cheap and labor expensive; thus it made economic sense to squeeze fertility from the land and go elsewhere when production dropped.

Various extractive industries were another major growth sector of the American economy in the colonial period, which included lumbering, trapping, fishing, and mining. These resources were both vast and profitable, so Americans were encouraged to squander them without regard for their possible limits. Not until the advent of the twentieth century was attention focused on the prospect of domestic nonrenewable resources being exhausted, or on the need to husband renewable resources like forests, fish, and wildlife.

By the time of the Civil War, industry was well developed in the United States. With government firmly in the hands of national leaders committed to economic growth after the war, the further development of industry moved rapidly into the twentieth century. The demands of manufacturers for raw materials entailed reckless plundering of the environment and the errant dumping of wastes. The union of science and technology generated whole new industries—electronics, aviation, petrochemical, automotive—in the short span of fity years or so, each with its own potential for depleting resources or fouling the environment.

After the setback of the depression years in the 1930's, the American economy leaped ahead during World War II. The GNP shot from a bit less than three hundred billion (in 1958 dollars) to nearly eight hundred billion dollars between the end of the war and the early 1970's. Much of this growth was linked to the production of luxury items that came to be regarded as necessities. The production of electronic goods like television sets, radios, and stereos rose over two hundred percent, and the manufacture of household electrical appliances increased over a thousand percent. The consumption of such merchandise was stimulated by high-powered advertising in mass media. Consumer convenience became a watchword of the American way of life. Private cars using extravagant amounts of energy displaced public transportation, and a host of minor electrical appliances hummed away in the average home. Disposable bottles and cans drove out returnables, and planned, deliberate waste became endemic. Americans achieved the world's highest per capita consumption of energy and other resources, an affluence that was outstripped only by their impact on the environment.

New technology, or new uses for old technology, facilitated economic growth and had a frequently pernicious environmental impact through the substitution of synthetics for natural organic materials. Chemical fertilizers, pesticides, detergents, plastics, and synthetic fibers produce more environmental damage than the natural materials they have replaced. In *The Closing Circle*, Barry Commoner argues that much environmental deterioration since World War II stems from the appearance of new productive technologies with high pollution to unit of output ratios (CEQ, 1972b:66; Commoner, 1971:140–177).

Paradoxically, the relative affluence of most Americans has been a factor in arousing environmental awareness. The present outcry over environmental quality is as much a function of American economic well-being as it is of the actual state of the environment. Studies have shown clearly that awareness and willingness to act on behalf of the environment are more common among people with education who are on a comfortable rung of the socioeconomic ladder. The degree of commitment probably is linked as much to the individual's sense of security and isolation from the more disruptive consequences of effective environmental protection as to his horror of the pollution around him.

The hallmark of contemporary American industry is bigness. One half of all manufacturing assets are held by the hundred largest companies. Most large industries are oligopolistic—auto, steel, paper, petrochemical, oil, power—and the dominant firms in these areas adopt more or less similar positions on environmental issues. Concealed behind a public-relations smoke screen of exhortations about the need to balance environmental protection with continued industrial growth, they consistently resist the enactment and enforcement of legislation designed to promote the former (Pirages and Ehrlich, 1974:81–29).

The central American industrial institution is the corporation, which is characterized by a separation of ownership and management, a feature that is environmentally significant in several ways. The performance of management is gauged by shareholders according to the profits they receive, obviously a poor indice of the company's environmental record. Indeed, the profit nexus between management and stockholders often shields the former from the critical scrutiny of the latter, that is, unless profits drop. The result is incentive to stress profit-making activities, usually at the expense of costly, ostensibly unprofitable spending to reduce pollution. It follows that criticism of unsound environmental practices is not likely to come from the management team, for promotion and other rewards are the prize of those who play the corporate game of seeking higher profits. The rewards of production employees are tied to the firm's success or failure, so they also have a vested interest in company profits. While it is true that unionized employees in recent years have fought for better environmental conditions in the context of their work, most have defended their pollution-prone companies, especially if a company is the chief employer in town. Should there be a choice between a cleaner environment and job security, most unions and the workers they represent commonly show a strong preference for the latter (Mintz and Cohen, 1971: Introduction).

The development of multicorporation conglomerates has presented further complications. Stockholders in such monster enterprises are even less likely to be informed or worried about the polluting activities of a subsidiary than are stockholders in a single firm. Moreover, the management of a conglomerate has more latitude to shirk environmental responsibilities than is the case with single corporation managers.

American business has normally been quick to adopt organizational, financial, or technological innovations that promise steeper profits. There is now some recognition that sensible environmental practices are not intrinsically unprofitable. Thus one can find businessmen who have accepted reform and change where it is clear that existing technology can reduce environmental impact *and* support profits by cutting waste. On the other hand, industry has been reluctant to invest significantly in the development of new antipollution technology; it has done so only when faced with legal pollution abatement deadlines beefed up with a vigorous enforcement program (Rosenberg, 1972; Mishan, 1970).

Another salient feature of the economic system that has proven hostile to environmental protection is the close association of industrial and commercial interests with government. Not only have government leaders and industrialists shared the same enthusiastic outlook on economic growth as the foundation of national welfare, government bodies must reckon with formidable business lobbies. In many instances the nation's major labor unions have contributed to antienvironmental pressures in spite of their differences with management on other issues. Indeed, both have been able to mobilize an impressive array of lobbying techniques based on wealth, influence on voters, and skill in negotiating with—and even penetrating with their own personnel—federal and state regulatory agencies in order to dilute conservation and pollution measures. Only in recent years, with the increased political stature of proenvironmental groups and the creation of environmental agencies at federal and state levels, have government and business moved into an adversary relationship. This is not to say, however, that the entire spectrum of government agencies dealing with these questions is hostile to industrial, commercial, and trade union interests. Rather the debate over the environment and its protection has been internalized by the government, and various agencies are battling it out in cooperation with their respective clients in business and industrial groups and major environmental lobbies.

THE SOVIET UNION

An outstanding feature of Russian history in the last century has been the transformation from an agricultural economy to an industrial economy. Transcending even the significance of the 1917 revolution, economic development has intertwined with radical political change to create a centralized, industrial state second only to the United States. Taken together, these changes have created a pollution potential of staggering dimensions and a set of economic institutions handicapped in coping with a deteriorating environment.

Past industrial development has followed an uneven course. Despite limited industrialization before the revolution, the economy remained essentially agricultural. Over eighty percent of the nation's wealth came directly from the land, which was tilled by technologically crude agricultural processes. Existing industry lay chiefly in the hands of foreign investors and technicians, but when capital was available, foreign or domestic, development was rapid. From 1890 to 1914, industrial output quadrupled.

The First World War temporarily ended industrial growth, for the tsarist society's productive and distributive capability eventually broke beneath the pressures of the struggle. In the turmoil of the Civil War that followed the revolution of 1917 there was some restoration of war materials production through the application of military discipline and forced centralized planning. However, normal economic relations between city and countryside collapsed totally, goading the embattled Bolsheviks to confiscate foodstuffs from hapless farmers (Sherman, 1969:53–59).

The end of the Civil War inaugurated a period of relaxation known historically as the New Economic Policy (NEP). Faced with a devastated economy, as well as hostile farmers and industrial laborers, who resented the confiscation of food and military discipline in the factories, authorities restored a limited market economy in 1921, although the "commanding heights" of heavy industry remained nationalized. These measures did much to restore the consumer economy to near prewar levels, though worsening trade terms between urban industrial centers and the agricultural hinterland limited severely the regime's ability to extract fresh developmental capital from the agricultural sector. This dilemma provoked dispute among political leaders in the years after Lenin's death in 1924. Some argued that the pace of further industrial development should be linked to the slow accumulation of capital from the normal operation of the market relationship between city and countryside. In practice this meant excruciatingly slow development and the concentration of political and economic power in the hands of the richer peasants. Trotsky and then Stalin advocated rapid industrialization by a forced extraction of capital from the agricultural sector. Stalin defeated his political opponents and ordered a two-pronged offensive to advance industrial growth. Central planning was resumed for virtually the entire economy, with the highest growth rates reserved for heavy industry. To provide necessary capital, collective farms were organized to enforce the compulsory low-cost delivery of agricultural commodities to state authorities. Millions of peasants were compelled to surrender their small holdings and join collective or state farms. The immediate results were disastrous. Agricultural deliveries plummeted and millions of livestock were killed by peasants who refused to surrender them to the collective. In the long run, however, collectivization was the means of siphoning precious investment capital from a reluctant and backward rural economy (Sherman, 1969:60–78; Shapiro, 1971:271–403).

The development of heavy industry began in earnest with the first of the five-year plans in 1928–1929. By official Soviet estimates, production grew over nineteen percent a year between 1928 and 1932. Even the most critical Western observers place the growth rate between 8.8 and 16 percent annually. The second five-year plan from 1933 to 1937 (it was proclaimed fulfilled in four years) achieved nearly as high a rate of growth, with the official figure put at 17.1 percent annually. The early years of the third five-year plan showed a dramatic sag in the growth rate, which was pegged in official statements at 9.4 percent annually, and in unofficial Western estimates as low as 1.8 percent. The Second World War caused severe economic dislocations as strategic raw-material sources fell into German hands and factories were relocated into less endangered areas. According to one high Soviet official, the war retarded industrial development by roughly two five-year plans (Sherman, 1969:79–126; Mickiewicz, 1973:91–100; Bush, 1973:1–7).

Economic growth since the war has been considerably slower than the prewar pace. Having recovered from wartime destruction by the early 1950's, Soviet planners discovered that economic growth is linked to technological sophistication and labor productivity and not merely to gross capital investment. From 1955 to 1969, the average annual rate of growth dropped to 5.7 percent. In 1970 it climbed to 9 percent, only to dip to 6 percent in 1971 and a low 4 percent in 1972. While more recent growth figures have inched slightly higher, it is likely that Soviet authorities will keep a close watch over future policy decisions that will affect the nation's further growth (Bush, 1973:7–9; Mickiewicz, 1973:91–100).

While the overall pattern of industrialization had a negative impact on the environment, the economic structure that emerged and the types of industries that received highest priority differed from their Western counterparts, and thus entailed a different mix of environmental problems. The high percentage of economic effort devoted to food processing and lumbering contributed to a rapid worsening of water quality because of the contamination potential of these activities, even though the extensive use of polluting chemical fertilizers and pesticides was delayed until the 1950's. Heavy industrial development also exacted an environmental toll, but the absence of a consumer orientation and the relative simplicity of early Soviet industrial technology reduced its total disruptive effects. Soviet industry sacrificed consumer goods to producer goods for the development of industrial infrastructure, which left the average Russian in the position of consuming less energy and natural resources, thus generating fewer pollutants and causing less of a disposal problem. Technological simplicity also limited the disruptive potential of early Soviet industry, for many of the most polluting industries did not develop until relatively late in the course of industrialization. As Barry Commoner has noted in *The Closing Circle*, levels and types of pollution are related in part to levels and types of technology in a nation's industry. The development of Soviet oil and petrochemical enterprises illustrates this point. Largely because of low-level technology in much of the economy, oil and petrochemical grew at a slow pace (Mote, 1971:134). There was little need in Soviet industry for sophisticated products derived from the catalytic cracking process of refining, which proved to be an unintended environmental boon because of that process' high pollution effects. This is not to say that industry during the early years avoided the creation of severe pollution at times, but merely that environmental

impact would have been far greater had consumer production and technological innovation kept pace with the growth of the GNP.

Economic institutions created by the Soviet regime have been chronically
insensitive to environmental considerations. By mandating fast growth as
the highest national priority, Soviet leaders activated psychological pressures
and institutionalized incentives that have blinded planners and managers
to the effects of industry on the environment. At the national level, plans
for each year channeled the bulk of scarce investment capital into heavy
industrial construction; few, if any, funds were reserved for pollution abatement or conservation. Economic growth and sheer bigness became a
compulsion for policy makers, justified by the needs of national defense
and by the desire to catch up with the West.

For central planners and ministerial officials, the task of determining
the environmental impact of their decisions has been difficult, and incentives
for pollution control have been virtually nonexistent in the past. Not only
have they been restricted by the priority granted heavy industry, they have
been deprived of adequate information to make ecologically sound decisions. Since the national income accounting system does not count pollution-control expenditures as "productive" investments, both planners and
ministry-level decision makers are reluctant to divert scarce capital to
investments that do not enhance their reputations with superiors (Kramer,
1973b:364–373; Goldman, 1972a:314–327; 1972b:9–76). Some economists
have suggested a modification of the accounting system so as to list such
nonproductive investments in a more favorable light, and one has proposed
a measure of bioeconomic costs rather than strict national income, but
little has been done thus far to reorient the system by which economic
success is measured (Oldak, 1970:11; VF, February 1973:50–52).

The price system for raw materials has also made it impossible to allocate
raw materials in a rational manner. Since prices are set arbitrarily rather
than by the market mechanism, they reflect the ideologically motivated
decision that water, land, and raw materials are free goods or are given
nonscarcity prices. The use of water illustrates a common result of these
assumptions. Industry is charged no fee, or only a nominal nonscarcity
fee, for the water it uses; hence there is small incentive either to conserve
it or to utilize water otherwise not fit for human consumption. It has been
estimated that industry could be induced to conserve thirty percent of its
water if a true scarcity price were charged (Kramer, 1973b:372). Soviet
economists and environmentalists have vigorously advocated for years that
a more realistic fee be imposed for industrial water use. The 1970 water
law provides that a fee may be charged in water-scarce regions at the
discretion of republic-level officials. While such fees exist in many cities
such as Moscow or in areas of chronic shortage, they are set generally

below costs and provide little incentive for conservation (Pryde, 1972:145; Goldman, 1972b:112-114; Powell, 1971:630).

The absence of a scarcity price on land has led also to irrational allocations, because there is no way to assess precisely how alternative uses are related to its productivity. Millions of hectares of fertile agricultural land have been diverted to industrial use or have been swallowed up by urbanization. Other huge tracts of land and timber have been flooded by water-control projects, all because planners viewed land as a free good. The recent Principles of Land Legislation asserts the priority of agricultural usage for land, but so far little has been done to implement this goal. In order to deter the indiscriminate use of land, some republics have attached a flat price to its use. In Latvia, organizations that take agricultural land must compensate the collective or state farm 350 rubles per hectare, while in Estonia the rate is 480 rubles. In practice, however, these expedients are marginally effective in promoting rational land use, since the flat rate does not discriminate between fertile land and less valuable tracts (Kramer, 1973a:159-160).

Similar limited price reforms have been attempted with respect to the evaluation of raw materials. The July 1967 price reform introduced fixed payments in the form of rents for most extractive industries designed to reflect the cost of natural resources, thus providing an incentive for their rational use. However, the reform has failed to achieve its purpose; the fixed rent is far below the actual scarcity prices of the resources extracted, and certain important items like coal were excluded (Kramer, 1973a:150-153; Goldman, 1972b:48).

From the perspective of the factory director, there are few incentives to be concerned with environmental quality; like his superiors at the ministerial level, he is judged in terms of gross output or the profitability of his enterprise. Until recent profit-oriented reforms were enacted, the sole criterion of success was the total output of a factory; nothing else mattered—not the product quality or sales, and certainly not the environmental consequences of production. Under the new profit system, the enterprise is evaluated by a profit standard, but this has not heightened notably the environmental consciousness of factory managers, for pollution-control expenditures are regarded in most cases as unproductive ones that diminish the firm's profit. Halting steps have been taken in the Russian Republic to list funds for certain factory sewage-treatment projects as productive expenditures, but with little impact thus far (Powell, 1971:626; Bush, 1972:27; Khramov, 1973:3).

JAPAN

After a hundred years of modernization and one devastating military defeat, Japan has become the world's third largest economic power. Rising like a phoenix from the ashes of war between 1945 and 1950, the nation quickly attained the top prewar GNP of 10 billion dollars. Environmental problems were minimal in the early 1950's, as they had been in the prewar era. Thereafter the steep ascent of productive capacity and consumption was accompanied by worsening pollution. The GNP climbed to the 39 billion level in 1960, to about 200 billion in 1970, and to more than 430 billion in 1974,* with an average growth rate of ten percent in real terms. Before the energy crisis imperiled continued rapid growth, Japanese economists had predicted an average growth rate of over ten percent for the first half of the 1970's, and a GNP of some 400 billion by 1975. The Ministry of International Trade and Industry projected this rate of growth through the second half of the decade and arrived at a GNP of 800 billion by 1985. While it is premature to assess the future impact of energy shortages (though one intuitively expects profoundly negative consequences), it nonetheless remains true that Japan's postwar industrial metamorphosis has been unique and unprecedented (Guillain, 1970; Kurihara, 1971:1–6; Nakayama, 1970).

A second factor bearing on present environmental disruption is the postwar development of a technically sophisticated industrial structure capable of generating prodigious quantities and types of pollutants never before experienced. At the core of this new structure are the steel, oil refining, petrochemical, paper-pulp, power, and automobile industries. Steel production before World War II was about 7 or 8 million tons at most. Production in 1956 was in excess of 10 million tons and is now well past the 100-ton mark. The goal for 1980 through 1985 is a stupendous 173 to 178 million tons. The massive iron and steel complexes along the Pacific seaboard have become major sources of air and water contamination. Oil refineries were first built in the 1950's to process imported crude oil and thus eliminate the cost of refined foreign products. Now Japan's refining capacity ranks second in the noncommunist world. Refining complexes have proliferated along the Tokaido Megalopolis, most of them equipped with docking facilities to receive giant tankers. A chronic oil-pollution menace has resulted both at home and along overseas shipping routes. Prior to 1955 Japan had virtually no petrochemical industry. Spearheaded by Mitsubishi, Mitsui, Sumitomo, and Nippon Petroleum since 1960, a switch has been made from coal-based acetylene to oil-based ethylene chemistry, and output has jumped tenfold. Ethylene production is second in the world, with 4.8 million tons turned out in 1971 and a goal of 15

---

* The precise figure is 131,500 billion yen, representing an increase in real terms of 2.5 percent over the previous year (*MF*, 1974:4).

million tons set for 1985. Other forms of chemical production tripled in the 1960's. Several huge centers for ethylene production were constructed in 1968, no less than three on Tokyo Bay near the Ise Shrine and a fourth to the north near the temple of Kashima. Predominantly oil-using power plants have sprung up everywhere to support the surge in urbanization, population growth, and industrial expansion (see the energy section of the next chapter). The automobile industry began to flourish only after the 1965 recession, but the number of vehicles is already past the 20 million mark and 37 million are projected for 1985. Urban air pollution cannot be ameliorated with the near doubling of such a major pollution source in a mere decade *(OE,* 1972: *BS,* 1972; *EPA,* 1974; *JT,* 14 September 1974; Fujii, 1970; *IRJ,* 1975; *WEIS,* 1975).

Pollution-prone industries have spread across the nation in response to regional development schemes promoted by the government in the 1960's under legislative umbrellas such as the 1961 Industrial Development Promotion Law for Underdeveloped Areas. The Doubling National Income Plan, drafted by the Economic Planning Agency in 1960, officially sponsored growth through an emphasis on heavy and chemical industry and the industrialization of sparsely populated rural areas. Attracted by promises of tax relief for local government, local authorities vied with one another to offer sites for oil, steel, petrochemical, and other *kombinato* (industrial complexes). The consequences were mixed and ambiguous. Quiet villages were transformed into industrial towns. Financial as well as environmental burdens were imposed on unsuspecting communities. To widen the financial base, village and town mergers were enforced. Administrative powers were integrated to promote efficiency, thus strengthening local dependency on industry and the central government, and predisposing provincial officials to defend polluters against their victims. The extension of a new industrial structure into rural communities was not cushioned by antipollution measures, which were all but nonexistent before 1965. The terrible pollution and the local protests of recent years have not dimmed high-level plans for as yet "undeveloped" regions. Large-scale industrial bases are in the works for Tomakomai in Hokkaido, Mutsu-Ogawara in Aomori Prefecture, the Subo Sea stretch bordering Yamaguchi Prefecture, for Fukuoka and Oita prefectures, and for the Osumi Peninsula, which contains Shibushi Bay *(EPA,* 1972b; *EPA,* 1968; *EPA,* 1970; *JT,* 23 September 1974; *OECD,* 1975c).

A last factor worth considering is the recent emergence of a new middle class dominated by an avid desire to enjoy the fruits of a consumer-oriented economy. Millions of people for the first time in Japan's long history are in a position to enjoy a materially good life, and Western consumer-oriented values are in the ascendency. Wages went up ten percent a year in the period 1961–1969, and real consumption has shot upward at a dizzying pace. As a society of affluent consumers Japan may well eclipse in due time anything so far beheld in the West, with predictable environmental consequences (De Mente and Perry, 1967; Vogel, 1971).

Certain features of Japan's economic structure discourage realistic environmental reform. One can cite first the well-known "double structure" of the economy in which goliaths in steel, oil, shipbuilding, petrochemicals, and manufacturing coexist side by side with innumerable small shops employing from twenty-five to fifty persons. These small, labor-intensive shops, which comprise the vast bulk of Japanese industry, have facilitated Japan's spectacular economic growth, but most of them are marginally capitalized and have little to invest in such "frills" as pollution control (DSJP, 26 April 1972).

A second observation is that the success of the great kombinato in steel and petrochemicals has been dependent on a Pacific seaboard strategy. Many industries receive raw materials in their own ships at their own docks, and the same ships commonly depart laden with finished products. This coastal system was born in 1953 with the Chiba steel works, which reclaimed part of Tokyo Bay through extensive landfills. The Tobata works followed suit in the Shimonoseki Straits, the Sakai complexes in the Bay of Osaka, and the Fukuyama and Mizushima works in the Inland Sea, all within the past fifteen years. The construction of other mammoth complexes on the same formula is proceeding north and south of the Tokaido Megalopolis. Any attempt to dismember or relocate these complexes will meet with stiff resistance because of the very circumstances that inspired their creation and nourished their prosperity. The astounding success of Japanese steel, for example, is inconceivable without the Pacific seaboard strategy (History of Steel in Japan, 1974). The most powerful segment of Japan's economy is locked into a polluted and congested Pacific coast by the very nature of its structure.

A third feature is the close relationship between government and industry. Policies affecting business are never implemented without consultation with top echelons of the zaikai, or economic and financial circles (Yanaga, 1968:30–35). Business-oriented ministries, particularly the Ministry of Finance and the Ministry of International Trade and Industry, retire their top bureaucrats at the age of fifty or fifty-five, who then provide a reservoir of potential board members for large companies.* In these executive positions former vice-ministers maintain close relations with their former ministry subordinates, often protégés who have moved into the vacated govern-

---

*Two recent studies have shown that out of 123 public corporation officials, 105 were retired government officials, and that in 1974 no less than 188 high-ranking government officials slipped into significant industrial posts immediately upon retirement (JT, 1 April 1975).

ment posts. Ever since Japan's economic "takeoff" in 1952, the ruling Liberal Democratic Party (LDP) has showered industry with tax breaks and tariff shields, and has enabled business earnings to be recapitalized by avoiding expenditures for public welfare, most notably antipollution measures. In return for such cooperation, business has donated generously the funds essential to the LDP's continuance in power.

A fourth problem is that economic growth has been fostered by massive deficit financing. Normally various industries have only twenty-five percent of their capital in equity; the remainder is debt, just the opposite of western practices. Banks lend up to ninety-five percent of their deposits at high rates of interest and are propped up by the Bank of Japan. The debt service borne by Japanese industry affects profoundly its ability to cope with pollution. Less capital is available for pollution-related investment because of debt payments, and in order for enterprises to meet financial commitments, even though interest payments in Japan are tax-free, the economy must continue to grow at no less a rate than five or six percent a year. Further growth, however, entails more loans, thus perpetuating a scheme of things difficult to control or alter.

Fifth, the paternalism governing employer–employee relationships minimizes the likelihood of a confrontation between management and labor over the issue of pollution. Whether the enterprise is a huge steel works or a tiny rivet shop, the entire working staff is viewed as a family whose solidarity is upheld by carefully defined relations based on *giri* (obligation) from subordinates and *ninjo* (human feeling) from superiors. In the larger firms, employment is for life. Under the system of salaries and promotions known as *nenko joretsu* every individual moves up the ladder simultaneously with his or her peer group, which is structured on the principle of seniority. The actual distribution of responsibility within a peer group will vary but great care is taken to preserve everyone's self-esteem so as to avoid friction. Above all, the company offers emotional security and a sense of belonging. The president (shacho) is a good "father" to his staff, which in turn works hard with undeviating loyalty; each employee perceives his or her own destiny as identical with that of the company. In such an atmosphere hostile criticism of company policy is nearly unthinkable. Most existing laboi organizations are company unions that take all comers, not just persons in a given trade. Their fate is linked with that of the company, and union activity is bent chiefly on reminding management of its fatherly responsibilities (Ballon, 1969; Nakane, 1972:33–36, 43–45; Ike, 1973:35–41,64–70).

Sixth, the "economic miracle" would not have been possible had the Japanese not relied on large-scale technological borrowing. Rather than plow capital into domestic research and development, Japanese industrialists have licensed patents from abroad, which were then adapted to domestic needs.

The significance of this practice with respect to environmental protection is that Japan is largely dependent on antipollution technology and processes contrived in foreign countries, whose environmental problems may not be like those in Japan. In any event, the Japanese are at a disadvantage without a mature domestic source of ideas and instrumentation (Ike, 1973:67).

At present Japan's economic institutions are resistant to change which would diminish pollution, but it would be well to caution the reader on this point. Should there be a new consensus on national priorities and a willingness to bring economic structure into line with environmental imperatives, several characteristics of the Japanese system could serve noneconomic ideals as easily as they are now serving material growth. The close association of business and industry and the relative unity of the Japanese business world could smooth the way to an ecologically sound national economy. Furthermore, Japan's people—well-educated, alert, disciplined, accustomed to self-sacrifice—could be mobilized to accept and fulfill that ideal with more ease than could western peoples. Unfortunately, as in the past, a catastrophe, or the imminent threat of one, may be necessary to deflect the Japanese from their immediate direction.

CHAPTER
2
SCOPE AND NATURE OF THE PROBLEM (1)

POPULATION

THE UNITED STATES

America's population grew so swiftly in the seventeenth and eighteenth centuries, doubling about every twenty-five years, that Benjamin Franklin predicted the center of the British Empire would shift eventually across the Atlantic. Although the rate of growth gradually declined, the population had reached some 76 million by the year 1900. The downward trend continued before the thirties, accelerated during the depression years, and modulated into a "baby boom" after World War II, continuing upward for about ten years. In spite of a return in the mid-fifties to a general pattern of decline in the rate of growth, the number of Americans had risen to some 210 million in 1973, with a doubling time at present of seventy years. Even should the birthrate remain low—it dropped to fifteen births per thousand in 1973—population size will not stabilize for seventy years because there are so many children from the baby-boom years who have attained child-bearing age. For the remainder of the twentieth century the rate of growth probably will remain in the vicinity of one percent a year, which will result in a maximum number of people somewhere between 280 and 300 million by the turn of the century *(CPGAF,* 1972: 10–21).

Throughout American history population growth and urbanization have been closely associated. Urbanization has speeded up since World War II. About seventy percent of all Americans now live in urban areas of over five hundred thousand population, or in the immediate environs thereof. The percentage is likely to increase in the decades ahead, and if current trends continue, urban areas will take up one sixth of America's continental land area and contain five sixths of the population by the year 2000 *(CEQ,* 1971:297–310; *CPGAF,* 1972:25–35).

The total size and geographic concentration of America's population has enormous impact on resource and energy consumption, air, water, and noise pollution, waste disposal, and land use. Since the average American's standard of living depends on the use of energy and nonrenewable resources in prodigious amounts, from both domestic and foreign sources, it is of real moment from an environmental perspective that the population of the United States will not stabilize for at least seventy years. Although it is well known and often said that six percent of the world's people gather up thirty-five percent of the world's resources each year, the ramifications and doleful significance of this fact seem to have little effect on the thinking of Americans. In the course of his expected life span, an American consumes fifty to a hundred times more than an Indian or a Chinese. Another fifty million Americans in twenty years or so can mean only one of two things: a greater share than thirty-five percent of the world's raw materials and energy will be sought, or the standard of living of many Americans will have to drop. Furthermore, there is a direct relationship between the level of pollutants generated, land used, and population size. The concentration of more people into urban areas merely intensifies environmental deterioration. Few Americans are disturbed by their role as the globe's champion polluters, a direct consequence of their life-style and consumption patterns, both of which are difficult to alter. Since population growth and urbanization are areas traditionally excluded from national planning, there has been no serious move to limit or direct either of them *(CEQ,* 1970:150–152; *CEQ,* 1972b:53–60; *CPGAF,* 1972:56–73).

THE SOVIET UNION

Despite enormous losses in two world wars and a civil war, the population of the Soviet Union has increased very rapidly to nearly three times what it was a century ago, Table 2.1. As of mid-1973, it had reached the 250 million mark, with further growth to 330 million projected for the year

Table 2.1 Population Growth of the USSR (in Millions)

January 1, 1870	86.3
January 1, 1897	124.6
End of 1913	159.2
January 1, 1940	194.1
January 1, 1950	178.5
January 15, 1959	208.8
January 15, 1970	241.7

Source: S.I. Bruk, Ethnodemographic Processes in the USSR (on Materials from the 1970 Census), Sovetskaia Ethnografiia, 1971, no. 4, pp. 8–34, in Soviet Sociology, vol. 10, no. 4 (Spring, 1972), pp. 331–380.

2000 (PRB, 1972b). Nevertheless, the growth rate has declined markedly since World War II. The rate of natural increase, or births minus deaths, had dropped sharply from the year 1950 to the present. In 1950 it stood at 17 per thousand, but by 1969 it had dropped to 8.9 per thousand. Expressed as a percentage of total population, the present growth rate is 0.9 percent, a figure that has dropped in recent years to parallel the declining rate of natural increase. Population doubling time has risen to seventy-seven years, a rate consistent with that of other industrial nations (PRB, 1972b; Bruk, 1972:345; Eason: 1968:208–210).

The primary cause of this declining growth rate lies in the rapid decline of the birthrate from 1960 onward. From a high of 24.9 per thousand in 1960, the birthrate fell to 17 per thousand by 1969. By mid-1972, the rate had gone up slightly to 17.4 per thousand because of more marriages in the age group born immediately after the war. While such minor shifts in the birthrate undoubtedly will continue in response to the age-group composition of the population as a whole, the average will remain far below the pre-World War II rate, largely because of the decline in birthrate historically associated with industrialization and urbanization (Bruk, 1972:343–345; Eason, 1968:208–210).

Birthrate slippage for the nation as a whole conceals important differences among regions and between urban and rural settings. While rates of birth and natural increase have dropped sharply in the more developed European areas, both have remained high in the less developed southern regions and in central Asia. The former are well below the national average rate of increase of 8.9 per thousand, while areas such as Uzbekistan, Kazakhstan, Kirgizia, Tadjikistan, and Azerbaidjan far exceed it (Bruk, 1972:345). In 1969 the birthrate was far lower in the cities (15.9 per thousand) than in the countryside (18.3 per thousand), and although the rate of decline has been far more rapid in urban areas, the gap has been narrowed since 1955. The rate is especially low in the largest cities, with Moscow and Leningrad registering 11.2 and 11.9 births per thousand in 1969, far below the urban average of 15.9. The large cities of central Asia are an exception to this pattern, with the birthrate in Frunze at 19, in Tashkent at 20, in Ashkhabad at 21.9, and in Dushanbe at 22.2, but even these are generally lower than those found in the surrounding countryside (Bruk, 1972:334–335; Eason, 1968:214).

Rapid urbanization since the turn of the century has upset ecological balances because of added demands for food, living space, and recreational facilities, and the inevitable weight of domestic and industrial waste. Largely in response to industrialization, the urban population has grown four and one-half times since 1913. In real numbers, it has grown from 28.5 million just before World War I to 136.7 million, while the rural population has declined from a high of 130.7 million in 1913 to a present low of 105.7 million. Thus the urban population has risen from eighteen percent of the total in 1913 to fifty-six percent in 1970 (Bruk, 1972:337–338). In earlier times, most of this urban expansion was due to the migration of worker-peasants to the new industries situated in urban areas. In recent years, the role of such migration has declined as authorities have taken steps to stem the flow of bodies into already congested cities. However, despite these shifts and the declining urban birthrate, Soviet experts predict that seventy-five to eighty percent of the population will live in urban centers by the year 2000 (SL, July 1972:19; Listengurt, 1971:120–123; Eason, 1968:205).

Still another good indicator of urbanization is the multiplication of urban communities; the number of cities with populations of five hundred thousand or more has increased threefold since 1939 from 11 to 33, with similar increases for smaller urban areas (SL, July 1972:19; Bruk, 1972:339). Since the revolution of 1917, over 950 new towns or cities have been created, usually in connection with the placing of industry in sparsely populated areas. While the trend toward further urban concentration has been unflagging in the European sections of the country, which began to industrialize

Table 2.2   Increase in the Number of Urban Communities in the USSR

Population of Urban Community	Number of Urban Settlements		
	1939	1959	1970
Under 10,000	1758	3043	3576
10,000 to 100,000	915	1428	1707
100,000 to 500,000	78	123	188
Over 500,000	11	25	33

Source: Bruk, p. 339.

before the revolution, the highest percentage gains are in those areas where extensive industrial development began with the first five-year plans. Since 1926, East Siberia has experienced a ninefold growth of urban population, and West Siberian urban regions have expanded ten times. The Far East and Kazakhstan, even more sparsely settled before industrialization, have increased eleven- and thirteenfold, while in the heavily industrialized Donbass, the urban population has grown twenty-seven times (Bruk, 1972:336–339). Table 2.2 depicts the growth of urban communities.

JAPAN

Japan is the world's sixth most populous nation. With 110 million people in September 1974, the Japanese archipelago exclusive of Okinawa has a bit more than 3 percent of the world's population, an annual growth rate of 1.3 percent, and a doubling time of fifty-eight years. At the present growth rate (on which Table 2.3 is based), a population of 120,798,000 is predicted for 1985, and one of 131,838,000 is projected for the year 2000 (*IPP*, 1972; *SAPC*, 1972; *PC*, 1971). Compared with most countries, Japan's population seems to be growing at a sensible pace and in the past twenty years has been set forth as something of a demographic model.* This benign picture alters significantly, however, when placed in the ecological frame of reference and in the context of finite resources.

Several recurring patterns are detectable from the late Tokugawa period onward (Taeuber, 1958: Chapter 1). First, growth rates have tended to be low, seldom exceeding 1.5 percent annually since the survey of 1872.† Nevertheless, in relation to land under cultivation and accessible resources,

Table 2.3   Japan's Future Population Growth

Year	Total
1972	106,000,000
1975	109,925,000
1985	120,798,000
1995	128,344,000
2005	134,960,000
2015	138,614,000
2025	140,619,000

Source: Institute of Population Problems, Research Series No. 192 (1969).
Note: This is a medium estimate. The period 1975–1985 is a prediction. The period 1990–2025 is a projection.

---

*The net increase between October 1, 1973, and October 1, 1974, was 1,380,000 people, by no means a negligible rate of growth.

†The survey in 1872 was for a civil registration system. The first population census by sex and age was in 1920.

substantial increases have occurred. Second, a proclivity for family limitation has been fostered by custom and tradition, and there is a well established precedent for a government-sponsored population policy, though in the past such policies have commonly aimed at opposing downward trends in fertility. And, finally, Japanese population growth has been closely associated with intensive urbanization.

The long Tokugawa peace sustained conditions favorable to rapid growth. When population pressures became evident in the late seventeenth century, villagers began practicing abortion and infanticide, which helped to stabilize growth between 24.9 and 27.2 million up to 1852. This slowdown in growth during the last 150 years of the Tokugawa era must be put in perspective. Population density was already high, about 235 commoners for each square mile of the total land area, excluding Hokkaido.

After the Restoration of 1868 almost three quarters of a century were needed to shrink Japan's premodern birth and death rates. In the meantime total population surged upward from about 35 million in 1872 to 72.2 million by the end of World War II. Thus population more than doubled in less than seventy-five years, spurred on by modernization of agriculture, employment opportunities in a new industrial complex, improved public health, and legislation against infanticide. The annual rate of increase was generally below 1.5 percent, but growth was sufficiently rapid to provoke social uneasiness (the "rice disturbances" of 1918) and debate about population policy as a result of the worldwide depression in the 1930's. The coming of war silenced public discussion of the matter. The government embarked on a conscious policy of further population growth by repudiating contraception and abortion and urging fertile Japanese to reproduce for the glory of the East Asian Co-Prosperity Sphere (Price, 1971:270).

After World War II, during the five years from 1945 to 1950, Japan's population mushroomed from 72.2 to 83.2 million. The annual average rate of increase was a formidable 2.9 percent, higher than at any previous time in Japan's history. This phenomenal growth was due to the repatriation of nearly 7 million Japanese, a decline in the mortality rate (especially infant mortality), and a postwar baby boom. After 1950, Japan experienced a remarkable demographic transition which coincided more or less with the advent of twenty years of unprecedented economic expansion (Taeuber, 1951; 1960). The birthrate plummeted from 34.3 per thousand in 1947 to 17.2 per thousand in 1957.

Urbanization (Table 2.4) has been the most dramatic and environmentally significant manifestation of population growth since the war (Tachi and Muramatsu, 1971:187). As a direct corollary of economic expansion, nearly 72.2 percent of all Japanese live in cities of over ten thousand, while in 1950 the number was a mere 37.5 percent. However, these figures alone fail to convey the peculiar peril of urbanization in Japan. Since 1950,

Table 2.4 Population Growth in Select Japanese Cities

City	Year	Population
Tokyo	1950	6,277,500
	1969	11,454,000
Osaka	1950	1,956,136
	1969	3,018,000
Nagoya	1950	1,030,635
	1969	2,014,000
Yokohama	1950	951,189
	1969	2,144,000
Sapporo	1950	313,000
	1969	957,000
Kawasaki	1950	319,000
	1969	932,000
Fukuoka	1950	392,649
	1969	825,000

Source: United Nations *Demographic Yearbook* (1970).

population has tended to concentrate in a region known as the Tokaido Megalopolis. In 1970 it contained 57 percent of Japan's population on about 13 percent of the total land area. Since the census of 1960, Japanese demographers have been inspired by events to contrive the notion of "densely inhabited districts" (DIDs) of over four thousand persons per square kilometer (*IPP*, 1971). Of the 1960 total population, 43.7 percent lived in DIDs comprising one percent of the total land area. In 1965 it was 48.1 percent on 1.3 percent of the land, and in 1970 it was 53.5 percent on 1.7 percent of the land.* There continues to be a steady drain on Japan's rural population as millions flock to the Tokaido Megalopolis in search of lucrative jobs in an expanding economy. A comparison of the 1960 census with that of 1965 reveals that 83 percent of Japan's villages have become areas of declining population, and many simply have ceased to exist as viable communities (*JT*, 22 October 1974; Goto, 1974).

A few cities on the periphery of Japan's heartland have begun to attract population as a result of improved transportation, expansion or relocation of industry, and the flight of disillusioned people from the Tokaido Megalopolis. There is little evidence, however, that the western corridor will cease to "develop" in the next few decades.† By 1990 it is expected that sixty-five

---

*The glut of people in small areas can also be expressed as the density level of cultivable land (16 percent of the total land area). On that basis, Japan holds 5,300 people per square mile, the highest density in the world.

†The National Land Agency has predicted that Japan's population in 1985 wll reach 124,310,000, or 19,640,000 more than in 1970, a substantial revision upward from estimates of the Institute of Population Problems. Most of this increase will be concentrated in the three main urban areas of the country (*JT*, 29 July 1974).

Table 2.5 **Density of Population Per Square Mile of**
Arable Land in Japan (16% of the Total Land Area)

Year	Total Population	Density
1920	56,000,000	2,800
1940	73,000,000	3,500
1955	89,000,000	4,500
1965	98,000,000	5,000
1970	104,000,000	5,300
1972	106,000,000	5,400

Note: Rounded figures are used.
Source: Taeuber, *The Population of Japan. Selected Statistics Indicating the Demographic Situation of Japan.*

percent of Japan's citizens will be living in that area (*IPP,* 1965; *HUD,* 1972).

The demographic prospect for Japan is not encouraging, for in a mere thirty years the nation is likely to add the same number of people it had in 1872 after 1,500 years of historical development. The pressure on resources, land, water, recreational facilities, urban institutions, and the environment will be immense, while the time available for complex adjustments is pathetically short. (See Table 2.5.) Japan's population growth must be viewed also from an international perspective. The present level of per capita income for each Japanese has an impact on the environment many times that of an Indian or an Indonesian.

CONSUMPTION OF ENERGY AND NONRENEWABLE RESOURCES

THE UNITED STATES

As in all industrial states, there is a direct correlation between the standard of living enjoyed by Americans and the amount of energy they consume. About forty-three percent of the energy used in the United States goes to industry, twenty-four percent to transportation, and nineteen percent to home consumers. Another fourteen percent is divided among commercial users such as stores and offices, agriculture, various government agencies, and other small consumers.

The total demand for all forms of energy doubles roughly every fifteen years. By the year 2000, assuming a low rate of population growth, demand will be four times greater than at present. Even before the 1973 Arab oil embargo, much of the northeastern quarter of the nation, where population and industry are concentrated, experienced a shortage of energy supply during periods of peak demand, and voltage reductions were not uncommon. (*CEQ*, 1970:159–161; *NY Times*, 31 March, 13 November 1974).

Oil yields about forty-five percent of all energy used (Table 2.6). In 1970 some 15 million barrels a day were consumed, but only 10 million were produced domestically; the difference was made up from imports. By 1980 consumption is expected to rise to at least 20 million barrels a day, while production is expected to increase only by 11 million, thus doubling the gap between the two figures. Even should oil begin flowing from the Alaskan North Slope field in the late 1970's, new offshore deposits be developed elsewhere in the nation, and the Arab boycott be lifted permanently with some reduction of prices, there will still be a serious deficit. Of even greater long-term significance to a nation intent on energy self-sufficiency in the 1980's is the limited size of known domestic reserves. The American Petro-leum Institute, whose figures may be deliberately low, estimates the proved recoverable oil reserves of the United States at 36.3 billion barrels. At projected rates of consumption, these reserves, even if supplemented by new discoveries, will be exhausted by the middle of the twenty-first century. The importation of oil will grow more costly as America competes with other industrial states in the international market, and as smaller oil-producing countries move for higher profits and outright nationalization of their oil fields. The situation worsened in 1973 when most of the Arab oil producers halted exports to the United States to force a change in American policy toward Israel. About six percent of American oil supplies were coming from the Arab states (*NY Times*, 9 December 1973, 10 February 1974).

Shale deposits in several western states are a potentially significant but as yet untapped source of oil. Until recently the major oil companies were not drawn to the recovery of shale oil because of the costly process involved. However, the new price structure of both imported and domestic oil has sparked a reassessment of the economic feasibility of exploiting shale reserves, which have been estimated at six hundred billion to three trillion barrels, or more than double the current known world reserves (*NY Times*, 23 February 1974).

Twenty-three percent of America's energy comes from natural gas, a relatively clean source in even shorter supply than oil. The proven recover-able reserves in the country are down to 266.1 trillion cubic feet, but the nation continues to consume in excess of 22 million cubic feet a year. The costs of gas exploration are high. Even though the Federal Power Commission recently has allowed gas prices to rise in some situations, the gas producers maintain that prices are too low to justify the expensive search for new sources. The Nixon administration was sufficiently concerned about declining reserves to ask Congress to permit the marketing of fresh

Table 2.6 United States Energy Sources

Source	Percent
Oil	45
Natural gas	23
Coal	17
Nuclear	6
Other	9

Source: The First Annual Report of the Council on Environmental Quality, 1970, pp. 159–161.

gas sources without government price regulation, so as to stimulate explora-tion for new sources. It is expected that liquid natural gas imported from Algeria, Iran, the USSR, and several other countries, beginning in the latter part of the 1970's, will lessen the drain on domestic reserves (NY Times, 27, 30 March 1974; 15 September 1974).

Coal is the most abundant form of energy in the United States, but its extraction and use often cause severe environmental damage. Present consumption is over five hundred million tons a year, or seventeen percent of the nation's total energy consumption, from a known reserve of some two trillion tons. About half the coal now used is produced by strip mining, a relatively cheap but environmentally destructive process. The restoration of land that has been strip-mined to partially its original state costs about two to four thousand dollars an acre. Mining interests say this price tag is prohibitive. Most of the four million acres that have been strip-mined are as yet unrestored; moreover, the scarred land is highly susceptible to erosion and pollutes waterways through the runoff of rain (NY Times, 16 June 1974).

In the not remote future the domestic supply of fossil fuels will be depleted. Precisely when this limit is reached will depend on the future rate of demand and the discovery of further reserves. A widely accepted government estimate projects that about 90 percent of all oil and gas will be gone by the year 2035, and that coal will be exhausted by 2300. The only promising alternative source of energy under development is the nuclear reactor. Twenty-five years ago nuclear energy was seen as a panacea for the nation's future energy needs, but thus far the promise of the atom has been realized only moderately. As of January 1974 the United States had 42 fully operational nuclear power plants with a capacity of 25,675,000 kilowatts, which amounted to 5.6 percent of the country's total electrical power. Another 56 plants are being built with a capacity of 53,679,000 kilowatts, and 101 others are in the planning stage with reactors able to generate 125,119,000 kilowatts. The full capacity of nuclear stations presently operational, under construction, and being planned is 204,473,000 kilowatts, or 37 percent of present generating capacity. It will be years, however, before most of these plants are operative. At present nuclear power supplies only 6 percent of the nation's electricity (NY Times, 9 November 1973, 15 March 1974).

The slow development of nuclear-powered electrical generators is due to unexpected design problems and protests by environmentalists about reactor safety and the environmental impact of nuclear stations. Manufacturers say their reactors could be producing electricity eighty percent of the time, but in practice the reactors operating in 1971 were supplying power only sixty-one percent of the time, which is far below the efficiency level of conventionally fueled units. Faulty design is most often at the root of these difficulties (NY Times, 3 February 1974).

Various other techniques are being investigated to produce the heat needed to drive steam generators. Nuclear fusion, as opposed to the fission process now used, may be technically feasible by the end of this century, but such a development would require massive funding. There is interest in drawing heated water from within the earth to drive generators; before long, sites are to be leased on federal lands for the mounting of such projects (NY Times, 23 January 1974). Solar energy has great potential, and Congress is now thinking about a fifty-million-dollar research program to develop it (NY Times, 23 February 1974).

The demand for energy, especially in the form of electricity, is certain to increase even should the present rate of population growth remain constant. A slowing of per capita demand would relieve the problem somewhat, but would entail substantial changes in the average American lifestyle. Conserving rather than wasting energy would not be possible without a radical shift in existing practices, since any form of conspicuous consumption ends up being conspicuous energy consumption.

American industry is also a voracious consumer of mineral resources. In the course of the nineteenth century, demand was met largely from domestic reserves, a measure of self-sufficiency that no longer obtains in the last quarter of the twentieth century. While some economists argue that growing demand in conjunction with dwindling supplies will inspire a search for new sources, encourage the use of lower grade ores, promote the introduction of substitutes, and mandate extensive recycling, the best evidence suggests that American dependence on foreign sources will increase.

The National Minerals Advisory Board reports that the United States is completely dependent on foreign mines for twenty-two of the seventy-four nonenergy minerals essential to a modern industrialized society.

The Department of the Interior claims that needs for copper, sulfur, and phosphates can be met from domestic supplies; however, imports account for between thirty and one hundred percent of the iron, aluminum, nickel, lead, zinc, chrome, and tungsten used. At the present world rate of consumption, proven reserves of these minerals, with the exception of iron ore, will be depleted by the year 2150 (*NY Times*, 17 November 1974).

In summary, it is virtually certain that vital fossil fuels and minerals will be in short supply by the end of the century. A higher level of imports can be only a temporary expedient for the United States. Furthermore, international competition among the developed nations will drive prices up and compel frequent, painful adjustments of production and employment patterns. While technology can take up some of the slack by providing substitute materials, the basic substances needed for substitutes are themselves increasingly in short supply, and their manufacture and disposal pose an intensive threat to the environment.

THE SOVIET UNION

Energy consumption in the Soviet Union is a good index of pollution potential, for the production of energy, as well as industrial and domestic activities through which it is used, is closely linked to air and water contamination. By this standard, the USSR is among the high energy-using nations of the world, with an annual per capita consumption of 4.4 metric tons of coal equivalent in 1970. This figure places it slightly above Japan (3.2 metric tons per capita) and considerably above the world average (1.9 metric tons per capita). Compared with the industrialized states of North America and Western Europe, however, the Soviet Union falls far behind, with the USA consuming 11.1 metric tons per capita, Canada 9.1, Sweden 6.3, and West Germany and the Netherlands 5.1 each. (*UN Stat Ybk*, 1971:175–180).

Energy consumption in the Soviet Union in 1969 was 1,030 million metric tons of standard fuel equivalent, which in 1970 increased to 1,106 million metric tons (each metric ton equals 7 million kilocalories). It has been estimated (Table 2.7) that by 1980 consumption is likely to reach 1,704 million metric tons (*USDI*, 1969:749, 1970:799, 1971:856; Elliot, 1974:6–12).

With respect to individual power sources, there has been a shift from coal fuels (lignite, anthracite, bituminous, and coke) to oil and natural gas. While coal contributed over half the primary energy balance in 1960, it dropped to a bit more than forty percent by 1969. By 1980 it may provide less than a third of the USSR's energy, although in recent months energy specialists have urged a return to coal for some industrial purposes in order to conserve less abundant fuels. Equally important from the environmental perspective has been an increase in the use of cleaner fuels, especially

Table 2.7 Total Primary Energy Balance in the USSR (Million Tons of Standard Fuel Equivalent)

Year	Total Primary Energy	Coal (Lignite, Anthracite, and Bituminous, and Coke)	Crude Oil and Petroleum Products	Natural and Associated Gas	Peat	Oil shale	Fuelwood	Hydro-electric Power	Nuclear Power
1960:									
Production	699.1	373.1	211.4	54.4	20.4	4.8	28.7	6.3	......
Imports	12.3	5.6	6.7	......	......	......	......	......	......
Exports	65.6	16.0	49.3	.3	......	......	......	......	......
Apparent consumption	645.8	362.7	168.8	54.1	20.4	4.8	28.7	6.3	......
1965:									
Production	976.7	412.5	346.4	149.8	17.0	7.4	33.5	10.0	0.1
Imports	10.6	7.6	3.0	......	......	......	......	......	......
Exports	123.0	27.7	94.6	.5	......	......	......	.2	......
Apparent consumption	864.3	392.4	254.8	149.3	17.0	7.4	33.5	9.8	.1
1969:									
Production	1,193.4	438.0	470.0	214.0	19.0	8.0	30.0	14.0	.4
Imports	10.0	8.0		2.0	......	......	......	......	......
Exports	173.4	27.0	143.0	3.0	......	......	......	.4	......
Apparent consumption	1,030.0	419.0	327.0	213.0	19.0	8.0	30.0	13.6	.4
1975:									
Production	1,515.0	461.0	636.0	330.0	20.0	10.0	30.0	27.0	1.0
Imports	31.0	9.0	7.0	15.0	......	......	......	......	......
Exports	237.0	29.0	185.0	22.0	......	......	......	1.0	......
Apparent consumption	1,309.0	441.0	458.0	323.0	20.0	10.0	30.0	26.0	1.0
1980:									
Production	1,796.0	483.0	772.0	436.0	21.0	12.0	30.0	40.0	2.0
Imports	40.0	10.0	14.0	16.0	......	......	......	......	......
Exports	292.0	30.0	223.0	37.0	......	......	......	2.0	......
Apparent consumption	1,544.0	463.0	563.0	415.0	21.0	12.0	30.0	38.0	2.0

Source: U.S. Department of the Interior, Minerals Yearbook, volume 4, Washington, D.C.: U.S. Government Printing Office, 1971. p. 749.
Notes: The figures for 1969, 1975, and 1980 are estimates. The 1980 figure is a revised estimate. A metric ton of standard fuel equivalent has a calorific value of 7 million kilocalories (7,000 kilocalories per kilogram) or the equivalent of 27,780,000 British thermal units (13,100 Btu per pound).

oil and natural gas. In 1960, oil and gas contributed twenty-six and eight percent respectively of the nation's power. By 1980, oil consumption will have increased to 635 million tons, or thirty-nine percent of the domestic energy balance. Even more dramatic is the expected growth in gas consumption, set at 416 tons, or twenty-five percent of the total, by 1980 (*USDI*, 1969:749, 1970:799; Pirages, 1973:9–10; Elliot, 1974:13). The effects of this shift can be seen already in Soviet cities, where the change from coal to oil or gas heating systems has reduced air pollution noticeably.

It is also instructive to note the per capita increase of energy consumption. In the period 1960–1968, the growth rate of energy consumption for the entire country was 6.1 percent annually. When population growth is taken into account—1.3 percent annually for the same period—energy consumption per capita falls to 4.7 percent (*UN Stat Ybk*, 1971:180).

The comparative growth rates of energy consumption and GNP from 1950 onward indicate that the Soviet Union now consumes less energy per unit of GNP growth than in the past. From 1950 to 1960, energy consumption grew annually by 7.8 percent, while GNP showed an increase of 6.2 percent: from 1960 to 1968, however, the margin narrowed to a 6.1 and 6.0 relationship (*UN Stat Ybk*, 1971:180–182). The meaning of this change is that further economic growth has become less reliant on gross increases of energy consumption and more dependent on the expansion of less-energy-absorbing parts of the economy, such as light consumer and service industries. There is no implication here that energy consumption will stabilize in coming years, but rather that future economic growth will require less energy per unit of growth than in the past.

In an age of energy shortages, the Soviet Union is in the enviable position of being an industrialized state that produces more energy than it consumes. Indeed, energy exports have become the rising star of Soviet foreign trade, going from nine percent of total energy production in 1960 to fifteen percent in 1969. Over fifty million tons of oil were sold to Western Europe and Japan in 1970 alone. Some conservationists have warned against indiscriminate sales to the West, but oil exports probably will increase in the next decade, motivated largely by the Soviet need to import advanced technology (*USDI*, 1969:749, 1971:830; Pirages, 1973:10–15; Smith, 1974; Elliot, 1974:252–259). Natural gas also has great export promise. Negotiations are already in progress with the United States, Austria, France, Italy, Finland, West Germany, and Sweden. Several gas and oil pipelines to Western Europe are presently in use or under construction, and Soviet officials have expressed interest in constructing natural gas liquefication facilities to increase potential foreign markets (Pirages, 1973:15).

Despite a growing awareness of limitations on domestic fuel resources, Soviet extractive industries have been very wasteful. The coal industry is typical. Because of economic incentives to maximize the output of high-grade ores, mine officials frequently leave lesser-grade ores untouched. On the national average, thirty percent of the coal in a mine is not extracted, and many oil and gas wells show only a fifty percent recovery rate. Over ten billion cubic meters of natural gas are wasted annually in the act of extracting oil, for it is a common practice to burn off or release the gas at drilling sites. Substantial quantities of crude oil are also lost each year through spillage onto the land near drilling rigs, or into the sea at underwater extraction sites (Kramer, 1973a:147, and 1973b:371–372; Goldman, 1972b:48; Pryde, 1972:102–104; Elliot, 1974:243–246).

If the present rate of increase in fuel consumption remains unchanged in coming years, Soviet fuel supplies should last well into the twenty-first century (Pirages, 1973:6). Even when increased exports are taken into consideration, the Soviet Union emerges as a fuel-rich nation in comparison with the United States and Japan. The picture with respect to coal reserves is typical. The Soviet Union has an estimated total coal reserve of 7,765,300 million tons. Reserves of crude petroleum are placed at 195,160 million tons, and natural gas reserves are thought to be 24,400,000 million cubic meters. In all of these instances the other two countries lag behind (Elliot, 1974:21, 80–81, 130–133).

Despite this seeming abundance, Soviet officials have already begun to investigate alternate energy sources. A number of nuclear generating plants are now providing electrical power, and several others are slated for construction in the next decade (Pryde and Pryde, 1974:26–34). Experiments have been carried out with tidal generating plants that utilize the ebb and flow of oceans to produce electrical power. An experimental station has been built on Kislaia Bay near Murmansk, and larger stations are planned for Lumbovskaia Bay and Mezen Bay on the White Sea (Pryde, 1972:131). Other sources, such as geothermal energy, are also being explored (Mangushev and Prikhodko, 1972:18).

The Soviet Union is equally rich in nonfuel resources. Of all the major industrial powers, it is the only nation that is not a net importer of metals. Moreover, it has been judged self-sufficient in twenty-six of the thirty-six minerals crucial to a modern industrial economy. The United States, in comparison, is self-sufficient only in seven. Only two mineral imports exceed twenty percent of internal consumption: bauxite, imported largely from Yugoslavia and Greece, and tin, obtained from Great Britain and Malaysia (Pirages, 1973:10–11). On the other hand, the Soviets export a wide assortment of raw materials. While the bulk of these exports are to socialist countries of Eastern Europe, sales to the Western industrial states and Japan are expanding rapidly.

Historically, the extractive industries have been poor stewards of Russia's mineral wealth; the result has been much loss and wastage. Improper loading and storage facilities have done more damage than wind and rain. The transportation of raw materials has been poorly supervised, resulting in further losses en route. Individual industries show a low recovery rate in extracting primary ore; thus the nonferrous metals industry in Kazakhstan recovers only fifty to sixty-five percent of the total value of the components from raw ore. Other industries show similarly high loss rates, discharging quantities of valuable raw materials with the unwanted ore tailings. For the most part this is an economic rather than a technical problem; the means exist in most cases to achieve higher recovery rates, but there is little economic incentive to employ them (Kramer, 1973b:371–372; Goldman, 1972b:51–52).

Known mineral reserves can supply the needs of domestic consumption well into the next century. The USSR possesses, for example, thirty-three percent of the world's iron ore, twenty-five percent of the manganese, and forty-seven percent of the platinum metal groups (Meadows et al., 1972:56–60). Holdings of other raw materials are equally impressive: twenty-two million tons of zinc, seventeen million tons of lead, five million tons of nickel, and thirty-five million tons of copper, to cite but a few (*USDI*, 1969; Pirages, 1973:10–14). While even these plenteous reserves will be exhausted in time, the Soviet Union will feel the pinch of resource depletion much later than other industrial powers.

JAPAN

The Japanese economic machine and 110 million consumers absorb fabulous draughts of energy, amounting to better than five percent of the world's marketable supply in 1970. During the years 1960 to 1971, energy consumption increased 3.4 times from 100 million to 340 million kiloliters (in crude oil equivalent), which represents an annual growth rate of better than eleven percent, or twice the world rate for the same period of time. Moreover, Japan's economy is so structured that energy consumption goes up by 1.18 times the rate of growth measured in GNP, compared with 0.8–0.9 for advanced western countries. Among noncommunist nations Japan ranks second (after the USA) in energy consumption; however, the amount used per acre of arable land is the world's highest, eight times higher than in the United States. Consumption for 1980 has been put at 620 million kiloliters, only eight percent of which can be supplied domestically (*OECD*, 1975d).

In the wake of the oil embargo and new energy price structures, Japanese planners have become more cautious about previously heroic expectations of economic growth.* Hastily revised projections anticipate energy demands

---

*In July 1970, the Japan Energy Council projected an energy requirement of one billion kiloliters (in oil equivalent) by 1985.

of 7 percent annually for 1970–1980, 5.5 percent for 1980–1990, and 4 percent for 1990–2000. Thus by 1985 some 800 million kiloliters (2.3 times the present level) would be needed, and by 2000 the demand would soar to 1.7 billion kiloliters (4.8 times the present level). In the meantime Japan's share of the world's trade in raw materials other than fuel may rise from ten percent to nearly thirty percent annually by 1985 (*MITI*, 1974a; *OE*, 1972; *MDN*, 12 July 1974; Miyoshi, 1971).

Japan's sharpened appetite for energy has fostered a perilous dependence on imports. In 1955 about seventy-five percent of the nation's energy requirement was met domestically; only a quarter of all energy materials had to be imported. This favorable ratio was drastically reversed in the 1960's when oil replaced coal; now imports of fuel stand at better than eighty-five percent of the total amount used, with forty-five percent of imported oil coming from the Arab nations.

Oil is at the center of the nation's energy picture in the next decade. In 1974 petroleum (99.7 percent of which is imported) constituted seventy-five percent of Japan's primary energy supply,[†] though some planners are optimistic about a reduction to sixty-eight percent by 1980. For the time being, a petroleum-oriented industrial structure will have to navigate the heavy weather of skyrocketing prices. In 1974 alone the cost of Arab oil for the Japanese rose from seven to fifteen billion dollars.

In the hope of becoming less dependent on Arab countries, the Japanese have begun an extensive quest for oil closer to home. More than ten Japanese companies have mounted projects in Canada, Indonesia, and Alaska. The recent establishment of diplomatic relations with the People's Republic of China and improved relations with the Soviet Union have also laid groundwork for access to oil and other resources, although neither country would be able to supply more than a small part of Japan's total need for crude oil. Under a bill entitled "Promotion of Mineral Resources in the Continental Shelf," dozens of exploratory wells have been sunk. Offshore areas are being probed near Hokkaido and Honshu, particularly in the Sea of Japan, and some oil has been found off Akita, Yamagata, and Niigata prefectures. However, total domestic production of fifteen thousand barrels a day remains a negligible contribution (*BMA*, 1971; Hennessy, 1971; Emmerson, 1971:324–325).

Coal will continue to decline in significance through the 1970's, contributing well below ten percent of total energy supplies. The energy crisis and the resulting pressure for Japan to become more self-sufficient has sparked a fresh look at the domestic coal industry. In 1960 about fifty-two million tons of domestic coal provided thirty-five percent of the country's energy;

[†]Japan consumed 9.4 percent of the world's total oil production in 1973. Of all crude oil exports in that year, 16.9 percent went to Japan (*JT*, 4 November 1974).

the twenty-two million tons produced in 1974 supplied less than six percent. Although coal production in Japan has accounted for as much as fifteen percent of the total amount consumed, the reserves are shrinking and are not of high quality. The Ministry of International Trade and Industry has announced that new mines will raise production by roughly two million tons a year, but it is clear that additional sources must be secured abroad. Imports are to be sought from Australia, the USA, Canada, the USSR, and the People's Republic of China. Vietnam and Poland may each be able to supply up to one and a half million tons a year. The Japan Coal Mining Council estimates that ten million tons will be needed in 1980 and twenty tons or more in 1985. Two methods have been suggested for tapping foreign coal reserves. One would convert coal into methanol on the spot and then ship it to Japan. The other would process imported coal into synthetic natural gas (SNG). Japan's first SNG plants are scheduled for operation by 1976. At present all of Japan's coking coal, vital to the steel industry, comes from North America, so Japanese interests have taken the bold step of investing heavily in the state of Virginia's production facilities. A similar arrangement has been worked out with British Columbia (Hymans, 1974; *MDN*, 13 July 1974). Should Japan manage to increase its consumption of coal by the joint expedients of home production and foreign imports, the effects will be further scarring of the landscape in Hokkaido and elsewhere as new mines are opened and more severe atmospheric pollution, unless liquification and gasification techniques are perfected.

Hydroelectric power and natural gas also are expected to fulfill only a small part of energy requirements, accounting altogether for some five percent. Practical sites for dam construction are nearly exhausted, for water power was exploited in the earliest stages of Japan's industrialization.* Although the Energy Council believes natural gas production will increase from 2,500 million cubic meters a year to 20,000 million cubic meters by 1985 (an eightfold jump), the addition will amount to no more than a fraction of all energy supplies. This increment may well be purchased at heavy cost to the environment. It will be achieved largely by drilling into the continental shelf and by further exploitation of dissolved gas in ground water, thus aggravating the problem of ground subsidence (see the following section on water pollution).

Alternate sources of energy are being explored. The recently launched "Sunshine Project" is concentrating on solar, geothermal, and hydrogen energy, as well as synthetic natural gas. The oil equivalent of potential solar energy available in Japan is estimated at 288 million kiloliters a

---

*Remaining potential is estimated at twenty-nine million kilowatts.

year, which might be compared with the 224 million kiloliters of oil imported in 1971. Currently two experimental "solar houses" are in existence. Experts are less certain about the potentialities of geothermal energy, though Japan is well suited to provide it. The thermal energy of volcanos and dry, hot rocks might yield in excess of twenty million kilowatts of power a year. The geothermal power station built in 1966 at Matsukawa in Iwate Prefecture is producing twenty thousand kilowatts. Although government plans aim at six million kilowatts in 1985 and twenty million by the twenty-first century, twenty-seven of the thirty sites in which surveys are to be conducted are located in national or quasi-national parks; the plans have been rejected by the Environment Agency, which fears heavy metal pollution and environmental disruption. The liquification and gasification of coal and the development of hydrogen fuel are being studied as foundation stones of a new energy system. None of these alternatives are expected, however, to have much impact before the year 2000. Oil will remain king, with perhaps a slightly higher profile for coal (*MITI*, 1974a; *JT*, 26 October 1974; *OECD*, 1975a; *OECD*, 1975b).

On the other hand, reliance on nuclear power has an imposing future, second only to oil by 1985. Japan's Atomic Energy Commission has said in a 1972 report on long-range nuclear power development that "nuclear-powered generators must be built at an unexpectedly rapid rate in future years." By permitting a huge increase of electric power consumption in the balance of this century,[†] Japanese planners are effectively relinquishing any real choice. Exigencies will force nuclearization, while the high cost and uncertain supplies of oil will serve to accelerate the transition. Thus 1972 estimates already have been raised to 32,000 megawatts of nuclear power by 1980 and 180,000 megawatts by 1990. As the inertia of uncritical growth and the uncertainty of fossil fuel supplies box the Japanese in more tightly, further inflation of these estimates can be expected in the next decade, peaking well beyond the 1970 estimate of forty-two percent as the share of nuclear energy in total output by 1990.[‡]

As in the case of virtually all other key resources, Japan has only small deposits of uranium ore, the primal fuel for every type of reactor; most of it is now imported from Canada. In order to power some fourteen stations by 1980, uranium stores elsewhere in the world will have to be tapped. Needs are conservatively estimated to reach 5,600 metric tons a year by 1979, while indigenous reserves in 1969 were only some 2,500 tons. This prediction does not take into account the probability of greater commitment

---

[†]Total demand for electric power is estimated to increase from 421,800 million Kw in 1973 to 990,400 million Kw in 1985. Nuclear power plants are to bear 27.2 percent of this load.

[‡]In 1973, six nuclear power plants produced 2,283,000 Kw, or 2.7 percent of Japan's power. The share by 1981 is set at 19 percent.

to the atom by 1985. The United States is now supplying large quantities of enriched uranium, but since that country has an ambitious nuclear program of her own, exports to Japan could well be cut in the near future. In addition to working on a domestic uranium enrichment facility, the Japanese are prospecting abroad, especially in Canada and Australia, on the assumption that digging for uranium is more pragmatic than drilling for oil (*JAEC*, 1972; Emmerson, 1971:327–334; *AEN*, 13 July 1974; *JT*, 24 August 1974).

Though the full impact of higher prices for oil has not yet been felt, it is possible to see the tentative outlines of future developments (*FEER*, 29 July 1972; Kiuchi, 1971). The rate of economic expansion will surely fall. After a drop to near zero growth in 1973–1974, officials of the Ministry of International Trade and Industry have revised their projections downward to about seven percent annual growth to 1985 and six percent thereafter. Even these estimates are based on highly optimistic assumptions open to doubt (*AEN*, 21 June 1974; *MDN*, 28 March 1974). A precipitous drop in the growth rate will mean a decline of industrial output, domestic consumption, and export earnings, the latter being a key to the financing of Japan's economic miracle, including fuel imports. To many Japanese environmentalists, including some officials within the Environment Agency, the shock of the energy crisis provides new opportunities for improving environmental quality. Decreased growth rates and industrial production will mean less pollution; already the output of plastics and paper has dropped sharply. Perhaps energy consumption can be reduced deliberately and further industrial growth seek an outlet in pollution-control technology. On the other hand, there is the temptation to switch to high sulfur fuels and the danger that inflation will limit government expenditures on the environmental front. In brute fact, however, business and government are preoccupied with how to consume more and not less.

Japan ranks second among the free world's consumers of all raw materials, and reliance on imports has been rising. In the case of iron ore, imports amounted to seventy-seven percent in 1963 and will move toward ninety percent in 1975. The need for copper will reach two million tons by 1980 and, unless new sources can be found, Japan will absorb sixty percent of the Philippine's exports and fifty percent of Australia's. In 1969 twice the amount of copper was imported as in the previous three years. Agreements have been reached permitting Japan to exploit sources in Chile, the United States, Canada, and the Solomon Islands. As the world's second largest tin consumer, Japan imported fifty-five percent more in 1969 than in 1968, mostly from Malaysia. Three quarters of imported aluminum comes from the United States and Canada, and half of the bauxite, crucial to aluminum production, from Australia. In spite of being the world's fourth largest producer of aluminum, the domestic supply was short in 1969 by eight hundred thousand metric tons. Foreign sources also supply tungsten and molybdenum, and while ranking third in the production of primary lead and zinc, substantial imports are inescapable. Japan's dependence on the world for vital resources in an age of swelling population and growing expectations among poor nations justifies Miyoshi's remark that "availability of raw materials is proving itself in the 70's to be the 'Achilles' heel' of the Japanese economy" (Miyoshi, 1971:284–286; *OE,* 1972; *DSJP,* 1972a).

CHAPTER
3
SCOPE AND
NATURE OF
THE PROBLEM (2)

AIR POLLUTION

THE UNITED STATES

Atmospheric pollution is concentrated in the densely populated, urbanized, industrialized northeastern and midwestern sections of the country where factories, power plants, and millions of vehicles congregate. Most of the select thirty-seven areas threatened by vehicular air pollution are in the heavily developed northeast and midwest, but others are scattered about the country in populous economic centers like Houston-Galveston, Mobil-Birmingham, and Los Angeles (CEQ, 1970:61–62).

Fifty percent of the country's air pollution comes from transportation sources, especially automobiles and trucks. Twenty-one percent comes from the combustion of fuels, much of it for the generation of electricity. Industrial activity contributes about seventeen percent of all atmospheric pollutants, the major sources being iron and steel; grain processing; cement, lime, paper, asphalt, and phosphate manufacturing; and coal cleansing. Two percent is attributed to the disposal of solid wastes, and another ten percent to miscellaneous sources like forest fires (CEQ, 1973b:270). When air pollu-

Table 3.1 Air Pollution in the United States

Source	Percent
Transportation	50
Combustion of fuels, including generation of electricity	21
Industry	17
Solid waste disposal	2
Miscellaneous	10

Source: The Fourth Annual Report of the Council on Environmental Quality, 1973, p. 270.

tion occurs in other than urban areas, it is usually associated with copper smelters, paper mills, or some other specific source. (See Table 3.1.)

Once regarded as a mere nuisance, air pollution is now acknowledged to have a negative effect on human health and the environment. Although health suffers the most, this fact was the last to be admitted in spite of dramatic incidents like the Donora, Pennsylvania, "killer fog" of 1948. It is now common knowledge that air pollution feeds the incidence of chronic diseases like emphysema, bronchitis, heart failure, and cancer. Knowledge about the health effects of specific contaminants has made strides, but there is still a great deal that remains in the dark (CEQ, 1970:66–70). More studies are needed like the recent one in Los Angeles that showed how inhalation of even small amounts of carbon monoxide by automobile drivers can aggravate a cardiac condition (NY Times, 20 December 1973). Other airborne pollutants have been linked to pollution-induced illnesses, especially in the case of workers whose daily routine exposes them to commonly used substances like asbestos, which is carcinogenic.

For a long while it has been known that air pollution inflicts costly damage on plants and nonorganic materials (CEQ, 1970:70–71). A 1972 study by the Stanford Research Institute estimated that American farmers lose 132 million dollars each year because of air-pollution impact on crops. As might be expected, losses were most severe in the northeast and middle Atlantic states where people and factories clot together. The study also found that air pollution had made the growth of certain crops impossible in some areas and had reduced or destroyed the value of recreational areas by killing of the foliage. These indirect losses were not included in the cost estimate given above, though undoubtedly it must be great (NY Times, 12 May 1972).

Examples are numerous of damage to construction materials used in buildings, bridges, public monuments, and the like. One need only inspect the blackened facades along the streets of most American cities. Stone, bronze, steel, and aluminum are not only darkened but eventually corroded by sulfur oxides. Particulates hurled about by the wind not only catalyze the injurious action of other pollutants, but function themselves as an industrial, urban sandstorm that assaults impartially both flesh and steel. Millions of dollars are disbursed each year for the cleaning and maintenance of clothes, cars, homes, and apartments, all due to air contamination (*CEQ*, 1970:72).

Cities must endure financial as well as other types of loss from the poor visibility that accompanies air pollution. Thus air traffic is either slowed or completely disrupted from time to time because of smog, smoke, and haze. There have been epic chain accidents on major highways in or near Los Angeles and New York, in part a result of low visibility caused by air pollution. Another economic cost is the increased use of energy to provide illumination in the midst of urban smog and haze. In a self-defeating pattern of events, pollution-clouded skies compel the consumption of more energy, which in turn produces its fresh burden of air contaminants (*CEQ*, 1970:71).

It is difficult to be precise about the financial loss imposed on the United States by air pollution, but an estimate of 16 billion dollars annually has been ventured. An estimated 100 million dollars a year goes for the repainting of steel structures; commercial laundering, cleaning, and dyeing of soiled fabrics costs another 800 million dollars; washing cars dirtied in part by air pollution runs 240 million dollars; the impact of air pollution on air travel runs some 40 to 80 million dollars. More problematic is the cost with respect to health, property values, and the resources wasted through incomplete combustion of fuels. Even more elusive in dollar terms is the aesthetic factor; after all, how does one measure or calculate the value of a beautifully clear day (*CEQ*, 1970:72)?

In summary, it is clear that American air pollution is a major problem and that it has profound implications for health, economic well-being, and the aesthetic quality of natural surroundings. Furthermore, air pollutants from American sources are contributing significantly to the world air-pollution load, and may play a major role in changing world climate patterns, for there is wide agreement among students of this subject that even small variations in the earth's temperature over an extended period of time can have great influence on the weather. The atmospheric waste of the United States diffuses to the rest of the world with no discernable respect for national boundaries.

The Soviet Union

The Soviet Union is no exception to the seemingly universal rule that rapid economic development produces extensive air pollution. The deterioration of Moscow's air in the 1930's and 1940's was undoubtedly typical of most other rapidly industrializing areas. Moscow scientists first noted the decreased growth rate of local trees in the 1930's and attributed it to the widespread air pollution that began with the first five-year plan. The fate of Izmailov Park, a verdant expanse of forests on Moscow's industrialized east side, became a microcosm of both industrial growth and environmental deterioration. As new residential housing and industry developed in the 1930's, the air over the park was increasingly polluted with smoke and acid fumes. The withering of the park's pines was first noted at that time by residents and local naturalists. The increase in auto and truck traffic near the park also added its share of pollutants to the already potent effluents of industry and power stations. By the 1940's, virtually all of this rambling and once unspoiled park had felt the sting of local industry (*AICE*, 1969, Vol. 2:62–64; Goldman, 1972b:123).

By the mid-1960's the average Russian did not need a scientist or a monitoring station to tell him that the air he breathed was increasingly fouled by pollution. Especially in industrialized areas, the withering of trees and the yellowing of pine needles became commonplace, and in the Urals officials admitted that tree kills for a ten-kilometer radius around some factories were the norm (Pryde, 1972:152). Moscovites noted the absence of birds from local parks, and winter too brought its special warning in the form of black snowfalls in industrial centers such as Kaliningrad (Goldman, 1972b:137). The residents of Magnitogorsk, seven kilometers from the Magnitogorsk metallurgical combine, complained of constant gas odors discharged by the plant. Many noted that the gases caused difficulty in breathing, eye irritation, headaches, and coughs, and others found it impossible to sleep with the windows open because of the foul odors. Metallurgical factories seemed particularly offensive to those unfortunate enough to live nearby. In one study, well over half of the residents living within a one-kilometer radius of such a factory objected to air pollution. Thermal power stations were even more offensive. The same study revealed that over eighty percent of the residents within a one-kilometer radius of a thermal power station complained of strong odors; even beyond the two-kilometer limit, over half of the population still objected to the malodorous discharges (*AICE*, 1971, Vol. 7:15–31; *AICE*, 1969, Vol. 2:25; Mote, 1971:218; Goldman, 1972b:142).

Despite the public recognition that pollution has become widespread and the official admission that in heavily industrialized areas the concentration of harmful pollutants has frequently exceeded the maximum permissible limits, the intensity in the Soviet Union today has remained far below that of the United States (Tables 3.2 and 3.3). While the local impact of high-polluting industries has been as severe as in any industrial nation, the total national impact has been estimated by Western experts to be from one-quarter to one-half that of the United States. The gross weight

Table 3.2 Industrial Air Pollutants in the USSR, 1968–69 (Percentages of Total Air Pollution)

Air Pollutants	Percentage of Total
Carbon monoxide	31.9
Total suspended particulates	28.3
Sulfur dioxide	27.0
Hydrocarbons	10.7
Nitric oxides	1.1
Others	0.5

Source: K.A. Bushtuyeva, *Some Problems in Improving Environmental Sanitation in the USSR, with Special Reference to Air Pollution,* United Nations, World Health Organization, 1971, p. 5.

of pollutants released into Soviet skies is far lower than in the United States, with roughly a two-to-one ratio separating the two concerning emissions of dust and sulfur dioxide and much higher margins occurring for carbon monoxide, hydrocarbons, and nitrogen oxides (Mote, 1971:231–236; Carey and Dockstader, 1972:18; AICE, 1972, Vol. 14:75).

Three factors account for this relatively advantageous situation. First is the lower level of economic development of the Soviet Union, and especially the late development of air-pollution-prone industries such as plastics and chemicals. Second is the relative scarcity of automobiles, although a growing smog problem has been observed in many cities that will intensify as auto production increases in the 1970's. Finally, the lower population density of the Soviet Union as a whole and the relative infrequency of large population and industrial agglomerations reduce the per capita impact of pollution, although further urbanization into existing population centers (opposed by Soviet authorities) will worsen the situation.

While neither Soviet nor Western environmentalists have estimated the total economic costs of air pollution in the USSR, they have been high. Air pollution has cost the Soviet economy in a number of ways. It has increased production costs for industries that must depend upon relatively pure resources, and has resulted in high rejection rates for others, such

Table 3.3 Gross Weight of Air Pollutants: USA–USSR (in 10^6 Tons per Year)

	Dust	Sulfur Dioxide	Carbon Monoxide	Hydrocarbons	Nitrogen Oxides
USA	28	33	100	32	21
USSR	17	16	19	7	1

Source: V.L. Mote, (1971) "Geography of Air Pollution in the USSR." Ph.D. dissertation. Seattle: University of Washington, p. 231.
Note: Data is from the late 1960s.

as electronics, with close engineering tolerances (Goldman, 1972b:140). Secondly, millions of rubles of valuable raw materials are discharged annually into the atmosphere, although attempts are being made to recover these resources (Pryde, 1972:152). The economy bears a third burden in the form of the power needs of areas whose skies are blackened by industrial and vehicular emissions (Powell, 1971:621). And finally, the costs in terms of the destruction of agricultural crops and forests and soil pollution have become worrisome to Soviet officials, who are beginning to realize that the supply of arable land and exploitable forests is not as inexhaustible as once believed (Kramer, 1973b:364-373).

The intensity of air pollution varies from region to region within the Soviet Union (Mote, 1971:238). The central and southern Urals area clearly ranks first in terms of pollution density because of heavy industry and mining operations. The combined Donbass (Donets Basin) and Azov region of the West Ukraine ranks second and shares many of the industrial characteristics of the central and southern Urals. Third is the Kuzbass (Kuznetsk Basin) in northern Kazakhstan and West Siberia, with its rich supplies of raw materials and heavy industries. Originally developed in the 1930's, it has become one of the major production centers of the USSR. The Fergana Basin ranks fourth. Stretching eastward from the Caspian Sea, it includes the more diversified industrial centers of central Asia. The Angara-Baikal area occupies fifth place, with its industrial heart at Irkutsk and its food processing, timber, metal, and petroleum industries lining the banks of the Angara River. Sixth is the central Transcaucasus, which includes the wide strip of land separating the Caspian and Black seas. The Caspian shore region, especially around the oil and chemical industries of Baku, is more intensely polluted than the less industrialized West. The region's two other major cities, Tbilisi and Yerevan, have been spared the extensive pollution of the Baku area by the development of local food and textile resources instead of heavy industry. Ranking last in this catalogue of afflicted areas is the central industrial region, including Moscow. Bordered by Kalinin on the northwest, Vologda in the north, Gorky on the east, and Tula on the south, it is poor in natural resources and high-grade fuels. It developed historically as a center of the textile industry, which to this day occupies a dominant place in the local economy. While other industries have been added—metallurgy, chemicals, food processing, metal fabrication, and secondary assembly operations—the region has retained a significant percentage of medium and light industry and thus been spared the fate of more extensively polluted heavy industrial regions. It must also be noted that the central industrial region, especially around Moscow, has received preferential treatment from Soviet officials anxious to offer it as a showcase of environmental action.

Table 3.4 Air Pollution by Industry in the USSR

Source of Pollution	Percent of Total Pollution
Thermal power stations	27.0
Iron and steel industry	24.3
Oil and petrochemical industry	15.5
Automobiles	13.1
Nonferrous metallurgy	10.5
Construction materials industry	8.1
Chemicals industry	1.3

Source: K.A. Bushtuyeva, *Some Problems in Improving Environmental Sanitation in the USSR, with Special Reference to Air Pollution*, United Nations, World Health Organization, 1971, p. 4.

In his study of air pollution in the USSR, V. L. Mote (1971:192–198) has noted some characteristics common to the twenty most intensely polluted areas.* Three quarters are centers of iron and steel production and associated metallurgical activities. Nearly all are over one hundred thousand in population, making it likely that emissions from autos and domestic boilers are important factors. Thermal power stations are significant polluters in twelve of the twenty areas, with their local impact dependent upon the quality of fuels burned and their location in relation to residential areas. Surprisingly the oil and petrochemical industry was seen as an important source of pollution in only one of the twenty regions.

Thermal power stations, which emit twenty-seven percent of the nation's air pollution (Table 3.4), present an acute problem (Bushtuyeva, 1971:4). Many of the over two hundred stations now in operation were built in the early years of industrialization when inattention to environmental needs permitted their construction in densely populated areas. Although many are slated for conversion to oil or gas, the remaining coal and peat-burning stations, which generate over half the nation's power, still pour out annually over five hundred thousand tons of sulfur dioxide alone (Mote, 1971:124).

The thirty-seven iron and steel production complexes of the Soviet Union produce almost a quarter of the nation's air pollution, due in large measure to the use of coke in the manufacture of ninety percent of all steel (Bushtuyeva, 1971:4; Mote, 1971:128–136). Despite periodic efforts to hasten conversion to cleaner fuels and to install better emission control devices,

---

*They are, in approximate rank order; Magnitogorsk, Krivoi Rog, Novokuznetsk, Donetsk, Dnepropetrovsk, Nizhnii Tagil, Zaporozhe, Makeevko, Yenakievo, Cheliabinsk, Ulan-Ude, Angarsk, Temir-Tau, Angren, Kramatorsk, Belgorod, Beloretsk, Konstantinovka, Lipetsk, and Irkutsk. The rank ordering changes slightly, especially for the last half-dozen, depending on the specific pollutant in question. Leningrad ranks 71st in air pollution; Moscow a surprising 253rd.

these production facilities continue to have a disastrous impact on the environment.

Emissions of the nonferrous metal industry, accounting for 10.5 percent of air pollution, have serious impact on health (Bushtuyeva, 1971:4). Excessive accumulations of lead have been found in both animal and plant tissue near processing plants, and concentrations many times the maximum permissible levels have appeared in the atmosphere in these areas. Lead has also polluted the soil and entered food chains near such factories (*AICE,* 1969, Vol. 2:24; Zykova, et al. 1970:12–17).

The oil and chemical industries contribute together 16.8 percent of the nation's air pollution. The production of synthetic fibers, which has increased tenfold since 1953, is an increasingly potent threat (Bushtuyeva, 1971:4; Mote, 1971:134). The 400 percent increase since the early 1960's in the production of plastics and resins has also added its burden of new pollutants to the atmosphere, to say nothing of the eventual disposal problem created by massive quantities of plastic consumer goods.

Photochemical smog has become an increasingly serious threat to the air quality of most large Soviet cities (Bushtuyeva, 1971:4). First noted in Moscow in the mid-1950's, its presence has now been observed even in smaller cities. Although nationwide pollution from auto exhaust is estimated to be only two percent of the American total, the local impact in a city like Moscow, with over six hundred thousand cars, can drive pollution density far above acceptable norms. The planned increase in auto production in the 1970's (2.6 million from 1971–1975) will intensify the problem since many of these vehicles are likely to be concentrated in urban areas (Mote, 1971:143–144; Goldman, 1972b:125–131; Bush, 1972:22–24; *AICE,* 1972, Vol. 14:45–95).

The construction materials industry, which accounts for slightly over eight percent of the nation's air pollution, annually pours thousands of tons of dust and other particulates into the atmosphere (Bushtuyeva, 1971:4). Among the worst offenders are cement plants, which yearly emit over four hundred thousand tons of cement dust, although the introduction of dust traps has cut emissions in some areas (Kramer, 1972:3–4).

Air pollution is regarded as a serious health hazard in the Soviet Union. While "killer fogs" similar to those in Donora and London have occasionally been noted, a more insidious impact is found in the high incidence of pollution-related health complaints in large industrial areas (Goldman, 1972b:142; Mote, 1971:27–28). Soviet doctors estimate that from thirty to sixty percent of all eye disorders are a result of air pollution. Controlled comparisons of high- and low-pollution areas have shown that the incidence of pneumonia in the former was 3.5 times above the norm, and acute respiratory infections, bronchitis, and infectious diseases were found two to three times more frequently than in the control group. Doctors have noted that residents in high-pollution areas frequently complain of headaches, nausea, dizziness, and disturbances to the central nervous system which produce excessive fatigue and excitability (Mote, 1971:28–29; Kaliuzhnyi, 1961:74; *AICE*, 1971, Vol. 7:24–26). More esoteric diseases such as fluorosis (caused by the excessive intake of fluorine) and berylliosis (a product of beryllium poisoning) have also been traced directly to industrial effluents (*USDC*, 1968, Vol. 17:3).

JAPAN

Air pollution has become a serious problem for Japan since World War II. The gross quantities of harmful gases and particulates are less nationwide than in the United States or the Soviet Union, but their concentration and toxicity in urban centers is greater. In 1971 the atmosphere over Japan was burdened with over five million tons of nitrogen oxides, over a million tons of hydrocarbons, and at least one half million tons of particulates containing more than a dozen metallic elements, including cadmium and lead. Sulfur content rose from two hundred thousand tons in 1955 to two million tons in 1971. The central government has named forty major cities that have concentrations of sulfur dioxide well above the advised level. In recent years soot, ash, dust, and assorted tars have been deposited on Japan at the rate of ten to twenty tons per square kilometer each month. No less than 85,487 facilities in the nation have been officially identified (in 1972) as heavy smoke and soot polluters (*OECD*, 1974).

Unfortunately no complete and reliable figures are available to permit a secure ranking of all pollution sources. Private homes and apartments in Japan seldom have central heating, but the portable oil and gas stoves used in individual rooms create together a heavy load of waste gases. Trash burning is a relatively minor source of air pollution because most solid waste finds its way into landfills and reclamation projects. In general the chief contributors seem to be industry (approximately sixty-five percent) and motor vehicles (approximately twenty percent). In large metropolitan areas like Tokyo and Osaka, vehicles are probably the leading source of air pollution, and in Tokyo the automobile is blamed by local officials for recurrent photochemical smog. The total number of motor vehicles in Japan grew from 610,000 in 1960 to more than 22 million by March 1972. At present Tokyo swarms with nearly 2.5 million of the nation's vehicles. Their annual emissions are prodigious and will continue to increase (*QEJ*, 1973:74–87; *JEA*, 10 December 1973, Vol. 1, No. 7:3–4).

The role of industry must be seen in the context of population growth, urbanization, government encouragement of certain types of industry (power, petrochemicals, steel, oil, paper and pulp), and increased energy consumption based primarily on petroleum. The proliferation of huge industrial complexes in thickly settled areas since the 1950's is a significant cause of Japan's atmospheric havoc. Fuji City has been labeled *kogai depato* (pollution department store), but the term is appropriate for dozens of other places as well. Tokyo's air pollution is partly attributable to the fact that twenty percent of the nation's industry is concentrated in that one city and its environs. Iron, steel, and petrochemical enterprises crowd the vicinity of Yokohama and Kawasaki cities. Japan's largest chemical complexes are in the Yokkaichi region southwest of Nagoya. The Hanshin industrial belt in the Osaka-Kobe area, concentrated mostly near Amagasaki City to the west of Osaka, specializes in iron, steel, power, and chemical products. Paper and pulp plants are to be found everywhere (*QEJ*, 1972:54–55; *JEA*, 1972a; *AEN*, 7 February 1973; *TMG*, 1971:51–81).

In conjunction with industrial and urban expansion, energy consumption nearly tripled between 1954 and 1964 and then doubled again by 1969. Much to their recent discomfort, the Japanese have become dependent on Middle East oil, which is high in sulfur. The relation between consumption of ever larger amounts of high-sulfur oil and aggravated air pollution is obvious.

The negative impact of air pollution on property, plants, and people in Japan is now beyond argument. The synergistic effect of mixing so many gases and chemicals together in the atmosphere has produced sulfuric acid mist and photochemical smog on a grand scale, with destructive consequences throughout the country. Leather and fabrics are weakened and rotted away; metals and cement are corroded and pitted; the life-span of buildings is reduced. As yet there has been no systematic attempt to estimate the damage to property caused by air pollution, but if the American value of some sixteen billion dollars a year is taken as a crude reference point in a vast country where the concentrations of population and industry are not as severe as they are in Japan, the annual cost probably runs to several billions in the Japanese archipelago.

Plant life also suffers from contaminated air. Sulfur dioxide and hydrogen fluoride have been identified as agents harming rice crops, and the same pollutants figure heavily in the death of silk worms feeding on contaminated mulberry leaves and in the defoliation of mandarin orange trees. Along major highways and in heavily industrialized areas, pine trees have withered by the tens of thousands, and zelkovia and pasania trees have virtually disappeared from Tokyo (*RIEP*, 1972:1–15).

More ominous and dramatic are the effects of air pollution on human health. In December 1970, the Japanese Ministry of Health conceded that half of Japan's largest cities are unsafe for human habitation because of air pollution. In 1970 Tokyo experienced severe photochemical smog that brought four thousand cases of skin, eye, and respiratory complaints crowding into local hospitals. In the following year there were two dozen further instances of heavy smog (1967 saw forty-six smog warnings, and the composition of the air appears to have grown more toxic since then),* and some twenty-eight thousand people saw fit to complain about diverse physical discomforts. A now celebrated incident was the near collapse of forty-three female students of the Tokyo Rissho Senior High School on July 18, 1970, when they were taking exercise out of doors. At peak traffic hours Tokyo policemen working in congested intersections take "oxygen breaks" at nearby vans equipped with oxygen tanks (*APTIC*, 13881 and 19869). Nevertheless, Tokyo's air is superior to that of some other cities. In nearby Kawasaki a perpetual haze of sulfur dioxide and nitrogen oxides signifies an unacknowledged disaster area (*APTIC*, 21722). Medical surveys indicate that at least ten thousand people are afflicted with chronic respiratory disorders traceable in the main to air pollution (*TMG*, 1971:51–83; *JEA*, 10 September 1973, Vol. 1, No. 4:2–3).

The city of Yokkaichi has given its name to a peculiarly virulent form of asthma. Fifteen years ago there was no serious air pollution. Now, as a result of regional economic development, fourteen large plants discharge 140,000 tons of sulfurous gas annually, in addition to a variety of other pollutants (Ui, 1972a:30–33; *JEA*, 1972i:23–24; *APTIC*, 21680).

Japan's polluted air contains several other noxious substances whose domestic effects are yet to be clarified. Millions of city dwellers seem to be absorbing excessive quantities of lead from the air they breathe. Asbestos may well become an acute problem, especially in the shipbuilding and construction industries, which number among Japan's major economic enterprises. Prolonged exposure among American workers has been linked to high incidences of chest cancer. Another airborne hazard is the acid rains which result from the mixture of sulfur and nitrogen oxides with moisture in the atmosphere. Destructive of both construction materials and human health, these rains eat away at steel and concrete with surprising effect and subtly undermine the metabolic functions of organisms and the leaching rates of soil nutrients.

The future does not look bright. Assuming there is no change in Japan's industrial structure, and allowing for a more sluggish growth rate than in the past (say eight percent in real terms), the sulfur content of the air

---

*In 1971 there were 176 petrochemical air-pollution emergency warnings in ten prefectures and five cities.

is expected to increase from 2 million tons in 1971 to 7.2 million tons by 1985. Faithful execution of all existing controls will not be able to neutralize the impact of further economic expansion (*EPC*, 1974:7–8).

WATER POLLUTION

THE UNITED STATES

Americans have been more or less cognizant throughout their history that adequate water resources are crucial for the development of industry, transportation, farming, and urban life. Any future growth will be severely limited by an insufficient supply of relatively clean water, and the general quality of life will suffer accordingly (*CEQ*, 1970:29–30).

The demand for pure water has been closely associated with population growth. Past experience indicates that when the number of Americans doubles, the requirements for water triple. In 1960 the public used approximately 1.1 million cubic meters a day; by 1980 it will consume something in the range of 2.4 million cubic meters a day. Even if the current low rate of population growth is sustained, the demand by 2000 will be 4.6 million cubic meters daily. The average American uses six tenths of a cubic meter of water each day in and around the home, which reflects both level of affluence and geographic location. The more affluent one is, the more water one is likely to consume. However, consumption of water in the home accounts for about one percent of total water usage in the United States (Hunt and Garrels, 1972:39–40).

Agriculture requires water of about the same quality as that used in households, and drinks up more than forty-six percent of the total used. Out of 460 million acres of cropland in the country, 44 million need irrigation; those irrigated acres produce twenty-five percent of all agricultural output. It is predicted that by 1980 agriculture's share of water will rise from forty-six to sixty-three percent, chiefly because of increased irrigation (Hunt and Garrels, 1972:42–44).

Approximately half of all the water used by Americans is consumed by industry, even more than agriculture. Of that amount, about sixty percent goes for the production of electrical energy, either in boiler-powered steam generating plants, or in the turbines of hydroelectric plants. A variety of production and service industries also use staggering amounts of water, which frequently must be good enough for human consumption (Hunt and Garrels, 1972:44–45).

Americans presently use about one third of the total flow of all the nation's waterways. With the expected growth of consumption, the amount of water used by the year 2000 will be roughly equal to the entire available stream flow, excluding that needed by hydroelectric plants. Water can be used repeatedly, providing heat, chemicals, and other pollutants are removed before it is returned to the streamflow. The technology to accomplish this recycling is available, but the cost of doing so will be high (Hunt and Garrels, 1972:48).

Water pollution is universal in the United States, with some degree of pollution affecting ninety percent of all waters. The problem is most serious and extensive in the industrialized northeast, the Ohio River Basin, the southeast, and the Pacific Coast, but western areas are hit by the runoff of nitrate fertilizers and salinization from irrigation projects (CEQ, 1970:32–33). Horror stories are abundant and easy to compile. In 1969, Cleveland's oil and chemical saturated Cuyahoga River burst into flames. The Pursumscot River in Maine exuded vapors powerful enough to turn the white paint on nearby houses yellow. In 1970 the Detroit River was found to contain six times the amount of mercury judged to be safe by the Public Health Service. In Alabama a plant manufacturing DDT leaked a substantial amount of it into a wildlife sanctuary that also contained a drinking water reservoir for a nearby city. Hundreds of such incidents threatening to life and property have been reported in recent years.

Viewing the nation as a whole, major sources of water pollution are industry, agriculture, and municipal communities. Well over half the volume of industrial waste comes from five enterprises: food processing, paper, organic chemicals, petroleum, and steel. More than three hundred thousand factories use water in their productive activities and discharge over three times as much oxygen-gulping waste back into the water supply, more than all the municipal sewer systems in the country. Since industrial waste is expected to grow several times faster than municipal waste, the trend will continue toward even greater contamination. Industrial waste water, in addition to its biological oxygen demand (BOD) content, often harbors toxic materials such as cadmium and mercury. When studies in 1970 revealed dangerously high levels of mercury in many waterways, fishing was prohibited on a number of lakes, including Lake Erie and Lake Champlain, and the federal government advised against fishing in nearly one hundred polluted rivers. Many other toxic metals are discharged as well, with little regard for their potential danger to human life (CEQ, 1970:33).

In the context of gross industrial sales, much of this waste can be treated at low cost; indeed, it would be less than two percent on the average for all industries. In some cases the cost is much higher because of how water is used, while in others the technology is not yet available. In Appalachia, the Ohio Basin, and a few additional areas, water contamination is a result of mine drainage that contains copper, lead, zinc, and other metals dangerous to aquatic life as well as to humans. Streams measured in tens of thousands of miles have been polluted in this manner, especially near open pit mining operations (*CEQ*, 1970:39).

Thermal pollution is a growing problem. Its chief source is electric power plants, which claim huge amounts of water for cooling purposes. Other culprits are the petrochemical, petroleum, steel, and paper-pulp industries. Because of the growing demand for energy, thermal effects on water will intensify in coming years. By 1980, it has been estimated, twenty percent of the total fresh water supply will be used for cooling operations by the electrical power industry alone (*CEQ*, 1970:33–34).

Agriculture is a second major source of water pollution. Population growth has meant more crops and livestock and thus more pollution. Modern techniques of cattle, poultry, and swine production jam animals and fowl into feedlots, which concentrate their wastes and aggravates the danger of harmful runoff. Crop production since the 1930's, and particularly since World War II, has relied heavily on the use of nitrate fertilizers. Much of this nitrate washes into rivers and streams or leaches into subterranean water supplies. In the western United States, salinization has become a problem on extensively irrigated land with a high salt content. Pesticides and herbicides have raised agricultural productivity but have also entered water systems in substantial amounts. Pesticides such as DDT and herbicides such as 2,4,5-T may be carcinogenic and mutagenic; circulating in water they undermine wildlife and eventually climb the food chain to man (*CEQ*, 1970:36–37).

A third major source of water pollution is the discharge of wastes from municipal sewage treatment plants that handle both domestic and industrial wastes. Somewhat less than a third of the nation's people live in regions served by adequate sewer systems and treatment plants. Another third lives in regions wholly without sewerage. The remaining third are served by inadequate treatment facilities. The gravest municipal waste treatment problems are in the northeast where people are most closely packed into urban areas. There are several complicating factors one should note here. In many cities the waste and storm sewers are part of the same system, thus frequently overloading treatment facilities during a storm. Furthermore, these facilities often cannot accommodate the burgeoning load of wastes, or have no technical means of coping with certain pollutants. And even after treatment, wastes frequently retain phosphates and nitrates from detergents and foster algae blooms (*CEQ*, 1970:35–36).

Streamflow in the United States is polluted further by oil spills of one sort or another. Of the 1.3 million cubic meters of waste oil disposed of by service stations each year, a significant proportion of it ends up in the water supply. Still more oil leaks from the two hundred thousand miles of pipeline that crisscross the country. Heavy leakage also flows from barges on inland waterways and rivers, and such oil carriers spill their loads in collisions like the recent one on the Mississippi River (*CEQ,* 1970:38–39).

Of lesser importance is the pollution caused by commercial and private watercraft. Oil, gasoline, and sewage are regularly dumped into waterways, with generous doses of garbage. Hence the wide growth and popularity of recreational boating has degraded the environment it depends on. The worst record is on the Great Lakes and major rivers like the Mississippi, where both commercial and recreational vessels have dumped raw sewage (*CEQ,* 1970:39).

Water pollution touches virtually every aspect of American life. It poses such a health problem that most water used for human consumption must be thoroughly treated before it is safe to drink. A disturbing study of public water systems has even raised doubts about the quality and safety of treated water. Once pleasant lakes have become odorous and algae laden because of septic tank and detergent pollution, and many beaches have been closed as unsafe for bathing. At a time when American leisure hours are increasing, outdoor areas where they can be spent are declining in usability because of water pollution. Both sportsmen and professional fishermen are deprived by spectacular fish kills from industrial and agricultural wastes, or by their indirect destruction as breeding grounds are ruined (*CEQ,* 1970:40–41).

The pollution that sluices into domestic waterways eventually finds it way to the oceans; other, more direct sources are oil spills, garbage dumping, untreated sewage discharges, and thermal pollution. The oceans have long been treated by the United States and other countries as expedient, cheap disposal sites. Until recently no one paid much attention to the effects of waste poured indiscriminately into the sea, for it was commonly assumed that immense bodies of water could absorb, dilute, or conceal all pollutants in any volume. Only in the past decade has accumulated scientific evidence sounded an alarm and shown conclusively that the oceans are being damaged to an ominous extent. A report in 1972 by the National Marine Fisheries Service discussed the severe ecological disruption caused by forty-five years of sewage and sludge dumping in international waters east of Sandy Hook, New Jersey. The population of marine species in the area had declined, numerous crustaceans such as lobsters and crabs were diseased, and abnormally high concentrations of bacteria and traces of heavy metals were observed. The whole problem is exacerbated by waste deposited in that region by the Hudson River. Similar environmental disaster areas exist at the mouths of other rivers or at offshore dumping sites (*NY Times,* 15 June 1972).

Another worrisome source of oceanic pollution is the discharge of oil from offshore wells and tankers. Over the past fifty years, spillage from ruptured loading or offloading lines, the flushing of ship's tanks, and leakage from damaged vessels has added some five to ten million tons of oil to the sea. In the summer of 1972 a tanker entering Casco Bay in Maine struck a submerged rock, tore a gash in her side, and left 378 cubic meters of oil in the water, and this is only one of many such incidents. In recent years the large numbers of offshore wells drilled in the shallow waters along the Gulf and California coasts have spilled thousands of cubic meters of oil into the Gulf of Mexico. The oil leak at Santa Barbara, California, became a national *cause celebre* and eventually released over 3,780 cubic meters. The growing demand for oil and more reliance on domestic sources will entail the construction of still more offshore wells, with a certain escalation of environmental hazards unless adequate controls are imposed (*CEQ*, 1970:38–39).

Federal investigations of waters off the eastern coast of the United States have detected massive pollution in the form of tar, plastics, and floating oil. Although the sources of this contamination could not be identified with certainty, a major part of it seems to have come from coastal chemical plants and oil tankers. About fifty percent of the waters surveyed are polluted. The study noted that the presence of tar had been negligible until the closing of the Suez Canal in 1967, which increased the volume of tanker traffic around Africa, thus leading to more sludge dumping in the Atlantic. The sludge was borne on currents to the Atlantic coast of the United States. Plastics sighted were in various forms, but most of it appeared as pellets commonly shipped from manufacturer to fabricator. Scientists are now studying the effects of such pollutants on fish eggs and young fish, especially cod, flounder, and haddock. Analyses of plankton samples taken in the summer of 1972 indicated that more than half were impregnated with oil (*GS*, 1970:293–294; *NY Times*, 13 February 1973).

There is no comprehensive estimate at present of how much water pollution damage has cost the nation, but it is likely, on the basis of local studies, that hundreds of millions of dollars are involved, perhaps even billions. Commercial and recreational fishing has been ruined along coastal areas and in streams and inland lakes. Industrial equipment and home appliances have been damaged by chemicals in water. Outbreaks of illness have been caused by polluted water supplies. The cost of cleaning up the waterways will run into the tens of billions, but such costs, however unpalatable, must be weighed against the imponderable but inevitable losses of continued pollution (*CEQ*, 1970:40–43; *CEQ*, 1973b:74–80).

THE SOVIET UNION

Rapid industrialization in the 1930's began the slow but inexorable process of fouling Soviet streams and rivers which today has assumed dimensions of national tragedy. By the 1960's, few Soviet citizens needed the testimony of scientists and naturalists to tell them that the nation's waterways were in serious danger. Fires blazed on the Iset and Volga rivers in the late 1960's, forcing the Volga steamers to carry signs warning the passengers against throwing lighted cigarettes overboard (Powell, 1971:622; Goldman, 1972b:231). Near the town of Vitebsk, residents watched the Dvina River hourly change color depending on the volume of dye discharged by a local factory (LaMothe, 1971:13). Fish kills also became common on major waterways, forcing the fishing industry to turn increasingly to the now-threatened fisheries of the Pacific and North Atlantic (Pryde, 1972:76–79; Goldman, 1972b:109). Oil spills were also commonplace, with 65,000 tons of crude oil—twice the capacity of the Torrey Canyon—seeping annually into the Caspian Sea near the oil production center of Baku (Bush, 1972:22; Pryde, 1972:76). In recent years, Soviet naturalists have also noted spreading algae growths on stagnant rivers and reservoirs (LaMothe, 1971:11; JPRS, 1970a:76–77).

The direct impact of water pollution on man quickly became apparent. Health problems were the first to be recognized (LaMothe, 1971:15–43). At one point, residents of the industrial city of Kharkov were advised to boil drinking water because of bacterial pollution. For residents of Ivanovo the problem of tainted drinking water from the Uvod River was so severe that city officials had to build a one-hundred-meter canal to draw water from the less polluted Volga (Goldman, 1972b:106). Algae growths have caused numerous health problems including nausea, infectious diseases, and allergic reactions, to say nothing of odors suffered by those living near algae-covered waterways (LaMothe, 1971:11). The recreational use of Soviet rivers and inland seas has also been affected by pollution. Swimming in a number of important rivers has been banned from time to time, and the Caspian Sea beaches near Baku and other oil production centers have been frequent victims of oil slicks from offshore drilling operations and local refineries (LaMothe, 1971:9–15).

Growing awareness of water pollution has led Soviet scientists to consider the impact of industrial and domestic wastes on the nation's future water needs. While the USSR seemingly has ample fresh water to meet present demand, it is unevenly distributed throughout the country. The underdeveloped areas of the Far East and the North receive the lion's share, and local rivers funnel it north to the Arctic and Pacific oceans instead of to the south and west where water is needed for industry and agriculture (LaMothe, 1971:77–78; Goldman, 1972b:78–79). From those water sources tapped for use by man, the Soviet Union annually withdraws 270 cubic kilometers, or about nineteen percent of the yearly runoff. In return, the nation annually pours back into Soviet waterways sixty cubic kilometers of waste water, less than half of which has received any treatment. Since these effluents pollute from twelve to fifteen times their volume of pure water, the total national impact is staggering. One Soviet scientist estimates conservatively that between 700 and 850 cubic kilometers of pure water are polluted each year, and this represents more than half of the nation's total runoff (Kudelin et al., 1971:339–342; LaMothe, 1971:30,78–79; Lvovich, 1969:109; Georgiev, 1972:4–5).

The sober realization that water supplies are not as inexhaustible as once believed has led Soviet scientists to startling conclusions about the nation's future water needs. According to their projections, two thousand cubic kilometers of clean water will be needed annually for the dilution of industrial and domestic wastes by the year 2000, even assuming a high level of waste treatment. If other consumption requirements are added, water needed by the nation as a whole just about equals the runoff that could be realistically controlled. For the densely populated and industrialized European regions, the annual deficit of local water resources needed for the dilution of waste waters would reach nine hundred cubic kilometers of stable runoff by the year 2000 (Kudelin et al., 1971:342). Accordingly, these specialists recommend extensive water recycling in industry and grandiose projects to divert northward-flowing Siberian and northwestern rivers to the south to meet water needs.

A vexing problem closely linked with the availability of adequate water supplies is that Soviet industry and agriculture waste millions of cubic meters of water each year. One economist has estimated that technological norms in industry and agriculture require less than thirty million cubic meters of water annually instead of the over forty million which are consumed (Goldman, 1972b:110; Kramer, 1973b:364–370). Water use in agriculture is an especially acute problem since it consumes three times as much water as industry. But while industry returns two thirds of its used water to streams and rivers—water presumably recoverable through proper treatment—four fifths of the water diverted for agricultural uses and irrigation is lost through seepage and evaporation. Only about half of the water from the rivers and streams tapped for irrigation ever reaches the fields, and only fifty percent of that is ever recovered for future use (Lvovich, 1969:111; Goldman, 1972b:111,260).

Soviet industry also wastes massive amounts of water, consuming from four to six times more than needed. In his study of environmental problems in the USSR, Marshall Goldman (1972b:110) has noted that the production of a ton of steel in the Ruhr valley requires two cubic meters of water. American industry consumes 100 cubic meters for the same ton of steel, and Soviet industry, which according to published technical norms should consume only 115 cubic meters, actually uses between 140 and 250 depending on the efficiency of the mill. Soviet industry will grow even more thirsty as it shifts to the production of synthetics and other high-water-use commodities. The production of one ton of synthetic fabric (the use of which has risen tenfold since 1953) requires from two hundred to eight hundred times the amount of water used in the production of a ton of cotton cloth grown on an unirrigated field, and aluminum (up almost fourfold since 1953) requires six to ten times more water than steel.

In comparison with the United States, the Soviet Union emits only two-thirds as much water pollution on a per capita basis (Carey and Dockstader, 1972:15–17). However, when the GNPs of the two nations are compared, it becomes evident that the USSR is a more intensive polluter of its waterways. Since the USSR has roughly only one half of the GNP of the United States and still emits two-thirds the gross tonnage of pollutants, this means that per unit of GNP, Soviet industry and agriculture emit approximately one-third more water pollutants. One cause of this higher GNP-pollution ratio is that intensive water polluting activities such as animal husbandry, fertilized agriculture, and food processing comprise a greater percent of the total Soviet GNP. It may therefore be safely assumed that were the GNPs roughly equal (barring extensive structural change in the Soviet economy), the USSR would emit a far higher total output of water pollutants.

Domestic and industrial sewage constitute the major threat to Soviet waterways. Only one fifth of Soviet cities have any form of waste treatment whatsoever, and over sixty percent of all waste is discharged without preliminary treatment (Pryde, 1972:138). Even in the relatively well-developed areas of the Russian Republic, only forty percent of the cities have treatment facilities, and the figures fall lower for less favored regions.

Soviet industry has had a woeful impact on water quality. For the nation as a whole, sixty-five to seventy percent of all industrial wastes are discharged without treatment into municipal sewer systems or directly into rivers and streams (Goldman, 1970:38). While the impact of individual industries will be considered below, it must be noted that the thrust of Soviet industrialization has concentrated on industries with high water-pollution potential—iron and steel, oil, pulp and wood processing, and, more recently, chemicals and plastics.

Thermal pollution must also be counted as an industry-related hazard. This problem is especially acute around thermal power stations, which frequently discharge water directly from their boilers, and it is likely to become increasingly severe in the future since Soviet hydrologists predict that Soviet industry will demand a far greater volume of water for cooling purposes (LaMothe, 1971:7; Pryde, 1972:139).

Open-pit mining operations also represent a hazard to nearby streams and rivers. Mine wastes constitute the most serious water-pollution problem in the heavily mined Donets Basin. One mining and processing combine alone discharges over forty-five thousand cubic meters of raw wastes into local rivers each day, with another contributing over twelve thousand cubic meters daily. The prospects for improved water quality around such operations are bleak. Not only have local mine officials resisted or ignored pollution-control measures in the interests of maximizing output, the regime has decided to expand open pit operations to a point where one third of the nation's coal was mined from these sources by 1975 (Bush, 1972:25; LaMothe, 1971:9–10).

In the less industrialized sections of the USSR, the primary sources of water pollution are agriculture and logging. Nitrate- and phosphorous-based fertilizers already take a heavy toll, and their use is slated to increase tenfold by 1980. The runoff from livestock feedlots is also a grievous source of water pollution in the countryside as Soviet officials strive to increase meat production (Carey and Dockstader, 1972:1; Bush, 1972:22). Pesticides and herbicides play an especially insidious role in water pollution since the runoff from treated areas carries a residue of the poisonous metals, chlorinated hydrocarbons, and organic phosphates on which these compounds are based. Soviet scientists have found lead accumulations in fish at levels similar to those discovered in the United States, and DDT residues have been discovered in various processed foods (Pryde, 1971:16–24; Mote, 1971:75–76; Rakhmatullaeva, 1971:115–116; Okunkov et al., 1971).

Logging operations also contribute to the pollution of Soviet waterways since up to a quarter of the cut timber sinks to the bottom of streams and lakes as it is being rafted to processing areas. Sunken logs, which now completely cover some river bottoms, smother fish breeding and feeding areas and absorb valuable oxygen needed by aquatic life. The rotting logs also emit toxic chemicals as they decompose. Inadequate reforestation leaves barren vast areas of once dense forest, permitting uncontrolled runoff to carry both silt and chemicals leached from the soil into streams and rivers (Pryde, 1972:98–100,139; Goldman, 1972b:167–168; Powell, 1971:632).

For the Soviet Union as a whole, the water-pollution story is best told in terms of the fate of the nation's major waterways. Virtually all of the important rivers and inland seas are dotted with numerous sources of industrial and domestic effluents. The Volga River is undoubtedly the greatest victim, for it alone carries nearly one half of all the nation's industrial wastes southward to the Caspian Sea. In recent years, the amount of pollution dumped into the Volga has increased fourteen times, now totaling several million cubic meters a day. These wastes come primarily from industrial sites and include petroleum products, dyes, and chemical salts from the refining, wood processing, and textile industries which line the shores. Domestic sewage also flows virtually unchecked into the river at many sites. Most of the major cities along the Volga—Kuibyshev, Gorkii, Kazan, Volgograd, Ulianovsk, and Saratov, for example—have inadequate sewage treatment facilities, although a major effort to build new treatment plants is now promised by Soviet authorities (LaMothe, 1971:7; Bush, 1972:22; Vendrov et al., 1964:29–30; Pryde, 1972:140).

Also typical are the Ural and Desna rivers, which serve the highly industrialized regions of the Urals and the Ukraine. Before the advent of a recent program to cleanse the river, Soviet scientists had predicted that if present rates of industrial pollution were to continue unabated, the Ural River would be unable to support life by 1980. The city of Orenburg alone dumped nearly 600,000 cubic meters of waste into the river each day, and not one of the city's factories possessed adequate water treatment facilities. Further upstream, Orsk discharged 130,000 cubic meters a day, although its treatment facilities could then treat less than ten percent of that amount. Moreover, a large smelting plant was put into operation despite the report of local sanitary inspectors that its discharges contained from 150 to 300 times the maximum permissible concentrations of phenol (LaMothe, 1971:6–7).

The Desna River, which serves as a key source of water for Kiev, has also deteriorated rapidly in recent years. The chief problem has been untreated domestic and industrial sewage, which has caused health problems for local residents and numerous fish kills. Adding to the river's woes is the deforestation along its banks, causing silting and numerous forms of pollution (LaMothe, 1971:12).

Water pollution has become a critical problem in many lakes and reservoirs, such as lakes Onega, Ladoga, Baikal, and Balkhash, and the Ivanovo and Kama reservoirs. Lake Baikal, of special concern to Soviet environmentalists and industrial planners because of the purity of its waters, is increasingly the victim of the lumbering operations and pulp and paper mills which have sprung up on its shores (Pryde, 1972:139–150; LaMothe, 1971:16–18). The pollution of the Aral and Caspian seas, both major inland waterways, also concerns environmentalists. For both, the major problems are oil pollution, industrial and domestic sewage, and loss of water. The Caspian Sea is polluted by oil spills from offshore drilling operations and from the unpurified wastes of local refineries. While measures were begun in 1968 to prevent oil spillage, cleanse industrial wastes, and build municipal treatment facilities, progress has been slow (LaMothe, 1971:21; Goldman, 1972b:228–229).

The loss of water by both the Caspian and Aral seas has also had far-reaching environmental impact. Since the early 1930's, the level of the Caspian Sea has dropped three meters, with eighty to ninety percent of the loss due to withdrawals for agricultural use. The Aral Sea has experienced similar losses, and if present trends continue, it will be a dry salt marsh by the year 2000. Not only has this loss disrupted fish breeding areas of both seas—and virtually destroyed the local fishing industry—it has also reduced their ability to dilute to acceptable concentrations the increasing load of industrial, domestic, and agricultural effluents which flow annually from cities and farming areas along their tributaries (Goldman, 1972b:216–217; LaMothe, 1971:19–22; Pryde, 1972:126–127; Vendrov et al., 1964:23).

Pollution also besets international waterways touched by Soviet industry and agriculture. The Black Sea is fouled by the discharges of the Soviet merchant fleet, which dominates this all but landlocked sea. Despite measures to limit oil spillage and the dumping of wastes at sea, merchant ships continue to discharge oil-laden bilge water and other harmful effluents. Domestic wastes are also a problem, with untreated sewage discharged into the Black Sea at over two hundred points along the Soviet coastline. The construction of treatment facilities, approved on paper, meets frequent delays because of insufficient funds. The purification plants of all major coastal cities—Krasnodar, Sevastopol, and Yalta—are inadequate, and near Yalta contamination is severe enough to promote endemic intestinal disorders among swimmers during the bathing season (LaMothe, 1971:23–25).

To the north, the Baltic Sea has been badly damaged by Soviet industrial and agricultural wastes. Domestic sewage, industrial effluents, and pesticides from nearby agricultural areas are all major problems. Virtually all of the rivers flowing into the Baltic carry inadequately treated domestic sewage. Paper mills in Sweden, Finland, and the USSR are the major sources of industrial pollution, although metallurgical factories and food processing contribute their share of harmful wastes. Mercury concentrations are also quite high because of its use in the paper mills. While measures have been taken to reduce mercury emissions by substituting other chemical compounds in the manufacture of paper, Soviet scientists have realized that their victory was short lived, for the mercury substitutes have their own special harmful impact on marine life. Pesticides also present a problem, and Baltic seals have registered ten times the DDT concentrations of their western counterparts. Pesticide concentrations in fish have risen to a point that many species are no longer safe for human consumption. Although Soviet officials have recognized belatedly the threat to this important waterway and have taken measures to limit oil spillage and other effluents, including agreements with the other riparian states, progress remains slow, and the Baltic remains the victim of years of inattention (LaMothe, 1971:21–23).

The cost that water pollution exacts yearly from the Soviet economy is enormous. One Soviet economist has estimated that 6 billion rubles a year are lost because of polluted waters, and this says nothing about the millions of rubles which would have to be spent to clean up fouled waterways and install purification devices to prevent further deterioration (Kramer, 1973a:98–99; LaMothe, 1971:12). Industry is frequently the victim of its own effluents. Ironically the much disputed Baikal pulp mill now finds it necessary to treat water it uses because the lake's natural circulation returns the mill's own wastes to the intake pipes (Goldman, 1972b:199). The fishing industry has also been a major victim of deteriorating water quality. Estimates of monetary loss range from 100 million to 350 million rubles a year, to say nothing of the unestimated capital costs involved in retooling the Soviet fishing fleet to draw this important national food product increasingly from the high seas instead of polluted inland waterways (Powell, 1971:622; Kramer, 1973a:100; Pryde, 1972:139).

The fish have not been the only victims of water pollution. Soviet health officials admit that health complaints are widespread and most often linked to the contamination of drinking water sources. Soviet medical research has only recently focused attention on more esoteric water-pollution-related health problems, and although much research is currently in progress concerning pollutants such as pesticides and metals, there has been little progress in isolating their specific impact (LaMothe, 1971:14–43; Pryde, 1970:31).

Colossal Soviet water-management projects, aimed at diverting the unused waters of north-flowing rivers to productive use in industry and agriculture and at controlling the seasonally uneven flow of the nation's most important waterways, have had a tremendous effect on the environment (LaMothe, 1971:75–83; Goldman, 1972b:211–270). Huge dams have disturbed the normal river gradient, interrupted the flow of silt and nutrients, and made it difficult for fish to find their way to spawning areas upstream (Pryde, 1972:82–83). Man has also suffered from the unintended consequences of these massive water-control and irrigation projects. While irrigation has opened millions of hectares of land for agricultural use, the land is itself mortally wounded by salinization from the minerals and salts in the water. For the country as a whole, ten percent of the irrigated area is affected by salinization. More strikingly the amount of land abandoned each year because of salinization roughly equals the area of new land brought into irrigated production (Pryde, 1972:124–125). Changes in weather patterns may also be expected in connection with the creation of reservoirs and other water projects. One Soviet scientist estimates that the impact of central Asian irrigation and water-management projects will shift the climatic zones in European Russia southward about a hundred kilometers (Zhakov, 1964:52). Others caution that any reversal of Siberian rivers that significantly reduces the flow of warmer water into the Arctic Ocean could lead to an expansion of the ice cap and bring on another Ice Age or possibly affect the rotation of the earth (Goldman, 1972b:261–263). The extractive and forestry industries have seen vast mineral and forest resources swallowed up by reservoirs, to say nothing of the loss of valuable agricultural land (Pryde, 1972:115; Goldman, 1972b:257–258). Worry over the effects of these water-management schemes has grown in recent years, and several projects have been reviewed or scaled down in light of their consequences for the environment and natural resources. Other major projects, especially those connected with the Volga, have dropped totally from view. It is also evident that Soviet officials are rethinking the ambitious Siberian and northwestern river-diversion schemes (Pryde, 1972:17).

JAPAN

Until recently Japan was favored with copious and relatively pure water supplies. Rapid industrialization and urbanization since 1955 have occasioned a water crisis of sobering magnitude, the ramifications of which are only beginning to penetrate official and public consciousness. Both the quantity and quality of fresh water in Japan are diminishing rapidly. The agents of this deterioration are industrial sludge and effluents, untreated sewage, pesticides, commercial fertilizers, oil, and a continual rain of pollutants from the atmosphere, including lead, cadmium, nickel, mercury, vanadium, and polychlorinated biphenyl (PCB). Oceanic pollution in Japan's coastal waters also has become an imposing menace, especially to the fisheries which supply a large portion of the country's protein.

The problem encompasses all of Japan. The central government has designated eighty-two major bodies of water as degraded enough to need control measures. Much of Japan's industry and fifty-four percent of the nation's population are to be found in the basins of those designated lakes and rivers. In 1969 and 1970 water supply sources damaged by pollutants totaled 583 in more than thirty-nine prefectures, whereas less than 50 were damaged in 1960. The Environment Agency believes "it is safe to suppose that the damage extends well over the entire country" (*JEA*, 1972l:1–10).

Of the 117 rivers in the Tokyo area, 5 are of special importance: the Sumida, Edo, Ara, Tama, and Naka. With the exception of the Edo and the upper reaches of the Tama, all of them have a BOD of more than five parts per million, a level above which most fish normally have trouble surviving. The Tama supplies a third of Tokyo's tap water, yet more than 10 ppm of BOD at the Chofu treatment plant forced suspension of operations, in part because of pollutants associated with "Kaschin-Beck" disease, which causes bone deformation. The Sumida has a BOD of 10–20 ppm in spite of an effluent treatment program and dilution with water drawn periodically from the Tone River. In many places the river gives off potent gases that corrode metal and injure health (*RIEP*, 1972:16–27; *RIEP*, 1970:31–37).

Government surveys have established that 56 out of the 104 major ports are heavily polluted. Future surveys of the remaining harbors will no doubt produce similar results, since virtually none escape the presence of industry and urban populations. The once magnificent and ecologically fascinating Tokyo Bay is now too contaminated in many parts even for industrial use. Japan's celebrated Inland Sea, with its swirling waters and picturesque, pine-studded islands, is metamorphosing into a coastal sewer. Of forty-two bodies of water designated as polluted before 1969, only two were coastal (the Yokkaichi-Suzuku and Otaka-Iwakuni areas). Of the forty bodies of water newly designated since 1970, coastal areas account for fifteen (*QEJ*, 1972:80–88; *JEA*, 1972l:46–49).

Where does it all come from? Sewage and fertilizer runoff are significant contaminants. At present, sewerage facilities throughout the country drain only twenty-three percent of the inhabited area and serve a mere thirty-five percent of the population.* Human and animal wastes are commonly disposed of in waterways, although more of it is used directly as fertilizer than in other industrial nations. Hakodate City, for example, discharges human waste into the sea four thousand meters offshore through long pipes. On some rivers like the Sumida and Tama, household waste water is a worse pollutant in certain spots than that of local industries.

Japan is one of the world's leading consumers of commercial fertilizer and chemical pesticides. Considering that Japan is no longer primarily a farming nation, the quantities of fertilizer added to the soil are staggering,

Table 3.5   Fertilizer Consumption in Japan (100's of Metric Tons)

Year	Commercial Nitrogenous	Commercial Phosphate
1961–		
1966	7,246	4,930
1967	8,420	6,093
1968	8,894	6,653
1969	9,067	7,018
1970	8,789	6,967
1971	8,657	6,529

Source: United Nations Food and Agriculture Organization *Production Yearbook* (1971).

---

*When the third five-year sewerage plan is completed in 1975, the ratio of areas with sewers to total urban area will be only 38 percent. Sewer service ratios in western countries run from 60 to 90 percent.

151,860 metric tons of nitrates and phosphorus in 1971 alone (Table 3.5). Nitrate- and phosphorus-rich waters pour through estuaries into bays and coastal fishing grounds, promoting severe eutrophication. Japan uses ten times more pesticides per acre than the United States, and the absolute amounts are remarkable for a small country with so little cultivable land. Parathion, phenyl mercurials, and benzene hexachloride (BHC) were for some time widely used in rice production. The first was abandoned because of numerous poisoning accidents among farm workers. In 1968 the government banned the use of organic mercurials in rice fields, but delayed this action until two years after investigations had revealed that Japanese body hair carried three to four times more mercury than was the case with people in other countries. Although Beta-BHC has also been forbidden, traces are still found in the fatty tissue of Japanese at thirty times the concentrations found in Europeans or Americans. Food contamination has also been extensive, for pesticides enter the soil and work their way up the food chain. According to Masahiko Ueda, chief researcher with the Sanitation Research Institute of Kochi Prefecture, Japanese foods contain six to sixteen times more chlorinated hydrocarbon insecticides than European and American foods. Studies by Japanese scholars suggest that river pollution by chlorinated hydrocarbons and other agricultural chemicals is fifty times greater in Japan than in England. Ironically this drenching shower of chemicals has not increased rice production significantly. Rather it has contributed, along with general water pollution, to the damage of paddy fields totaling 194,000 hectares in about 1,500 districts, a fifty-percent increase since 1965 (*FAO*, 1971:462–517; *QEJ*, 1973:115,144–146; Ui, 1972a:38).

Industry is also an important source of pollutants. The relationship between industrial growth and water pollution is direct and inescapable. Between 1962 and 1968 the GNP went up by 86 percent, mining and manufacturing by some 250 percent, and heavy oil consumption by about 425 percent. Industry's consumption of water increased 34 percent from 26,960,000 to 36,030,000 tons a day, excluding recycled and seawater.† Paper-pulp, food processing, and chemical industries consumed 61.3 percent of this water in 1968 (up from 40.5 percent in 1962). Until 1958 there were no controls whatever on industry with respect to the treatment of sludge and effluents or their disposal in water systems. A generally laissez-faire attitude by government toward industry in the matter of pollution, combined with a concentration of toxic industries unique in the world, has generated a dangerously septic condition. For example, along the Tama River, whose basin covers 1,200 square kilometers, or 60 percent of the Tokyo area, there are no less than one hundred metal-plating factories

---

†The amount used by industry in 1970 was 41 million cubic meters of freshwater, excluding recycled water, a day.

whose effluents contain cyanide, cadmium, ammonia, and other deleterious substances. The high cyanide level in waste water has forced several shut-downs of water intake for domestic purposes.

Paper and pulp waste also pose a great threat to inland and offshore water resources. Japan's 679 pulp mills use an incredible amount of water; a large mill may consume more water than a city of 50,000 people. Waste water flowing from these mills totals millions of tons a day, and is accompanied by tons of sludge containing grease, loose fibers, pulp lignin, mercury, assorted chemicals, and, lately, PCB. In combination with water the sludge gives off poisonous sulfur acid and hydrogen sulfide gases. The mills dot Japan's shoreline, but Shizuoka Prefecture accounts for 191 (twenty-one percent) of the total, and Fuji City, with a modest population of 180,000, is burdened with 140. In addition to 3,000 tons of sludge a day, the hapless port of Tagonoura receives 2 million tons of waste water daily. Fully loaded ships can no longer enter the harbor because of sludge buildup. In 1970 an effort to dredge the bottom was abandoned when ten workers succumbed to sludge gas, and in 1971 thirty-three Japan National Railroad workers fell ill from hydrogen sulfide gas while working on tracks near the water. An attempt by mill owners to dump sludge at sea was blocked by irate fishermen. A current "solution" to the problem is dumping in and along the Fuji River (Ui, 1972a:64–67).

Much of Japan's water-pollution load finds its way ultimately to the sea by way of streams, rivers, coastal drainage, and the six hundred billion tons of rain that bear contaminants downward from the air each year, all of this apart from the direct and frequent dumping of wastes at hundreds of offshore sites. Among all potential sources of oceanic pollution, oil enjoys a special status. In 1971 oil accounted for some eighty percent of officially acknowledged pollution offenses in Japan's coastal waters. Seventy-two percent of these oil incidents occurred in Tokyo, Ise, and Osaka bays, and in the Seto Inland Sea. Waste oil enters the sea from most of the 5.5 million vessels that use Japanese harbors each year. Spills are the most spectacular source, such as the breakup of the Liberian tanker *Juliana* in 1971 off Niigata, which spilled 6,000 tons of crude oil.* Many tons of oil also debouch into the ocean by way of rivers choked with effluent and sewage. One visible manifestation of this oil influx is the presence of numerous oil clots in the Japan Current. Government studies conclude that the ocean surface of the Black Current area carries an average of thirty tons of oil (160 tons maximum) for every hundred square kilometers. The coastlines of the Chishima Islands, where the Black Current collides with the Kurile Current, are badly polluted with drifting oil scum, and many

---

*In January 1975, a petrochemical tank burst on the eastern shore of Shikoku and released 250,000 gallons of oil into the Inland Sea.

other areas are also adversely affected. There is every reason to believe the pollution of Japan's coastal waters will be aggravated by future expansion of industrial and private oil consumption. Moreover, the likelihood of massive spills is sure to grow as more and bigger tankers ply coastal waters,† especially tankers of the Globtik-Tokyo class (477,000 D/W tons), now the world's largest; Japanese shipbuilders are planning even more gigantic tankers of 500,000 tons and above (*JEA*, 1972l:46–49; *JT*, 12 November 1974; Ui, 1972a:68–70).

Japan illustrates for the world a bizarre consequence of tampering with underground water. As a result of pumping out subsurface water for domestic and industrial purposes, ground levels have dropped in forty-six districts in thirty-one prefectures. The Nakanoshima area in Osaka (comparable in many respects to New York's Manhattan) has subsided to zero sea level or below and is threatened with flooding at high tide. In Tokyo some areas are subsiding 210 millimeters a year and 124 square kilometers are already at sea level. At Niigata the earthquake of 1964, aided by ground subsidence, flooded 121,300 homes. Industrial sites and business districts usually escape these inconveniences because they are located on high ground. The chief victims are citizens in residential areas, but so far government regulation and control of this environmental problem has been negligible (*JT*, 23 October 1974; *QEJ*, 1973:135–137; *MDN*. 26 May 1974; Ui, 1972a:57–58).

Closely related to water pollution in Japan are several spectacular instances of chemical and heavy metal poisoning. PCB has entered water directly and sifts down indirectly from the air. The substance is a chloride with insulating properties which make it useful in the production of electrical appliances, carbonless copy paper, paint, ink, and other items. About 11,000 tons were used in 1970, up from a mere 200 tons in 1954. Consumption dropped to 6,780 tons in 1971, because of prohibition of its use as a solvent in the manufacture of carbonless copy paper (large reserves are still being sold), but an upswing in production is expected as new applications are developed. PCB first came to national attention as a dangerous pollutant in 1968 when 10,000 people in western Japan were afflicted with Kanemi Yusho, or Kanemi Rice Oil Disease. The source was the Kanemi Soko Company in Kyushu, which uses PCB as a medium for heat transfer in the manufacture of rice bran oil. The victims exhibited unsightly and painful symptoms: virulent acne over the body, loose and falling hair, joint and stomach pains, numbness and palsy, vomiting, impaired vision and memory. At first this incident was dismissed as an isolated case of food poisoning. Now it is clear that PCB has entered the environment through

---

†There were 21 tanker collisions in Tokyo Bay in 1973. Ise Bay and the Seto Inland Sea have a similar problem because of the proximity of great petroleum complexes.

the burning of PCB-laden products and by means of waste industrial water. Sea bass from Tokyo Bay have concentrated PCB at a maximum of 120 ppm, compared with 0.1 to 1.0 ppm in other parts of the world. Carp from southern Lake Biwa have concentrations of 10 to 20 ppm and 1 to 5 ppm in other sectors. High PCB levels have been detected at monitoring stations off Yokohama, Kawasaki, at the mouth of the Tama River, and many other places. Between 1968 and 1972, 29,126 tons of PCB were used domestically, only 3,600 tons of which were recovered by late 1972. It is in the breast milk of mothers everywhere in the country (*QEJ*, 1973:148–152; Ui, 1972a:25–27; *JEA*, 10 August 1973, Vol. 1, No. 3; *JT*, 22 December 1972; *DY*, 24 July 1974).

Mercury poisoning, to which we shall return in a later chapter, has affected thousands, especially in Minamata and Niigata. Tokyo public health officials have warned Tokyoites to dine sparingly on tuna because of high methyl mercury concentrations.

One of the most dreadful exhibits in Japan's gallery of pollution horrors is cadmium poisoning, dubbed Itai-Itai (ouch! ouch!), after the tormented cries of those unfortunate enough to contract it. This disease decalcifies the bones, thus promoting skeletal deformation and disintegration. The accompanying neuralgic pain is excruciating, especially in the pelvic region. In time the victim actually becomes shorter in stature because of crumbling fractured vertebra. Eventually all body movement becomes agonizing and the patient dies from inability to eat or sleep. Thus far more than a hundred people have died of Itai-Itai and 280 have the disease, though fewer cases are recognized by the government. Itai-Itai has appeared on Tsushima Island where the Toho Zinc Company has a mining facility, in Toyama Prefecture where the Kamioka Mine of the Mitsui Mining and Smelting Company operates at the headwaters of the Jinzu River, and in the cities of Kurobe, Annaka, and Bandai as well, all of which are host to copper and zinc mines. The Kamioka Mine has been discharging waste into the Jinzu River for many years, and there is also considerable runoff of zinc, copper, lead, and cadmium from slag heaps. The cadmium-tainted river flows through Toyama City. Its water is drawn off by rice farmers to irrigate their paddy fields, thus contaminating a staple food; indeed, cadmium-bearing rice has become a national problem that was officially acknowledged only in July of 1970, when the Ministry of Health and Welfare relented to public pressure and established a ceiling for the concentration of cadmium in rice. Wheat and cabbages in the vicinity of Annaka have also been shown to carry cadmium. Thus far seven areas have been designated as candidates for cadmium pollution, specifically in the prefectures of Miyagi, Gumma, Nagasaki, Oita, Toyama, Fukushima, and Fukuoka. When one considers that about a thousand industries process or use cadmium in Japan with relative freedom from stringent controls, the ominous dimensions of the problem become obvious *(JEA,* 1972i:18–23; *QEJ,* 1973:158–161; Ui, 1972a:17–20).

The rampant pollution of Japan's water resources is expected to intensify as demand rises. Thus total requirements for freshwater are likely to shift from 79,380 million tons in 1970 to 126,290 million tons in 1985. Per capita demand annually for the same two years is put at 765 and 961 tons. During this time period the BOD load is predicted to rise from 6.4 million tons in 1970 to 21.2 million tons by 1985, or 3.3 times the 1970 level. How the Japanese propose to reconcile their future needs for water with such massive pollution loads remains, for the present, an enigma. In the meantime, there is no clear understanding of how severely water pollution is affecting health and ecosystems, for the worst aspects of the problem have emerged only in the past fifteen or twenty years *(JT,* 28 August 1973; *EPC,* 1974:9; *OMG,* 1971:19–20).

CHAPTER
4
SCOPE AND NATURE OF THE PROBLEM (3)

SOLID WASTES

THE UNITED STATES

On a per capita basis, Americans probably generate more garbage and trash than any other people in the world. Every man, woman, and child discards five pounds of solid waste each day that somehow must be disposed of, often at palpable risk to the environment (CEQ, 1970:106).

In the United States an obvious form of environmental pollution is the garbage dump and landfill that blots the landscape near urban areas. Litter and trash also are scattered on roadsides and city streets, in picnic areas and parks, and around homes from one end of the nation to the other. The problem has become critical in recent years with the wide use of plastics, nonreturnable glass bottles, metals for packaging, and a taste for prewrapped convenience foods (CEQ, 1973b:200).

Solid wastes threaten the environment near mines, industrial plants, cattle farms, and poultry establishments. In 1973 some five billion tons of industrial solid wastes were unloaded on the nation. Not only are they aesthetically displeasing, they are resources down the drain and often contribute to air and water pollution. Agricultural wastes, which account for about half of all solid wastes produced in the country, include remains from slaughtering operations, chaff from harvesting, trimmings from vineyards and orchards, and residues from greenhouses. In the agricultural sector, feedlots are the worst offender; mountains of manure accumulate and press on water quality.

Mineral wastes collect in slag heaps, culm piles, and mill tailing dumps and constitute some forty percent of all solid waste. Industry contributes scrap metal, slag, rags, plastic shards, fly ash, and paper to the tune of one hundred million tons a year. Four fifths of these wastes come from the iron, copper, steel, bituminous coal, phosphate rock, lead, zinc, aluminum, and anthracite industries. Residential, commercial, and institutional wastes include thirty million tons of paper, one hundred million tires, thirty billion bottles, sixty billion cans, millions of automobiles and worn out appliances, four million tons of plastics, and millions of tons of sewage sludge and garbage. The bulk of these wastes land in dumps and landfills in and around cities, which are quickly running out of space for such purposes. The solid waste deluge is increasing by four percent a year, so the burden on disposal services is additive (*CEQ*, 1970:107–108).

In the meantime, the technology of solid waste collection, disposal, and recycling is poorly developed. Over ninety percent of the existing landfill disposal operations and seventy-five percent of the incinerator facilities of the nation are substandard. Many local attempts to gather waste materials for recycling have foundered because of public and business indifference. Moreover, financial incentives are weak. In the past decade the percentage of recycled as opposed to virgin raw materials in use has declined, chiefly because the latter are not so expensive. The situation with respect to recycled paper illustrates the point. From 1960 to 1969, the percentage of recycled paper consumed, compared to the use of original fiber material, dropped from twenty-three to eighteen percent; it cost less to use virgin timber (*CEQ*, 1973b:202–204).

The Soviet Union

Like any industrial society, the Soviet Union must dispose of an ever-increasing burden of solid wastes. Economic growth has proliferated not only industrial solid wastes but also the problem of what to do with manufactured goods once their productive life has ended. Urbanization has concentrated these and other human wastes into sprawling urban centers, creating severe local problems.

Unfortunately no national figures are available on the amount of industrial wastes cast yearly into the environment, although it is probably safe to assume that their quantity has increased at roughly the same rate as industrial growth as a whole. The production of general manufactured goods has increased over eleven times from 1940 to 1970, suggesting parallel growth in the volume of industrial wastes *(TsSU,* 1971:135). Metallurgical industries have experienced acute disposal problems, for as much as three thousand tons of slag may be produced by a single blast furnace each day, and production has increased over threefold since 1953 (Mote, 1971:75; *TsSU,* 1971:190–195). Soviet managers are faced with a vexing dilemma by these disposal problems. On the one hand, the need to meet a production quota stiffens their will to resist any "diversion" of the factory's efforts into secondary activities such as waste recycling. On the other hand, their labor costs are frequently low in relation to raw material costs, creating pressures to salvage as much as possible for future productive use (Goldman, 1972b:280).

The problem of domestic refuse—"garbage" in the everyday parlance—has increased with the standard of living, especially in crowded urban areas. One official laments that the average Muscovite produces twice as much garbage as he did in 1965 (Shirokov, 1973:6). On the national average, each citizen generates somewhere between five hundred and one thousand pounds of domestic solid wastes annually, while the average American, a heavyweight by comparison, generates nearly a ton a year (Mote, 1971:74). While these wastes create disposal problems for local officials, especially in densely settled areas, their impact on the environment is less visible and lasting than in the West. A greater portion of the offensive items, such as glass bottles, paper, and scrap metals, which pile up by the millions of tons in other countries, are eventually recycled for use because of the low labor costs involved. Abandoned and junked autos, a major problem in most American cities, are virtually nonexistent in the Soviet Union. Given the scarcity of vehicles and spare parts, autos are driven to the last mile and then cannibalized for spare parts (Goldman, 1972b:74–75).

The disposal of packaging is still a minor problem. Most items are sold unpackaged, with the buyer responsible for providing the container for transporting his purchase home. Tin cans are relatively few in number, and with the exception of a few items—occasional egg crates, for example—most foodstuffs are sold loose over the counter. However, Soviet authorities have recently given greater emphasis to container production. The development of self-service stores somewhat like small-scale supermarkets has also increased the need for better packaging, and officials have expressed interest in importing packaging technology from the West (Bush, 1972:24).

In general, the biodegradability of these wastes is relatively high. Most of the items that are completely nonbiodegradable, or that decay only after prolonged exposure to natural processes, comprise a small percentage of the total or are recycled in large quantities. The most important exception is the huge quantity of plastic consumer goods first produced in the Khrushchev years (the production of plastics rose four times from 1962 to 1970). In providing the Soviet consumer with a wide assortment of plastic kitchenware and other gadgets, Soviet leaders introduced into the environment the first significant accumulation of nonbiodegradable wastes (Promyslov, 1973:2).

Industrial wastes are usually disposed of in open dumps as close to the factory as local officials will permit. Domestic waste disposal is usually handled through a combination of surface dumps and landfills. In some areas composting in biothermic chambers is used since the resulting compound can be used as fertilizer. Open burning of trash is rare in large cities such as Moscow and Leningrad, which have large incinerators, some linked with thermal generating plants. In these developed areas, refuse is collected roughly every three or four days and directed through local recycling facilities, if available, and eventually into the city's landfills and incinerators (Mote, 1971:74–75; Bush, 1972:24; Goldman, 1972b:173–174). Moscow is now experimenting with pneumatic underground tubes to speed household wastes to collection points, and several new processing plants or incinerators have recently been completed or are on the drawing boards (Shirokov, 1973:6). In smaller towns and rural areas, collection is more sporadic and the use of surface dumps and open burning more common.

JAPAN

Before 1945 there were few problems concerning waste disposal. Human and animal wastes were collected as fertilizer; garbage was fed to hogs; paper, scrap metal, and discarded glass were commonly salvaged for reuse. Most homes were equipped with simple wooden baths fueled with household trash and useless bits of wood. The slag, metal tailings, sludge, and discards of industry were not as yet overwhelming. A possible exception was the mining industry, whose considerable wastes inflicted serious damage on local environments quite early (Strong, 1972; Ui, 1972a:48–50).

As a result of population growth, rising incomes, urbanization, rapid industrialization, and the emergence of a consumer-oriented economy, the Japanese since 1945 have been confronted with a growing annual torrent of industrial wastes, urban effluent, and garbage (*JEA*, 10 May 1974, Vol. 2, No. 5). The premium on habitable land and the delicacy of Japanese ecosystems both magnify the problem. Although it is difficult to bring statistics from scattered and often conflicting sources into focus, the total amount of solid waste for the country in 1973 was in the vicinity of seven hundred million tons, coming primarily from industrial, urban, and household sources (*JEA*, 1972d; *QEJ*, 1973:140–142; Ui, 1972a:59–62).

Industry is by far the greatest offender. In 1970 the Ministry of International Trade and Industry (MITI) polled 5,000 large factories, and from the 2,443 replies received, estimated the production of 39,360,000 tons of waste and projected an annual total of 59,000,000 tons for all 5,000 concerns, which are far from accounting for all of Japanese industry. A projection of 100,000,000 tons was made for 1975, with the same 5,000 factories taken as the base. Tokyo alone generates over 35 million tons of refuse a year in industrial wastes.

The annual total for household wastes in 1972 was close to 27 million tons. This category of refuse includes garbage, paper, plastics, discarded furniture, television sets, refrigerators, and other appliances. The Japanese people were once amenable to saving, conserving, and recycling resources, but values have changed in the wake of a new affluence and consumerism. Millions of citizens are now locked into a waste and discard economy which thrives on built-in obsolescence and expensive, elaborate packaging. (QEJ, 1973:141).

Tokyo is once again a barometer of trends throughout urban Japan. Household waste in 1972 came to 13,000 tons a day, up from 9,600 tons in 1970, and 11,210 tons in 1971. In 1975 the quantity of refuse was about 25,000 tons a day, or some 4.3 million tons a year. At present Tokyo churns out about sixteen percent of the national total; in 1968 the cost of disposal was forty million dollars and had doubled over the previous seven-year period. Some feeling for the whole of Japan is conveyed by statistics for a few other key cities. In 1969 Yokohama had a turnover of waste amounting to 662,337 tons, and the Osaka-Kobe area managed to come up with no less than 730,000 tons in a single month in 1969 (RIEP, 1972; TMG, 1971:222–224; JQ, 1972b).

The composition as well as the bulk of refuse has changed over the years. Most striking is the quantity of discarded plastics, which doubled from 5.4 percent to 10.3 percent of all solid household waste between 1966 and 1970. The tantalizing convenience of plastic containers and utensils, as well as the lure of cheaper costs for industry, has set the Japanese consumer on a dangerous road. The manufacture of plastics is a central activity of the Japanese petrochemical industry and a formidable vested interest. Total production of plastics was 1,600,000 tons in 1965, more than 5,100,000 tons in 1970, and approached 10,000,000 tons in 1975 (RIEP, 1972:34–39).

The options for disposing of a yearly total of more than seven hundred million tons of wastes, short of massive recycling, are limited. Incineration contributes to thermal and air pollution but is nonetheless a growing industry in Japan. Many cities use landfills, but available land for such purposes is rapidly disappearing. A related expedient is the building of large artificial islands out of garbage and refuse, like the 112 acre "Yume no Shima" (Dream Island) in Tokyo Bay. A "New Dream Island" is already taking shape as garbage is piled into a 470,000 square meter area, and there are plans for still another area of 270,000 square meters. The ecology of Tokyo Bay has been given low priority in these desperate attempts to keep Tokyo's head above the garbage level *(TMG,* 1971:99–100).

Still another means of disposing of solid wastes is composting. It is not as yet widespread, although Kobe, Tokyo, and Amagasaki have fairly large operations. The most shameless recourse is ocean dumping. Chiba City in Chiba Prefecture disposes of some three hundred to four hundred tons daily in this way, and all other Japanese cities near the sea are similarly inclined. In Tokyo about seventy percent of all solid waste goes into landfills; the rest is incinerated or dumped in the ocean. The problem is developing far ahead of any solution either available or in sight.

RADIOACTIVE POLLUTION

THE UNITED STATES

Mankind has always been exposed to a certain amount of natural background radiation from the sun and from materials in the earth's crust. This natural radiation causes at least part of the natural mutation rate among humans, and has also been linked to incidences of cancer and leukemia. It would appear, then, that any human activity that raises the level of exposure to radiation is hazardous and should be treated with great caution.

Since World War II, human beings have been exposed to new sources of radiation. Radioactive fallout from nuclear weapons testing includes the highly dangerous strontium-90 and cesium-137, which persist with half-lives of twenty-eight and thirty years, respectively. Although the United States and the Soviet Union signed a treaty in the 1960's to stop their own atmospheric testing of nuclear weapons, the People's Republic of China and France have continued such tests. The other major source of radiation developed in the past thirty years has been the nuclear power plant. Several dozen nuclear generating plants are now operational in the United States, and over a hundred more are in various stages of planning and construction. Every one of them is a potential source of radiation leakage, and all raise problems concerning the safe disposal of their radioactive wastes *(CEQ,* 1970:143).

The National Academy of Sciences estimated in 1970 that the American population is exposed to an average of 182 millirems per year from all sources of radiation; 73 are from medical sources, 4 from nuclear fallout, and 3 from miscellaneous sources like television sets. Exposure from nuclear power generating systems amounts to only .003 millirems at present. The average amount of man-made radiation exposure is about 3.5 percent of the Environmental Protection Agency's safety guidelines for such exposure, but this total undoubtedly will rise as more nuclear systems come into operation to satisfy future energy requirements. The Atomic Energy Commission has established reactor design regulations that will limit the exposure of people living near nuclear power plants to about 5 percent of the background radiation, although this standard has been deemed unsafe by groups opposed to the development of nuclear power (CEQ, 1973b:190).

Another point of controversy between certain environmentalist groups and advocates of nuclear power development is the adequacy of emergency systems designed to cool a reactor core should the normal cooling system fail. Overheating of the reactor due to failure of the emergency system could result in an extensive release of radioactive materials into the surrounding environment. Long hearings were conducted by the Atomic Energy Commission in 1971 and 1972 on the adequacy of emergency core cooling system standards. With the conclusion of these hearings in late 1973, new standards were issued for the design of such systems, and are to be applied to both existing plants and those under construction (CEQ, 1973b:194; NY Times, 30 December 1973).

The disposal of reactor wastes promises to become a more acute problem as nuclear plants gain in size and number. Such wastes are classified as either low or high level. The low-level type consists of gases, liquids, and solids from reactors and other nuclear facilities. Until 1971, low-radiation gases and liquids were merely released into the atmosphere and into waterways, since their levels were well below the Atomic Energy Commission's (AEC) safety standards. Beginning in 1971, the AEC required installation of new air and water effluent controls in nuclear plants to stop those emissions. The low-level solid wastes are now stored in a small number of AEC-owned and AEC-licensed burial sites, and their volume is growing rapidly as more reactors are put into operation; several million cubic feet of such wastes are buried at approved sites.

The high-level wastes, principally in the form of used fuel rods, are shipped to reprocessing plants where the rods are reworked into liquid wastes and further processed into new solids for burial. This procedure reduces the physical volume of the wastes by some ninety percent, but with the multiplication of reactors, a large volume of such wastes must be disposed of each year. The AEC has estimated that by 1980 commercial reactors will have produced 3.5 million gallons of liquid waste that will be converted into solid matter totaling 35,000 cubic feet. Disposal of these toxic substances presents horrendous difficulties. Burial at sea invites leakage and serious oceanic pollution. Burial in the ground invites the contamination of underground water. The disposal situation will worsen by the end of the century when sixty to seventy percent of the country's energy is tied up in nuclear power (CEQ, 1970:145–146).

The Soviet Union

Historically neither the user nor the victim of nuclear weapons, the Soviet Union has largely avoided the degree of emotionalism that attaches to the debate over nuclear weaponry and the peaceful use of atomic energy in the United States and Japan. While Soviet leaders are fully cognizant of the consequences of nuclear test fallout and the environmental hazards of the industrial use of atomic energy, the public at large seems blissfully unconcerned. The development of military and civilian uses of atomic energy may even be regarded as a cause for pride for the average Russian, since it testifies to his nation's scientific achievements and new-found stature.

The environmental threat of fallout from nuclear testing has declined markedly since the 1963 Test Ban Treaty was first implemented. Following the conclusion of the treaty, the amount of radioactive aerosols dropped by ninety-five percent, and the presence of other radioactive particles fell almost as much. However, Chinese nuclear testing in the atmosphere since 1967 has again caused the level of strontium-90 and cesium-137 to rise six times above the pretest level (Goldman, 1972b:128). Future tests of even larger weapons are likely to worsen this new fallout hazard since both the People's Republic of China and France do not adhere to the Test Ban Treaty and regard themselves free to continue atmospheric testing.

Little is known about the industrial uses of nuclear energy in the Soviet Union, although we must assume that the relative scarcity of these resources and the tight security provisions attached to their use probably mean that industrial use is more limited than in the West. Soviet scientists have used low-yield nuclear explosions to increase the output of gas and oil fields. While Soviet officials claim that the gas and oil then extracted are free of radioactive contamination, Western specialists are skeptical since similar experiments in the West have shown that such fuels retain a low level of radioactivity (*Environment*, 1971:28).

The Soviet Union presently has in operation nine major nuclear generating plants, with several more under construction. By the year 2000, it is conservatively estimated that the Soviet Union will annually produce well over two million kilowatts of electrical power through nuclear power stations (Pryde and Pryde, 1974:26–29; Goldman, 1972b:142–143; Emelianov, 1971:41). The operation of this ever-growing grid of nuclear power stations will inevitably increase the potential for nuclear pollution, to say nothing of the danger of accidental catastrophic discharges of radiation through the failure of reactor cooling systems or other accidents.

The USSR is ahead of the United States in the development of liquid metal fast-breeder reactors. However, according to the testimony of visiting American scientists, much of the speed of development has occurred at the expense of safety precautions. Few of the safety problems for which control measures have been developed in the West have been considered serious by Soviet technicians (Pryde and Pryde, 1974:29–30; *Environment*, 1970:S-3).

The manufacture of nuclear fuels for both civilian and military uses releases small quantities of radiation into the environment. The processing of uranium ore into fuel contaminates large quantities of water, and fuel enrichment processes further heighten the danger. Radioactive solid wastes in the form of ore tailings are also created and are usually disposed of in large dumps near the processing plants.

The operation of nuclear power reactors routinely releases radiation into the air and water. Krypton-85, a radioactive gas, is simply discharged up the station's high stacks to be dissipated in the atmosphere. The water used in the reactor is contaminated by tritium, which binds to the water molecules by replacing the hydrogen atoms. While Soviet officials claim that this discharged water is adequately treated, the experience of such stations in the West suggests that such treatment is less than fully successful (Goldman, 1972b:142–144).

The disposal of nuclear wastes also creates special environmental difficulties. The rapid growth of nuclear power stations and atomic-powered ships has led Marshall Goldman (1972b:143) to estimate that Soviet officials will be faced with the disposal of thousands of tons of radioactive wastes by the year 2000. Evidence suggests that presently solid wastes are simply dumped untreated into the Black Sea and possibly other locations, and liquid wastes are either solidified for burial or pumped into underground storage chambers, each alternative presenting its own threat of long-term contamination of the environment (LaMothe, 1971:19,48; Pryde and Pryde, 1974:32–33).

Soviet medical officials have shown increasing interest in the health consequences of the peaceful uses of nuclear energy. The Labor Hygiene and Occupational Diseases Institute of the USSR Academy of Medical Sciences has five research departments which deal with questions of radiation safety and health, and the Institute of Radiation Hygiene of the USSR Ministry of Public Health also deals with such questions. In 1969, radiation safety standards were strengthened to permit 5 rem per year exposure for workers in nuclear-related industries and 0.5 rem per year for the general public (*HEW*, 1970:680–699; *USDC*, 1970:7). Concern for worker safety seems well founded in light of the lax standards applied in the early years of nuclear power development in the USSR. From 1946 to 1948, workers in atomic plants developed an abnormally high frequency of cataracts. As late as 1963, it was rumored that outbreaks of leukemia in Moscow were caused by the careless disposal of radioactive wastes. Safety standards are now tighter and seemingly better enforced, but doubt remains among those who come into occupational contact with radioactive fuels or live near nuclear facilities (Goldman, 1972b:143–144).

The potential danger of accidents in nuclear power stations and other facilities using such fuels has not been regarded as a serious threat by Soviet officials. There are no backup cooling systems in conventional burner reactors, and thus a failure of a reactor cooling system would permit the superheated fuel elements to melt their way through the reactor wall and contaminate an extensive area around the installation. The fast-breeder reactors program in the Soviet Union has, in the opinion of some Western observers, been less than thorough in providing safety precautions. The transportation of nuclear fuels and wastes also poses a potential threat of contamination. At the present time such radioactive elements are transported in clearly marked trucks and vans, with seemingly few precautions against loss or theft (Pryde and Pryde, 1974:30–33; *Environment,* 1970:S-3). Conventional accidents are also a problem, as in the case when an explosion aboard a nuclear submarine at the Gorky naval base released considerable quantities of radioactive pollution along that segment of the Volga (Pryde, 1972:154–155).

JAPAN

The Japanese are unique among the world's people in their direct, traumatic experience with the destructive potential of nuclear energy. Survivors of the Hiroshima and Nagasaki bombings continue to sicken and die of cancer and leukemia in atomic bomb hospitals. At least 230,000 people still suffer from radiation diseases. As a result of this encounter with atomic radiation, the Japanese contracted a "nuclear allergy," a profound and widespread uneasiness about nuclear energy.

Although the Japanese public is still nervous, government policies are free of aversion to the peaceful use of the atom. Thus it is a matter of national policy to encourage 686 corporations and companies to use radioisotopes for a variety of purposes, even though environmentalists have charged that uninformed workers are frequently exposed to dangerous conditions of radioactivity. Japan has built a commercial nuclear-powered ship, the *Mutsu,* which was completed in 1973 and promptly developed a leak in its reactor once at sea. There is every reason to believe, however, that in the future Japan will become the world's leading producer of nuclear commercial vessels (*JT,* 9 March. 1974; Ui, 1972a:71–72; *JAEC,* 1972:14–15).

The most dramatic evidence of increased reliance on the atom, however, lies in the construction of nuclear power plants. Six are now in operation, some fourteen are presently slated for activation by 1977, and future development will probably be even more rapid given potential energy shortages and the high cost of fossil fuels. By the year 2000, some forty districts will be in close proximity to large-scale nuclear facilities. Current government intentions are that nuclear fission will provide 180,000 megawatts by 1990.* Hence a nation intimately acquainted with the devastation of nuclear war now promises to become an imposing source of nuclear pollution. In its long-range statement on nuclear energy, Japan's Atomic Energy Commission admits that "with the scale of nuclear installations becoming bigger and the kinds diversified, the level of radiation near these installations and the discharge of heated water are becoming serious problems." *(JAEC,* 1972:12; *AEN,* 1 November 1972).

There is very little natural uranium in Japan,† but the processing of even a small quantity generates huge amounts of polluted water. At present there are no enrichment facilities in Japan. However, a fuel reprocessing plant for the extraction of remaining fissionable material from used fuel is expected to be ready in 1975, and still others are being planned. Radioactive wastes from a reprocessing plant are especially potent and are ineptly controlled by existing technology. Stacks emit krypton-85, and waste water is tainted with tritium, which has a nasty habit of binding itself to water molecules. Reprocessing a ton of spent fuel generates 100 gallons of waste boiling with the heat of its own radioactivity, 50,000 curies of assorted fission products, and 1,000 curies of strontium-90. An extraordinarily vulnerable public would do well to ponder the Japan Atomic Energy Commission's comment that "a spent fuel reprocessing plant involves many as yet unsolved problems" *(JAEC,* 1972:10).

The sanguine claim of technologists that nuclear reactor systems are "safe" is not supported by evidence from Japan. Out of the six currently active stations, at least three have reported accidents or dangerous incidents involving radioactivity. The Tsuruga power station, for instance, was obliged to replace four defective fuel rods in November 1970. In June of the same year the entire reactor was closed down because of a leak in the primary cooling system. Other defects have been detected subsequently *(JT,* 24 October 1974).

Apart from the intrinsic probability of malfunction in Japan's reactors, it is worth pointing out that they perch on a major earthquake zone. The Tokai station is only sixty-five miles northeast of Tokyo, which was devastated by earth tremors in 1923. The Tsuruga station is located in Fukui Prefecture, where an earthquake in 1948 destroyed Fukui City. It is only a matter of time before major earthquakes occur again, and the Japanese

---

*It is now admitted that the cost of nuclear power will exceed that of thermal power using oil in the future *(JT,* 26 October 1974)

†A project is under way to extract it from seawater.

government has no means of providing convincing assurance that nuclear power stations will escape lethal damage.

The disposal of nuclear wastes has found no environmentally sound solution in Japan, though it is hoped that a new Radioactive Waste Disposal Center created in 1974 will come up with something (*JT*, 20 August 1970). Ocean dumping is the most expedient procedure; between 1955 and 1965, volatile radioactive wastes in the amount of 1661 drums were dropped to the sea bottom. Official plans for most kinds of waste are tentative. Low-radiation wastes are to be solidified and disposed of on land and at sea; by 1975–76 "research" will tell authorities precisely where.* Medium-radiation materials, such as ion exchange resins, are stored presently at nuclear installations and await a decision, promised by 1980, about disposition. High-radiation wastes, that is, spent fuel rods, are stored and also await a decision about disposal. The problem is truly monumental in light of Japan's ambitious nuclear power program, the limited area of the country, and the nation's reliance on food resources of the ocean. According to Japan's Science and Technology Agency, the amount of spent fuel supplies will be 1,600 tons a year by 1985. Overall radioactive wastes are expected to reach a volume of 45,000 cubic meters, or 225,000 drums, a year by the mid-1980's, presenting a monumental disposal problem (Ui, 1972a:74; *JAEC*, 1972:12–14).

NOISE POLLUTION

THE UNITED STATES

In America the plague of noise is integral to a prevalent urban life-style, with its din from autos, trucks, buses, construction projects, subways, railways, and jet aircraft. Although city dwellers may regard noise as a mere irritant, they are commonly unaware that prolonged exposure to high levels of sound can injure health and result in loss of hearing. An authority on noise has observed that "environmental noise is one of the most serious public health problems, urgently requiring solutions and public controls." A variety of studies support this conclusion. A Wisconsin Medical School psychiatrist has shown that housewives' complaints of headaches, nausea, and nervous tension were related to noise. Other studies indicate a correlation between high noise levels and birth defects in animal fetuses, as well

---

*In the meantime the sea will have to live with the consequences of thermal pollution. Kajiwara and Kikuchi point out what nuclear cooling systems do to water: "An atomic power station which generates 1,000,000 kilowatts of power uses 5,000,000 tons of seawater a day as secondary cooling water and radiates 360,000,000,000 kilocalories of heat. This much heat can raise the temperature of 3,600,000 tons of water from zero to one hundred degrees" (Ui, 1972a:74).

as physiological changes such as elevated pulse and blood pressure levels. Further research is needed on these matters, but it is already conceded that noise is a conspicuous form of urban pollution.

Much of the phenomenon is due to the proximity of residential zones to major transportation facilities and industry. Noise is often most severe in the vicinity of highways and airports, a consequence of unplanned growth in cities and suburbs. The expressways that ring and cut through cities have introduced a steady noise level of 70 to 90 decibels, to which prolonged exposure can damage hearing permanently. Subways in places like Boston and New York are even noisier at times. The 115 to 120 decibel level produced by a four-engine jet on takeoff has provoked formal complaints and lawsuits from residents in the vicinity of fifty major airports; altogether, some fifteen million people live close enough to airports to be disturbed by intense aircraft noise.

Other major sources are foundaries, auto assembly plants, saw mills, and a host of additional industries. Some of the larger concerns have promoted safety programs to guard their employees' hearing, but an estimated ten to twenty million industrial workers are exposed regularly to noise levels in excess of eighty-five decibels. Due to the location of older residential housing near industrial sites, many nonworkers are also victims of high noise levels. Bulldozers, jack hammers, cranes, and other types of equipment used in the construction of highways, subways, skyscrapers, shopping centers, and sports stadiums have swelled the cacophony impinging on Americans (*CEQ,* 1970:124–128; *CEQ,* 1972b:206,211–216).

In addition to impairing health and mental peace, noise inflicts other kinds of significant damage. The World Health Organization maintains that excessive noise costs the United States some four billion dollars a year in compensation payments, accidents, inefficiency, and absenteeism. Noise depreciation of real-estate values mounts into the billions, especially in the vicinity of jet airports. Sonic booms, a noise-pollution spectacular, have caused damage of one sort or another throughout the country, obliging the air force to pay out more than a million dollars in compensation (*NY Times,* 3 September 1973). With further industrial growth, more people, and attendant construction projects, the problem is likely to intensify rather than diminish.

THE SOVIET UNION

Long seemingly unaware of the abrasive presence of high noise levels in their cities and factories, Soviet environmentalists have only recently acknowledged that noise pollution has become a bothersome and even harmful consequence of industrialization and urbanization. One suspects that this official recognition of the problem has lagged far behind general public awareness that the average Soviet city dweller lives in a world of noisy factories and streets and poorly sound-proofed apartments.

Like their American counterparts, Soviet medical officials have also noted the health consequences of noise pollution. A high-level Ministry of Public Health official has admitted that noise not only affects hearing but also contributes to nervous disorders and cardiovascular diseases, disturbs body metabolism, causes fatigue, and reduces work capacity. Doctors now refer to the phenomenon of "noise sickness" as a common malady of harassed urban dwellers. The problem is regarded as very serious by medical researchers and public health officials, and a special interdepartmental commission has been created by the Ministry of Public Health to deal with noise-pollution problems (JPRS, 1970c:5-9; Pryde, 1972:158; Khotsianov, 1973:13).

Noise from autos and trucks is a major problem in Soviet cities. Street noises have been measured up to ninety-five decibels under normal traffic conditions, which is equal to standing twenty feet from a roaring subway (JPRS, 1970b:15-16). Autos and trucks are poorly muffled when first built, and inadequate servicing means that thousands of vehicles with old or damaged mufflers go untended. Russian drivers are also given to racing their engines at intersections, and apartment dwellers frequently complain that car owners start their cars several times on especially cold winter nights to warm the engines (Bush, 1972:24-25; Promyslov, 1973:2).

Airport noise is less of a problem than in the United States. While Soviet aircraft are no quieter than their Western counterparts, the airports tend to be located further from the center city. Moscow's three civilian fields are all located well out of the city. The impact of dense air traffic around urban centers is also diminished by a ban on overflights (Bush, 1972:24). During a year's residence in the Soviet capital, I cannot recall any occasion when aircraft could be heard in the vicinity. It is likely, however, that the development of a Soviet supersonic transport will create added noise-pollution problems.

Factory noise is a problem for Soviet workers. Foreign observers report that work area noise tends to be far higher than in the West. Factory location in residential areas has also added to the impact of industrial noise pollution. While factories and residential housing are supposed to be separated by a carefully specified distance depending on the nature of the industry (this is primarily designed to diminish air pollution, but its usefulness in noise abatement is evident), the rules are frequently violated. Factories spring up in already established residential areas, and managers frequently build their own housing near the factory as a convenience for the workers. The commonplace result is that the rules to the contrary, there is an uncomfortably close proximity between the workers' machines and the residents' ears (Bush, 1972:24–25).

Soviet apartment dwellers also find their lot a noisy one. A recent study conducted in Riga indicates that noise bothers people more at home than on the street or at work. Housing construction has lagged far behind the pace of urbanization, meaning that thousands of families are crowded into much smaller accommodations than mandated by Soviet housing regulations. The buildings themselves leave much to be desired. Construction is poor, leaving ill-fitting doors and windows to transmit high noise levels. Sound-damping insulation has been totally absent until recently, and even now it is used in only a small number of buildings. Soviet contractors also frequently stint on the basic construction materials both to save money and to speed completion of the project, thus making the walls and floors less soundproof. Pressure regulators are not used in the plumbing, making the pipes sing a discordant chorus each time a tap is opened. Elevators are also a noise problem in larger dwellings, and one Moscow official has proposed that apartments adjacent to elevator shafts be declared unsuitable for occupancy. There is considerable evidence to suggest that the high noise level commonly found in these apartment complexes takes a high toll in terms of frayed nerves and shortened tempers (*JPRS*, 1970c:4–6). The vast majority of cases brought before the pseudo-judicial Comrades' Courts— councils of building residents who hear minor complaints and mete out small penalties—concern noise and other social frictions which arise out of endemic overcrowding. Clearly the average apartment dweller needs no decibel meter to remind him that his walls are thin and his neighbors noisy.

JAPAN

Silence and tranquility have become luxuries and rarities in modern Japan, snatched away by the deafening roar of traffic and aircraft, the hammering and hissing of ubiquitous construction machines, the clamor of hundreds of thousands of factories, and the unending babble of millions living cheek by jowl. Noise pollution has become the single greatest environmental complaint of the Japanese people. National surveys in 1968 and 1972, touching on most forms of pollution, found noise and vibration most frequently cited as major complaints of forty-five percent of the respondents (*QEJ*, 1972; *JEA*, 10 March 1974, Vol. 2, No. 3). In Tokyo the figures rose to fifty-seven percent. A similar response emerges from most of Japan's urbanized areas, and even the countryside does not escape the consequences of automobile traffic. There is reason to believe that noise pollution has undesirable effects far beyond those uncovered by polls. In *Tokyo Fights*

Pollution, (*TMG,* 1971:156) we read that "it is safe to say that there are many latent victims of noise and vibrations; in other words, the filed complaints are only the tip of the iceberg." Only Japanese patience and stoicism in the face of discomfort have obscured the problem until recently.

Certain conditions in Japan exacerbate the effects of noise; among these are endemic crowding, the poor insulation of wooden houses which still predominate everywhere (the average Japanese house can screen out only ten decibels), and the location of multitudinous small industries in residential and commercial areas, often right next to domestic dwellings. The effects are varied. Japanese doctors have found that noise disturbs sleep, contributes to fatigue, promotes tension and stress, raises blood pressure, alters the proper functioning of the autonomic nervous system, and at ninety decibels or more can temporarily or permanently damage hearing. There is still another effect everyone understands: the irritation of not being able to obtain a modicum of peace and quiet for the normal purposes of life. For example, 387 schools in the Tokyo system (twenty-two percent of the total) complained of distracting noise in 1969. The noise level in most of the schools was sixty-five to sixty-nine decibels, although 14 reported levels as high as seventy-five decibels. The order of contributing nuisances were autos (sixty-eight percent), planes (twenty-three percent), trains (six percent), and factories (slightly under two percent).

As in the United States, Japan is in danger of being taken over by the automobile. In congested urban areas a high level of traffic noise is commonplace, even without the boost afforded by rush hours. The problem is worsened by the Japanese passion for revving up engines as a form of ego-assertion and the practice of many young Japanese (known as the "kaminari tribe") of knocking out their mufflers or replacing them with ingenious noisemakers.

All major Japanese airports are near or adjacent to residential areas. The noise potential of aircraft can be illustrated with Haneda International Airport in the Tokyo area. Haneda handles up to 500 planes a day, which means that an airplane is landing or taking off every three minutes; at peak hours, the time gap is a minute and a half. Most of these aircraft are big four-engine jets that at takeoff register eighty decibels at a point six kilometers away. Tokyo's confrontation with aircraft noise will grow even worse when the operation of a new international airport at Narita begins.

Factory noise is very nearly omnipresent because of the close physical juxtaposition of urban dwellers and various enterprises. Some eighty-six percent of Tokyo's more than eighty thousand factories employ less than twenty people. Most of Japan's small industries are located in residential areas, where they fill the air with the whine of machines. One can add to factory noise the din of a seemingly interminable construction boom. In most of Japan's big cities one is seldom far from a rude symphony of concrete breakers, pile drivers, rivet guns, compressors, diesel and vibro hammers, and an incessant parade of trucks. Moreover, highway construction, architectural projects, subway excavation, civil-engineering schemes, and the like, tend to reach a peak during the summer months when most people are out of doors *(RIEP,* 1972:52; *QEJ,* 1973:132–134; *JEA,* 5 June 1973).

To this tidal wave of sound must be added the myriad television sets, radios, loudspeakers and public address systems, and the continual hum of millions going about their business in Japan's packed cities. As in the case of other forms of pollution, noise is expected to become an even more formidable nuisance in the future, for the simple reason that sources discussed above are expected to multiply *(MDN,* 15 June 1974).

ECOSYSTEM DETERIORATION

THE UNITED STATES

Ecosystems have been assaulted ferociously in recent American history. The countryside has been ripped up to build cities, extract minerals, and dispose of wastes. The atmosphere and waterways have been impregnated with waste with no thought of the impact on fragile or even hearty ecosystems. The more "civilized" an area, the more likely that local ecosystems are disrupted by a general depression of biological activity.

Man has inadvertently unseated the stability of ecosystems in the name of "progress," and then has attempted to control the instabilities by applying technology. In agriculture, for example, American farmers have deliberately boosted production by using hybrid seed and tons of artificial fertilizer to make the soil temporarily hyperfertile. More tons of DDT and other pesticides have been added to control insects in lieu of natural predators. The final result of these expedients for the sake of production and profit has been the creation of artificial ecosystems, highly simplified and unstable, that cannot exist without the constant support of technology (Commoner, 1971:146–153).

In some isolated regions of the United States, such as wilderness areas under federal protection, ecosystems may still exist in a balanced state without having felt the hand of man. In other, less isolated areas, the hand of man is only lightly felt. Throughout most of the nation, however, especially where industry and people are concentrated, most ecosystems are badly disrupted, or a tenuous balance is preserved by technological juggling.

In the past few decades, Americans have subjected the land and water to an entire new range of influences without the slightest comprehension of their total impact. A recent example of ecosystem meddling occurred in California. The destruction of sea otters that feed on sea urchins has led to a sea urchin population explosion which is now threatening the survival of major commercial kelp beds. Leaving the otters in peace may restore the balance, but at this point no one can be sure *(NY Times,* 14 March 1972).

Intensified pressure on ecosystems is inevitable as more and more land is used for cities, roads, airports, agriculture, recreation, and industry. As population grows, not only will habitats and breeding grounds of wildlife disappear, but recreational hunting and fishing will contract its range. Most game species have been thoroughly studied and are both propagated and protected by legislation. Hence the numbers of all game species in the nation has remained stable for decades, a situation that may not continue as habitats are decimated.

Information about nongame species is generally quite limited. The Endangered Species Conservation Act of 1969 has improved the situation by clearing the way to more significant research on rare and endangered species *(CEQ,* 1973b). In 1970 the Department of the Interior published a revised list of threatened native species; these included 101 species of birds, mammals, fishes, reptiles, and amphibians. Some zoologists have estimated that a third of the mammals in the United States should be on the list *(CEQ,* 1972b:191).

The populations of many nongame species of wildlife appear to be declining, particularly the larger predators and birds high in the food chain. A few, such as eagles and wolves, are hunted or poisoned as reputed threats to domestic animals *(CEQ,* 1973b:225). More fundamental for birds is the load of pesticides and other toxic substances in their environments, which pass along the food chain in ever greater concentrations from one creature to the next. The result is either death by outright ingestion of these poisons, or a more dismaying interference with reproductive functions (Carson, 1962).

THE SOVIET UNION

Evidence of ecosystem deterioration is abundant in the Soviet Union, indicating that the economic and social systems of twentieth-century industrialized and urbanized Russia have come to have a fundamentally unsettling effect on the balance of nature. Without doubt, man has always pressed on nature; a Russian peasant of the nineteenth century affected the soil, the forests, and the wildlife surrounding him. But until recently this impact has been contained by the ability of ecosystems to maintain an equilibrium.

People were neither so numerous, nor so demanding on the environment, that a wide range of other life forms were endangered. This situation has changed in the past seventy-five years.

Ecological effects are felt in two ways. First is man's direct impact on other forms of life, seen most easily in the hunting and fishing of certain species to near extinction. Like most nations with a rapidly growing urban population, the Soviet Union has been forced to draw more deeply from natural stores of food and animal resources, frequently taking more rapidly than nature can replenish. The sheer size of spreading urban areas has encroached on the life space of many species, driving them deeper into a shrinking wilderness. The complex ecological balance of forest areas has also been upset by the exploitation of easily accessible areas and inadequate replanting of valuable timber.

Industrialization has endangered ecological balance in a second way—it has polluted virtually all major waterways and a large portion of the atmosphere in which all life forms must exist or from which they obtain food. Thus air and water pollution touch virtually all living things, either directly through the progressive deterioration of their immediate life space, or indirectly through their impact on the food chain (Pryde, 1972:71-78; Kirillin, 1972:2-3).

Evidence of ecosystem deterioration due to air pollution is widespread, as we have noted above. Trees yellow and die in the biting presence of industrial effluents, and birds have deserted highly polluted areas for cleaner skies. Airborne pollutants have entered the food chain at numerous points and ultimately work their way up to higher forms of life, including man.

Even more evident is the deterioration of a wide range of interlocking ecosystems which are affected by water pollution. Hardest hit are the fish which live in fouled waters, although higher life forms which rely on fish as a dietary staple are ultimately touched. Some index of the impact of water pollution on aquatic ecosystems may be derived from the declining fish catches from polluted waterways. The total fish take from the Caspian Sea has fallen over two and one-half times since industrialization began in earnest in the 1930's. The decrease in the catch of valuable fish such as sturgeon has declined even more rapidly, falling four hundred percent since the turn of the century, while the take of less valuable species has risen. Even with this shift to less desirable fish, the Soviet fishing industry has been compelled to divert its fleet to ocean fisheries because of polluted domestic waters; only twenty percent of the fish consumed in the USSR is now harvested from inland waterways (Pryde, 1972:79; LaMothe, 1971:8).

Further environmental disruption of aquatic ecosystems has occurred because of the destruction of fish feeding and spawning areas. Logging operations and industrial effluents have killed off valuable feeding areas, and the construction of dams and hydroelectric power stations has cut fish off from their upstream spawning grounds and disrupted the flow of natural nutrients downstream (Pryde, 1972:79–83).

Soviet commentators admit that many rivers and lakes have lost their self-cleansing capacity, a problem which will worsen in coming years with increasing industrial and agricultural demands for water and an ever-increasing load of wastes (Goldman, 1972b:109). Several important inland waterways such as the Caspian and Aral seas face the additional problem of decreasing water levels. The level has dropped to such a point in the Aral Sea that the concomitant increase in salinity has led to an attempt to breed saltwater fish where freshwater fish once flourished (LaMothe, 1971:19; Pryde, 1972:126–127). The increasing frequency of eutrophication and spreading algae blooms on still waters must also be counted as evidence of man's disruption of the aquatic ecosystem, for much of the overfertilization which causes such growths comes from extensive use of fertilizers in agriculture (LaMothe, 1971:11).

Further evidence of ecosystem deterioration is found in the growing list of endangered species in the Soviet Union. While conservation efforts have scored notable successes in preserving and even increasing the numbers of certain species such as beaver, sable, otter, and bison, the list of endangered and protected animals remains long. The threat to wildlife has come both from commercial overhunting, as with the whale, and from a loss of natural habitat through deforestation, urbanization, and pollution. The depletion of game birds is typical of man's unintended harmful impact on nature, for the primary cause of their declining numbers has not been overhunting but man-made dangers such as deforestation, marsh drainage, urbanization, and pollution. The increasing use of pesticides in agriculture has intensified the problem, and sizable game kills have been reported, especially in connection with the dispersal of pesticides by aircraft (Pryde, 1972:45–91; Fisher et al., 1969; Kirillin, 1972:2–3; Gerasimov, 1970:217; Powell, 1971:622; Sapozhnikov, 1970:2).

JAPAN

Pollution, destructive regional development, and the pressure of a hundred million people are corrupting hundreds of ecosystems in Japan. A decline in the quantity and quality of aquatic life is especially apparent. It is sadly ironic that the Japanese, who depend on fish for up to fifty-three percent of their protein, should loot and poison the sea so cavalierly. While the demand for fish, shellfish, and water plants edges upward each year, domestic and oceanic waters must absorb millions of tons of effluent, nitrates, phosphorus, oil, sewage, and assorted chemicals. Heavy metals and chlorinated hydrocarbons are firmly established in food chains here as elsewhere in the world. Oil films are screening out sunlight and reducing photosynthesis in phytoplankton. Japan's estuaries, the habitat of mollusks and shellfish as well as the feeding and spawning grounds for many species of fish, are clogged with waste. Red tides (akashio) now bloom in most bays and inland seas. The bays at Ise and Tokyo, and the Seto Inland Sea, are especially hard hit. Tokyo Bay was once a superb shallow-water fishing area, producing bumper catches of laver, goby, and short-necked clams. Fishing dropped off after 1955 because of red tides and became chronically bad in the 1960's. Land reclamation projects like Dream Island and heavy metal pollution have further encroached on fishing grounds. In 1962 the ecological collapse of Tokyo Bay was symbolized by government payment of ninety-two million dollars in damages to four thousand fishermen, a gesture that cancelled traditional fishing rights. Tokuyama Bay in the Seto Inland Sea is a sump for the daily discharge of many tons of waste from a nearby petrochemical complex. A three-year study of the bay's luxuriant red tides confirmed the close relationship between these "blooms" and the presence of nitrate and phosphate in huge amounts (*QEJ*, 1973: 126–128; *TMG*, 1971:99–100; *JEA*, 1972l:49; *QEJ*, 1972:99–101; *JT*, 2 April 1973).

The total cost of pollution to the fishing industry in 1969–1970 was in the billions, amounting to nearly four percent of all revenue earned. The strangulation of rivers, bays, inland seas, and estuaries, wedded to the appetite of a growing population, has driven fishing fleets into the remotest waters. Thus thirty percent of the catch in 1971 was trawled from distant fishing grounds.* Depletion of marine resources in the East China and Yellow seas has led Japan to fix its eye on the Mediterranean (*QEJ*, 1973:116–117; *MAF*, 1972:2).

Japan's plant cover is shrinking rapidly as a result of pollution and commercial exploitation. Forest reserves have been plundered of late to supply vast domestic needs. The paper industry has been markedly insatiable, producing twenty percent more paper in 1971 than was needed. The drain has been so substantial that in 1970 forty-nine percent of the nation's timber requirements were met by imports, compared with twelve percent in 1960. Log production has stagnated for much the same reason that whaling has declined—overexploitation of profitable stocks. Air and water pollution are stripping away vegetation. Thus trees in the southern Kantō region are expected to disappear in fifty years, poisoned by toxic air, deprived of supplemental moisture by the removal of ground water, and starved chemically by the death of essential bacteria in the soil. Trees in many

---

*An international 200 mile limit would mean that 45 percent or more of Japan's catch would come from waters controlled by other nations.

industrialized cities are doomed. The cypress, cryptomeria, and chestnuts of Tokyo's National Park for Nature Study are expected to perish by 1980 because of heavy air pollution. The Himalayan pine, ginkgo, and cherry trees may slip into oblivion shortly thereafter. A nationwide survey of national greenery in 1974, the world's first, produced gloomy results. There is virtually no greenery at all in Osaka City, and eighty-seven percent of Tokyo's twenty-three wards are barren *(TMN,* August 1972:3–4; *QEJ,* 1973:168–170; *MAF,* 1974a; *AEN,* 1 June 1974).

Bird life is also a sound indicator of stable ecosystems. About seventy-five percent of Japan's 471 bird species migrate; the winter species fly in from China, Alaska, and West Siberia, the summer species from China and Southeast Asia. They include the swallow, snipe, plover, swan, goose, duck, and crane. The migrations have thinned out in recent years as habitats have been disrupted or taken over by man and pesticides have infiltrated the water. In 1943, for example, 62,300 wild geese nested in 149 refuges; in 1971 a mere 27 refuges harbored 5,160 geese. At present twenty-eight species of birds are close to extinction, including regal creatures like the Japanese crane, white stork, crested ibis, and golden eagle. All of them are in danger because of human interference with the environment. The crested ibis, to choose an example, was known in ancient Japan as *toki.* Once fairly numerous, hunting and deforestation of the wooded wetlands where it nested have reduced its population to a precarious nine individuals on Sado Island, Ishikawa Prefecture (Yanagisawa, 1972; *JEA,* 1971d; *NY Times,* 23 January 1972).

Direct aggression by man takes a heavy toll of bird and animal life. Altogether thirty-two species of birds and seventeen of mammals are legally accessible to hunters. Moreover, government regulations permit the "extermination" of creatures classified as a nuisance, such as sparrows, crows, bulbuls, rabbits, bears, and monkeys (the famous snow monkey is too isolated to be threatened in this way, and is protected). In 1970 hunters eliminated 13,560,000 birds and 1,110,000 mammals. The truth of the matter is that hunting occurs all over the country and government regulations are inadequate to conserve wildlife *(JEA,* 1971a).

THE ENVIRONMENTAL CRISIS AND THE QUALITY OF LIFE

THE UNITED STATES

Americans have defined "quality of life" normally in terms of comfort, possessions, and material standard of living. Their hopes for a bright future have been hitched rather openly and shamelessly to industrial might and technology. Now the pall of environmental deterioration has intruded a new dimension with respect to the meaning of "quality" in human life. Many citizens in the United States are aware of that dimension, and have begun to evince a mounting distrust that the future is not so bright as they thought it might be. A recent study of public attitudes toward the future shows in the past quarter century a decline of confidence in the nation's prospects for making a better life for generations to come; these doubts are fed in part by a growing cognizance that problems touching on the quality of life cannot be solved by an exclusive stress on material production (*NY Times*, 29 July, 20 August 1973).

At present some 210 million Americans enjoy a standard of living far exceeding that of most other nations in the world. They are such insatiable consumers of energy that even before the Arab embargo more energy was used than could be produced during periods of peak demand. The outcome was occasional electrical voltage cuts—the so-called brownouts—in the summer when air conditioners were overextended, and temporary shortages of gasoline and heating oil. It is obvious that growing shortages of energy and nonrenewable resources are a thundercloud on the horizon of further improvement of the American standard of living. Population growth will push up the total demand for goods and services for at least the next seventy years. There is no assurance of this demand being fully met, or that per capita consumption and the rate of economic growth will not decline. Foodstuffs are likely to be in shorter supply as fertile land is poisoned by pollution or diverted to other uses, and as fuel shortages reduce the crops that can be planted and harvested. Shortages will drive up the cost of once cheap, plentiful commodities, and sometimes force a painful readjustment of consumption patterns.

The effects of environmental decay on health must be taken into account. Air pollution causes or aggravates a host of diseases. Water pollution has sparked bacterial epidemics as well as heavy metal and chemical poisoning. Noise pollution is connected with various nervous disorders. The number of lives shortened or burdened with suffering is difficult to estimate, but it must be considerable, and a large segment of the American public is aware of a relationship between illness and poor environmental quality.

Environment-related quality of life problems are most intensely felt in the urban areas of more than fifty thousand people, where the majority of Americans live. Parks, recreation areas, beaches, and green spaces have shrunk; city streets are often dirty, the air foul, and nearby waterways rancid with waste; yet Americans seem to have little choice but to reside in such conditions, for the city is where economic opportunity is greatest.

The environmental crisis has had a profound effect on the life-style of the suburbanite. Locked into the automobile out of necessity and for convenience, he is the victim of fuel shortages and price hikes brought on by inept government and industrial planning, and can find no relief in poorly financed, often primitive public transportation systems. As the bedroom suburbs expand and swirl around the industrial areas that ring most American cities, factories add their pollutants to those of the ubiquitous automobile, further begriming the good life. Furthermore, the suburbanite pays handsomely for the pollution display around him, not only through diminished environmental quality, but through higher taxes for sewage treatment and waste disposal. Careless land-use planning and inadequate zoning regulations invite the expansion of housing into wilderness or sparsely settled regions, with little regard for the ensuing annihilation of delicate ecosystems that sustain wildlife. In an ironic cycle, flight from the crowded, polluted cities merely duplicates those conditions in the suburbs and the country, where meagre tax bases and weak local government are even less equipped to fight or check environmental decline than urban centers (*USEPA*, 1973; *NY Times*, 2 June 1974).

The financial burden of pollution is staggering. Not only must the direct costs of abatement be carried by taxpayer and consumer, there are many indirect costs as well. Four types of costs have been set forth by the Council on Environmental Quality: damage costs that tie directly into pollution; avoidance costs resulting from attempts to avoid or reduce the impact of pollution; costs associated with pollution monitoring and the enforcement of abatement laws; and the abatement costs of controlling existing environmental decay. Damage costs include medical bills for the treatment of pollution-related diseases, cleaning bills, crop losses, and the like, which may run to 25 million dollars or more each year. The second category is more difficult to estimate because the avoidance of pollution often is intertwined with imponderables like the decision of urban residents to flee to the suburbs; it has been suggested, however, that such costs amount to tens of billions every year. In 1972 the federal government alone spent 861.5 million dollars in this area. Abatement costs are even higher. The federal government spent nearly 2 billion dollars in 1973, and expenditures by private industry were close to 4.5 billion in 1972. The Council on Environmental Quality has put all environmental expenditures from 1972 to 1981 at 274.2 billion dollars; thirty-seven percent of this great sum will be paid by the taxpayer, and sixty-three percent by private industry, with the lion's share provided by increased prices for the consumer (*CEQ*, 1973b:74–117).

But there is more to the cost of environmental degradation than dollars and cents. One can compute medical expenses for pollution-related illnesses, but not the suffering and anxiety of the victim and his family. Economic losses due to pollution are readily quantified, but the value of smog-free days, clean, sparkling rivers, and green, quiet neighborhoods remains elusive in terms of money. Few Americans are likely to admit satisfaction with the quality of their lives, and few would not agree that it would be enhanced by more congenial natural surroundings. Even hardened denizens of New York yearn occasionally for a breath of air in the country or a lakeside stroll. These feelings have little to do with considerations of material gain.

Yet improvement of the environment can be won only at the expense of other forms of production and consumption, which will confront Americans with difficult choices about national priorities and economic trade-offs. Whether Americans are willing to accept both the social and economic costs associated with ending environmental disruption is a debatable question. Even the comparatively trivial dislocations and inconveniences that surfaced during the recent oil shortage provoked selfish, petulant behavior among many individual citizens, especially at the gas pump, and set in motion political pressure to ease environmental restrictions; the environmental crisis, it appears, is easily forgotten when upstaged by more traditional economic or political crises. The need to make personal sacrifices, to reorder national priorities, to reshape personal life-styles, and to bear a considerable financial burden, accompanied by a loss of many conveniences, may well cause many citizens to reconsider their commitment to environmental quality.

THE SOVIET UNION

Soviet citizens also find the quality of the lives they lead affected by environmental deterioration. In small ways and in large—from the minor nuisances of noise and vibration to the major tragedies of deteriorating air quality and poisoned waterways—the average Russian finds the quality of his life touched by his own deleterious impact on the environment.

It is virtually impossible to assess the total social cost of environmental pollution in the Soviet Union because of the complexity of the many issues involved and the secrecy which surrounds valuable data. It has been estimated, for example, that water pollution alone milks the economy of six billion rubles a year (Pryde, 1972:98). For the average Russian, these costs are born primarily in the form of higher living expenses. Laundry and cleaning bills in polluted industrial sites must run annually into the millions of rubles, to say nothing of the deterioration of other durable goods and increased medical costs. Eventually the Soviet consumer is saddled with higher production costs experienced by Soviet industry because of pollution. The misuse of scarce resources also affects the cost of manufactured goods, although the absence of a free-market pricing system operating on the basis of supply and demand, and the Soviet Union's relative abundance of raw materials, softens the impact.

Soviet citizens also bear the direct cost of pollution control and clean-up programs initiated by the government. It has been estimated by Soviet environmentalists that seventeen to twenty billion rubles would be needed to clean up the nation's waterways *(PKh*, 1969:17). While current appropriations come nowhere near that figure, there have been sizable expenditures, and it is likely these sums will increase gradually in coming years. But such investments will force difficult decisions. Faced with a declining growth rate, Soviet leaders would undoubtedly be reluctant to divert large sums into pollution control without substantial cutbacks in other areas.

The Soviet consumer will probably bear pollution-related costs in two ways. First, his taxes will go up. Since the Soviet government derives its income primarily from turnover taxes (a sales tax attached to most commodities as a part of the regular price), the cost of most goods and services will probably rise (Sherman, 1969:19). Since the amount of these turnover taxes is determined by the state, it is probable, given past performances, that the lion's share of these new revenues will be collected through increased taxes on consumer goods and household staples and will bear little relationship to the amount of pollution caused by a particular industry. The consumer is likely to suffer in still another way. Given the declining growth rate of the Soviet economy and the regime's fondness for heavy industry, the growth rate of the consumer goods is likely to yield first to environmental pressures.

Environmental pollution has also exacted a higher incidence of disease and a shortened life-span. As we have noted, air pollution has been linked with increased rates of respiratory and eye disorders, and residents of highly polluted areas show less general resistance to disease. Water pollution is associated with numerous health problems. Tainted municipal water supplies and bacterial pollution of some major rivers have increased the rate of disease.

Soviet medical science has only recently acknowledged this important link between the quality of the environment and national health. In the past, medical research was largely restricted to the question of worker safety in pollution-prone industries. Only within the last decade have pollution-related health problems of the entire population seriously been considered (LaMothe, 1971:33). Although no precise measurement is possible, high pollution levels are undoubtedly related to a decreased life-span, especially in urbanized areas. While improved health service and sanitary standards offset these new hazards somewhat, environmental pollution shortens in some measure the lives of city dwellers and workers exposed regularly to its effects.

The cumulative impact of population growth and environmental deterioration will hinder the production of adequate food supplies. Even the best soils are low in minerals. While the expansion of fertilizer production will compensate in part for this shortcoming, it also will cause further pollution. Secondly, the existing pattern of rainfall makes Soviet agriculture susceptible to frequent drought. In *The Hungry Planet*, Georg Borgstrom calculates that the Soviet Union runs almost a four times greater risk of food calamity caused by water shortage than the United States. The increasing water demands of industry and urban areas will only worsen the problem, as will the greater flood of pollutants from industrial and municipal sources. And Soviet officials now admit that virtually all arable land is under cultivation. A former Minister of Agriculture, himself relieved of office in 1973 because of agricultural failures, candidly admitted that from 1958 to the present time, the amount of arable land per person has decreased from 1.06 to 0.94 hectares, a trend that doubtless will continue. This relative decrease is due both to population increases and to the destruction of once productive land by salinization, wind and water erosion, and flooding by massive water-management projects. Clearly the only possible solution aside from imports lies in the intensification of production on existing land (Pusta, 1971:1–3; SL, July 1972:15).

The aesthetic quality of the average Russian's life is directly affected by surrounding environmental deterioration. At work he is assaulted daily by an array of environmental hazards, ranging from intense pollution released by industry itself to excessive noise. Pollution-control measures at the work site have a lower priority than planned quotas, thus leading to high rates of illness and disease. The asbestos industry is typical, with its high rate of asbestos-related health problems (Goldman, 1972b:142). Workers on collective and state farms also face pollution hazards. Accidents with pesticides and other chemical products are reported frequently, and Soviet medical journals show concern with treating pollution-related medical ills of the nation's agricultural workers (Pryde, 1971:16–24).

The rapid development of Soviet industry has resulted in a form of visual pollution in major industrial centers. A forest of belching smokestacks has replaced once green wooded areas, and acre upon acre of drab, undistinguished apartment compounds have sprung up to meet the demand for more housing. Spared only the eyesore of commercial billboard advertising in cities and along roadways (save only the display of political propaganda put up before the November 7 and May Day celebrations), the average urbanized Russian has seen once striking cities succumb to a visual blight fostered by industrialists and uninspired urban planners.

Urbanization and poor housing have had great impact on the quality of life. Living in overcrowded apartment complexes in close proximity to polluting industries has taken its toll of the average Russian. As we have noted, residents in areas of dense air pollution have been quick to complain about the everyday annoyances of dirt, soot, and odors. While planners have called for better control measures and the construction of forest belts and parks near residential areas to mitigate the negative effects of industry, little has been done in practice.

Crowded into urban areas, the Soviet industrial worker finds it increasingly more difficult to escape cities of concrete and steel for untouched recreational areas. Swimming has been banned on some major waterways because of pollution, and park areas in large industrial centers are plagued by bad air. Moscow's situation is typical. Although nearly a third of the city's area is occupied by some form of green vegetation, population growth has been so great that park land per resident has declined despite new planting programs. Most Soviet cities are ringed by a green belt of forests used for recreational purposes. Moscow has over 460,000 hectares of woodlands at a radius of fifty kilometers from the center city, and Leningrad enjoys an area of 149,000 hectares. But the growth of industry and population in the satellite towns will undoubtedly destroy some portion of these forests and reduce per capita park and forest area unless effective control measures and planting programs are undertaken quickly (SL, July 1972:14; AICE, 1969, Vol. 2:61; Pryde, 1972:157).

Throughout this catalog of ecological woes, it must be kept in mind that environmental quality lies in the eye of the beholder. The average Russian has shown no great willingness to sacrifice continued development in the interest of environmental quality. To him, the quality of life is undoubtedly more closely linked with enjoying the plethora of consumer goods long denied him by an economy oriented toward heavy industry. Although there is a discernible and growing core of environment-minded people in the Soviet Union who perceive the crisis facing their nation, the average Soviet industrial worker or peasant does not regard the death of birds and fish, or urban smoke and haze, as anything approaching a national crisis, especially when the "quality" of his life is connected with a desire for better clothing, a television set, and a private car. This is not to say that environmental awareness has not risen notably in recent years or that complaints against polluters do not appear frequently in the Soviet press (see the following chapter). But it does mean that the problem is regarded as not very serious and easily tractable; it is viewed as almost an accident under a socialist economy, something that has occurred because of a massive national oversight and which, with proper attention, can be solved without extensive economic or social dislocation. It is something that "they"—the political leaders, the engineers, and the scientists—are expected to solve with only marginal impact on the man in the street.

JAPAN

In his formal address to the Stockholm Conference, Dr. Buichi Oishi, former director-general of the Environment Agency, expatiated on the quality of life in Japan:

The Japanese people, who had thought that greater production and greater GNP are the guidelines for human happiness and had passionately bent their efforts to those objectives, were disillusioned and awakened to their mistaken idea. Many beaches were reclaimed to construct industrial complexes. Nature with green foliage was defaced to construct roads and housing. Green had disappeared from the cities; even scarce parks are not adequately tended and flowers are neglected. People are unaware that they are losing the feeling of sympathy for nature. Their sense of public morality to cherish nature is being dulled. The destruction of the environment is now beginning to degrade the spirit of man *(QEJ,* 1973:265–266).

By their own admission and bitter complaint, life has become extraordinarily unpleasant for millions of Japanese. As of 1973 more than ten thousand persons were *officially* designated as suffering from pollution-related diseases, many of whom are crippled or otherwise ruined for life, and it is impossible to say precisely how many more unreported cases exist. The estimate for Minamata disease alone runs to ten thousand in western Kyushu, and respiratory diseases have claimed thousands more in key industrial areas *(QEJ,* 1973:153–162).

The cost of restoring the environment to past levels of quality has moved upward in substantial increments in recent years and the general financial loss sustained by society has become formidable. Money spent to clean up pollution cannot be used to build homes, send young people through college, or plan for an auspicious retirement, not to mention buying food, clothing, and medicine. In 1970 the estimated losses due to pollution came to more than 6 billion dollars, encompassing health, household matters (new clothes, laundry bills, painting, and so on), damage to fisheries, agriculture, and forestry, and antipollution expenditures by industry and government. The overall figure amounts to six percent of Japan's GNP for that year and represents a tenfold increase over the previous decade. The share paid out directly by citizens increased nearly eight times between 1960 and 1970 *(QEJ,* 1972:10–14).

The unfavorable ratio of people to habitable land area has created a host of vexing problems which affect the quality of life. Land prices in Japan, which may already be the world's highest, have been rising at ten to sixteen percent a year since 1969; they jumped thirty-one percent in 1972 alone. High-rise construction is beginning to dominate the Japanese urban landscape, for there is literally no place to go but up, or out into the sea. In a desperate attempt to alleviate a critical housing shortage, developers have flung up millions of wooden apartment blocks consisting of one- and two-room flats, thus increasing the vulnerability of tenants to the ravages of fire and earthquake. Although living space averages a cramped 3.5 square yards per capita, rents tend to be exorbitant. Units in modern high-rises, whether purchased or rented, are accessible only to the very affluent, and there are long waiting lists for cheaper housing. High rents and crowding have forced urban dwellers in large numbers to locate at points distant from their jobs, thus creating a massive commuter problem (*JT*, 23 January 1973; Hibino, 1973; *HUD*, 1972:3).

The commuter's way of life in Japan could well become the subject of a black comedy. Yukata Sasayama describes a typical commuter train experience: "Every train car packed to two and three times its capacity; on every platform young people are employed part-time to push against the backs of men and women and cram them into trains they could never board under their own power ... We are crammed in as tightly as we are because we are human beings. If pigs were crammed in so tightly they would all die within thirty minutes" (Sasayama, 1969:410; *TMN*, June 1972:5–7).

The tyranny of the automobile has become overwhelming. The fact that a vehicle of some kind is operating for every 120 square yards of land area in the nation, and one car per 50 meters in the streets of Tokyo, suggests that people may soon be displaced altogether by machines. Traffic in large cities has become perpetual and hapless pedestrians must negotiate steep overwalks in deference to an endless stream of autos.* Freeway construction has gobbled up valuable land for the exclusive use of vehicles, but without easing traffic jams. The impact on Japan's once beautiful landscape has been devastating, especially in those areas most attractive to the tourist. Twelve million tourist cars a year inundate and ruin the once quiet beauty of Kyoto. One can reach Mount Fuji from Tokyo by taking a speedway to Lake Kawaguchi, and then a toll road, known as the Suburu. The Suburu is clogged annually with 520,000 autos, three times more than enterprising local officials believed would come. The pall of exhaust kills twenty thousand subalpine trees a year, and the noise of crowds and machines brings the tumult of the city to the country. Over the past ten years, motorized visitors have strewn the slopes of the sacred mountain with nearly a thousand tons of refuse (*JQ*, 1972a:7–9; *JT*, 27 August 1973).†

The unwary observer is often surprised to learn that Japan's miraculous economic growth has failed to provide certain obvious amenities as compensation for environmental ruination (Tadashi, 1967). Considering the rate of economic growth, the Economic Planning Council admits that living standards are not very high. The cost of living increased 25.4 percent

---

*Perhaps with grim good reason. Traffic deaths in Japan for 1974 totalled an appalling 11,200 persons. Even more are expected perish in 1975 (*JT*, 27 April 1975).

†I was shocked to see the multitude of dead and withered pines during an ascent to the top of Mount Fuji in the summer of 1974. Trash was commonplace.

between August 1973 and August 1974, which was tops among industrial states. There are 2.4 square meters of park area per person in Japan, compared with 22.8 in the United Kingdom and 20.3 in West Germany. The distribution ratio for flush toilets is 9.2 percent, which ranks with Nepal and Jordan, the world's lowest. The proliferation of gadgets and department stores can be deceptive. Many citizens are beginning to experience the anomaly of cramming appliances into shoddy apartments where there is barely room to stretch out. The mania for travel in Japan is no doubt related to the discomforts of home. In the wake of exorbitant land prices, shortages of lumber, inflation, and overpopulation, the prospect of owning a private home in Japan has all but disappeared for the majority. The estimated cost of a small two-story home on a 99 square meter lot in the suburbs of Tokyo is sixty-five thousand dollars* (*JT*, 18 October 1974; *AEN*, 25 April 1974; *DY*, 8 May 1974).

There is reason to believe Japan will have trouble sustaining an adequate and not utterly expensive food supply. The pressure of humans and animals on cultivable soil is already intense. In spite of elaborate water development projects, mechanization, and massive infusions of pesticides and chemical fertilizers, overall production declined in 1969–1970. Cultivated land has been decreasing since 1962 and in 1973 was 0.6 percent less than the previous year; the Japanese have 0.06 hectares per capita, well below the world average of 0.4 hectares per capita. In order to extract the last iota of productivity from the soil, fertilizer and pesticides will be poured on even more lavishly than in the past, with predictable environmental consequences, but probably without concommitant increases in yield. Japan appears to have nudged the outer limit of what can be wrung profitably from the soil (*JT*, 19 April 1974, 31 October 1973; Iinuma, 1974; Barse, 1969; Borgstrom, 1972: Chapter 9).

Major fishing grounds around Japan have been seriously contaminated by PCB, mercury, factory wastes, and urban drainage. It is ironic that the Japanese, who take fifty percent of their animal protein from fish, were compelled in 1973 to cut back on consumption because of unprecedented government guidelines on how much of certain species should be eaten. At the end of 1972, the Ministry of Agriculture and Forestry released a PCB survey of 2,273 fish taken from fourteen water-zones. Some 153 fish from nine water-zones in eight prefectures showed PCB counts at the highest permissible level (3 ppm). The public was stunned, fish sales dropped, and a national "Let's Refrain from Fish" movement was launched. Westerners cannot grasp the significance of these events unless they understand how much the Japanese love *sashimi*, or strips of cold, raw fish (*JQ*, 1973c; Ui, 1972a:25–27).

---

* 308 yen to the dollar.

The loss of intangibles that make up the quality of life can evade precise expression and yet be keenly felt. Japanese civilization manifested until recently a special relationship with nature, one suffused with awe, wonder, and admiration. This relationship has been reflected in art, literature, customs, religion, and architecture. A sense of closeness with the natural world has inspired flower arranging and bird watching, parties to note the turning of autumn leaves, festive gatherings on waterways to celebrate holidays, excursions into the back country or along the seashore in search of uniquely shaped rocks to adorn domestic gardens, and an affection for animal life. I have on my desk as I write an exquisite *netsuke* carved from ivory, a miniature figure of a cormorant fisherman with his two diving-birds. Barefoot, dressed simply, smiling with open pleasure, he clasps one bird to his chest, the wings spread as though to embrace him, while the second bird nestles quietly at his feet. The figure strikes me as profoundly expressive of man and nature in harmony. It is this intimacy that Japan seems to have lost, and the Japanese themselves will have to assess how much has been sacrificed in the name of modernization. Life has become materially richer but not inevitably better (Barber, 1974).

CHAPTER
5
AWARENESS OF
THE PROBLEM

THE UNITED STATES

In the twentieth century Americans have come to see gradually that population growth, urbanization, economic development, and technological change are at the root of distressing environmental problems. This awareness showed itself first among scientists, who then influenced the thinking of government officials, the business community, and the general public.

THE SCIENTIFIC COMMUNITY

In the latter nineteenth century a few natural scientists began expressing concern about the environment. They noted particularly the depletion of resources, for the closing of the frontier brought sharply to mind their finite character. The conservation movement of those years was basically a scientific one aimed at persuading the nation to heed advice about the sensible utilization of resources. Several academic disciplines were involved, including geology, forestry, and hydrology, each of which looked piecemeal at the environment rather than at the whole. During the same period the study of ecology spread to the United States from Europe. Until the 1930's, ecologists wrote primarily for other ecologists, and little of what they knew about man's impact on the world of nature found its way to a wider audience.

In the thirties, some implications of ecological studies were brought to the attention of government and the public by professional conservationists like Aldo Leopold, a leading champion of wilderness preservation and a forester with the U.S. Forest Service. He left government service to take a professorship in game management at the University of Wisconsin, from which vantage point he emphasized the need for mankind to develop an "ecological conscience" (Nash, 1967:182–199; Fleming, 1972:23–27).

In the twenties and thirties, other members of the scientific community began to give attention to the impact of pollution on health and economic activity. Professional journals increasingly devoted articles to air and water pollution, the dangers of misusing chemicals and pesticides, noise pollution, and industrial diseases like asbestosis. Comprehension gradually dawned among some scientists about the significance of unrestrained resource consumption, the proliferation of wastes, and the spread of pollution. A. G. Tansley, in an *Ecology* article of 1935, coined the term "ecosystem," which he defined as "the whole system, including not only the organism complex, but also the whole complex of physical factors forming what we call the environment" (Fleming, 1972:23–24; Tansley, 1935).

Man's impact on the environment received greater attention from the scientists after World War II. A major factor contributing to this heightened awareness was concern about nuclear fallout, but soon other questions were to be raised about the effects of technological innovation. In 1968, the American Association for the Advancement of Science (AAAS) held symposia on the environmental consequences of technology. The AAAS created a permanent Committee on Environmental Alterations and charged it with a continuing review of man's impact on nature. Sessions on environmental matters have become a fixed part of subsequent AAAS meetings (Fleming, 1972:40–51; Cooley, 1970:xi).

Since 1970 a new discipline called environmental science has developed in the laboratories and seminar rooms of universities, industries, and government agencies. Environmental science, according to a 1971 report of the National Science Board of the National Science Foundation, is "the study of all systems of air, land, water, energy, and life that surround man." Emphasizing a systems approach, it draws on the work of more narrowly focused disciplines such as physics, biology, chemistry, oceanography, and ecology (*NSB*, 1971:vii–viii). Much environmental research is being conducted by university scientists with financial aid from philanthropic organizations and government agencies. About seventy-five percent of the Environmental Protection Agency's research is done under contract with private research centers and in four National Environmental Research Centers of its own (*USEPA*, 1972:97–102).

GOVERNMENT AND INDUSTRY

Environmental awareness on the part of the government roughly parallels that of the scientific community in its development. To the middle of the nineteenth century government at all levels saw the environment only as a provider of natural resources and a capacious dump for refuse. In the late nineteenth century the federal government and many state governments set up special agencies to deal with some environmental problems; hence the origin of the National Forest Service to manage national woodlands and timber production, the Reclamation Service to provide water for irrigation of western lands, and the Army Corps of Engineers to improve navigable waterways and prevent floods. Similar agencies sprang up on the state level.

A fear of resource depletion up to World War II stimulated extensive federal legislation based on the "multiple-use" approach. The gist of this concept was to regulate the use of resources on federal lands so as to assure the greatest good for the greatest number of Americans over an extended period of time. In practical terms, it meant a simultaneous pursuit of exploitation, focused on the extraction of resources, and preservation, focused on the value of land as recreational areas. Although the federal government acted generally in accordance with this vaguely defined multiple-use theory as far as its own lands were concerned, little or nothing was done to regulate the use of privately owned property. A farmer could destroy his soil; a forest owner could strip his holdings and allow erosion to develop; a factory owner could dump his wastes in a segment of stream without regard to his neighbors (Hays, 1958).

The multiple-use idea was expanded and modified as groups competed with one another for resources, finally reaching accommodations with one another and with government supervisory agencies. The complex of agency-constituency interests that emerged over the years tended to resist suggestions for changing established methods of dealing with environmental problems. The rules of the game were hammered out through legislation, regulation, and mutual understandings; the players, once familiar with the rules and their nuances, had a vested interest in not changing them (Ekirch, 1973:88–99).

The best known experiment with the multiple-use theory was the Tennessee Valley Authority of the New Deal in the 1930's, which was mounted to develop resources, power, and flood control, and generally to improve living standards in the region. Government experiments with multiple use ended with World War II, when the country once more geared itself for war production, but with no deep worry about the effects of accelerated industrialization on the environment.

The Eisenhower administration was largely indifferent to environmental issues. On the other hand, Congress authorized in 1955 a federal program of assistance to the states for research on air-pollution control. Shortly thereafter the Federal Water Pollution Control Act was passed. The 1960's saw a marked growth of awareness in government. In May 1962, the Kennedy administration held a White House Conference on Conservation that was attended by five hundred delegates and observers from both public and private institutions. The conferees talked less about resource management than about an increasingly obvious deterioration of the environment. In his "Great Society" address in May 1964, President Johnson argued for preservation of the environment as a great public issue, and called a White House conference in the following year to explore means of protection and restoration (Cooley, 1970:xiii–xv).

Environmental legislation poured from Congress and the state legislatures in the 1960's but until the end of the decade, most of it continued to be reminiscent of the earlier piecemeal approach. Bills were passed on such matters as wilderness protection, recreational areas, and solid waste disposal. In addition, several air- and water-pollution measures were approved, but were ineffective because of weak enforcement provisions (Cooley, 1970:xv–xvii). Only in the 1970's did it become evident that a fragmented approach to mushrooming environmental problems would not do, a realization that led to a new wave of legislation and the creation of two new federal environmental agencies, steps that are discussed in Chapter 7.

Environmental consciousness in the business community is a recent phenomenon. It has been traditional for businessmen to believe that vast resources should be exploited freely in the nation. Convinced either of their inexhaustibility, or that technology would unerringly develop substitutes, the industrialist and the entrepreneur have firmly resisted all government restrictions on the use of resources. In the 1960's, however, some businessmen finally acknowledged the reality of environmental problems, but often accused environmentalists of exaggerating the magnitude of them. The tendency to oppose government restriction in the environmental field survives, but when it can be demonstrated that sound environmental practices are attainable with extant technology, and in the long run profitable, there is a counter tendency to accept change. On the other hand, regulations and guidelines not within reach of available technology, or that threaten in other ways to cut profits, are stoutly resisted.

A prime index of awareness in business is the amount of money it gives up for pollution research and control. Industry is conducting a major share of environmental research in the United States, especially the development of pollution-control technology. In 1970, industry spent about 741.5 million dollars in research and development, and the figure rose in 1971 to an estimated 925.8 million dollars. A recent study suggests that air- and water-pollution control cost the business community 1.6 billion dollars in 1969, 2.5 billion in 1970, 3.3 billion in 1971, and 4.5 billion in 1972 (*CEQ*, 1973b:91). From 1967 to 1973, private investment in air- and water-pollution control facilities has grown at a rate of 32 percent a year, a figure far higher than the 9.4 percent annual increase of expenditures for industrial plants and equipment (*CEQ*, 1973b:88).

THE PUBLIC

The public has been aware of environmental deterioration in a limited, localized context for generations. The extinction of the passenger pigeon and the near extinction of the buffalo provoked amazement. The destruction of virgin forests was noted as a melancholy but inevitable result of economic progress, as was the fouling of water and air. Despite muted warnings from the scientists and misgivings among some ordinary citizens, the general public remained largely apathetic. Most people simply did not have an adequate basis for judgment.

Following World War II, a sequence of dramatic incidents alerted the public by stages to the environmental debt of the past. The air-pollution disaster in 1948 in Donora, Pennsylvania, captured public attention and initiated a flurry of articles on the causes. The public was further aroused by scientific reports on the dangers of nuclear fallout from testing programs in the 1950's, especially when a connection was made between strontium-90 and milk.

In the past twenty-five years, scientists like Rachel Carson, Barry Commoner, and Paul Ehrlich have done much to arouse public consciousness about the dangers of pesticides, the shortcomings of chemical fertilizers, the implications of unregulated population growth, the mixed blessings of technology, and the necessity for developing values around ecological imperatives.

The growth of public awareness has left its traces in public opinion polls of the 1960's and 1970's. In a Michigan Survey Research Center study in the early sixties, forty-eight percent of the respondents thought the government was spending enough on environmental protection, while fifteen percent wanted a reduction of such expenditures. By the middle of the decade a notable change had occurred. A Harris survey in 1965 showed forty-three percent of the respondents actively concerned about the environment, and by the later sixties, as the federal government introduced stronger air and water measures, and as works of Carson, Commoner, Ehrlich, and others were being published, public consciousness intensified even further. A 1967 Harris survey indicated that half the public placed environmental pollution above all other domestic problems, although, oddly enough, a third of those surveyed were uninterested in more government activity in the environmental field. In the same year another study suggested that seventy percent of urban residents regarded air pollution as a serious problem; only thirty percent of rural residents seemed to share this conviction. Two years later, National Wildlife Federation surveys showed fifty-one percent of the respondents "deeply concerned" and thirty-five percent "somewhat concerned" about the environment. In 1970, a Congressional Quarterly poll showed ninety percent of those polled worried about water pollution, and a Gallup poll indicated that fifty-three percent of the public viewed air and water pollution as priority issues (*AIPO*, 1969; *AIPO*, 1970; Trop and Roos, 1971:52–63).

Better media coverage of environmental questions was partly responsible for heightened public awareness, with television probably taking honors in this educational offensive. A good deal of attention has been given to environmental disasters in regular news programming, and many special reports have featured issues like the eutrophication of Lake Erie, the overcrowding of national parks, and the inexorable growth of population.

According to a recent survey, newspaper editors expect the environment to be an important topic of news and discussion through the seventies, and a significant number of large newspapers have full-time editors and reporters riding herd on environmental developments. More newspapers are running series, such as the Chicago *Tribune's* "Save Our Lake" campaign. In the past few years a plethora of magazines, journals, and newsletters have been published by environmental groups. While their readership is limited, these sources frequently influence the opinions of community leaders attuned to pollution and its consequences. A visit to any good bookshop will turn up dozens of volumes on every conceivable facet of the environmental crisis, a tribute to the speed with which publishers exploit a popular issue (Maloney and Slovonsky, 1971:64–78).

Publishers have been quick also to offer environmental teaching materials to elementary and secondary schools. Thousands of school districts are either developing environmental curricula (this can be had directly from publishers) or integrating environmental materials into other curricula. Many colleges and universities have developed environmental programs as well.

THE SOVIET UNION

During the 1960's the Soviet Union witnessed a quiet revolution in environmental awareness. While environmental deterioration and resource conservation have occupied a handful of scientists and naturalists since before the revolution, the current upsurge of public and governmental interest is a recent phenomenon. The unchallenged success of industrialization has created striking environmental problems which can no longer be ignored.

THE SCIENTIFIC COMMUNITY

Awareness dawned first among the members of the scientific community, and they have been among the most aggressive advocates of pollution abatement and conservation programs. Even during the heyday of industrialization, scientists described the deterioration of air quality in major industrial centers and the progressive pollution of rivers and streams, although virtually no one took serious note of their findings (Pryde, 1972:11). Scientists remained in the forefront of the growing environmental movement as new attention focused on pollution in the late 1950's and the 1960's. More than any other group, they have raised the level of national awareness and pressed for effective abatement programs, frequently waging an uphill battle against hostile government bureaucrats and industrial managers, sceptical fellow scientists, and an apathetic public.

Within the scientific community, researchers in the medical and biological sciences have played the largest role, with the staff specialists of state pollution-control and conservation agencies a close second. On occasion noted scientists in other fields have voiced their support, as did the physicist Andrei Sakharov in his officially banned essay *Progress, Coexistence, and Intellectual Freedom*, which noted the common environmental concerns of industrial nations. Research on environmental questions has been centered in a relatively small number of institutes subordinated to the Ministry of Public Health, the Academy of Sciences, the Academy of Medical Sciences, the Chief Administration of the Hydrometeorological Service, and the State Committee on Science and Technology. Highly compartmentalized specialization is typical, with separate institutes dealing with specific fields of activity (for example, occupational hygiene) or individual pollutants. Republic-level ministries of public health and academies of science conduct their own investigations of local environmental problems, and limited research is done in the academic community. Industrial ministries are also frequently involved, at least tangentially, in pollution research. Effective coordination of these diverse research activities has always eluded Soviet officials, despite the creation in 1966 of a Scientific Council for the Study of Natural Resource Problems under the State Committee on Science and Technology. Acknowledging this shortcoming, Soviet officials early in 1973 called upon the State Committee to join with the USSR Academy of Sciences in the creation of an interdepartmental scientific and technical council on environmental problems, although past experience suggests that the council will probably find it difficult to guide research within a number of institutes subordinated to and funded by different agencies (Kramer, 1973a:42–46,74; HEW, 1970:158–159; Pravda, 10 January 1973:1).

Despite the preeminence of scientists in the development of environmental awareness, serious limitations still restrict environmental research. As already noted, research is poorly coordinated and ill funded. The not infrequent subordination of research functions to industrial ministries has also tended to suppress accurate disclosures of the magnitude of the problem; polluters simply refuse to appropriate funds to point up the negative aspects of their activities. Even among the nonproduction ministries and the semi-independent research agencies, pollution research has been limited both by the desire to further research in more productive areas and by the general unwillingness in the past to acknowledge the problem. Only in recent years have scientists such as M. V. Keldysh, former president of the USSR Academy of Sciences, spoken out for more research (Gerasimov, 1971:208–209; Pravda, 10 January 1973:3).

Soviet geographers have joined with their counterparts in the physical sciences in calling for greater environmental awareness. Having fallen on hard times in the intellectual community, geographers are seeking to refurbish the discipline through the introduction of the man–nature orientation and the concept of a unified biosphere. Such a perspective inevitably suggests greater attention to environmental considerations, and some geographers have lauded Western attempts at ecosystem modeling (Gerasimov, 1971:211–218; Lopatina et al., 1970:142; Sochava, 1971:288).

The active role of scientists and geographers in raising the level of ecological awareness must not be taken to mean they have become unqualified critics of further economic growth. Most speak instead of the "rational" use of nature, that is, a balanced program of exploitation and conservation that would alleviate the worst environmental offenses without severely limiting growth. Leading scientists such as Keldysh and I. P. Gerasimov, the dean of Soviet geographers, still speak of the need for massive projects to irrigate arid areas and to alter the course of major rivers, although they admit that greater consideration must be given to the secondary environmental and human costs involved (Gerasimov, 1969:24; Gerasimov et al., 1964:3–15). Opinion is subtly divided even on Lake Baikal, with scientists and environmentalists such as P. L. Kapitsa and Yevgeni Fyodorov, former head of the Hydrometeorological Service, cautioning their more eager colleagues that protection of the lake must be balanced against the wise use of its unique resources (Fyodorov, 1972:15–18; Shabad, 1973:15).

A word must also be said about the role of the nonscientific intelligentsia in raising the level of environmental awareness. Social scientists have contributed very little to the growing public discussion, although a few bold economists have proposed that industry be compelled to pay for clean-up programs or that the nation consider a reduction of the growth rate to divert funds to reclamation projects (Oldak, 1970:11; Pryde, 1972:165; Bush, 1972:27; Fedorenko and Gofman, 1973:38–46). The legal profession is also responsible for a growing body of literature on legal and administrative problems of pollution control. A paradoxical situation exists concerning the literary intelligentsia. In part the paradox stems from the conflicting focus of prerevolutionary and Soviet literature. Still venerated prerevolutionary writers such as Tolstoy stressed the importance of a harmonious relationship between man and nature, and before the revolution a substantial body of literature emerged which was highly critical of the environmental and human costs of economic development. In contrast, much of the literature of the Soviet era has glorified the march of industry and ignored, until recently, its unintended environmental consequences. It was only in the 1960's, when the degradation of Lake Baikal and other important waterways was first discussed in the press, that members of the literary intelligentsia began to speak out. Curiously, this new-found environmental awareness has cut across conservative and liberal lines. The deterioration of the environment has been condemned both by literary dissidents writing in officially banned underground journals and by long-approved conservative writers such as Mikhail Sholokhov, who complained bitterly at the Twenty-third Communist Party Congress in 1966 of the pollution of the Don River (Sakharov, 1968:48–50; Solzhenitsyn, 1974:21–26; Sholokhov, 1966:354–362).

GOVERNMENT AND INDUSTRY

Soviet industrialists and government officials were long aware that industry annually poured millions of tons of pollutants into the nation's air and waterways, although they lacked, until recently, sufficient scientific knowledge of the ecological impact of these wastes. While the Soviet government enacted a number of environmental or conservation-related laws in its early years, enforcement was halfhearted. The late 1940's witnessed a timid reawakening of interest in the environment as new measures on air and water pollution were passed. Additional enactments came from the Supreme Soviet in the 1950's, and in the late fifties and early sixties, all of the union republics passed comprehensive environmental and conservation measures.

The enforcement picture suggests, however, that the real awakening among governmental leaders came only in the 1960's when a series of pressing environmental problems were recognized. Only then were special projects undertaken to cope with the worst problems such as Lake Baikal or the Volga and Ural basins. The late sixties and early seventies saw enacted stricter and more wide-ranging environmental regulations, and measures were launched to overcome the enforcement problems inherent in administrative decentralization. With increasing frequency, high-level officials have called for stricter protection measures, and joint party and state resolutions—viewed as the most authoritative and forceful pronouncements on policy matters—have been issued on environmental questions. In September of 1972, the Supreme Soviet devoted an entire session to pollution and conservation problems, and more legislative interest has also been seen at the republic and local levels. At both the Twenty-third and Twenty-fourth Communist Party Congresses (1966 and 1971), delegates noted the need for better protection of the environment (Kramer, 1973a:6–10).

Despite this increased governmental activity, Soviet leaders remain reluctant to acknowledge the full magnitude of the problem. A part of their reluctance stems from a sense of embarrassment and the long-standing practice of suppressing unfavorable information about state activity. Soviet leaders and scientists have had to contend with the ideologically motivated belief that pollution problems could exist only in capitalist systems. Thus they have tended to write off the political outcry in the West on pollution questions as an attempt to divert public attention from more fundamental political and social issues. Only in cautious ways such as the American-Soviet agreement on environment matters have they officially admitted that virtually all industrial nations must cope with pollution. The traditional penchant for secrecy has also restricted the level of awareness, especially regarding the regime's frankness with the Soviet people. M. D. Millionshchikov (quoted in Bush, 1972:26), first deputy chairman of the USSR Academy of Sciences, sums up this attitude in his reaction to the open debate in the West:

> We treat these problems a little differently. Open discussion in the press and in public does not always produce a review of the problem from the right point of view. We try to consider this in scientific discussion, not in public.

While officials have recently begun to permit fairly open discussion of environmental problems in the otherwise censored media, at times they have denied publication even to modest critics. In September 1970, for example, the party banned further discussion of environmental problems, leading *Izvestiia* to cancel a proposed series of articles on the pollution of the Volga. By early 1971, however, the ban was lifted, apparently after discussion among top leaders (Gwertzman, 1970b:52; LaMothe, 1971:1). But even this new-found candor was relative, for authorities censored a Russian language edition of the July 1971 *UNESCO Courier*, deleting an article by Marshall Goldman on pollution in the USSR (which liberally cited Soviet sources) and substituting instead a bland piece by the president of the Ukrainian Committee for the Protection of Nature.

Soviet industrialists undoubtedly have long been aware of pollution, although they have shown a clear disregard for its consequences. While managers have lacked a sophisticated scientific understanding of the environmental degradation surrounding their factories and mills, they have of necessity been acutely aware of pollution-related health complaints among their workers and of their own conscious violations of poorly enforced environmental laws. In their defense, it must be noted that there were powerful incentives to violate pollution-abatement regulations, for a factory's bonuses and a manager's prospects for advancement depended upon meeting gross production quotas and not on the quality of the environment.

THE PUBLIC

General public awareness of environmental problems has been limited both by restrictions imposed until recently on discussion of the question and widely held attitudes which deemphasize environmental concerns. Although early polls show that workers living near polluting industries were clearly aware of the problem, wide-scale public attention was not focused on the deteriorating quality of the environment until the 1960's (Kaliuzhnyi, 1961:102–114). In the late 1950's and the 1960's, the discussion of pollution spread from the scientific journals to popular journals and newspapers such as *Literaturnaia Gazeta, Novii Mir, Nash Sovremenik,* and *Komsomolskaia Pravda* (a reader familiar with the Soviet press will note the intellectual and liberal bias of these sources, or their youthful orientation as in the case of *Komsomolskaia Pravda*), and finally to the mass-circulation dailies *Pravda* and *Izvestiia.* The primary journal to bridge the gap between specialists and the general public before the 1960's was popular biology journal *Priroda (Nature)*, which frequently cited environmental problems long before less aggressive publications. Since the mid-1960's, the number of environment-related articles appearing in mass-circulation media has grown rapidly, and film makers have also taken up the question (Bush, 1972:26; Gwertzman, 1970a:6).

An examination of this enlarged debate reveals that while the problem is now discussed more openly, the most frequent participants remain scientists and other specialists in environmental affairs. From his prolonged study of the handling of environmental questions in the Soviet media, John Kramer (1973a:25–26) points out that the most frequent participants are scientists and academics (holding nearly a two-to-one margin over the nearest group), deputies of local or the Supreme Soviet (who focus primarily on local offenses), members of conservation or pollution abatement agencies (who attempt to use the press to generate pressures against uncooperative officials and factory managers), and economists (but *not* factory managers).

Deeply held public attitudes toward man's relationship to nature and the pressing desire to enjoy the consumer benefits of industrialization have also dulled the environmental awareness of the average Russian. The view that nature's wealth is virtually inexhaustible and that it is man's fate to conquer and reshape nature is widely held. Moreover, the average citizen undoubtedly places the satisfaction of his own material desires well above environmental considerations in ordering his personal priorities; in a work-now, consume-later economy, the argument that increased production, especially of consumer goods, must be even further delayed in the interests of environmental quality is destined to be unpopular.

JAPAN

National consciousness of environmental problems has arisen only since 1965, although awareness of localized pollution stretches back to the late nineteenth century (Ui et al., 1970:31). The mainstream of environmental awareness tends to focus on readily perceivable damage inflicted on health and property rather than on "invisible," potentially long-range ecological disruption. Moreover, the concept of environmental quality is commonly associated with limited pollution-control measures and only infrequently with more fundamental social, political, and economic questions. Thus pollution is widely viewed as a "side effect," a troublesome anomaly open to correction without strict controls on economic growth, consumption, and waste.

The Scientific Community

In the past, only a handful of Japanese scientists have addressed themselves to a broad range of environmental issues. The most notable is Jan

Ui of Tokyo University. He has edited a wide-ranging, provocative volume entitled *Polluted Japan,* and published a comprehensive, pessimistic article in *Japan Quarterly* which was later featured on the editorial page of the *Asahi Shimbun,* Japan's most prestigious newspaper. Although other Japanese scientists have published much useful material on specialized aspects of pollution and the environment, there is no figure in sight with Ui's blend of knowledge, sweep, political sophistication, and moral outrage (Ui, 1972b).

Somewhat more obscure are a few scientists and physicians who have struggled against heavy odds to establish the truth about pollution-related diseases. Such was the case with the late Hajime Hosokowa, who first investigated the origin of Minamata disease as director of the Chisso Factory Hospital in Minamata City, and with Noboru Hagino, who traced cadmium poisoning to the effluent discharged in mining operations and saw his findings vindicated only after a long period of bureaucratic evasion (Ui et al., 1970:48).

Occasionally social scientists speak out. Among economists, Kiyohara Murata of Chuo University applauded the historic court decision that forced the Chisso Corporation to compensate victims of mercury poisoning in Kumamoto Prefecture, and Kenichi Miyamoto of Osaka City University urged that Chisso be compelled to clean out the mercury–laden sludge at the bottom of Minamata Bay and the surrounding Shiranui Sea. Most economists, however, are preoccupied with analyzing the structure and perturbations of the economy. New attitudes have appeared among sociologists. Those who participated in the 1970 international symposium on pollution in Tokyo endorsed a general resolution that proclaimed environmental destruction as "one of the greatest issues in modern times" and affirmed a healthy environment to be "a basic human right."

On the negative side, too many scholars and scientists have been less than candid, objective, and informative about the extent and gravity of environmental problems. Their low profile can be explained as a result of social conventions and certain institutional patterns. Scientific loners who seek to inquire and publish in controversial fields are likely to be shunned and isolated. Like nearly everyone else in Japan, scientists are bound by a network of obligations and loyalties reaching throughout the social order. They are no less vulnerable than anyone else to the abrasive change of being *kojin-teki* (individualistic), which implies an unseemly, self-centered indifference to the collective interests of the group. The wise Japanese scientist must remember that expert scientific opinion, particularly on matters embarrassing to politicians and industrialists, is subject to adjustment within a larger picture.

The recent emergence of the environmental crisis has caught scientists without a well-organized, independent forum for the frank expression of their views. The great national universities are without ecology departments; the creation of such departments has been only just recommended by the government, subject to approval by the universities. In the meantime Japan has no equivalent, for example, of the Scientist's Institute for Public Information, the American body whose aim is to link scientists with nonscientists by supplying technical information on environmental issues; the newspapers are the closest approximation, or perhaps Jishu-Koza (Independent Forum), an evening forum that brings together concerned citizens and scientists at Tokyo University.

In Japan authority emanates from a group rather than from an individual context. Most scientists outside the universities are associated with industry or with perfectural and national research institutes, which limits independence of thought and inquiry. Industrial "think tanks," like that of the Mitsui combine, sponsor research largely on economic questions. University professors do very little consulting with government and industry, nor are they often asked for advice. The academic world tends to be closed off and aloof from public affairs. Young scientists may break out of the ivory tower from time to time, but they do so with extreme caution, and with the knowledge that colleagues may be offended and superiors contemptuous.

Despite these difficulties, research on environmental pollution has grown fast in recent years, encouraged both by government support of new research centers and by spreading awareness of the problem. Myriad research projects have been initiated on virtually every facet of pollution with characteristic Japanese élan. These include not only conventional studies of the origin, nature, and effects of pollutants, but exotica like the development of a diffusion model of auto exhaust fumes on a superhighway and a hydraulic scale model of the Seto Inland Sea. A growing number of national, prefectural, and private research institutes are involved as well as various government ministries and agencies, all purportedly coordinated by the Environment Agency. Some effort is being made to enlarge the hitherto peripheral role of the universities. In 1974 the government opened a forty-nine million dollar National Institute for Environmental Protection in the Tsukuba Academic City now under construction in Ibaraki Prefecture. The institute will function as a "think tank" for environmental problems in general and will direct special attention to the long-range impact of pollution on ecosystems and heredity. Still another "think tank" was begun in the autumn of 1973 as a cooperative venture involving business federations, large enterprises, and government, the latter to be represented by the Economic Planning Agency. Scholars, private specialists, and the mass media are to have roles in setting up this institution, whose range of economic, social, and public opinion studies is to include criteria for optimum economic growth, guidelines for a national consensus on environmental problems, and attitudes of business and industry toward their social responsibilities *(QEJ*, 1973:245; *JT*, 20 August 1973).

GOVERNMENT AND INDUSTRY

The central government has been compelled by public outcry to acknowledge the fact of worsening environmental conditions. During the Sato administration anti-pollution laws were passed, environmental appropriations increased, an Environment Agency created, and a spate of pollution policy statements issued, mainly in the form of "white papers" flowing from various ministries. The Economic Planning Agency's *New Economic and Social Development Plan, 1970–1975 (EPA*, 1970) concedes that "unless further strong and effective measures are taken, the deterioration of the environment will be accelerated, and to secure a safe ... existence for the people will not only become difficult, but sound development of the economy will also be obstructed" *(EPA*, 1970:55).

The Environment Agency has published several booklets crammed with ominous findings. In *Quality of the Environment in Japan (JEA*, 1972j) it is said that "concern over environmental pollution seems to have reached the point of explosion. Each citizen has come to feel the worsening of environmental conditions in his ... daily life, and the nation as a whole is paying a great price for its neglect of environmental considerations." In the national report submitted to the Stockholm Conference a key remark is that "deterioration of the human environment is one of the most crucial problems that Japan will have to face in the 1970's." A long-range forecast by the Ministry of Health and Welfare sees seventy percent of Japan's citizens willing to sacrifice economic growth for an unpolluted environment by the year 2000 *(QEJ*, 1972:2; *JT*, 6 January 1973; *JNR*, 1971:1).

Concealed behind these expressions of concern, however, is a profound ambivalence on the highest government levels. In *Jiyu-Shimpo* (The Liberal Democratic Party paper) former Prime Minister Tanaka seemed to take a pro-environmental stance in July 1970, in arguing that "the task which we must tackle is to change the order of priority in economic policy, which stems from the standpoint of restoring human rights, and to carry out a modern industrial revolution, with the aim of preventing public nuisances." But in the same interview he also lauded continued rapid economic growth, taking obvious pride that the economy was then projected to grow at the rate of ten percent a year and the GNP to reach about three hundred trillion yen (about one trillion dollars) by fiscal 1985. The essence of Tanaka's solution to environmental problems is simple—more economic growth at breakneck speed, which is a bit like prescribing a bottle of brandy for a massive hangover.

Compared with the central government, municipal governments are embued with a greater sense of urgency. Mayors of towns, cities, and autonomous regions like Tokyo are closely in touch with day-to-day environmental problems, for they receive complaints more directly and must cooperate with prefectural governors to enforce pollution-control standards. Overwhelmed by urban ills, they have been critical of the central government for token environmental funding, lax emission standards, and local powerlessness to curtail the march of industry. The peppery mayor of Tokyo, Ryokichi Minobe, has denounced the ruling party's favorable treatment of industry, and his administration has published one of the best introductions to Japan's environmental dilemma, *Tokyo Fights Pollution (TMG,* 1971; also see Kunimoto, 1972).

Until recently the business world contented itself with vague rhetoric about higher standards of public responsibility, while proceeding to do much as it pleased. The most impressive sign of a change is a daring proposal set forth in March 1973 by the Industrial Planning Council, an influential private organization with a membership of thirty-one top business figures. The council aims to reduce pollution and deal with an increasingly apparent energy and natural resource crisis by freezing, scaling down, or phasing out nine types of industry, including steel, petrochemicals, oil refining, electric power, paper and pulp. The plan is remarkably cognizant of Japan's vulnerability to pollution and shortages of raw materials, and is an implicit challenge to unrestrained consumption and production. Kiichiro Sato, head of the Council and leader of the Mitsui group of financiers, calls the report a negative view of the idea that "consumption is a virtue." It has not been received with enthusiasm by the mainstream of Japanese business and industry, which is mostly worried that public hostility might hurt sales and impede growth. Toshiwo Doko, president of Keidanren (the Federation of Economic Organizations), the "supreme coordinating body of big business," said in 1974 that Japan's resource-consuming industrial structure would have to change in the direction of knowledge-intensiveness *(LJ,* 10 October 1974; Yanaga, 1968:42). The Japan Committee for Economic Development (Keizai Doyukai), composed of younger business executives, has warned that mounting protest against the excesses of industry could result in "severe ordeals" for business. The "polluter-pays principle" and the need for antipollution reform are regarded more favorably, but the committee urges that government and the public share the cost and that emission standards not be unreasonable *(AEN,* 23 March 1973).

There are other signs that the business world is turning to face reality. In 1970 and again in 1972, the Japan Broadcasting Corporation polled one hundred top company presidents about the trade-off between economic growth and pollution. In 1970 only 34.5 percent would stop pollution at the cost of slowing economic growth; in 1972 the figure had risen to 63 percent. What people spend money on always says something about their values. It is encouraging that antipollution investments in Japan have been rising steadily, if not spectacularly. Thus antipollution spending in 1975 represented 18.9 percent of all investments, up from 16.4 percent in the previous year *(QEJ,* 1973:29; *JT,* 27 November 1974).

The Public

Coverage of environmental issues in the mass media has been expanding since about 1965. Television is an important source of information and has carried full reports of mercury and cadmium-poisoning incidents. Newspapers have been by far the indispensable forum for activist lawyers and scientists doing "people's research." The amount of space devoted to environmental problems in news articles rose from 0.4 percent in 1960 to 2.8 percent in 1972, and news coverage in general quadrupled between 1965 and 1970. In one prominent paper, articles on pollution in a single year numbered 14 in 1960 and 124 in 1971. Japan's leading dailies, the *Asahi Shimbun, Mainichi Shimbun,* and *Yomiuri Shimbun,* have published critical editorials on population growth, the energy crisis, pollution, and the connection between economic growth and the environmental crisis. Less prestigious papers have also responded to the challenge of pollution. The *Minamata Times,* otherwise a one-man, local scandal sheet, did a thorough job of reporting to its one thousand readers the appalling outbreak of mercury poisoning in Kumamoto Prefecture *(QEJ,* 1972:3). Junior high school textbooks for use from April 1975 have been revised to give considerably more space to pollution, the relationship of pollution and health, and citizens' movements against offending industries *(AEN,* 28 June 1974).

Opinion polls indicate a striking surge of awareness in recent years. A national poll conducted by the Prime Minister's Public Information Office in 1973 produced these results: 50 percent of the sample believed a cleaner environment should have first priority, while only 20 percent put economic growth first; 70 percent affirmed that nature is being destroyed close-at-hand; 61 percent had suffered from one form of pollution or another; and 87 percent were pessimistic about improvement in the future *(JEA,* 10 January 1974, Vol. 2, No. 1:2–3). Numerous regional polls have uncovered an abundance of worry and complaint. A survey of three thousand people in Chiba Prefecture showed 96.6 percent to be concerned about pollution, and nearly 60 percent felt victimized by it. As to fixing responsibility, 59 percent pointed their fingers at thoughtless industrialists.

The number of official complaints has risen sharply from some twenty thousand in 1966, to sixty-three thousand in 1970, to eighty-eight thousand in 1972, and no part of the country is unrepresented; noise, odors, and air pollution are the most frequent targets of complaint, in that order. Officially registered discontent may be regarded as the tip of a gigantic iceberg, for the Japanese are inclined to bear suffering and hardship silently (*JEA*, 10 March 1974, Vol. 2, No. 3:3-4).

CHAPTER
6
THE POLITICS
OF
ENVIRONMENTAL
QUALITY

THE UNITED STATES

POLITICAL ISSUES AND NATIONAL PRIORITIES

After three centuries of vigorous economic growth and its attendant environmental disruption, a fresh perception of national priorities has emerged in the past two decades; some attempt is now being made to balance the claims of material growth with those of ecological integrity. The latter issue gained considerably in stature during the 1960's, reaching a culmination in 1969 with passage of the National Environmental Policy Act (NEPA), which set forth comprehensive guidelines for the first time (Sprout, 1971). The NEPA declared it to be the responsibility of the federal government, working with state and local authorities, "to use all practicable means, consistent with other essential considerations of national policy," to assure each generation of Americans of a "safe, healthful, productive, and aesthetically and culturally pleasing" environment. It is clear in this announcement that environmental considerations are to share the stage with other national goals, but are to be honored by "practicable means" that do not encroach on economic growth or national security (Public Law 91-190; Utton and Henning, 1973:83).

At present the need for environmental protection and restoration is not at issue; rather it is the pace and thoroughness of abatement programs, and who shall bear the cost of pollution control which incite argument. Although few political leaders question the need for action of some kind, this has not always been the case. The road to existing environmental legislation has been a turbulent one marked by protracted struggle at all levels of government—between interest groups and their political sympathizers on the one hand and business and industrial lobbies on the other. Political alignments on environmental questions appear to have been connected less with partisan affiliation than with the anticipated effect of pollution-control measures on a legislator's constituents or on special interests supporting him. Legislators face hard choices which almost never reflect a simple confrontation between the unchallenged desideratum of a clean environment and the unqualified villainy of a polluting industry. Choices normally take the form of seemingly incalculable trade-offs. In the short run, more investment for pollution control means palpable inconvenience in the guise of higher consumer prices and, in extreme cases, factory closings and the disruption of long-standing industrial operations. Such negative effects must be weighed, in a thus far vague, embryonic social calculus, against prospects of future economic benefit and the more intangible profit of a salubrious environment. These questions have touched the widest possible spectrum of the body politic, throwing up new political alignments that pit newly mobilized environmental groups against sometimes well-coordinated alliances of industrial, commercial, and trade-union interests determined to blunt the cutting edge of environmental protection measures (Cooley and Wandesforde-Smith, 1970).

More fundamental, perhaps, is the question of whether traditional assumptions about economic growth are best for the nation. While most political debate has focused on how to divide the economic and social costs of pollution abatement, and environmentalists and environment-minded economists have argued that economic growth itself is the proper subject for discussion. Several alternatives have been advanced. Some advocate a "steady state" or no-growth economy, some a slow-growth economy, while still others recommend an alteration of national income accounting so as to discriminate between environmentally destructive and environmentally sound investment policies.* At the core of all proposals

---

*The term "economic growth" is ambiguous. It is commonly used to mean the production of material goods—cars, TV's, and the like—but is perhaps better understood as net national product per capita, or "the sum of consumer, government, and business expeditures on final goods and services, including investment in new capital, minus an estimate for the depreciation of capital" (Olson and Landsberg, 1973:5). Thus economic growth becomes largely a matter of rising per capita income. A stationary or even a slow-growth economy entails many knotty problems with respect to income distribution, the age structure of a society's population, and the diminution of net investment (Olson and Landsberg, 1973:94–97). It is significant

is a common denominator—the idea that persistent economic growth, hitherto the gyroscope of American national purpose, should be pursued only with great caution.

The steady-state concept is not widely accepted by government and business leaders, or by the man in the street, in part because of an unwillingness to face the political and social consequences of submitting to stringent limits on future growth. The former groups, along with many environmentalists, think that pollution control is largely a matter of applying money and technology that need not detract seriously from economic growth, although painful short-term adjustments might be necessary on an industry-by-industry basis. The prevailing consensus seems to be that in the long run, pollution control will be good for the economy by reducing health costs, by curtailing the wasteful use of resources, and by creating jobs in the field of pollution-control technology. Rightly or wrongly, it appears to be difficult for Americans to envision a society and economy founded on no-growth assumptions. It has been much easier for legislators to deal with pollution control than with the more radical idea of forging a completely new structure of national priorities (*NY Times*, 2 June 1974).

This pattern of response is well illustrated by attitudes and public programs that have tried to cope with the nation's energy crisis. In 1973, most Americans realized for the first time that impediments to the domestic production and importation of oil threatened economic prosperity and their consumer-oriented, mobile life-style. In their efforts to deal with the crisis, political leaders have evidenced a typical strategy, that of concentrating on narrowly short-term technical problems, such as increasing domestic production of oil and other fossil fuels, tapping new energy sources, and mounting limited conservation programs. Few, if any, of these people have suggested forcefully that Americans must alter their style of living, be reconciled to a fundamental restructuring of the economy, or accept future retrenchment in economic production. Programs have been shaped more around the notion of national self-sufficiency than a change in basic consumption patterns, or a shift in public attitudes, both of which glory in the consumption of energy in colossal amounts (Holdren and Herrera, 1971:19–22). Technology and astute diplomacy are taken to be the keys to solving the problem; sacrifices that must be endured are regarded as temporary rather than long-term adjustments, and it is expected that the problem eventually will disappear. It is perhaps too much to ask politicians

that pro- and anti-growth advocates are busy sorting out the arguments. A more attractive approach to traditional economic thinking is to supplement GNP with a new concept of welfare: Tobin and Nordhaus' measure of economic welfare (MEW), or Samuelson's version of the same thing, net economic welfare (NEW). Both are new methods of national accounting which stress consumption, hence household welfare, rather than production. Thus defense spending would not contribute to a measure of NEW (*NY Times*, 29 July 1973).

in a democracy to accept the short-term risks of demanding that their constituents fundamentally reorder their lives, but the ultimate risk of political expediency and traditional behavior among those responsible for the nation's welfare is that elections will be won while the country runs aground on the shoals of an energy shortage. (*NY Times*, 9, 10, 22 October 1974; 13 November 1974).

GOVERNMENT AGENCIES

Final responsibility for the implementation of environmental policy rests with the president, but he is supported by a number of advisory, administrative, and enforcement agencies within the federal government. The leading advisory body is the Council on Environmental Quality (CEQ), which owes its existence to the NEPA. The CEQ has the task of reviewing the effect of federal programs and activities in the environmental sphere through analysis of impact statements whose submission is required by the NEPA. The CEQ publishes a monthly summary of impact statements filed with it by other agencies, and issues an annual report, *Environmental Quality*, which capsulizes the state of the environment, federal programs, research in progress, and similar matters. The council is a three-member body whose chairman, as of this writing, is Russell W. Peterson, former governor of Delaware, a man with a strong environmental record. As part of the president's executive office, the council is free to recommend policy guidelines to him (*CEQ*, 1973b:405; Public Law 91–190). The president, in turn, is free to ignore the advice or to play it off against that of other agencies. Some environmentalists believe the council and its activities have been downgraded significantly over the past few years, leaving it with only limited monitoring and educational functions.

Administrative responsibilities are widely diffused throughout the executive departments and their subordinate agencies (Rosenbaum, 1973:98–100, 107–108). Moreover, the range of environmental functions performed by executive agencies is very wide; environmental advocates have virtually no concern that is not shared, more or less, by some federal agency. If nothing else, all agencies must file impact statements whenever they propose something, such as the construction of an interstate highway, that might leave a deep imprint on the environment. (Public Law 91–190).

In addition to the Environmental Protection Agency (EPA), discussed below, there are others with major environmental responsibilities. These include the National Forest Service, Soil Conservation Service, National Oceanic and Atmospheric Administration, Army Corps of Engineers, National Park Service, Bureau of Land Management, Bureau of Outdoor Recreation, and Bureau of Reclamation. The Land and Natural Resources

Division of the Department of Justice handles all federal civil suits involving natural resources and pollution abatement, and is also in charge of criminal prosecution for violations of air- and water-pollution laws *(OFR, 1972–1973; Rosenbaum, 1973:86–88)*.

Several independent administrative agencies are directly connected with environmental affairs. Until recently, the often controversial Atomic Energy Commission (AEC) virtually monopolized the nuclear field, including research and development, regulation of civilian use of nuclear materials and reactors, encouragement of nuclear power applications, and the management of radioactive wastes *(OFR, 1972–1973)*. Environmental groups, particularly the Consolidation of National Intervenors, accused the AEC of subordinating safety precautions to the development and use of atomic energy *(NY Times, 10 November 1974)*. It was also charged that the AEC in its dual role of advocating nuclear energy development and regulating its use was embroiled palpably in a conflict of interest. Congress responded to such criticism by dividing the functions of the AEC between an Energy Research and Development Agency and a Nuclear Regulatory Commission *(NY Times, 10 October 1974)*.

An independent agency with an impressive title, but of relatively little significance, is the Citizen's Advisory Committee on Environmental Quality. Chaired by Laurance S. Rockefeller as of this writing, it is supposed to advise the president on such important matters as the reconciliation of environmental and economic goals, and occupy itself with the promotion of private environmental groups and industry-initiated abatement programs. The committee's reports to the president have recommended more federal expenditures and the founding of a national environmental institute. These counsels have been ignored for the most part, probably because the committee's functions overlap with those of the CEQ *(CACEQ, 1972)*.

As a counterweight to the Citizen's Advisory Committee, former Secretary of Commerce Maurice Stans pushed successfully for the creation of the National Industrial Pollution Control Council (NIPCC), a conduit for the views of industry on environmental problems. The NIPCC advises the president and the CEQ through the secretary of commerce. It is composed of executives from major industrial firms and is divided into twenty-six specialized subcouncils representing different branches of industry *(OFR, 1972–1973)*.

The stellar federal agency dealing with environmental problems is the EPA, which was established in December 1970 and took over from other agencies a variety of research, monitoring, and enforcement functions, rapidly becoming the principal instrument for pollution abatement. Its eighty-eight hundred employees staff the national headquarters in Washington, ten regional offices, and four National Environmental Research

Centers charged with the study of pollution-control technology, ecosystems, the effects of pollution on health, and environmental effects of radiation. The budget for the EPA in 1972 was 32.5 billion dollars, 2 billion of which was diverted to the construction of sewage treatment plants *(USEPA, 1972; Trzyna, 1973).* *maybe 3.25*

Most of the EPA's routine monitoring and abatement duties are handled by its branch agencies. The Office of Noise Abatement and Control studies the causes and effects of noise pollution and works out projections of future noise levels in urban areas. The Office of Pesticide Programs sets up pesticide residue tolerance levels for foodstuffs and monitors the presence of such residues in the environment; it also registers commercial pesticides and defines restrictions on their sale and use. The Office of Radiation Programs pursues a national surveillance of radiation levels and evaluates the impact of new radiation technology; it also develops methods for the measurement and control of radiation exposure, and provides technical assistance to other government agencies with radiation protection programs, including the training of personnel. The Office of Solid Waste Programs researches solid waste management, emphasizing recovery and recycling programs rather than simple disposal; through grants-in-aid to state and local governments, it encourages the development of solid-waste management systems *(USEPA, 1972; USEPA, 1971a; Trzyna, 1973).*

The Office of Air Programs develops air quality and source emission standards, and provides technical as well as financial support for regional air-pollution control activities. It has broad powers under the Clean Air Act of 1963 (with its 1966 and 1970 amendments), the Motor Vehicle Air Pollution Control Act of 1965, and the Air Quality Act of 1967 to make direct grants to state and local governments for air-pollution control, regulation of motor vehicle emissions, and the definition of air quality standards. Should a state fail to enact and enforce air quality regulations up to federal standards, the EPA has the legal authority to make them do so *(USEPA, 1972; USEPA, 1971b; Trzyna, 1973).*

The Office of Water Programs functions much like the Office of Air Programs. One of its major tasks is to administer a huge program of grants for the construction of sewage-treatment and water-purification facilities. Programs of the office also help to train technicians for water quality projects, and provide wide-ranging technical assistance to state and local governments. Comprehensive interstate river basin planning for pollution control and abatement is encouraged; moreover, the office has power to enforce water quality standards on interstate waterways. Finally, it enforces laws directed against oil and vessel pollution of interstate waterways, and in cooperation with the Corps of Engineers, administers the Rivers and Harbors (Refuse) Act of 1899 *(USEPA, 1972; Trzyna, 1973).*

The EPA's first administrator, William D. Ruckelshaus, was an attorney whose political experience was limited to one term in the Indiana legislature and an unsuccessful 1968 bid for the Senate. He was chosen to head the EPA after serving as chief of the Civil Division of the Justice Department. His credentials as an environmentalist were marginal, amounting to membership in the Audubon Society and an attraction to outdoor life. His successor, Russell E. Train, who was the first chairman of the CEQ, has a much stronger environmental background, having served as president of the Conservation Foundation before entering government service. Both, however, are self-proclaimed political realists who have spoken out publicly for a balance between traditional national goals and environmental protection (*NY Times*, 6 August 1972; 27 April, 18 September 1973).

In many states, steps have been taken to centralize environmental responsibilities in one agency, as was done with the EPA on the national level. Some twenty percent now have agencies similar to the New Jersey Department of Environmental Protection, which exercises sweeping authority over various forms of pollution, pesticides, coastal and tidal lands, fish and game, water resources, and state forests and parks. Perhaps the most comprehensive powers are those of the Pennsylvania Department of Environmental Resources, for it presides over all environmental concerns except fisheries and water-pollution control. Other states with centralized agencies are Connecticut, Delaware, Nebraska, New York, and North Carolina (Trzyna, 1973).

Five additional states have taken somewhat less exacting steps toward centralization. In Alaska, following a 1971 reorganization, environmental responsibilities were divided between the Department of Environmental Conservation and the Department of Natural Resources. Montana, Ohio, Vermont, and West Virginia have come fairly close to the Alaskan pattern (Trzyna, 1973).

Several other states have adopted a somewhat different approach to the coordination of their environmental efforts. Thus in Hawaii the Office of Environmental Quality Control coordinates all of the state's programs but does not administer them directly. It has developed a pollution-monitoring system to help achieve its objective, and also handles environmental research and educational programs. The director sits as chairman of an Environmental Council, which is composed of representatives of the media, private environmental groups, and professional environmentalists. In Oregon the assistant to the governor for natural resources coordinates the activities of all state natural resource agencies and organizes the annual Governor's Conservation Congress (Trzyna, 1973).

The appearance of centralized or semicentralized state agencies has had two important results: public health offices, usually poor stewards of environmental quality, no longer control pollution abatement, and the political influence of local industrial interests has been reduced. Prior to these changes, it was commonplace for scattered pollution-control agencies to be packed with representatives of the very industries ostensibly being regulated. One should not infer from this shift the demise of industry as a political force, but at least there are now state agencies whose sole *raison d'être* is to protect the environment, and their number is likely to grow as the EPA applies pressure to states without centralized organs to create them (Haskell and Price, 1973:243 ff).

In addition to the federal and state agencies, there are over fifty interstate bodies that deal more or less directly with environmental affairs. The activities of the Coastal States Organization are typical of this third type. Based in Savannah, Georgia, this agency comprises the thirty-two states and territories with coastlines on the Atlantic and Pacific oceans or on the Great Lakes. One of its principal functions is the shaping of a common policy with respect to national coastal zone management legislation, and to aid member states in the solution of mutual resource problems on coastal zones. The organization also serves as a clearinghouse for information on the coastal and marine activities of member states, and acts as their spokesman on coastal zone management to the federal government (Trzyna, 1973).

POLICY MAKING AND PRESSURE GROUPS

Environmental policy making in the United States is marked by intense rivalry between environmental and industrial lobbies, and takes place against a background of decentralization in both policy-making and administrative functions. From the perspective of all contending forces, the system is extraordinarily open, in the sense that competing interests can organize and lobby with few restrictions, and because key federal and state agencies offer multiple points of access. Underpinning this process of competitive advocacy is the assumption that all sides will have their say in some appropriate forum. Compromise and adjustment in the process of formulating environmental policy usually reflect the underlying political sinew of the contending parties. When environmental lobbies have lacked power, the situation throughout much of American history, policy usually has expressed the interests of business and industry.

The range of clashing interests is broad in this pluralistic policy-making milieu. At one extreme, environmental advocates are represented by numerous organizations which are either new or newly powerful. At the other extreme, one finds their opponents represented by venerable, long-familiar lobbies associated with powerful business interests (Utton and Henning, 1973:26–34).

More than 250 national and regional organizations are dedicated to environmental protection, ranging in size from a few dozen to over a million members, with an aggregate enrollment of better than seven million (DeBell, 1970:333–338). Since many of the people in these groups are well educated, articulate, and politically active, the organizations have become a potent force in the American political system on all levels (Trzyna, 1973; Rosenbaum, 1973:75–80).

There are different shades of commitment to political activism, but all of the organizations direct part of their resources to environmental education. The Scientists' Institute for Public Information has been energetic and persuasive in its campaign to inform and educate public opinion. National organizations like the Conservation Foundation, the National Wildlife Federation, the Izaak Walton League, and the Audubon Society have cooperated with the EPA to establish public information programs on the environment, and have been a valuable source of feedback to government officials (USEPA, 1972:86).

A number of environmental and conservation lobbies have pursued distinctly political goals. Best known is the Sierra Club, a militant organization that sacrificed its tax-exempt status in the early 1960's to enter the political arena. By the late 1960's, its forty-one regional associations counted over 140,000 members, a peak that has now dipped somewhat. The club's point of view is "preservationist," which means that it opposes the violation of wilderness areas for almost any purpose. This purist stance has put the club at odds with more moderate environmental groups that hold a modified version of the multiple-use theory (Trzyna, 1973:302–303).

Still more militant is the Friends of the Earth, a smaller organization of some twenty-five thousand members created by the Sierra Club's former executive secretary, David Brower, after a split over tactics in the latter group. With its focus mainly on the restoration of already polluted areas rather than on the conservation of surviving wilderness, it has fought industrial interests in the courts and in the political sphere (Trzyna, 1973:281–282).

The 1974 elections contain evidence of the new political influence possessed by environmental organizations. In the battle line's front rank were Environmental Action and the League of Conservation Voters. The former published a list of the "dirty dozen" in Congress whose election it opposed, two of whom were defeated in primaries and six of whom went down in the general election; the bad environmental records of the candidates seem to have been a factor in their defeat. The latter group distributed eighty thousand dollars to the campaign chests of environment-oriented Congressmen; of the thirty-eight candidates the league supported or endorsed, thirty were elected (NY Times, 7 November 1974).

Table 6.1 Activities of Environmental Groups in the United States

Type of Activity	Percentage of Groups Participating
Information dissemination	65
Public meetings and discussions	57
Participation in hearings	46
Recycling	23
Legislative research and drafting	19
Lobbying	17
Litigation	7
Protests and demonstrations	2

Source: The Fourth Annual Report of the Council on Environmental Quality, 1973, p. 387.

Other environmental lobbies are more concerned with conservation measures rather than pollution abatement. The Audubon Society, with a current membership of over two hundred thousand, is probably best known. Although usually middle of the road on pollution abatement questions, it has sided occasionally with the more aggressive Sierra Club. The Izaak Walton League, with some fifty-six thousand members, concentrates on the management of wildlife and recreational facilities. Conservationists and sportsmen dominate its membership, a juxtaposition that has helped bridge differences between the two groups on resource management. The National Wildlife Federation is principally geared to the sportsman's concern with wildlife use and conservation. As a federation of state councils representing rod and gun clubs, it has well over two million members on paper, but few of them are active in the organization. Because it wishes to provide hunting and fishing opportunities for its members, as well as promote conservation, it has proved vulnerable to attack by the militant environmental groups (Trzyna, 1973:284–285, 296–297).

Also important are organizations like Planned Parenthood and Zero Population Growth. Small but highly vocal, they have conducted public education programs to warn of uncontrolled population growth and its deleterious effects. They have lobbied for government-sponsored antinatalist programs, including subsidized birth control and unrestricted abortion. While opposed by politically powerful religious sects, these groups have won a nunber of significant court battles on the dissemination of birth-control information and abortion (Trzyna, 1973:299–300, 313).

In addition to the many national and regional organizations, there are about four hundred state and an estimated twenty-five hundred local groups committed to environmental protection. By way of illustration, one finds in Massachusetts alone the Connecticut River Watershed Council, Inc., the Massachusetts Air Pollution and Noise Abatement Committee, and several dozen other state and local organizations. In most states, the non-national and local affiliates of national organizations run the gamut of environmental concerns. No one can survey these groups—including their range of interests and their proliferation in the 1960's—without recognizing the surge of public interest in the environment, a phenomenon the groups themselves generated in part and used to political advantage (Trzyna, 1973:419–424).

The profusion and diversity of organizations working at all levels of government have impeded effective national coordination of programs, ideas, and energies. Some of the more prominent national groups, such as the Sierra Club, do act to coordinate politically relevant activities, especially if their local chapters give them a national power base. It often happens that *ad hoc* coalitions form on specific questions, as was the case with the Citizen's Crusade for Clean Air, a coalition of thirty-eight separate groups, and National Intervenors, a band of sixty groups concerned with nuclear reactor safety and environmental effects of radiation *(NY Times,* 5 February 1973).

Environmental organizations at all levels have achieved considerable sophistication in winning their objectives. In the fifties and sixties, techniques for effective action were hammered out against politically favored, well-entrenched destroyers of the environment. The muscle of the environmental groups is the ground swell of public anxiety about environmental quality. By the 1970's, their cause had become respectable and their methods so refined that the Citizen's Advisory Committee on Environmental Quality published a booklet, *Community Action for Environmental Quality,* which details practical strategies, legal and political, that can be employed by aroused citizens *(CACEQ,* 1974).

By early 1973, more than 130,000 copies had been distributed, and the committee issued another booklet, *Citizens Make the Difference;* this one contained a half-dozen case studies of environmental groups in action, describing how they are started, organized, and financed, and how their battles are fought through publicity, education, lobbying, legal actions, political pressure, and petition and letter-writing campaigns *(CACEQ,* 1973).

The Environmental Defense Fund (EDF) exemplifies the new environmental organization that began small at the local level and grew quickly into an institution of national stature. The EDF was born in 1967 when a small group of scientists and lawyers on Long Island came together to resist the use of DDT for mosquito control. By 1972, the EDF had a national dues-paying membership of thirty-seven thousand, a newsletter, offices in New York, Washington, D.C., and California, a full-time professional staff of seven lawyers, five scientists, and two economists, backed up by advisory committees of volunteers in law and the sciences. Once the EDF is committed to action, it utilizes a variety of tactics, including suits in federal and and state courts, scientific petitions to administrative agencies, participation in legislative committee work, the courting of alliances with other citizen groups, and the airing of its recommendations in public forums. However, its tax-exempt status prevents lobbying. The EDF has been caught up in large and diverse projects during the few years of its existence. These have included the banning of DDT and certain other pesticides, stopping the Cross-Florida Canal, forcing water-management projects to comply with the NEPA requirement for impact statements, challenging the cost-benefit analyses used to justify such projects, opposing the trans-Alaska oil pipeline, and many more (Trzyna, 1973:279: *CACEQ*, 1973:55–61).

Attuned to public consciousness, adept at manipulating the political process, and possessed of numerical strength, environmental organizations in the past decade have begun to fight the mighty business and industrial lobbies. These lobbies are organized primarily along functional lines—the oil lobby, the highway lobby, the auto lobby, the agricultural lobby, and so on—with their individual efforts often coordinated by an interlocking network of trade associations and law firms, which pit combined political leverage of the business community against government actions judged harmful to its interests (Main, 1970). With perhaps eighty percent of the nation's one thousand largest corporations represented by more than five thousand lobbyists in Washington, and countless more in the fifty state capitals and local government centers, considerable pressure can be exerted at every level of government (*NY Times*, 4 February 1974).

Industrial and business groups have distinct advantages in their struggle with environmental lobbies. They are quite knowledgeable about the formal and, even more crucially, informal rules by which the system operates. Many lobbyists are lawyers or experts in technical fields; hence they can often participate, directly or indirectly, in the legislative process by suggesting policies or by providing industry-sponsored commentary on proposed legislation early in the drafting stage. Campaign contributions have become a weapon, with the implied threat of political sanctions should environmental measures discommode a legislator's constituents. Lobbyists may also evoke a blizzard of letters or other purported expressions of public opinion to justify their claims. Moreover, these lobbyists are better equipped with funds than their environmental counterparts, for most of the latter are dependent on voluntary contributions, which are not tax deductible. On the other hand, environmental groups with tax-exempt status are legally forbidden to lobby, whereas business firms can write off as business expenses many costs associated with their lobbying (*NY Times*, 5 May 1974; Green et al., 1972:21–37; Rosenbaum, 1973:80–86).

But environmental groups are not without resources, and the relative openness of policy making in the United States has given them some clear advantages. While the fragmentation of environmental authority has resulted frequently in administrative chaos, it has also created multiple points of access to decision makers. Put simply, the battle for environmental protection is never completely won or lost until a number of smaller skirmishes have been played out at the state or federal legislative, administrative, or judicial levels. When routine channels are unresponsive or dominated by pro-industry groups, alternative strategies are usually possible. Not uncommonly a form of political gamesmanship shifts issues among different branches of government, or from the state to the federal level (or vice versa), to search out the most receptive policy-making forum. While pro-industry groups are equally adept at this gamesmanship, it nonetheless provides great opportunities to bypass hostile policy makers and to neutralize the advantages of industry spokesmen.

Another advantage shared by environmental groups is their ability to politicize issues, so as to build up a ground swell of public pressure capable of diluting the influence of industrial and business lobbies. Many policy decisions on environmental matters occur at the legislative committee or administrative levels, where industrial lobbies have accumulated superior influence through a long history of cultivating and funding legislators and establishing close working relationships with bureaucrats. Environmental lobbies have been impelled, therefore, to develop strategies for shifting decisions to the floor of Congress, where they come to public attention, or to build counterpressures in a legislator's own constituency. It is axiomatic among students of American interest groups that business lobbies are most effective when operating at low levels of public awareness and visibility, which is normally the case when a circle of powerful decision makers is locked into a few legislative committees and regulatory agencies. While the glare of public exposure is no assurance that the balance of power will be shifted, it does, nevertheless, color the rules of the political game more to the advantage of environmental lobbies. One must bear in mind, however, that environmental issues cannot be politicized successfully without a public opinion in favor of stricter policies, a point well illustrated by recent congressional action to limit environmental challenges to the Alaska pipeline; this move would have been difficult if the public were not more concerned about energy shortages than about the ecology of the tundra.

THE ENVIRONMENT AND THE COURTS

In the face of growing demands for environmental protection, federal and state courts have been called upon to clarify frequently vague directives concerning the environment, and to move against offending industries. In suits brought by environmentalists, industry, and federal, state, and local authorities, courts have been forced to judge the precise meaning of recent legislation and to interpret legislative intent where public mandates are in conflict. In the process, courts have become a potent weapon in the hands of private environmental groups and government agencies concerned with pollution.

Some striking court cases at the federal level have involved the NEPA section 102 (2) (C), which requires impact statements from federal agencies when they recommend legislation that might affect the environment significantly. These statements must include a discussion of unavoidable negative effects, alternatives to the proposed action, differentiation between short- and long-term impact, and notice of any irreversible commitment of natural resources. It is also required that draft statements be circulated among agencies at all levels that have expertise or jurisdiction in the relevant area. The statement, with comments of other agencies, must then be made available to the president, the CEQ, and the public (Public Law 91–190).

In 1971–1972, the CEQ laid down careful guidelines for drafting of impact statements and for their circulation. The purpose was to clarify ambiguous language in 102 (2) (C) concerning what constitutes a "major action" or "significant impact" on the environment, and to spell out what federal agencies are obliged to participate in the filing and review of the statements (CEQ, 1973b:416–439). When such guidelines failed to remove all ambiguities, environmental organizations brought suit to force more precise legal definitions, especially concerning access to key documents.* In a typical case, *Natural Resources Defense Council v. Morton*, the District of Columbia Court of Appeals ruled that impact statements must contain a full analysis of the project's consequences and a "rigorous exploration of alternatives." Mere *pro forma* statements would not do. In subsequent cases, filed by environmental groups to compel disclosure of the impact of government projects, the courts have held that complete impact statements must precede action by federal agencies. One result of this interpretation has been delays of large-scale engineering projects as their environmental implications are debated by government and environmental groups. Of greater moment, however, is the fact that conflict over the use of impact statements has affirmed the right of environmental spokesmen to a strong say in federal projects potentially inimical to nature. While Congress has set a dangerous precedent in forbidding further delays in the construction of the Alaska pipeline emanating from court challenges of impact statements, it is likely that such fiats will be politically viable only in extreme cases (CEQ, 1972b:248–255); CEQ, 1973b:236–242).

Another dimension in the environmental role of courts is recent activism among pollution abatement officials in hauling offenders before judicial tribunals. When wedded to severe sanctions that the courts may increasingly apply, this type of activism is tantamount to an unspoken coalition of private and public environmental interests.

---

*The watchfulness of environmental groups has not been able to assure full benefit from impact statements (Kreith, 1973).

In the past few years, private environmental groups also have learned to use the courts. Recent federal and state legislation has allowed for private suits against polluters or inattentive pollution-control offices *(NY Times,* 12 November, 10 December 1974). This provision, first appearing in the 1970 Clean Air Act, is now integral to federal legislation on water pollution, noise pollution, and ocean dumping. It allows citizens to initiate civil suits against persons alleged to be in violation of antipollution laws, and also against the director of the EPA for neglecting to carry out a nondiscretionary enforcement act *(CEQ,* 1973b:395).

Several developments have strengthened the role of the courts. First, environmental groups are now accorded legal standing in pollution suits; until recently their role in court actions was limited unless they were victims of pollution. Second, the courts have permitted extensive class action suits against polluters, although indications were in late 1973 that the Supreme Court would impose tighter restrictions on this device *(NY Times,* 2 February, 8 June 1974). Ultimately the position of courts in the environmental picture is due to sustained pressure and litigation by environmentalists, and the intrinsic power of the bench to apply heavy sanctions.

It is important not to misread the posture of the courts in environmental litigation. Court decisions are based on carefully stated charges, skillfully marshalled evidence, and understanding of the law's ramifications. However just an environmentalist plea may be, it is not likely to go far before the bench if it is poorly organized and argued. Thus, in a recent case, *Ethyl Corporation* v. *Environmental Protection Agency,* decided by the U.S. Court of Appeals for the District of Columbia on January 28, 1975, the court effectively annihilated the EPA's program to eliminate lead from gasoline. The whole story is a melancholy chronicle of EPA blunders, errors, and fumbling inability to present evidence for a perfectly good case against ambient lead poisoning. The judge could hardly be expected to argue the EPA's muddled position in lieu of a better performance·(Reitze and Reitze, 1975:2–3).

A Case Study: Lake Erie

Lake Erie and its plight symbolizes hundreds of waterways in the United States. The lake's once pure water has nearly succumbed to the ravages of thoughtless industry and population centers in the Erie basin. In the political context, the story of Lake Erie epitomizes both the weakness and strength of efforts to protect the environment.

It is the oldest of the American Great Lakes, with three easily identifiable basins. To the west is the smallest and most polluted of the three, averaging twenty-two feet in depth; about sixty percent of the waste dumped into the lake settles there. The central and largest basin, averaging about sixty feet in depth, contains twenty percent of the lake's pollution, and the eastern basin, averaging seventy-five feet in depth, has some ten percent of it. The principal sources of contamination are municipal sewage systems and industrial plants dotting the lake's shores and tributaries (*CEQ,* 1973b:291; Dadisman, 1972).

Signs of trouble first appeared in the 1920's, with a radical decline of two fish species caught in the lake, and then in 1928 a drop in the water's dissolved oxygen content was noted for the first time. Similar evidence that something was awry gradually accumulated in the next two decades, peaking in 1953 with the disappearance of the mayfly population, a primary source of food for many of the lake's fish. Investigations revealed that oxygen-poor water had disrupted the mayfly's reproductive cycle. By this time the scientific community was aware that eutrophication was building up abnormally in Lake Erie, but their warnings were not heeded. Government officials and the public lolled about in ignorance of the situation until 1964, when scientists of the Federal Water Pollution Control Administration (FWPCA) discovered that twenty-six hundred square miles of lake bottom was nearly devoid of oxygen (Commoner, 1971:96–101; Zwick, 1971:188; Graham, 1966:101).

Alarmed by these findings, H. W. Poston, the Chicago regional director of the FWPCA, prepared a speech for the prestigious Cleveland City Club on the deterioration of the lake. The speech appearance was vetoed by James Quigley, assistant secretary of the Department of Health, Education, and Welfare (HEW), which had jurisdiction over the FWPCA, on the ground that it would be politically embarrassing to the secretary of the department, Anthony Celebrezze, a former mayor of Cleveland. This attempt to suppress knowledge of the unpleasant truth failed; a newspaper reporter ferreted out the story, and in March 1965, the *Cleveland Press* ran it under the banner "Critical Pollution is Found in the Lake." A few days later more information came to light at a Cleveland League of Women Voters seminar where two local FWPCA officials spoke. Within a week the *Washington Post* and the *New York Times* focused national attention on the condition of Lake Erie (Zwick, 1971:188–190).

Despite a rising furor over the condition of the lake, FWPCA officials were reluctant to implement even the weak enforcement powers available to them. Under the Federal Water Pollution Control Act of 1956, an "enforcement conference" could be summoned by the secretary of HEW if interstate waters were polluted, or at the request of a state governor if intrastate waters were involved. Public pressure finally moved Governor James Rhodes of Ohio to request an enforcement conference, even though industrial leaders in his state vigorously opposed it (Zwick, 1971:190).

Official participants in this conference included a federal representative, one from each of the state water pollution-control agencies with jurisdiction over the waters in question, and one from any interstate water quality agency that might be involved. Unsworn testimony was to be taken not only from these conferees, but from other interested parties, such as representatives from industry and environmental groups. When all who wished to speak had been heard, the conferees issued advisory recommendations to the secretary of HEW, who might or might not adopt them as cleanup principles. After a minimum of six months had passed, the secretary could convene a new conference to review developments since the last one and to seek fresh recommendations, a procedure that could be repeated indefinitely at his discretion. If the secretary decided that insufficient progress was being made, he could, six months after the conference, convene a hearing board, a formalized version of the conference, where more testimony was heard under oath and alternative recommendations were made to the secretary. The hearing-board stage was used sparingly, and even more rare was the final step in the enforcement process, which entailed the secretary asking the Department of Justice for an injunction against the polluters (CEQ, 1971:12–13).

The 1965 conference requested by Governor Rhodes was only the first of five such meetings. Environmentalists made good use of them to keep the public alerted to the septic state of Lake Erie, and to generate support for public bond issues to finance new sewage plants for the cities on its shores. Despite these pressures, conference deadlines for the implementation of pollution-control measures were pushed back. State and municipal governments, as well as industry, pleaded difficulties in the planning and financing of such projects. Until September 1969, the federal government did little to exact compliance with its recommendations; at that time, six-month notices were handed to the city of Toledo and to the Interlake Steel Corporation of Toledo and three other major steel companies in Cleveland, thus signaling the government's reluctant decision to initiate court action. In the end, threatened court action did not materialize, because all the polluters vowed to speed up their pollution-control schedules. The four steel firms also agreed to permit federal inspection of their efforts to meet standards. Nevertheless, in mid-1970 the Department of the Interior, which had by that time been given jurisdiction over water-pollution control, reported that 78 of the 110 cities polluting Lake Erie were behind their cleanup schedules, as were 44 of the 130 industries originally cited as offenders. This discouraging report provoked the issuance of six-month notices to Cleveland and Detroit, instructing them to move ahead with the new sewage-treatment facilities or face court action (Zwick, 1971:281–283). In June 1971, the above parties and the EPA, which was now in charge of water-pollution control, agreed on a six-year abatement program. Taken together, Toledo, Cleveland, and Detroit contribute about seventy-five percent of the pollutants that flow into Lake Erie from municipal sources: the upgrading of their treatment plants constituted a major step in relieving the lake's burden of pollutants. The federal government contributed significantly to municipal delays in treatment plant construction by failing to pay communities the matching funds owed to them for such construction *(CEQ,* 1971:13; *NY Times,* 9 April 1974).

Scientists have agreed since 1965 that a major cause of eutrophication in Lake Erie is the heavy flow of nitrates and phosphates from municipal sewage systems, a problem that can be dealt with by improved sewage treatment. However, since the construction of new sewage-treatment plants was costly and time consuming, environmentalists in the mid-sixties urged the federal government to force the detergent industry to eliminate phosphates from their products. In line with this suggestion, the Johnson administration extracted an agreement from detergent industry representatives to try to find a substitute for phosphates. In 1967 a Joint Industry-Government Task Force on Eutrophication, composed of four representatives from the Department of the Interior and nine from the detergent industry, was formed to investigate the problem. It was chaired by a man from the Soap and Detergent Association, a lobby for the industry. The very makeup of the task force virtually guaranteed its effectiveness; it focused on the idea that phosphates should be removed not from detergents, but rather from effluent going into the lake, by means of better sewage treatment. Under the Nixon administration, the detergent industry's position on phosphates was strengthened even further by the creation of NIPCC, the Detergent Sub-Council of which was chaired by the president of Proctor and Gamble, the industry's largest heavy detergent producer, whose products contained the most phosphates (Zwick, 1971:73–75). Close liaison with the administration was also provided by Bryce Harlow, a presidential aide who had been a former lobbyist for Proctor and Gamble (Rathlesberger, 1972:47–48). Senator Edmund Muskie has charged that the Nixon administration's lumbering pace in getting phosphates out of detergents is linked to a sixty-four thousand dollar contribution to Republican campaign coffers, in 1968 and 1970, by executives of seven detergent companies.

Even though the detergent industry appeared to be firmly in the drivers seat on the phosphate issue, it began to introduce a new chemical compound known as NTA (nitrilotriacetic acid) as a substitute for phosphates in some of its products, as a hedge against the remote possibility that phosphates might be banned. In mid-1970, government scientists began to investigate NTA for biodegradability and health hazards. Industry researchers had already said it scored well on these points. Scientists at the National Institute of Environmental Health Sciences came to an altogether different conclusion, and in December 1970 William Ruckelshaus of the EPA and Surgeon General Jesse Steinfeld jointly ordered the suspension of NTA, pending further tests (Zwick, 1971:87–90). As of the end of 1974, the Ford administration has refused to ban phosphates from detergents, even though a number of states and cities have made it illegal to sell detergents with a high phosphate content. In contrast, the Canadian government has effectively barred their use.

Pressure from environmental organizations and the press has been important in advancing the cleanup of Lake Erie. In addition to technical and fiscal obstacles encountered by municipalities and industries, the top federal water-quality administrators have failed to push the campaign unless pressured by environmentalists. Part of their failure can be laid to administrative confusion, a move of the FWPCA from HEW to the Department of the Interior, and later, in December 1970, into the newly created EPA, where it became known as the Water Quality Office. The confusion was compounded by changes in personnel which required time for the new administrators to become familiar with their jobs. Even more serious, perhaps, is that men appointed to head water quality programs generally have been political appointees lacking both administrative experience and knowledge of the programs (Zwick, 1971:54–66).

Solution of Lake Erie's pollution problem is complicated by its location between the United States and Canada. The federal structure of both nations has created further difficulties because authority was divided between the central and regional governments. Two other elements exacerbate the situation. The current sensitivity of Canadian political leaders to the question of what is commonly referred to as American "economic imperialism" has also made them sensitive to the environmental encroachments of American industry. The industrial heartlands of both nations are heavily dependent on waters of the Great Lakes, including Lake Erie. This means pollution abatement programs that cause extensive dislocations will cut deeply into the economic well-being of each nation.

Despite these problems, both nations have made efforts to meet the common environmental threat. Discovery of mercury in the waters of Lake Erie led to a September 1970 conference of the premiers of the three Canadian provinces and the governors of the eight American states located adjacent to the Great Lakes. The conference urged direct informal contacts about their mutual problems, including pollution of the lakes, without going through Toronto and Washington. They also anticipated that the International Joint Commission on Waterways would act as a clearing house for the exchange of information and research on problems of common interest (CEQ, 1973b:292; Dadisman, 1972).

Unfortunately, this movement by provincial and state governments toward better cooperation on pollution abatement in the Great Lakes has been undercut by recent actions of the American EPA. In 1971, after hearings on the problem of sewage dumping into the Great Lakes, the EPA decided that American ships sailing these waters will still be allowed to dump sewage overboard until onboard holding tanks can be installed and onshore treatment facilities are built. This decision stands at odds with the laws of most of the states on the Great Lakes and the province of Ontario, which already require pleasure craft to have holding tanks, and to dispose of sewage in onshore facilities.

A recent and more hopeful turn of events is the signing in 1972 of a joint American–Canadian agreement to clean up the Great Lakes. This agreement was preceded by a six-year study conducted at the request of the American and Canadian governments. The study's results were reviewed by a special group of representatives from American and Canadian federal, state, and provincial governments, who drafted what is formally known as the Great Lakes Water Quality Agreement of 1972.

The 1972 agreement establishes general and specific water quality objectives for the Great Lakes. The general ones call for elimination of toxic substances, reduction of nutrients that speed eutrophication, an end to oil spills and debris, an end to odors, coloration, and other nuisances, and removal of objectionable sludge deposits. The specific ones include the establishment of maximum ambient levels for specific pollutants and an absolute limit to the amount of phosphorous deposited. Under the agreement, both American and Canadian water quality standards and regulations must conform to these objectives. The International Joint Commission is assigned monitoring responsibilities. By the end of 1975, the major programs under the agreement are to be completed, or in the process of completion. By 1973, about four hundred million dollars in federal, state, and local funds had been appropriated for the construction of waste treatment plants to meet objectives of the agreement, but the spending of funds has been slowed by administrative red tape (CEQ, 1972b:83; NY Times, 9 April, 23 May 1974)

In long-term perspective, the consensus appears to be that Lake Erie can be salvaged if pollution abatement programs are effectively implemented within the next few years. It is less a question of whether existing technology can handle the problem than of whether political will exists in both the United States and Canada to make sacrifices necessary to save the lake. On this point, the record is mixed. Limited action has been taken at both the national and international levels, but further improvements in the lake's waters will depend on perseverance of environmentalists and their political allies on behalf of further legislation and strict enforcement of emission standards.

THE SOVIET UNION

POLITICAL ISSUES AND NATIONAL PRIORITIES

The concentration of power into the hands of a small elite historically committed to rapid economic growth has shaped a pattern of national priorities inhospitable to an ecological frame of reference. The high priority given heavy and military-related industry has limited recognition of the nation's growing environmental woes and severely retarded the diversion of scarce capital into pollution-control and cleanup projects. Moreover, the political imperative of retaining wide-ranging decision-making powers in the hands of top Communist Party officials has limited the power of environmental lobbies, which have played an important role in boosting environmental awareness in less centralized political systems.

This is not to say, however, that political conflict over environment-related issues in infrequent. Quite the opposite is the case, since the presence of central economic planning lodges important environmental decisions within a highly politicized and competitive bureaucratic structure (Kelley, 1974; Ploss, 1965:283–287; Skilling and Griffiths, 1971; Schwartz and Keech, 1968). Most environmental disputes involve, therefore, conflicts among different state agencies, as in the case of Lake Baikal, which pitted the Ministry of Timber, Paper, and Woodworking against several state environmental protection agencies, as well as a growing collection of conservationists, scientists, and other intellectuals. Unfortunately for the environment, this has usually meant that more powerful ministries associated with heavy industry have been able to overshadow less influential state agencies concerned with environmental protection. Thus bureaucratic conflicts over environmental quality are more frequently settled with reference to the political weight—and party connections—of the contending organizations rather than the objective merits of the case.

A critical political issue that will determine the fate of the environment is the question of the pace and nature of future economic growth. The issue may be divided into two interrelated parts: whether continued economic expansion will be pursued as the dominant national goal, and whether the economy will continue to emphasize heavy industry or shift greater attention to the production of consumer goods. Concerning the desirability of continued growth, few Soviet citizens would question the need for economic expansion, both to increase long-denied domestic consumption and to defend their homeland from potential enemies from whatever quarter. The official line is unambiguous and strident in tone: the economy must grow as rapidly as possible to facilitate the building of a strong communist system (Fyodorov, 1972; *VF*, April 1973:42–56). Contemporary leaders have been both frightened and embarrassed by the recent drop in the rate of growth and have taken far-reaching measures, including the importing of

Western and Japanese capital and technology, to get the economy moving again. Only a few economists and scientists have questioned the desirability of further growth from the environmental or resource-conservation point of view (Gerasimov, 1971:213; Oldak, 1970:11; *VF,* January 1973:48–60; February 1973:36–52; March 1973:52–73; April 1973:57–79).

The second issue is whether the economy will give priority to the development of heavy industry or consumer goods production. Continued high priority for heavy industry will inevitably step up the load of effluents poured into the environment. But the mere reordering of national priorities to accelerate the production of consumer goods—undoubtedly the preference of the man in the street, who has been promised a better material standard of living for years—would do little in itself to end environmental deterioration. Soviet consumer materialism, like its capitalist counterpart, could easily result in the creation of new high-pollution industries and an unending stream of disposable consumer goods destined for the junkpile. Any environmentally meaningful change would depend on a substantial reordering of personal priorities and a redefinition of the quality of life in ecological as well as materialistic terms. It is understandable that the average Russian thinks of well-being in the latter frame of reference. Long a victim of cramped housing, deprived of or made to wait on long lists for consumer goods, he is hesitant to accept further delays in the name of environmental quality.

A final, and perhaps more important, political issue involves the relative power of various government agencies and the jealously guarded policy-making prerogatives of top Communist Party leaders. Any reordering of priorities in favor of the environment would also involve restructuring the ministerial pecking order at the expense of long-powerful production ministries. Such changes would be opposed bitterly, not only by the bureaucrats themselves but also by higher party leaders who have formed political alliances with these ministerial power centers. In short, there is no politically viable pro-environmental constituency to draw the attention of competing Soviet leaders anxious to add politically powerful allies to their followings. Top party leaders at the Politburo level, and in the central party apparatus, would also be compelled to surrender some of their carefully guarded policy-making powers on environmental questions to scientists, conservationists, and environmentalists; at the very least, they would have to consult more widely on policy questions within these circles, thereby vesting *de facto* decision-making powers in the hands of technicians.

GOVERNMENT AGENCIES

Administrative responsibility for the implementation of environmental policy has been fragmented among a dozen or so separate ministries, agencies, and state committees. In practice, much responsibility for protection of the environment and natural resources has been vested in those agencies charged with their use and exploitation (Goldman, 1972b:192). Adding to the confusion is the federal nature of the Soviet system. While political power is centralized into the hands of the Communist Party, legal and administrative responsibility is divided between parallel national and union-republic ministries (Pryde, 1972:9–24). Since questions of pollution abatement and resource conservation are reserved to the union republics, national legislation has tended merely to suggest broad guidelines, leaving it to subsequent union-republic legislation to fill in details. Although guidelines are usually observed faithfully, the existence of overlapping and parallel agencies at both levels generates confusion. Special enactments of the USSR Council of Ministers and the Communist Party Central Committee on pressing environmental questions are sometimes offered to cut through the bureaucratic maze, but their successful implementation depends on the compliance of lesser administrative agencies.

A look at agencies involved in water-pollution control shows a common pattern of overlapping administrative bodies. Primary responsibility for water resources is vested in the USSR Ministry of Land Reclamation and Water Resources and its union-republic counterparts. However, the Ministries of Power and Electrification, Fisheries, Agriculture, Inland Water Transport, and Public Health also play a vital role. General questions of pollution control are the responsibility of the USSR Ministry of Public Health and its union-republic counterparts. The national ministry sets emission standards and deals with pollution in bodies of water touching more than one republic, while the republic ministries deal with local pollution. In addition, both national and union-republic economic planning agencies concern themselves with the development and protection of water resources, and special regional water-basin commissions have been created to oversee important waterways.

In practice, the formulation of pollution-control standards simultaneously —and usually chaotically—involves a wide range of agencies. Under current water-resource legislation, the emission of harmful pollutants must be licensed by state authorities, a process usually involving the local soviet (city council), the Sanitary Epidemiological Service, and a long list of water users. Effective coordination is usually the exception rather than the rule (Pryde, 1972:107–12; Fox, 1971:9,207–216; Bush, 1972:28).

The Ministry of Public Health sets air-pollution standards and polices their implementation through sanitary inspectors. Established in the late 1940's, these standards mandate maximum permissible concentrations of harmful substances that may be emitted over established time periods (*HEW*, 1970:162–163). The sanitary inspectors of the Sanitary Epidemiological Service are legally empowered to fine offending factories or municipalities and, in extreme cases, to order production stopped or the relocation or closing of polluting enterprises. In fact, these powers are circumscribed by bureaucratic and political realities. When pitted against powerful ministries working in close coordination with local officials intent on regional economic development, the sanitary inspector finds himself outmaneuvered and out-lobbied (LaMothe, 1971:25; Powell, 1971:629). Moreover, there are serious problems in terms of the heavy work load and in keeping sufficient numbers of trained personnel in the service. These inspectors are expected not only to police existing pollution-control standards but also to supervise the siting and construction of new factories and to deal with a wide range of other environmental issues (Kramer, 1972:11).

The Chief Administration of the Hydrometeorological Service of the USSR Council of Ministers also deserves attention. In January 1973 it was mandated to set overarching standards for monitoring air, water and soil pollution *(Pravda,* 10 January 1973). The exact powers awarded the agency remain vague, for the enactment creating its new role also instructed other existing agencies to strengthen their own pollution-control programs. Probably the service will focus on monitoring emission levels and on the explication of national policy guidelines, a function consistent with its previous research role. Its former director, Yevgeni Fyodorov, a middle-of-the-road environmentalist who stressed the compatibility of economic growth and pollution abatement, has become an increasingly prominent official spokesman on environmental questions.

The weakness of pollution-control agencies is a direct consequence of their low standing in the ministerial hierarchy and of their limited political influence. The Sanitary Epidemiological Service, the primary enforcement agency, is subordinated to the USSR Ministry of Public Health, itself a relatively unimportant agency in comparison with the ministries for heavy industry, machine construction, building, agriculture, and so on. Given the direct links between top Communist Party leaders and the production-oriented ministries and the emphasis placed on continued economic growth, environmental considerations are, with rare exceptions, given secondary priority. With neither effective legal controls nor political influence at their disposal, control agencies are limited to marginal harassment of polluters and must depend on the fleeting cooperation of higher authorities for more effective measures.

Recent attempts have also been made to strengthen the hand of the local soviets in the enforcement of antipollution measures. A 1971 decree granted these bodies wide-ranging powers to supplement the work of other state control agencies *(Izvestiia,* 20 March 1971). However, aggressive local action has been the exception rather than the rule. Since local officials frequently work closely with industry spokesmen—recent economic reforms even award a part of a factory's profits to local government, and fines levied against polluters used to end up in local coffers—there is little incentive to enforce controls if they interfere with the mutually profitable operation of the enterprise unless local environmentalists are able to mobilize public support (LaMothe, 1971:12; *LG*, 13 February 1974).

POLICY MAKING AND PRESSURE GROUPS

Policymaking in the Soviet Union takes place within the highest organs of the Communist Party, with virtually all important decisions being reached in the Politburo. In practice, policy decisions usually emerge as the product of informal bargaining between high-level Politburo figures and the party or bureaucratic interests with which they are linked (Kelley, 1974). Unfortunately, the spokesmen of environmentally oriented state agencies and semiofficial public conservation groups are usually closed out of high-level negotiations because of the long-standing dominance of party officials and industrial interests. Adding to the lack of influence wielded by environmentalists is the fact that many relevant policy decisions are made at the administrative level within government agencies charged simultaneously with the exploitation and use of natural resources. Until recently, most Soviet policy statements on environmental protection have simply outlined vague national goals and instructed the appropriate state agencies to take steps for their implementation. In such a setting, it is not difficult to understand how agencies whose primary responsibility is the exploitation of nature might well overlook vaguely worded environmental mandates.

While an attempt has recently been made to coordinate policy making on environmental questions through the creation of a legislative committee on environmental protection and resource conservation in the Supreme Soviet, it seems evident that the committee's role will be limited. In reporting on the activities of the committee in preparation for the December 1974 session of the Supreme Soviet, Yevgeni Fyodorov, the chairman, noted that his body had the authority to examine the draft economic plan for the coming year and make recommendations concerning pollution abatement and resource utilization. The tone of the report left little doubt, however, that the various government ministries, industrial interests, and resource users which testified before the committee had come primarily to inform that body of decisions reached elsewhere rather than to work out a coordinated environmental program. Further evidence of the low standing of the committee comes from the identity of its chairman, a middle-level technician who once headed the Hydrometeorological Service; in contrast, the important legislative committees are frequently headed by more prestigious members of the top party elite, sometimes including members of the Politburo (*Izvestiia*, 5 December 1974).

Most of the advantages enjoyed by the major industrial lobbies are closely linked both to their status as powerful bureaucratic organizations and to the close, symbiotic relationship between these state agencies and the Communist Party apparatus. In the former case, it is virtually axiomatic that organization is one of the prerequisites of power, especially when policy is made within a highly politicized bureaucratic setting. Organization means manpower, expertise, large and continuing budgets, legitimacy in a society concerned with official status, and the right to be consulted on a regular basis on matters of policy that touch upon the organization. The possession and skillful use of knowledge and expertise are also critically important, especially on questions of environmental policy making, where some of the most important battles are waged on the uncertain and shifting ground of determining the real environmental dangers of economic activities and estimating the technical feasibility and socioeconomic trade-off costs of pollution abatement measures. The use—and frequently the misuse—of "expert" testimony and research has become one of the major weapons in defending the prerogatives of industrial interests and discrediting the views of the opposition.

Industrial interests also benefit from their close working relationship with party *apparatchiki*—that is, full-time party employees working within the all-powerful staff agencies of the Communist Party's own bureaucracy. Both share roughly not only the same views concerning the priority of economic growth but also a mutual sense of organizational identity and purpose. Organizationally the political and industrial hierarchies merge at the top level through the extensive representation of party *apparatchiki* and the representatives of industrial interests on top party bodies. The Central Committee has become a cross section of the Soviet "establishment" in recent decades as industrial and other economic interests have become important elements along with the dominant apparatus group. And while the top-ranking apparatus assignments and the Politburo continue to be dominated by what Fleron has termed "professional politicians," that is, individuals with wide-ranging career experiences as political executives in the provinces, the emergence of these "generalists" is misleading, especially from the environmental point of view (Fleron, 1969:176–201; 1968:228–244). Although they have had little direct affiliation with industrial and commercial enterprises, most of these people have moved up the hierarchy either through assignments to regional administrative posts within the party machinery (*oblast* [province] first secretaryships are the most common route to advancement) or through assignment to party apparatus posts that control and regulate industry. In either case, the individual is unlikely to assimilate a frame of reference stressing environmental protection. In the former instance, regional party secretaries intent on advancement have had little incentive to favor environmental safeguards that may limit the productive capability of regions to which they are assigned. The case is much the same with industry-related party apparatus personnel, who are concerned with the productivity of the agencies for which they are responsible, and who would, in most cases, defend them against external attack (Hough, 1969:178–214; Azrael, 1966:152–182).

Further down the chain of command effective coordination is provided at the day-to-day policy-making and administrative levels through a parallel hierarchy of state and party agencies. In its simplest form, every state ministry or agency has a counterpart body somewhere within the party apparatus. Thus various government ministries concerned with heavy industry are paralleled by functionally specialized sections of the central party apparatus' Department of Heavy Industry, while the Ministry of the Chemical Industry and the Ministry of the Fuel Industry find their counterparts in the apparatus' Department of the Chemical Industry and Department of the Fuel Industry. Similar parallel agencies exist for virtually all aspects of economic and social activity for which there is a state ministry, agency, or committee on the books. The system extends downward in increasingly simplified form to the union republic, *oblast,* and local levels as well (Avtorkhanov, 1966:192–227,263–289).

From the environmental point of view, the existence of these parallel structures is important for two reasons. Although the primary functions of the party apparatus lie in supervising personnel assignments and overseeing the performance of the counterpart state agency, the relationship does have environmental overtones to the extent that the two are joined in a common purpose—the fulfillment of a shared production goal. Subtle interdependencies develop linking the two agencies, since the performance of each is determined at least in part by the achievements of the other. Party apparatus personnel quickly learn that they are evaluated in large measure by the performance of the state agency, and the government ministries find that their apparatus-related counterparts are useful in obtaining the ear of higher authorities and in cutting through red tape. This is not to suggest that conflict does not occur between the two; given the uncertain and overlapping lines of authority and the tendency of strong-willed party and state bureaucrats to defend their individual and agency prerogatives, conflict is frequent. The point is, however, that this conflict is internal to the party-state industrial complex itself, that is, among party and state bureaucrats sharing roughly the same mission and overall priorities. This symbiotic "fit" between party and state bodies provides a natural mutual-defense mechanism whenever the common interests of both are challenged. Such mutually advantageous defensive arrangements have long been known to exist at the local and regional levels. Termed "family circles" by Soviet authorities, they can also be shown to be operative in building opposition to the passage and subsequent implementation of environmental protection measures (Pravda, 6 July 1974). Simply stated, the "families" protect their members against pressures generated by environmentalists, with the balance of forces usually in favor of local industrial and commercial interests that operate to the benefit of local party and state leaders.

Second, the existence of this dual administrative structure provides yet another institutionalized point of access through which industrial interests can press their case against environmentalists. In a setting where channels of communication and access to top policy makers are severely limited, these institutionalized contracts prove valuable. The personal mobility of individual managers and specialists between the government ministries and the parallel party apparatus posts is also not infrequent, thus adding to the likelihood that personal cliques and contacts will persist and cut across formal bureaucratic lines of authority both horizontally across agency distinctions at the same level and vertically up and down the chain of command. Given the tendency to expedite decisions through such informal contacts —in other words, to avoid the confusion and delay built into this system of parallel hierarchies—these contacts play an important role in coordinating opposition to external opponents and in providing access to higher-level political and administrative authorities.

Note must also be taken of another advantage which industrial and commercial interests enjoy through their access to the media. In a setting where communications media are controlled by central authorities, the ability to make one's case to the public or to communicate effectively with and mobilize one's own constituency may prove a key asset. This is not to suggest, of course, that matters of environmental policy are decided through the media, but rather that the process of defining and politicizing a given issue (especially a new issue such as the environment) or of mobilizing supporters and other potentially helpful elite groups can be critical in shaping the outcome of the clash. In this regard, industrial and commercial interests usually have the advantage of sponsoring and/or controlling trade publications which can be used to mobilize virtually all segments of an industry to a common challenge.

In contrast, the influence of environmental lobbies is limited in the Soviet context by their organizational weakness, a lack of real social or political autonomy, and the countervailing power of proindustry groups. Largest of the environmental bodies is the All-Russian Society for the Conservation of Nature, which has nineteen million members in the Russian Republic and six million in the Ukraine, with lesser numbers in other union republics.

Most, however, are school children in the society's youth division. Although the society is permitted by law to participate in the drafting of economic plans with environmental impact, there is no evidence that it has been meaningfully consulted. While it has little political leverage at the national level, the organization has been more effective at the local level in educational work, in conducting unofficial inspection programs, and in reporting violations to appropriate state agencies. Other voluntary inspection groups also have a role in policing the environment, especially in the area of wildlife conservation, although they have no legal power to impose sanctions. Officials of the Ukrainian State Committee on Nature Conservation estimate that there are thirty thousand such voluntary inspectors in the Ukraine alone, and similar groups are active in other regions. In the eyes of more aggressive environmentalists, the effectiveness of these organizations is limited by their own self-imposed timidity in the face of opposing industrial lobbies (Goldman, 1972b:185–205; Kramer, 1973a:38–75; Clawson and Kolarik, 1974:31–33).

More effective are the *ad hoc* lobbies which form concerning concrete pollution problems. Most evident in recent years has been the wide-ranging coalition of naturalists, conservation officials, scientists, writers, and other intellectuals who have come to the defense of Lake Baikal. Having no formal organization through which to press their arguments, they have relied on existing scientific commissions, state-related conservation groups, and the personal prestige of their spokesmen to drive home their argument in the media. Similar *ad hoc* coalitions have sprung up on a number of other issues.

From his study of environment-related articles in both national and local newspapers, John Kramer (1973a:24–28) paints a revealing portrait of such an *ad hoc* coalition. Heading the list of those who demand stronger environmental protection are scientists and academicians, who were nearly twice as active as the next group. In second and third place are the deputies of various local soviets and the Supreme Soviet and members of state environmental protection agencies. In the former case, these were merely deputies and not top-level political or administrative personnel; given their relative powerlessness, it is unlikely that they would exercise great influence at either the local or the national level, although they might serve as a sounding board for local complaints. In the case of environmental protection agencies, it seems likely that many articles were designed to create pressure against uncooperative government officials and enterprise managers by citing continued violations. Theoretical economists—but not ministry or factory personnel—rank fourth on the list of environmental activists. Conspicuous by their almost total absence are the representatives of industrial and commercial ministries, and factory directors; only a few who were involved with low-pollution activities called publicly for better protection of the environment. Also conspicuously inarticulate were the wide range of Communist Party officials in both territorial administrative and apparatus posts at all levels of the party hierarchy. The handful that confronted the issue spoke only in vague generalities.

Regional commissions formed to deal with pollution in limited geographic areas and scientific commissions also occasionally act as environmental lobbies. Numerous water-basin commissions, such as that recently formed for the protection of Lake Baikal or the Desna River, are concerned with environmental quality and often press for stricter emission controls (LG, 4 December 1974; Pravda, 20 November 1974; LaMothe, 1971; LG, 13 February 1974). A number of scientific commissions, such as the Central Board of Nature Conservation of the Ministry of Agriculture, and the Academy of Sciences' Commission for the Study of Productive Forces and Natural Resources also handle environmental matters. Recently the Academy of Sciences and the State Committee on Science and Technology have been ordered to pool their resources in a new body to oversee research into environmental problems (Pryde, 1972:20; Pravda, 10 January 1973; Clawson and Kolarik, 1974:36–44). Evidence also exists that environmentalists and specialists are now more widely consulted in the policy-drafting stages concerning the environmental impact of proposed policies, although no formal procedures exist, as in the United States. A number of hydrologists and other scientists were influential in drafting the new Soviet water law, although one key recommendation that scarcity prices be charged from industrial water use was ignored in the final legislation (Kramer, 1972:4).

Special note must also be taken of the media in pressing for sterner pollution-control measures. Environmentalists frustrated in their attempts to urge stronger measures on ministry officials frequently turn to the media to dramatize issues in the hope that a public outcry will convince top party officials that steps must be taken. While state censorship obviously limits their independence, certain newspapers and journals have become identified with environmental issues. Most notable are Literaturnaia Gazeta and Komsomolskaia Pravda, in which the campaign to save Lake Baikal was first launched. More specialized geographic and biological journals have also opened their pages to environmental spokesmen, especially the popular journal Priroda (Nature). The mass distribution media have also begun to play a more important role in increasing environmental awareness and focusing attention of pollution offenders. The major dailies Pravda and Izvestiia carry stories each week on pollution abatement programs or continued violations. A tradition of moderately aggressive investigative reporting has developed on environmental questions, especially in response to readers' letters. Such actions frequently pressure local enforcement officials to take corrective action *(Pravda,* 6 July 1974: *Izvestiia,* 12 June 1974; *KP,* 25 January, 10 April, 25 June 1974: *NY Times,* 29 November 1974). This is not to suggest, of course, that the balance has shifted in favor of environmental forces, but rather that significant avenues for counterpressure have opened via the media in recent years.

THE ENVIRONMENT AND THE COURTS

In the Soviet case, the courts have proven largely ineffective in punishing pollution offenders because of both their own institutional timidity and the lax legal sanctions they may apply. Soviet courts have never developed an independent watchdog role over the activities of other government agencies; in the early years of Soviet power, they were purposely cast in the role of the handmaiden of state policy, and although the post-Stalin era has brought some procedural controls against arbitrary and capricious court action, they have remained instruments of government policy. Judges are appointed only with the approval of the Communist Party, as are prosecution officials at all levels.

Another reason for ineffective courts is the weakness of legal sanctions at their disposal. Until recently, many union republics did not consider pollution violations criminal offenses. Even today, most of the sanctions levied against polluters come from administrative rather than court action. State sanitary inspectors can fine an individual fifty rubles and an enterprise five hundred rubles, and a chief sanitary physician can impose lesser fines. The recently strengthened Russian Republic criminal code provides for a year's imprisonment or a three-hundred-ruble fine for pollution offenses, and up to five years' imprisonment for "substantial harm" to human health or agricultural production, or the disruption of wildlife. Despite these provisions, actual enforcement is lax. On the financial side, fines are usually paid out of the factory budget. Only recently, and on rare occasions, have factory officials been compelled to pay fines out of their own pockets or been subjected to liens against their salaries. Criminal sanctions are seldom imposed, although there are instances cited in the press in recent years of jail terms or periods of "corrective labor without deprivation of freedom" imposed in case of exceptional violations. It is likely, however, that these measures have been taken primarily to warn obdurate factory officials and do not signal a wave of widespread convictions (Pryde, 1972:137–53: Goldman, 1972b:30–33; LaMothe, 1971:7,25: Powell, 1971:629: *SR,* 15 February 1970; *SZ,* 18 January 1970; *Izvestiia,* 10 April 1975:6).

The impact of the courts is also restricted by the fact that individual victims of pollution cannot initiate court action against offenders. Their sole recourse is to file a complaint with the appropriate pollution-control agency and to rely upon its protective vigor and political strength to force curtailment of emissions. There have been no landmark cases in which courts have ordered compensatory payment to pollution victims, nor have municipalities or economic enterprises sought relief from the courts for economic losses suffered at the hands of polluters.

A Case Study: Lake Baikal

The political debate over the pollution of Lake Baikal, which began in the early 1960's as industry neared the shores of its exceptionally pure waters, has lined up environmentalists against industrialists in a battle that illustrates the pitfalls of Soviet environmental policy making. Two major protagonists have taken the stage. The Ministry of Timber, Paper, and Woodworking, whose cellulose mills represent a major threat to the lake, has lobbied for years for industrial development of the lakeshore and against stricter emission controls. In defense of the lake, a diverse coalition of local conservationists, scientists, and writers has emerged to work hand in hand with the Ministry of Land Reclamation and Water Resources, the Hydrometeorological Service, and the Ministry of Health, which are formally charged with defense of the lake against pollution (Kramer, 1973a:162-180; Goldman, 1972b:177-210).

Lake Baikal is a unique body of water by any standards. Fed by over three hundred tributaries and drained only by the Angara River, it contains some of the world's purest water and gives life support to over seven hundred kinds of animals and plants found only in its waters or on its shores. Long a subject of reverence by local residents and conservationists throughout the world, Lake Baikal first experienced the disruptive presence of man in the 1950's, when industrial development along tributaries and logging operations on steeply sloped shores began to upset its delicate ecological balance. Along the Selenga River, which supplies over half of the lake's water, about fifty factories and mills have been established since the revolution, and the city of Ulan-Ude, the capital of the Buriat Republic, dumped untreated municipal wastes into the river. Logging operations have taken their toll, since many logs rafted down tributaries or across the lake sank, thus releasing toxic chemicals as they decomposed and smothering fish-spawning and -feeding areas. The widespread stripping of the lake's steeply sloped shores has also altered runoff patterns and permitted the leaching of minerals into the lake's waters (Goldman, 1972b:179-182).

Urged by the Ministry of Timber, Paper, and Woodworking, Soviet planners decided in 1957 to permit construction of two cellulose mills in the Baikal basin, one at the southern tip of the lake at Baikalsk, the other on the Selenga River. The Ministry justified construction of these mills on the ground that pure water was necessary for the production of superpure cellulose cord needed for national defense. Construction plans were publicly announced in 1958, but it was not until July 1960 that the first conservationist outcry came from a local writer, who cautioned in a poorly circulated essay published in Ulan-Ude that the mills would have serious environmental consequences (Buiantuev, 1960). A year later the question was again raised by two local writers, but to little avail (Serova and Sarkisian, 1961). The first warning to catch the public eye came in 1962 from Gregory Galazii, director of the Limnological Institute of the Siberian branch of the Academy of Sciences. Writing in the popular youth-oriented newspaper *Komsomolskaia Pravda*, he cautioned that discharge from the mills would not only disrupt the lake's ecological balance, but also endanger the water supply of Irkutsk *(KP*, 12 December 1961). The usually conservative economic paper *Ekonomicheskaia Gazeta* offered a mild critique of the industrial development of the Baikal basin a month after Galazii's attack, but further debate was suppressed. Construction continued at the mill site, however, and the debate was reopened by Oleg Volkov a few years later in a stinging attack in *Literaturnaia Gazeta*, which was to emerge as a major advocate of the lake's protection. In the next few years, a public debate raged on the pages of *Literaturnaia Gazeta* and other journals which pitted the representatives of the Ministry of Timber, Paper, and Woodworking and their expert witnesses against representatives of pollution-control agencies and a growing band of scientists and influential writers (*LG*, 6 February 1965; 18 March 1965; 10, 13, 15 April 1965; 29 January 1966; 2 June 1966). The public outcry reached a high point in May 1966 in an outspoken letter in *Komsomolskaia Pravda* signed by over thirty distinguished scientists, writers, and creative artists, including several members of the prestigious Academy of Sciences (*KP*, 11 May 1966).

While public discussion over the fate of Lake Baikal raged on, a second battle was under way between conflicting state agencies, first over the initial certification of the Baikalsk plant and then over the setting of proper emission standards. The first confrontation brought the Ministry of Timber, Paper, and Woodworking up against the Ministry of Land Reclamation and Water Resources. When the latter's chief sanitary inspector refused to certify the mill as ready for operations until purification facilities were completed, the Ministry of Timber, Paper, and Woodworking simply found another sanitary inspector who was willing to sign the document. Permission to began production was quickly withdrawn when the Ministry of Land Reclamation and Water Resources complained to higher authorities, and the entire issue was handed over to the State Acceptance Commission, which had to give final approval before the mill could open. Through its representative on the commission, the Ministry of Land Reclamation and Water Resources continued to voice its opposition, and twice that body refused to permit production to begin at the Baikalsk plant. The deadlock was broken when the Ministry of Timber, Paper, and Woodworking unilaterally and illegally changed the composition of the commission to obtain a favorable decision (*KP*, 11 August 1970).

Having obtained certification from the State Acceptance Commission, Baikalsk plant officials found themselves involved in another dispute concerning emission standards governing the mill's operation. It quickly became apparent that the mill's original purification facilities could not meet established norms. In clear violation of an earlier 1960 enactment on the preservation of the lake, plant officials began operations before the purification facilities were completed and the staff trained. Breakdowns were frequent, and basic flaws in the equipment's design were soon discovered (for example, bacterial filters were used in waters too cold for the bacteria to survive) (*LG*, 29 January 1966). As pressures grew to speed the construction of new purification facilities or to force the plant to cease operations, Baikalsk factory officials responded with a request that emission standards be lowered "temporarily" until new facilities could be completed. The Ministry of Health approved the revised norms, noting that the mill's discharges would be fit for human consumption, but failing to observe that even this level of relative purity would severely endanger some of the lake's more delicate species. From its perspective, the Ministry of Fishing also sanctioned the new norms, for it was thought they would have little impact on already depleted fish harvests. The Hydrometeorological Service raised strenuous objections to lowering emission standards, and the Ministry of Land Reclamation and Water Resources, which had led the earlier battle against certification, was not even consulted, a clear violation of law. Outmaneuvered, out-lobbied, or simply ignored, the state agencies concerned with environmental protection found themselves helpless to reverse this unfavorable decision, and the "temporary" standards remain in effect to this day (*KP*, 11 August 1970; *LG*, 5 April 1970, 4 December 1974).

The advocates of the Baikalsk and Selenga mills demonstrated practical political skills by promoting these ecologically questionable projects as essential to the economy and national defense. With the aggressiveness and self-assurance of a land development promoter, spokesmen of the Ministry of Timber, Paper, and Woodworking turned aside proposals to expand existing cellulose mills in other locations with the argument that only the lake's pure water could be used to produce high-quality cellulose cord needed for aircraft tire production. Once the Baikalsk plant was well under construction, however, the Ministry redefined its production goals to reduce the output of cellulose cord and to include the production of ordinary paper; the Selenga mill underwent a similar metamorphosis and is now scheduled to produce cardboard cartons as well as cellulose cord. Ministry spokesmen also skillfully used another common ploy in purposefully under-estimating by one third the construction costs of the Baikalsk mill, raising their figures to realistic levels only after the project had received approval (Kramer, 1973a:163–166).

The Ministry of Timber, Paper, and Woodworking was not the only state agency to resist the introduction of adequate environmental safeguards. Opposition was also heard from many of the lake's other polluters. Industries which dotted the shores of its tributaries, like their counterparts elsewhere, resisted attempts to compel a diversion of scarce capital and manpower to pollution abatement programs, and little encouragement came from the central ministries. Local governments continued to operate completely without or with inadequate municipal waste-treatment facilities, although funds were finally allocated for their construction in the late 1960's (Pravda, 24 September 1971).

Despite the continued attempts by virtually all of the lake's polluters to evade or modify antipollution controls, Soviet leaders have since 1969 laid down stricter regulations governing industrial wastes at the lake as well as lumbering wastes and municipal sewage from nearby cities. Responding to the rising crescendo of complaints from the ad hoc coalition that had formed to defend the lake, the Council of Ministers issued new regulations in February 1969 (Izvestiia, 8 February 1969). The regulations provided for the creation of a special water conservation zone of some twenty thousand square miles around the lake. Restrictions were placed on lumbering activities within the zone, and timber was not to be cut on slopes steeper than twenty-five degrees. The law stipulated that sunken logs must be removed from stream and river beds, and that felled trees could no longer be dragged down the slopes but must instead be transported by cableways. The rafting of logs was also to be permitted only in large masses, which reduced the chance of sinking, and eventually overland transport was to replace the practice of log floating altogether.

The 1969 enactment also stipulated that the purification facilities at the Baikalsk mill were to be enlarged, and the Selenga factory was instructed not to begin production until its purification equipment was completed. Other industries on the lake's tributaries were to be similarly limited, and cities such as Ulan-Ude were instructed to purify their municipal wastes.

The result was the all-too-frequent pattern of professed adherence to the new regulations but continued de facto violations. The purification facilities at the Baikalsk operation continued to prove inadequate, but only small fines were imposed for the violation of standards. A report published in Komsomolskaia Pravda in the summer of 1970 indicated that pollution levels had actually increased since the 1969 enactment (KP, 11 August 1970).

Progress on the control of logging operations and the treatment of municipal sewage was also snail-paced.

Evidence of continued ministerial evasion prompted the passage of a new law on the protection of Lake Baikal in September 1971 (*Pravda*, 24 September 1971). This time the law was issued under the dual imprimatur of the USSR Council of Ministers and the Communist Party Central Committee, signaling that the highest priority was to be attached to its provisions. Essentially similar to the 1969 enactment (and the 1960 law as well), the 1971 decree ordered that the Baikalsk purification plant be completed by the end of the year, a deadline which it failed to meet. However, Soviet officials were sufficiently satisfied with the mill's progress to permit Russell Train, the chairman of the United States Council on Environmental Quality, to tour the purification facilities in October of 1972. He reported that the purified water released into the lake still remained tainted, although it was apparently fit for human consumption (*NY Times*, 5 October 1972). This judgment was shared by another team of Americans who visited the Baikalsk plant a year later and found the purification equipment "as good or better than" similar systems employed in the West (Goldman, 1973–1974:3). Sewage treatment facilities at the Selenga mill were to be completed before the end of 1972, when the factory was to begin operations. Mill officials promised the introduction of a complex three-stage treatment system, but environmentalists remained skeptical, pointing out that existing technology cannot adequately treat such potent wastes to a point where they will not endanger the lake. As with the Baikalsk plant, delays were experienced, and the mill did not begin operations until July 1973, with mill officials silent on the status of the treatment facilities (*NY Times*, 9 July 1973).

All other industrial enterprises and urban areas in the Baikal basin were instructed to draw up timetables for the construction of sewerage systems, with the systems to be in operation by the end of 1972. Ulan-Ude, the major urban complex and worst offender, was given an extra year. A report from the region in April 1972 indicated that such facilities were experiencing construction delays and might not meet the mandated deadlines (*LG*, 5 April 1972). Tacit official acknowledgment that such delays were continuing came a little more than a year later when Soviet authorities refused to permit a visiting team of American environmentalists to inspect the five worst polluting factories in Ulan-Ude. Water samples taken offshore near the delta of the Selenga River, which carries the city's wastes to the lake, indicated that a heavy load of industrial and municipal pollutants was still present (Goldman, 1973–1974:7).

The 1971 enactment repeated earlier instructions to the logging industry to clear stream beds of sunken logs and to reduce further sinkage. Earlier bans on cutting steep slopes were maintained, and an envigorated planting program was ordered, although climate, high winds, and poor soil make reforestation difficult (Goldman, 1973–1974:8). Subsequent reports from the area have noted some improvement in the operation of local forestry enterprises despite complaints from local loggers that financial assistance from the central government had been minimal. The clearing of stream and river beds has been begun, although local cutters have found it difficult to master the trick of floating logs in large "cigars" to reduce sinkage. The clearing of fish-spawning and -feeding areas has also prompted the Ministry of Fishing to construct several hatcheries for the Baikal whitefish, whose numbers had been drastically reduced by pollution. The overland transport of logs has increased, but any effective improvement must await the allocation of massive sums for road building in primitive areas (*LG*, 5 April 1972; *Pravda*, 14 March 1974).

Late in 1974, Soviet authorities finally approved comprehensive regulations governing the lake's future use. The product of several years of consultation among water conservation and pollution abatement agencies and evidently the subject of considerable conflict with industrial and municipal authorities, the new regulations stipulate current emission standards (to be revised upon the completion of an Academy of Sciences study of acceptable pollution levels) and set forth guidelines for the future industrial and recreational use of the lake. In commenting on the plan, I. I. Borodavchenko, the deputy minister of Land Reclamation and Water Resources, has noted that pollution-prone industries will be banned from the lake's entire water basin (*LG*, 4 December 1974). While the two existing pulp mills will be permitted to continue operation if proper treatment is given to their wastes, no new hazardous factories can be built. The ban also extends to prohibit the construction of any other new industries directly on the lakeshore or on its tributaries, although the enforcement of this provision will undoubtedly prove difficult in practice, especially since the region is slated for industrial and commercial development. The new regulations also call for the continued construction of purification facilities for industries and urban sites within the basin; while the number of such installations has "significantly grown" in the past few years, Borodavchenko leaves little doubt that much remains to be done. Already familiar instructions to the lumber industry to end log floating and clear log-covered riverbeds are repeated in the 1974 regulations, and new rules are offered governing the use of pesticides on nearby agricultural areas and the dumping of wastes by vessels on the lake (*LG*, 4 December 1974; *Izvestiia*, 20 April 1975; *Pravda*, 20 November 1974, 6 May 1975; Goldman, 1973–1974:9–10).

While it is too early to assess the impact of these new regulations, it is clear that many lessons may be drawn from the Baikal affair about the evolution of Soviet thinking concerning the fate of the lake and about the complex and highly competitive policy-making process through which such decisions are reached. It seems evident that the latest set of regulations reflects a twofold set of compromises between environmentalists and industrial and municipal interests. The first compromise concerns the compatibility of economic growth and adequate protection of the environment. Soviet authorities have clearly taken a middle-of-the-road position concerning the wisdom of exploiting the lake's unique resources. Rejecting the recommendations of both single-minded industrialists and conservationists, they have accepted the premise that continued growth is possible even in the delicate Baikal basin if adequate environmental safeguards are maintained. The second compromise is distinctly more political. The decisions reached about the protection of Lake Baikal have shown a clear and recurring pattern of short-term compromises reached among the various government agencies and *ad hoc* environmental groups. What is striking is not that such a pattern should exist in a milieu in which policy clashes rapidly translate into bureaucratic conflicts, but rather that Soviet environmentalists have been able to have any impact at all. In this regard, the political importance of the *ad hoc* environmental lobby which emerged and its favorable reception in some of the nation's leading journals cannot be underestimated. With few official channels open to the assertion of environmental interests—these are, after all, the normal decision-making channels usually dominated by production-oriented ministries—pollution-control officials and concerned scientists and intellectuals had to adopt the counter strategy of politicizing the dispute. Without the press and the personal prestige of key writers and intellectuals, the fate of the lake undoubtedly would have remained solely in the unprotecting hands of development-minded bureaucrats.

Several other political lessons can be drawn from the struggle over Lake Baikal. The deterioration of the virgin lake's waters certainly had nothing to do with an absence of appropriate legislation. The first enactment was passed in 1960, long before the impact of the cellulose mills threatened the lake. If adequately enforced, much of the deterioration of the lake would have undoubtedly been avoided. Nor have Soviet officials been reticent in offering new regulations for the lake's protection. The 1969 and 1971 decrees both offered roughly the same safeguards as the 1960 law, differing only in their increasing political weight and the sense of urgency that surrounded their release. It must also be said that environmental lobbies, and especially the *ad hoc* coalition of writers and scientists that identified with the preservation of the lake, had great success in securing tough environmental policy statements from top government agencies, although much time was lost in convincing high-level leaders that a serious problem existed.

If this is the case, what then explains the continued violation by the Ministry of Timber, Paper, and Woodworking and other offenders? The answer lies in the distinction between the success of environmentalists in securing tough policy statements and the ability of lesser government agencies to enforce these regulations against powerful production agencies. The breakdown came at the secondary level of policy interpretation and enforcement, at the stage where the general outlines were translated into specific emission standards or when the control agency inspectors took the field against the offending factories. With little political clout of their own, the control agencies found their authority frequently ignored or their limited legal sanctions inadequate. Their only recourse was to return again to the national level to seek even stronger mandates against continued violations, with the hope that new national attention to the problem would strengthen their hand.

JAPAN

POLITICAL ISSUES AND NATIONAL PRIORITIES

The central political issues facing Japan in the coming decade are whether economic growth should continue at the same high rate achieved in the 1960's and what proportion of the nation's wealth should be allocated to the protection of the environment and related welfare sectors. Emerging concern about environmental pollution and related questions of public welfare in the past few years has stimulated a widening debate about national priorities. This debate signals the end of a long-term consensus that economic goals are of primary importance, and the beginning of a complex struggle to establish a new consensus about the nation's future course.

For nearly two decades the Liberal Democratic Party (LDP) has ruled Japan from a virtually unbeatable posture. Its tenure in office has been associated with rising wages, prosperity, and the country's envied status in the world as an economic superpower. The four major opposition parties* have had little opportunity to overturn the LDP because the electorate has been content, in the main, to support a status quo that has meant increased consumer benefits. However, as the Japanese search for a fresh consensus on important domestic issues, especially pollution and inflation, there is

---

*They are, in present order of parliamentary strength, the Japan Socialist Party (JSP); the Japan Communist Party (JCP); Komeito (Clean Government Party), once the political arm of Sokagakkai, one of Japan's "new religions"; and the Democratic Socialist Party (DSP).

evidence that the LDP's continued rule is in jeopardy *(AEN,* 12 July 1974; *JT,* 28 October 1974; Kawata, 1974; Imazu, 1974).*

A continuing focus of national debate is former Prime Minister Tanaka's controversial plan to remodel the Japanese islands, which is expounded in his 1972 book *Nihon Retto Kaizo-Ron (The Case for a Remodeling of the Japanese Archipelago).* The remodeling program is predicated on several interlocking programs. The first is to create a high-speed network of railways, air routes, and highways, thus reducing travel time to a few hours between any two points in the country. This program is the foundation for the second, which is to redeploy industry away from the congested Pacific Coastal Belt to less settled regions inland and to as yet unexploited coastal areas. The objective is to reduce the share of industrial production along the Pacific coast from the present seventy-three percent to about fifty percent by 1985. The third program aims at building two new cities in each prefecture. A typical city will support 250,000 people and be laid out in proximity to industrial parks. This element of the plan presumably will drain off excess population from the great urban centers and redistribute it throughout the country. Tanaka's vision of the future is to be financed by issues of government bonds and various tax incentives, both positive and negative, to induce movement of reluctant industries. Institutional structures to implement this plan have already been created *(JT,* 2 August 1974). Ultimately the entire scheme will depend on an annual economic growth rate of at least eight or nine percent (Farnsworth, 1973:120).

Although the energy crisis has to some extent deflated the remodeling plan because of a dramatic drop in the growth rate, a spiraling rate of inflation, and the discrediting of Tanaka's leadership within the LDP, criticism was voiced by environmentalists and a few segments of the business community even before energy shortages became apparent. Environmentalists have pointed out that even if production on the Pacific Coastal Belt were reduced to fifty percent of the nation's total, production throughout Japan would still far exceed present total output. The consequence would be heavier pollution over a wider area because of the multiplication of individual emission sources. Moreover, the established urban-industrial

---

*The position of the LDP actually has been worsening through the 1960's to the present, probably because social welfare has not kept pace with economic growth. There is an inverse relationship between increments of GNP and the percentage of votes cast for the LDP. Thus in 1958 the party received 57.8 percent of the vote in the House of Representatives election, and less thereafter until the percentage had dropped to 47.6 percent in 1969. Elections in 1972 and 1974 were major setbacks, especially the latter, because of the huge amounts of money spent by the LDP and the open support by big business of LDP candidates. The party is now in a financial crisis. The Federation of Economic Organizations (Keidanren) has announced that it will stop handling political donations to the LDP, and scores of companies have defected from Kokumin Kyokai, a fund-raising organization for the party *(JT,* 19 August 1974; *MDN,* 15 August 1974).

complexes would not be much better off, for the remodeling plan would allow factories operative in and after 1962 to remain where they are. Many industrialists are also less than enthusiastic about Tanaka's proposals. Hiroaki Suzuki, managing director of Kobe Steel, voiced the doubt of many seaboard tycoons when he said in late 1972 that Japan could not have produced the world's least expensive steel without close proximity to the Pacific coast, and that it is unreasonable for the government to press for relocation of industry away from congested areas without considering production costs. Prominent industrialists have also complained that the government-sponsored relocation policy would result in massive social and economic dislocations. One firm that moved north voluntarily lost one hundred of its three hundred employees and fifty of its one hundred subcontractors, thus suggesting the traumatic effects of a dispersion policy. Keidanren (Federation of Economic Organizations) has formally registered its opposition to the proposed heavy taxes on factories as a spur to relocation, a protest the LDP cannot lightly ignore (Hoshino, 1973; Omori, 1972; AEN, 19 March 1973; JT, 8 March 1973).

The selection of Takeo Miki to replace Tanaka as head of the LDP in November 1974 will do little to reorient the party's attitudes regarding continued growth and regional development.* Although a former director-general of the Environment Agency, Miki has shown himself more concerned with political than environmental considerations in appointing Tatsuo Ozawa to head the Environment Agency. Ozawa served as minister of construction under the Tanaka regime and is clearly identified with the Tanaka faction of the party. With his background and factional connections, it is unlikely that Ozawa will place environmental concerns ahead of other long-established goals (NY Times, 26 November 1974; JT, 28 October 1974).

The four opposition parties have charged that Tanaka's plan is merely an extension of politics and policies of the 1960's; it is a confession that business and economic growth will continue to receive top priority, with just enough environmental and social welfare window dressing to blunt criticism and protest. Indeed, they say it is a simple task to show that Tanaka's plan is a more grandiose version of the income-doubling and regional development plans of the 1960's, an elaboration of the 1970 New Economic and Social Development Plan, 1970–1975. The true beneficiaries of this expansion, the opposition argues, will not be the people, or the environment, but a minority of powerful industrialists (AEN, 27 November 1972).

---

*In his major policy speech before the Diet in January 1975, Prime Minister Miki said most of the right things concerning environmental protection and restraints on economic growth, but so did former Prime Minister Tanaka (JT, 25 January 1975).

In the December 1972 parliamentary elections, the opposition parties blamed inflation, pollution, and inadequate living standards on "the policy of the successive governments for high-rate economic growth—a policy which benefits business exlusively" (this statement from JSP Chairman Tomomi Narita was paralleled by the chairmen of the other three parties). These charges were apparently substantive enough to win the JSP and the JCP additional seats in the Diet, a disarming erosion of LDP power that strengthens the possibility of a coalition between two or more opposition parties.* The LDP is in a delicate position. A trebling of GNP in fifteen years could aggravate environmental pollution and inflation severely enough to give a leftist coalition a controlling edge in the Diet. On the other hand, a substantial and permanent slowing of economic growth would eclipse the *raison d'être* which has sustained the LDP since 1955. A redefinition of goals in terms other than growth will be difficult for the ruling party because of its close identification with the industrial sector, and the opposition has already begun to seize the initiative in just such a redefinition. The upshot is a stormy, uncertain course for politics in the balance of the 1970's, with environmental and related issues pressing more urgently for solution. (*JT*, 18, 25, 17 November 1972; *AEN*, 1 December 1972).

GOVERNMENT AGENCIES

Until the creation of the Environment Agency under Premier Eisaku Sato on July 1, 1971, authority to deal with environmental issues was scattered among a host of ministries and agencies. The new Environment Agency is charged with preserving the environment so as to assure "a healthy and civilized life for the people of Japan." This responsibility includes conservation of nature as well as prevention and amelioration of pollution. Administrative consolidation has resulted in the formal elimination of environmental offices in other agencies. The core of the Environment Agency is four bureaus for planning and coordination, nature conservation, air quality, and water quality. The first of these controls the formulation of basic policy, estimates environment-related expenditures, including research funds, collects pollution data, and coordinates the work of all other agencies. The second presides over national parks and the protection of wildlife, and dispenses advice to relevant agencies about city planning. The third enforces laws relating to air pollution, noise, vibration, and offensive odors, sets air quality standards, and has a special division to ponder strategies for coping with the automobile, the chief villain behind

---

*In a rare show of cooperation, the four opposition parties took the governorship of Shiga Prefecture, a former stronghold of the LDP, in November, 1974 (*JT*, 21 November 1974).

Japan's thick photochemical smog. The fourth establishes and enforces standards relating to water pollution, ground subsidence, and soil contamination. To round out this structure, the Environment Agency also supervises the work of three ancillary councils on control of environmental pollution, parks, and wildlife, and works closely with two national institutes, one for pollution research and the other for the training of pollution-control personnel. The agency is staffed with some 542 civil servants.* However, there is not a single ecologist on the agency's staff; the official explanation is that health problems take precedence over problems of ecological disruption. The head of the agency bears the title director-general and holds ministerial rank. Like all other state ministers, he is a political appointee. Thus the former director-general, Takeo Miki, now prime minister, is a major faction leader in the Liberal Democratic Party. His immediate successor in the agency was Matsuhei Mori, a member of the Miki faction, though appointed by Tanaka. Mori was in turn replaced by Tatsuo Ozawa, a Miki appointee drawn from the Tanaka faction (*JEA*, 1973a; *JEA*, 5 June 1973, Vol. 1, No. 1:7-8; *QEJ*, 1972:151-153).

On paper at least, there can be no doubt that a substantive improvement has been made over past arrangements in which more than a dozen agencies were enforcing laws and setting standards in a peripheral and conflicting way. However, many problems remain. One of the most formidable is that the Environment Agency is a junior organization in Japan's pantheon of ministries. The mere fact of recent birth is enough to place it at the low end of the continuum with respect to prestige and the power to move events. In a highly status-conscious land like Japan, it is not necessarily the gravity of the problem with which one deals that attracts respectful attention and support, but where one stands in the pecking order. The Ministry of International Trade and Industry, the Ministry of Construction, and the all-powerful Ministry of Finance are heavily funded, politically powerful, and squarely on the side of business and economic growth. Their elite staffs have forged an intricate network of friendships, professional contacts, and understandings within government, business, and academic circles. Even under ideal circumstances the fledgling Environment Agency would require time to build up a similar profile of bureaucratic reach and power. There is reason to believe that in order to do so, industry would have to be treated with the utmost courtesy, in spite of the agency's mandate to enforce pollution abatement measures. Sobering evidence has already materialized to suggest that the agency may have no choice but

---

*Out of the agency's staff, 300 came from the Ministry of Health and Welfare, 150 from national park areas, 60 from the Ministry of Agriculture and Forestry, and 30 from the Ministry of International Trade and Industry. More than 50 percent of them are graduates of Tokyo University (Interview with agency personnel, August 1974).

to dilute its efforts to rectify environmental abuses, or else simply be ignored.

The implementation of an environmental law normally cannot evade a wide consensus that must include the wishes of both the political world *(seikai)* and the financial world *(zaikai)*. The interests of these mammoth cliques somehow must be harmonized, an ideal that tends to undermine or neutralize the best efforts of the Environment Agency.

The most notable recent example of a consensus between the worlds which weakened a significant environmental measure was the delay and interim modification of Japan's version of the Muskie air-pollution law. The implementation of the American law was put off in 1973, thus providing Japanese auto manufactures with the hope that Japan's air-pollution measure could be delayed as well. But the director-general of the Environment Agency refused to yield at first, declaring that "automobile exhaust standards were established to improve the serious air pollution in this country, and events taking place in the United States have no bearing upon our intent" *(JEA, 5 June 1973, Vol. 1, No. 1:4)*. The nine major auto manufacturers claimed inability to meet the standards. One of them invoked the oil crisis as an excuse, arguing that a car meeting the 1975–1976 standards would use more gas. The Air Quality Bureau of the Environment Agency retorted, ". . . if you talk about the oil problem, it will be a great contribution on your part if you do not produce automobiles" *(MDN, 22 June 1974)*.

In June 1974, Miki called the auto executives to a special meeting with the intention of attacking their arguments and demanding reports on the progress of their antipollution research. The executives came but refused to cooperate. In this crisis, the relative immaturity of the Environment Agency was a distinct handicap. Such arrogance and defiance would have been unlikely had the auto elite been summoned by MITI or the Ministry of Finance. As a result of business pressure and political compromise, the original measure has been delayed for several years and lenient interim standards have been substituted. The consensus was that the original standards would not be wholly given up (the wish of the auto manufacturers), only delayed, and that weaker interim standards would go into effect by 1975. Thus the government retains its law and the auto industry has a reprieve from adjusting to its full impact *(JT, 5 December 1974; 23 February, 31 March 1975)*.

Most of Japan's forty-six autonomous local government bodies (Tokyo, Hokkaido, and forty-four prefectures) have some kind of environmental bureau or council. They exercise what power they have with uneven determination, are poorly staffed, and generally struggle to do a monumental job with sparse resources. The strongest local antipollution agencies are to be found in big cities like Tokyo, Osaka, and Nagoya, which are led by radical mayors, usually socialists. Although local agencies have been authorized to enforce standards stricter than those set by the central government, few actually do so.

POLICY MAKING AND PRESSURE GROUPS

Policy making in Japan takes place through an elaborate process of consensus making, which has been dominated by the LDP, government bureaucracies, and industrial lobbies since the end of the war. While this approach minimizes overt political conflict, it results in a tightly restricted (although not totally closed) decision-making system in which the majority of policy proposals come either from the bureaucracies themselves (sixty percent) or from lobbyists (twenty percent) *(LJ,* 10 October 1974, Ike, 1972: Thayer, 1969: Chapters 8–9). The long-standing authority of the LDP has also lodged considerable *de facto* decision-making power in internal party circles. The weakness of the Diet as an effective policy-making forum has also contributed to the semi-closed nature of the policy-making process, as has the inactivity of individual legislators in sponsoring environmental legislation. In this setting, the impact of environmental lobbies is severely limited by the tight structure and industry-dominated consensus orientation of the policy process.* Environmental lobbies are themselves poorly developed in Japan and possess little effective political muscle against pro-industry groups. The Environment Agency, which may yet emerge as a central focus for lobbying activities, has proven mostly ineffective, itself the victim of counterpressures for unabated economic growth. Thus the normal process of consensus building usually fails to give an effective voice to environmental groups. While environmental spokesmen have won limited victories at the local level and have successfully turned to the courts, they have failed to forge a nationally powerful lobby.

Traditionally pressure groups have been viewed as not quite respectable. Their influence in policy formation is in large measure a consequence of weak party organization on the district level, which leaves dietmen vulnerable to organized pressure from extra-parliamentary groups. Another factor that strengthens pressure groups is the image that dietmen have of themselves as judges rather than initiators of policy; lack of initiative in the Diet forms a vacuum receptive to outside thinking. Within this roughly drawn context, pressure groups commonly express their will by means of a number of devices, including demonstrations, petitions, law suits, and

---

*Japanese consensualism is not unlike American "incrementalism" in some respects. The latter shapes public policy on the basis of past experience, consultation among affected parties, bargaining and compromise, and modest rather than radical change. As in Japan's consensualism, "incrementalism means that few policy problems are ever solved" (Rosenbaum, 1973:94–95).

carefully cultivated contacts with government bureaucrats and political leaders (Yoshimura, 1974:7). It must be remembered that Japan's most powerful pressure groups are in the economic sector. An organization like Keidanren (Federation of Economic Organizations), unlike many of the groups discussed below, has direct and powerful contacts with influential government officials (Yanaga, 1968: Chapter 2).

Three types of pro-environmental pressure groups are important in Japan. Least important are familiar groups like the labor federations, the League for Government Compensation of Expropriated Agricultural Lands, the Agricultural Cooperatives Association, the National Housewives Associations, and the eighty-seven-thousand-member Japan Medical Association. In addition to customary preoccupations, all of these groups, with the exception of the Japan Medical Association, have become sensitized to the issues of pollution and environmental quality, but it remains to be seen how much they can influence environmental policy. While there is some promise in the 1971 collaboration of two labor federations to organize massive antipollution rallies in forty prefectures which drew about eight hundred thousand people, the political impact of these groups has yet to be demonstrated.

The second type of group is devoted to the protection of animal life, the preservation of scenic areas, and other traditional conservationist goals. The Japan Association for the Protection of Nature estimates some 130 such groups are active throughout the country. They include a wide assortment of people, including students, workers, scientists, lawyers, agriculturalists, and fishermen. One such group is the Association to Preserve Nature in Nikko, which is engaged in a signature-collecting campaign in Tochigi Prefecture to block further economic development in Nikko National Park, one of Japan's most beautiful regions and a unique repository of alpine plant life (*JQ*, 1972a).

The third and most significant type of group is *jumin undo*, or "movement of inhabitants," denoting a plethora of *ad hoc* militant groups that have sprung up in direct response to pollution and its causes (Miyamoto, 1970). Participants in *jumin undo* have come to the defense of pollution victims, blocked the movement of industry into specific communities, held up the construction of power plants, and criticized the hitherto inviolable policies of regional development and intensive economic growth. In their scale of values, the "quality of life" is not necessarily synonymous with a swollen GNP. The political successes of *jumin undo* have been impressive, especially in blocking the further expansion of industry, and as we shall see in the case study of Minamata Bay, in winning compensation for pollution victims. Determined resistance by citizens has shelved construction plans for five power plants (one is nuclear) in the prefectures of Kyoto, Aichi, Mie, and

Miyagi, even though authorization had been obtained from the government in 1971. Residents in Ikata, Ehime Prefecture, have demanded reconsideration of a nuclear power plant to be raised in the area. On the northern island of Hokkaido, the Hokkaido Electric Power Company wants to build a thermal power station, with a seven hundred thousand kilowatt capacity by 1985, in the farming community of Date. In July 1972 fifty-six farmers, fishermen, and other citizens brought suit against the company to stop construction, and were unimpressed by the claim that without a new power facility Date would face an insufficient supply of electricity. In yet another case, in December 1971 the Kagoshima prefectural government concluded plans to develop the entire Osumi Peninsula of which scenic Shibushi Bay is a part. The huge industrial complex envisaged for the area is now regarded as a partial implementation of Tanaka's remodeling plan. In August 1972, however, the proposed *kombinato* was delayed for further review in deference to the Anti-Pollution Liaison Council, a pressure group consisting of twelve different circles of residents. Since the antipollution drive began, the political consciousness of residents in Osumi has undergone a transformation. A conservative outlook has yielded to fresh perceptions and attitudes about local government, economic growth, and the relationship between citizenship and the quality of community life. A combined pressure group has blossomed from the dozen original bodies and is fighting government intentions to open part of the Nichian Coastal National Park to development by the petroleum industry (Ui et al., 1970:III-3).

Since the beginning of the 1970's, citizen's movements have undergone some striking changes. First, the more than one thousand groups have tended to grow in size. Thus the Pollution Countermeasures Liaison Council of Aichi Prefecture, which elected a reformist mayor in Nagoya, has 230,000 members. Where these movements once consisted of no more than 100 people, they can now be divided into two groups, those with more than 500 members, and those with less. Second, the movements have greatly expanded their targets and tactics. The causes of *jumin undo* are virtually a catalog of the environmental and social ills of contemporary Japan. Tactics have matured from the posture of "humble request" (self-effacing petitions for reform) to that of an "appeal-pattern" (signature gathering and pamphlet distribution), to that of an "action-pattern" (sit-ins, demonstrations), to the latest stage of "intellectual tactics," which draws on the full resources of the legal system. Third, movements of the "resistance type," which have stood in the path of industries and government agencies, are down to a quarter of the total. For the remainder the trend is to exploit or compete with political parties, which were, until recently, either ignored or merely used as conduits. Many citizen's movements have begun to put up their own candidates for office, thus bypassing completely the familiar party lineup. Leaders of citizen's movements have been elected mayor in the cities of Kamakura in Kanagawa Prefecture, and Hino in Tokyo Prefecture. In the meantime, already established parties are carefully gauged as to their responsiveness and made use of accordingly. The transformation of citizen's movements into quasi-political parties has advanced to the point where they are widely thought of as a "fourth power,"* coequal with the excutive, legislative, and judicial powers (*JQ*, 1973c:368–373).

The antipollution movement is a dramatic manifestation of civic spirit in postwar Japan which has vitalized the all but inoperative Local Autonomy Law of 1947. The movement expresses a consumer point of view bearing on individual rights and welfare rather than on duties and group harmony (*JQ*, 1973b). Protesters are impatient with the thousand and one delicate compromises entailed by a consensus approach to decision making, and have chosen the traditionally odious path of confrontation and conflict. On the other hand, *jumin undo* is not a blind, reflex attack on economic growth as such, but a selective, critical rejection of certain methods of development and a call for readjustment in the scale of priorities.* The citizen's movement has no distaste for higher wages and living standards, but is convinced that affluence can exact too stiff a price if pursued ingenuously on its own terms. The movement's greatest strength is in the new industrial areas and in regions where the enterprises have future ambitions. People in long-established industrial zones take the factories for granted and do not perceive them as unwanted invaders (Simcock, 1974; Interview with Keikichi Kihara, special staff writer, *Asahi Shimbun*, August 1974).

The Environment and the Courts

In Japan the courts have played a vital role in environmental protection. By March 1973 four celebrated pollution court cases had ended with nearly complete victory for environmental interests (Stunkel, 1974b). In the first case, the Kumamoto district court ruled in March 1973 that the Chisso Chemical Company, a producer of plastics, chemical fertilizer, and organic chemicals in Minamata City, was guilty of killing and crippling hundreds of people through the discharge of mercury-laden wastes into Minamata Bay. The company was ordered to pay some 3.8 million dollars to 45 victims (18 of whom had died) and their families. The 45 victims constitute one of six groups totaling 397 persons (of whom 60 have died). The focus of the hearings in the Kumamoto trial was whether the company had been

---

*Gresser has listed some ninety civic campaigns in Japan for the prevention of environmental pollution, and details places, organizations and their founding dates, and precise activities (Gresser, 1973:Appendix I).

Jumin undo might be called a rash of "revitalization movements" (Wallace, 1956).

ignorant of potential harmful effects in its waste-dumping policy. The company maintained that available knowledge was insufficient to warrant a prediction of Minamata disease, and took its stand on a "no-fault" argument. The plaintiffs argued that the company had foreknowledge derived from two studies conducted by 1959, and that in spite of evidence pointing to mercury (effects of waste water on laboratory animals), the flow of toxic waste was not stopped. Moreover, the victims charged, Chisso persisted in dumping mercury waste even after the government officially pointed a finger of blame at the company in 1968. On handing down his decision, Judge Jiro Saito said, "No factory, through its productive activities, can be permitted to pollute and destroy the environment. Still more, no factory should be permitted to violate and sacrifice the lives and health of regional residents." The Kumamoto affair is the origin of pollution law suits in Japan and perhaps the biggest water-pollution case in its history (*JEA*, 10 August 1973, Vol. 1, No. 3:2-3; *AEN*, 12 April 1973).

In the second case, the Niigata district court ruled in September 1971 against Showa Denko Kanose for discharging mercury waste into the upper reaches of the Agano River. The company was directed to pay seventy-seven victims and their families about eight hundred thousand dollars. Presiding Judge Kiichi Miyazaki spotlighted negligence as the heart of the case and stressed the failure of Showa Denko to take precautionary safety measures (*JT*, 20 March 1973).

The Yokkaichi branch of the Tsu district court handed down the third important decision in July 1971 in finding six firms guilty of polluting the air in Yokkaichi. The court ordered payment of about 286,000 dollars to twelve victims of acute asthma and other respiratory ailments. In the fourth case, the Toyama district court ruled in July 1971 that Itai-Itai disease, which killed and disabled dozens of residents along the Jinzu River, was due to cadmium discharged by the Mitsui Mining and Smelting Company, and awarded 31 surviving victims some 159,000 dollars. More suits are likely to follow, since there were 150 registered victims in October 1971, 48 of whom had died (*KH*, 2 November 1971; *JEA*, 5 June 1973, Vol. 1, No. 1:5-6).

The basis in law for these rulings was Article 70 of the Civil Code, which provides for compensation in the event of injury or infringement of rights due to negligence. Prior to the four great pollution cases the burden was on the plaintiff to prove a causal relationship between his disease and the activities of an accused factory. These decisions have established new precedents and interpretations, shifting the burden of proof onto industry. The Minamata and Toyama rulings established that only circumstantial evidence is required to trace cause and effect involved in a case of mass-pollution sickness. In order to fix blame on industry, it is sufficient to confirm that waste is being discharged in conjunction with a pollution-related illness. Only two facts are needed: a statistically high incidence of disease, and a demonstrated polluter. Moreover, firms can be found guilty even if they are not the sole polluters, which means that an individual can sue a single corporation rather than be obliged to make a case against all polluters in the area. Solatium contracts, or damages paid outside of court, do not constitute a legal settlement and cannot be invoked by a company to block future litigation on the same case. Compensation can be exacted for loss of livelihood and income, such as resulted from the destruction of Minamata Bay fishing grounds, as well as for loss of health and life (*JQ*, 1973b).

Fortunately for the Japanese the postwar court system is independent of the government's executive branch, and judges are free under the consititution to render decisions in accord with conscience and individual readings of the law. Even so, Japan's Supreme Court has been reticent about defending civil rights from government infringement. It is the lower courts that have come forward as champions of the citizen against seemingly irresistible corporate and government interests.

The court settlements have encouraged direct negotiations between polluters and victims. The Shiohama complex settled out of court with 140 air-pollution victims in November 1972, agreeing to pay about 1,750,000 dollars in less than three months of talks. In February 1973 Mitsui Mining and Smelting consented to pay 2 million dollars to farmers along the Jinzu River who had abandoned their land because of heavy cadmium contamination.

Although systematic use of the new precedents could be a powerful weapon against polluters, there are constraining factors. An important one is the time needed for litigation. The Minamata case ended three years and nine months after the suit was filed and seventeen years after the first victim was detected. The Yokkaichi case dragged on for four years and ten months. Another inhibiting factor is the traditional Japanese distaste for litigation and confrontation tactics, which reflects a society in which differences are adjusted ideally on a personal rather than on a legal basis. Finally, many of the victims feel that monetary compensation (usually a compromise between polluter and victim) has distorted the reality of their suffering. They want health and vitality back. One man remarked that winning the damage suit was like selling ten years of physical and mental anguish for ten million yen. The court decisions have helped, but they cannot restore the dead to life or make the crippled whole.*

---

*Compensation payments have threatened Chisso with bankruptcy. A bizarre development is that the Japan Development Bank may advance Chisso a substantial loan, thus setting the precedent of using public funds to bail out polluters (*JT*, 22 April 1975).

Two Case Studies: Minamata Bay and Mishima-Numazu

The dynamic interaction of government policy, economic interests, scientific testimony, competing social values, and local civic culture can be isolated in two notable upsurges of protest against pollution and its effects: the first in Minamata City, Kumamoto Prefecture; and the second in the cities of Mishima and Numazu, Shizuoka Prefecture. Each case represents a different pattern of response to *kogai*. Citizen outrage in Minamata was concerned primarily with securing compensation for damages and fixing blame on the offending industry. In the second case, citizens organized to *prevent* pollution and set out aggressively to buttress local autonomy against the encroachments of large-scale industrial and government interests.

Mercury poisoning, or Minamata disease, transformed environmental disruption into an explosive social and political issue. The small industrial town of Minamata in western Kyushu has a population of about forty thousand, most of whom work as fishermen and farmers, or as laborers in one local industry, the Chisso Chemical Company. The town is provincial, conservative, and poor; the factory is its solitary monument to Japan's new industrial order. For years Chisso had sluiced its wastes into Minamata Bay, wastes containing substantial amounts of methyl mercury. Around 1956 local cats mysteriously began to exhibit signs of madness. Soon thereafter people succumbed to terrifying aberrations: loss of hearing and speech, convulsions and tremors, gnarled limbs, and chronic mental disturbance.* The one thing they had in common besides the symptoms was a diet of fish from Minamata Bay and surrounding waters. When children were born with the disease in 1958, it was shown to be congenital. Mercury had sped upward through the food chain of local marine life to man.

The relatively simple connection between these facts was not officially recognized for twelve years, while the victims who survived were obliged to wait until 1973 for legal redress of their grievances against Chisso. The path from 1956 to 1973 is littered with distortion, evasion, and the collusion of special interests to obscure the truth about Minamata disease. The entire story, as told by Jun Ui in his *Kogai no Seijigaku (Politics of Pollution)*, reveals cogently the power of big business and government and the strategy of *jumin undo*.

The composition of the Minamata antipollution movement can be reduced to four closely meshed strands. The first involves militant farmers and fishermen who were intuitively aware of Chisso's liability, and who tried to pry concessions from the recalcitrant company officials. Failure to elicit a sympathetic response provoked demonstrations and riots. In November

---

*The most poignant evocation of this pollution disaster is in W.E. and A.E. Smith, *Minamata: Words and Photographs* (1975).

1959 some three thousand people raided factory precincts, only to be driven away by police: leaders of the demonstration were arrested and jailed. Because Chisso dominated Minamata's social, economic, and political life, the victims of industrial pollution were bereft of a power base from which to conduct an organized, politically significant offensive. Weak local authority and community dependence on the factory for jobs, area prestige, and municipal revenues further encouraged many citizens to side with the company or to take refuge in noninvolvement. With a few rare exceptions, such as a one-man local newspaper and a local poet, Michiko Ishimure, the people of Minamata were reluctant to defend the victims, or to criticize Chisso.*

The second strand involved a flow of publicity, information, and assistance from outside the community. The violent collision of angry citizens with the local power structure, compounded by the horrible nature of the disease at issue, attracted the attention of intellectuals, scientists, lawyers, and journalists who tried in various ways to help the victims. Good press and television coverage created a framework of public opinion favorable to the victims.

A third strand was the tangled conflict between two species of scientific opinion, that of government and company-oriented researchers and that of nonpartisan investigators. The long dispute over what and who caused Minamata disease involved authorities from Kumamoto- and Tokyo-based academic institutions, government ministries, and scattered research institutes. In 1959, studies by Dr. Hosokawa of the Chisso Factory Hospital (he was subsequently directed by the company to cease his inquiries within the hospital) and by staff of the Kumamoto Medical School pointed to mercury as the disease agent and Chisso's effluent as the source. The company refused to admit blame and even denied that mercury was used in its operations, though in fact it was an essential catalyst in at least two processes. Denials were accompanied by refusal to cooperate with investigators who wished to inspect the plant and examine waste water prior to discharge. Technicians of the Chisso factory prepared counterarguments with the help of university professors brought into the company's orbit, including well-known figures from Hoho Medical University and Tokyo University. A committee of inquiry from the latter institution received financial assistance from the Japan Chemical Industry Association, a supporter of the company's position.

The government's point of view had been elusive. A committee of experts from the Ministry of Welfare confirmed at first the mercury-poisoning theory, but the committee was dismissed and ministry officials tried to

---

*With good reason. W. Eugene Smith, coauthor of the aforementioned book on Minamata, was attacked at the factory by thugs trying to intimidate petitioners. His cameras were broken along with several vertebrae, and he was nearly blinded.

suppress the report. A similar committee of the Ministry of International Trade and Industry held secret meetings and was dissolved for unknown reasons. The result of Chisso's counteroffensive was to create an impression in 1960 that Minamata disease was still cloaked in mystery. The factory continued to discharge its wastes, news of the incident subsided, and public attention was diverted by a furor over the Japan–American Mutual Security Agreement and Prime Minister Ikeda's announcement of an income-doubling plan based on a strong, expanding economy.

The fourth strand of the controversy involved the issue of compensation. If the victims and their supporters had not resorted to demonstrations, it is apparent that Chisso would have done nothing to recognize their predicament. But local officials, alarmed by the disturbances and the bad publicity, prevailed on the company to work out a settlement. The nature of that settlement accentuates the isolated, ill-organized, politically ineffectual situation of the victims in a community like Minamata. Families of the dead were to receive 800 dollars. Afflicted but living adults and children were to receive 280 and 80 dollars a year, respectively. This solatium was drawn up with the qualification that when "the factory waste is discovered not to be at fault, the whole agreement shall be dissolved; if the factory waste is shown to be responsible for the disease, the victims shall not request any further compensation." At this point Chisso was fully aware from its own tests that waste water fed to cats produced symptoms of Minamata disease.

Further work by Hosokawa in 1962, corroborated by Professor Irukuyama of Kumamoto University, proved conclusively that methyl mercury caused the disease. But official recognition of the fact was delayed until 1965 when a second outbreak of the disease occurred in Niigata, forcing the government to admit a connection between the two cases. The Niigata victims went to court, thus reviving the entire issue. The Minamata group met with them to compare notes and resolved to press Chisso for further compensation. Once more with aid from the outside, Minamata victims began to organize a more telling civic movement against the polluter. The legal success of these unhappy people in 1973 should not be allowed to mask the fact that compensation paid was far below the demand. Indeed, the expedient of seeking compensation is plagued with an inherent weakness, because the "adjustment of views" always puts the final amount about midway between what the victims want and what the polluter is willing to pay (Ui, 1972b:14–16; Ui et al., 1970:II-2; Simcock, 1972:16–18; Irukuyama, 1968; Ui and Kitamura, 1971:271–287).

* * *

In the Mishima and Numazu districts near Mount Fuji and Hakone National Park, an energetic, resourceful body of citizens organized to prevent pollution by barring Tokyo Electric Power, Sumitomo Chemical, and Fuji Petroleum from their communities. Action was motivated by an earlier unpleasant experience with Taho Rayon, which had built a large plant in the city and depleted its water supply. This triumphant example of *jumin undo* inspired similar movements in other cities and towns endangered by indiscriminate regional development. Unlike the Minamata movement, Mishima-Numazu contained ingredients favorable to the emergence of a widely based civic consciousness. Instead of impoverishment, modest affluence was the rule. Instead of a town dependent of one factory, Mishima and Numazu were proud, relatively self-sufficient communities fully aware of advantages worth preserving. Instead of a simple amalgam of despondent fishermen, farmers, and laborers, one found a complex and responsive social structure comprising well-to-do farmers, housewives and mothers with an alert eye for environmental quality, civic-minded professional men, and salaried people in a variety of jobs—in short, a dynamic middle class. In addition, progressive elements in local government contrasted sharply with conservative, subservient politicians and bureaucrats in Minamata.

In response to a government proposal that highly polluting industries take up residence in the area, the citizens of Mishima-Numazu originated study groups, women's clubs, Neighborhood Government Associations, and other forms of voluntary cooperation to examine and discuss options. Bradford Simcock (1972:19) has described the beginnings of the movement:

> In Mishima and Numazu cities, the citizen's movement began with a study group sponsored by backers of Mishima's young progressive mayor (elected in 1961) that was to look into matters of regional administration and development. It was formed basically as a response to a prefectural plan to build a petro-chemical complex there. When the intentions of the prefectural government were more fully known (they included a proposal to merge Mishima, Numazu, and Shimizu), the mayor's group organized a so-called "friendly discussion meeting" and a lecturer spoke on petro-chemical complexes and regional development, the impact on local communities, etc. Though the mayor's group was aligned with the progressives, specifically, the Japan Socialist Party (which in this case in the person of the mayor was a genuinely progressive force oriented to his constituents and not toward officials and politicians above him), they assiduously cultivated a non-partisan image.

In 1964, after many citizens of the Mishima-Numazu area had seen a television special on pollution in Yokkaichi City, about two hundred activists visited Yokkaichi for direct observation of the city's problems and talks with asthma victims. Among groups represented were the Women's League, several town-block associations, the Chamber of Commerce and Industry, and the PTA. Upon returning they gave speeches and reports portraying Yokkaichi as a pollution-disaster area enjoying minimal benefits from heavy industrialization. In a brilliant offensive move, teachers from Numazu Technical High School and a scientist from a nearby genetics research institute organized a private research team to evaluate data and conclusions in the prefectural government's report on industrialization in the area. The independent team thoroughly discredited the government plan and thereby boosted enormously the prestige of the resistance movement. The culmination of this self-motivated community education and action program was a demonstration of twenty-five thousand people in Numazu that heralded defeat for the prefectural government's construction scheme. All six major metropolitan cities now have "progressive" mayors, elected with socialist and communist help.

The resistance of Mishima-Numazu to regional development is a paradigm for the assessment of other citizen's movements in Japan. Unfortunately the social organization of the Japanese, with its intrinsic regard for authority figures, its preference for harmonious adjustment of views rather than confrontation, and its adaptation to a political tradition in which authority has always flowed downward from the top, is not well suited to a healthy expression of grass-roots democracy. Political initiative outside of and opposed to existing power structures has never been the Japanese way, and the sense of individual rights is still weak in spite of freedoms guaranteed by the postwar constitution. Nevertheless, the Mishima-Numazu victory proves that civic spirit can be galvanized (McKean, 1974).

CHAPTER
7
ACTIVE PROGRAMS

THE UNITED STATES

ENVIRONMENTAL LEGISLATION

Much legislation passed by Congress and state legislatures throughout American history was aimed at fostering the exploitation of nature for economic gain. Jobs, profits, and economic growth were the emblems of quality by which such legislation was judged. Until the end of World War II, most legislation seeking to stop pollution or the ill-considered waste of natural resources was enacted at the state and local level; however, these laws often were poorly enforced, for agencies charged with their implementation were hampered by inadequate funding and staffing. The federal government scarcely concerned itself with pollution control, although it did establish a number of programs that attempted in theory to apply multiple-use and maximum-yield concepts to the management of resources under its control.

In the late 1940's, a new array of attitudes toward the natural environment slowly emerged, encouraged by a generally high level of economic prosperity. In consequence, a body of legislation grew to the end of protecting and restoring the environment. The quality of life—clean air, clean water, quiet, open space, recreational opportunities, a variety of flora and fauna—developed tentatively as a new standard of measurement for the quality of legislation. Economic growth was not forgotten, but it was no longer the sole standard by which public policy was judged. The federal government moved into pollution control as it was recognized that the hodgepodge of state and local legislation could not deal adequately with what was, by its very nature, an interstate problem. In addition to the environmental logic of such national legislation, the expansion of federal law in other social welfare areas during the New Deal, was a great precedent.

Between 1948 and 1970 Congress passed five acts to abate and control water pollution, and between 1955 and 1970, five acts were enacted to deal with air pollution. (On pre-1970 legislation, see Kneese and Shultze, 1975:30–50). These laws used a variety of approaches, including the establishment of water and air quality standards, federal subsidies for pollution-control construction, and the creation of agencies to oversee the implementation of the legislation. Nevertheless, until 1970 the effective coordination of state programs and the successful enforcement of federal programs was the exception rather than the rule, in large part because there was no central environmental agency until the creation of the EPA in 1970 (*USEPA,* 1972:viii-x; Rosenbaum, 1973:136–158; Kneese and Schultze, 1975:51–57).

Legislation flowing from the pens of federal and state lawmakers in the 1970's has proven far more comprehensive, specific, and enforcement-oriented than that preceding it.* Less concerned with the multiple-use theory of resource use and conservation, it has focused more on the explication of emission standards and the organization of monitoring and enforcement agencies at all government levels. The scope of federal authority has been enlarged to provide a mechanism for the coordination and strengthening of state-based emission-control programs, and in many areas the federal government has become the direct monitoring and enforcement authority. In other abatement areas, such as air pollution, the federal government retains indirect powers through its ability to set minimal standards, below which state emission regulations may not fall, and to intervene directly in cases where state programs are judged deficient.

Federal environmental legislation, pollution control structures, and policy-making style have passed through three stages in the past two decades. The first, reaching into the mid-1960's, consisted in weak, largely futile gestures by the government with no cooperation from industry. The second

---

*There are serious exceptions, the most spectacular recent one being the Energy Supply and Environmental Coordination Act of 1974 (P. L. 93–319), an ambiguous, inconsistent measure at odds with existing law. Its muddled provisions seem to have great potential for weakening pollution control laws (Reitze and Reitze, 1974).

stage, reaching from the mid-1960's to 1970, was dominated by the "standards and enforcement method of pollution abatement," a decentralized procedure keyed into interest groups. It involved a cumbersome, time-consuming, inherently self-defeating process of setting goals, defining criteria for various pollution levels, formulating quality standards or ceilings on various pollutants, enunciating emission standards, and undertaking enforcement through a range of options from exhortation to court actions. Because the burden of proof was on the government at every stage, data collecting and evaluation seldom led to a meaningful enforcement program. Polluters exploited delays and uncertainties to go on polluting and sought to emasculate standards which eventually emerged from the long tunnel wherein cautious bureaucrats were busy justifying their goals, criteria, and standards. The third stage emerged with the Clean Air Amendments of 1970 which rejected the decentralized, state-by-state approach and shifted the burden of proof to industry (Rosenbaum, 1973: Chapter 5). Thus a potentially effective framework for pollution abatement has only just appeared on the scene and has most of its real battles ahead of it.

A general feature of federal pollution control is the extensive use of a regulatory approach to harness the polluter. Centralized regulation falls back on rules which specify what may or may not be done. Hence the incentive approach languishes. A pattern of incentive-oriented public policy would aim at channeling the self-interest of polluters in the direction of socially responsible actions. Under the present system there is no clearly visible incentive to use water (still widely regarded as a "free good") efficiently and rationally *beyond* the requirements of the law. In the meantime, regulations are there to be broken, circumvented, or complied with minimally, and "regulatory agencies have often become the captives of the industries they are charged with overseeing" (Kneese and Schultze, 1975:7; Utton and Henning, 1973:208–216).

Population Policy

The question of population control has long been considered outside the sphere of legitimate government regulation. However, as it became apparent in America that size and geographic distribution of population are causally related to air, noise, and water pollution, energy and resource consumption, and the disappearance of open spaces and various species of animals, demands for public action widened.

In 1969, President Nixon created the Commission on Population Growth and the American Future to study population growth and internal migration trends in the United States, and to recommend policies for dealing with a spectrum of problems bound to population growth in the remainder of this century. In its final report in 1972, *Population and the American Future* (*CPGAF*, 1972) the commission recommended the adoption of a national policy designed to stabilize the size of the population as soon as possible. It urged a slowing of population growth through wider dissemination of birth-control information, easier access to birth-control drugs and devices, and legalization of abortion (*CPGAF*, 1972:163–190). Support for these recommendations came from women's rights groups, and from organizations like Zero Population Growth and Planned Parenthood. Both President Nixon and various members of Congress, including Representative Gerald Ford, directly or indirectly attacked the report, as did private institutions, like the Roman Catholic church and antiabortion "right-to-life" groups. The result has been political stalemate, with little federal action to implement the commission's recommendations.

Due to ineffective national leadership with respect to population policy, attention has shifted to the state level and the courts, where advocates of population planning have won a number of victories. The Supreme Court has decided that states cannot prohibit the sale of contraceptives. In a landmark decision in January 1973, the Court held that states could not prohibit abortions during the first thirteen weeks of pregnancy, although they may enact health-related restrictions from that time on, and act to protect the legal rights of the fetus from the twenty-fourth week. Several states had revoked their antiabortion laws even before the Court's decision. The case in New York was typical; after a bitter battle between various women's rights and birth-control organizations, such as Planned Parenthood on the one side, and the Catholic church and numerous right-to-life groups on the other, the state legislature narrowly overturned previous restrictions. A subsequent attempt to pass a new antiabortion law was vetoed by Governor Nelson A. Rockefeller. Attention has shifted back to the federal levels as antiabortion advocates attempt to secure the passage of a constitutional amendment to prohibit abortion (*NY Times*: 6 September, 9 October 1974).

Given conflicting pressures, it is unlikely that a coherent national population policy will be adopted in the foreseeable future. Similarly, the commission's recommendation that the national government take a lead in guiding future internal distribution of population has also received scant attention from legislators. Traditionally, Americans have been a highly mobile people, and the national government has been reluctant to curtail movement directly. Nevertheless, recently a few states, such as Oregon, have acted to slow in-migration, and numerous local governments have done so through zoning codes (*CPGAF*, 1972:207–229).

Actually there is good reason to believe that government policy on the population issue lags well behind public understanding and flexibility. A national opinion survey by the Gallup organization in April 1974 asked the following remarkable question: "Some people feel that the world will reach a point some day where, because of population and economic growth, there won't be enough water, land, food, and other natural resources for everybody. Other people believe that the world can continue to grow without running into serious shortages because somebody will always be able to solve these problems. Do you yourself believe that sooner or later world population and economic growth will have to be regulated to avoid serious shortages or not?" (the sample queried was 1,865 persons, more than the usual national cross-section; NY Times, 1 December 1974). Sixty-four percent said yes and seven percent were undecided. When asked whether population and industrial growth should be controlled "in the area where you live," fifty-four percent said yes and nine percent were undecided. Evidently the view that America is "overpopulated" and consumes too much is not confined to an exclusive circle of ecologists (Davis, 1970).

RESOURCE MANAGEMENT

The most urgent resource management problem facing the United States in the 1970's stems from the so-called energy crisis. For the first time in history Americans find their demand for energy outstrips readily available supplies. In the summer of 1973, gasoline was already in short supply, primarily because of inadequate refining capacity in the United States rather than any shortage of crude oil. Major oil companies blamed environmental opposition for their failure to build more refining capacity, but critics retorted that the gasoline shortage was contrived to drive independent retailers out of business. Regardless of why the shortage existed, the Nixon administration refused to intervene despite prevalent demands for government action (NY Times, 10 February 1974).

As the gasoline shortage lessened in the early fall of 1973, shortages of propane gas and oil used for home-heating and industrial purposes loomed. Under strong pressure from congressmen from states where propane and oil are used heavily in the winter, the Nixon administration imposed an allocation system for the distribution of these two forms of energy. The shortage of natural gas used for home-heating purposes had been the rationale used by the administration earlier in 1973 to secure passage of a bill to de-regulate the price of natural gas at the wellhead in order to encourage exploration for new supplies (NY Times, 10 February 1974).

The already serious energy crisis was aggravated in the late autumn of 1973 by another outbreak of hostilities in the Middle East. New pressures came in the form of a temporary embargo—now lifted—on oil exports to the United States and other nations friendly to Israel, and through hikes in the price of crude oil, both coordinated through the Organization of Petroleum Exporting Countries (OPEC).

Shortly after imposition of the embargo, President Nixon delivered a special message on the energy crisis, stating that the nation's demand for energy would exceed supply by ten to seventeen percent in the winter of 1973–74. Predicting that the shortage would continue for at least the next few years, until new sources of energy could be developed, he recommended a number of steps to cope with the problem. In the short term, Americans were urged to alter habits of wasteful energy consumption by voluntary measures such as cutting down on driving speed and maintaining home temperatures at a lower level. He also proposed quick congressional passage of an Emergency Energy Act that would allow temporary relaxation of environmental regulations on a case-by-case basis, authorize the imposition of special energy conservation measures, such as restriction of working hours for commercial establishments, provide for the development of offshore oil reserves, reduce speed limits on federal highways, and expand the power of federal agencies to adjust common carrier schedules. Finally, under the title Project Independence, he proposed a massive effort to make the United States self-sufficient in energy by speeding the development of all domestic supplies, including coal gasification, shale oil, and advanced forms of nuclear power. Congress quickly began work on these proposals and enacted several of them before the end of 1973 (NY Times, 24 January 1974).

Despite partial success of the Nixon legislative package, far-reaching energy legislation was not forthcoming. Beset by the Watergate scandal, the administration did little to push energy proposals in its last few months of existence. When President Nixon's successor, Gerald R. Ford, outlined his energy program in October 1974, declaring that the United States has "a real energy problem," he urged such measures as a reduction of foreign petroleum imports, an increase in domestic coal production, and more haste in the development of nonfossil fuels. Although his goal was substantial energy self-sufficiency rather than total independence, President Ford's proposals differed little from those of his predecessor (NY Times, 29 October 1974).

Throughout the spring of 1975 President Ford and the heavily Democratic Congress remained at loggerheads over energy policy. Following his pocket veto of the strong strip-mining regulation bill passed late in 1974, the president put forward a more detailed energy program that called for a gradual end to price controls on domestic oil and natural gas to induce greater production, a heavy duty on foreign oil to reduce American dependency on foreign sources, and more rapid development of offshore oil reserves. Congress refused to act on his program and struggled futilely to develop its own energy program. It did pass another, somewhat stronger strip-mining bill which the president vetoed, as he had the previous bill, on the ground that it prevented the development of too large a portion of the nation's coal resources. Faced with congressional inaction on energy, President Ford used statutory powers he already possessed to impose a one-dollar-a-barrel duty on foreign oil in March and an additional dollar-a-barrel duty in June. In addition he threatened to veto any congressional action to extend price controls on domestic oil (NY Times, 28 May; 4, 6, 8, 11 June 1975).

Several other aspects of the Nixon and Ford administrations' energy proposals have proven controversial. The idea that the nation can become totally self-sufficient in energy within a decade has been rejected by many scientists, who argue that complete independence would quickly deplete domestic resources and exact an unduly high environmental price. Also controversial is the suggestion that environmental safeguards be reviewed on a case-by-case basis, with a view to delaying implementation of some regulations, especially air quality standards, so that "dirty" fuels like coal or high-sulfur oil can provide energy during the transition period. Environmentalists deem this strategy an open invitation to industry, utilities, and auto manufacturers to postpone emission-control deadlines indefinitely. As expected, industry spokesmen have been quick to plead special cases. The resulting picture of eased standards is mixed, however, with both industrial interests and environmentalists scoring occasional victories. For example, while the auto industry has secured a partial postponement of automobile emission controls and some utilities have been permitted to burn coal or high-sulfur oil, environmentalists have blocked the construction of new oil refineries in New England and nuclear generating plants (a more complete discussion of the pollution-control picture follows in the next section) (NY Times, 10, 23 October 1974; 13 November 1974).

Controversy has followed decisions to permit construction of the Alaska pipeline and to authorize selective offshore drilling for oil. Long under attack by environmentalists, the Alaska pipeline, which would carry heated crude oil from the North Slope oil fields south to port facilities at Valdez, had been blocked by a series of successful court challenges. These concerned the inadequacy of the environmental impact statements submitted and legal problems with leasing the right of way. Late in 1973, under growing pressure from energy producers and an energy-hungry populace, Congress passed special legislation prohibiting further court action by environmental groups and permitting construction to begin, with assurances from the oil industry that all possible measures would be taken to safeguard the environment (NY Times, 14, 17 November 1974).

The Nixon and Ford administrations' emphasis on nuclear power sources as the most feasible alternative to fossil fuels has drawn criticism from environmentalists (Curtis and Hogan, 1969). Reporting in December 1973 on the future growth of nuclear generating capacity, AEC Chairperson Dixy Lee Ray revealed that over half of the 10 billion dollars in funds recommended for research into alternate energy sources would be channeled into projects dealing with nuclear generators, especially the newer fast-breeder reactors. She projected that the new reactors would provide over twenty percent of the nation's power by the year 2000. Environmentalists and scientists have challenged the wisdom of this course of action on the ground that such reactors present a high risk of accident, and have charged the AEC with deliberate concealment of dangers (Novick, 1973; 1975). The battle is now in the courts, centered on the adequacy of environmental impact statements submitted by advocates of such reactor development (*NY Times,* 14 January 1974).

In the meantime, sanguine expectations that nuclear power will be the magic wand in America's energy crisis have been rudely deflated. Nearly half of the 191 reactors ordered or under construction have been either canceled (8) or deferred (86) anywhere from five years to indefinitely *(NW,* 17 October 1974). In January 1975 the AEC had bad news to announce about the fast-breeder reactor, whose commercial debut was pushed forward from the 1980's to the 1990's (*NY Times,* 18 January 1975). This clouding of the nuclear power horizon is attributable in large part to escalating costs and construction problems, but also relevant are safety factors, fuel scarcity, technical failures, and plutonium security (Novick, 1974). The fast-breeder reactor is dogged especially with financial difficulties and gives every indication of being a shaky buy in the energy market (Cochran et al., 1975).

Controversy also has wracked the Nixon and Ford administrations' fumbling attempts to organize an effective national energy agency. Even before shortages in the fall and winter of 1973–74, the Nixon administration proposed the creation of a Department of Energy and Natural Resources to exercise authority in energy conservation matters. Congress did not act, however, and the administration was forced to move at the executive-office level, creating an Energy Policy Office (EPO) in July 1973, headed by John Love, former governor of Colorado. The EPO was charged with coordinating national energy policy, but by late November it was apparent that for various reasons—mostly weak administration support—the agency was a failure. In November the EPO was superseded by the Federal Energy Office, which was upgraded subsequently to the Federal Energy Administration (FEA). Its first director was William E. Simon, a former Wall Street investment banker and chairman of the administration's Oil Policy Committee. With strong administration support, Simon (labeled an "energy czar" by the media) was put in charge of developing national energy policy, as well as the mandatory oil, gasoline, and propane allocation programs initiated during the oil embargo. When Simon became secretary of the treasury in the late spring of 1974, his former deputy in the FEA, John C. Sawhill, became the FEA's director (*NY Times*, 2 December 1973; 19 April, 30 October, 1974).

Sawhill, trained as an economist, publicly advocated strong conservation measures, including a heavy tax increase on gasoline, to deal with the crisis. His position was at odds with the Nixon and Ford administrations' emphasis on increasing energy supplies. President Ford requested Sawhill's resignation from the FEA when it became clear that he could not work with Secretary of the Interior Rogers C. B. Morton, head of the interagency Energy Resource Council that had been created to develop a comprehensive energy policy. Frank G. Zarb, an associate director of the Office of Management and Budget, was nominated late in 1974 to replace Sawhill (*NY Times*, 31 October, 26 November 1974).

As of this writing, the worst of the energy shortage seems to have receded; oil imports have increased, and once-familiar lines at gasoline stations have virtually disappeared, as has the outcry for nationwide rationing. Energy experts warn, however, that the problem of energy shortages is far from solved. Indeed, there exists a real danger that a return to seemingly adequate gasoline supplies—despite the high prices—will dull public awareness of the problem's long-range nature and encourage a repetition of wasteful consumption practices. With much public resentment pinning the blame alternately on Arab oil-producing states, large American oil companies, or government ineptness, minute attention has been given to harmonizing consumption patterns with the finitude of fossil-fuel supplies.

The country also faces a growing shortage of other nonrenewable raw materials but little government action has been taken to allocate available supplies. Rather, an informal allocation system, in which suppliers parcel out their stocks to favored consumers, has come into being for many scarce materials. Increased prices have acted as a rationing mechanism as raw-material-producing nations have begun to imitate the tactics of the Arab states and OPEC. Short of government-sponsored rationing programs, not much can be done in the open market to control available supplies. Government stockpiles of strategic materials may occasionally be sold off to affect the availability and price of raw materials, but this is a short-term solution at best. The only other alternative for the government has been in the field of waste recycling.

The federal government has enacted several programs to encourage state and local governments and private firms to develop solid-waste recycling programs for the recovery of valuable raw materials. The Internal Revenue

Service has ruled that industrial development bonds issued to finance recycling facilities are tax-exempt when sixty-five percent of the material recycled by the firm is solid waste. This ruling is an attempt to make recycled materials more competitive in price with materials produced from virgin resources.*

The EPA's Office of Solid Waste Management has made grants to most of the states, and to a number of interstate and regional agencies, to assist the development of waste collection and disposal systems. Grants are also being made for the establishment of recycling demonstration operations. In San Diego, for example, an EPA-sponsored 200-ton-per-day demonstration project will produce over a barrel of low-sulfur fuel oil, 140 pounds of ferrous metals, and 120 pounds of glass from each ton of refuse. In the same vein, the Bureau of Mines has encouraged research into, and demonstration projects for, the recovery of minerals from municipal incinerator residue. Another series of demonstration projects is being run by the Federal Highway Administration to test the feasibility of using waste materials in road building and parking-lot construction. Yet there is no true "national planning of solid waste management" (Rosenbaum, 1973:239–241). A number of measures integral to such planning have little chance, according to environmentalists, of becoming law in the near future. Among them are a national tax on disposable containers, tax incentives for the use of recycled materials and the elimination of depletion allowances on virgin materials, and substantial allocations of money to the development of recycling technology.

As nonrenewable resources become more scarce and prices rise, conservationists hope the economic incentives for recycling will draw industry in that direction.* In the short run, however, the percentage of recycled materials used in producing goods has actually declined over the past few years, in spite of improvements in resource-recovery technology. For example, recycled paper as a percentage of total paper production has dropped from 23.1 percent in 1960 to 17.8 percent in 1969. Virgin materials remain cheaper by traditional accounting methods than recycled materials; the reasons are tax depletion allowances, lower transportation costs (because factories have been located near them), and relatively easy extraction. Traditional accounting methods, however, fail to take into account environmental savings that come from the use of recycled materials. The production of a thousand tons of steel reinforcing bars from scrap rather than virgin ore requires seventy-four percent less energy and fifty-one percent less

---

*Due to recession, discriminatory federal taxes, and regulations favorable to virgin materials, recycling has declined in the past two years, according to the president of the National Association of Recycling Industries (*Environment*, June 1975:22).

*It has been suggested that "to properly recycle our wastes will require an industry perhaps as large as the present automobile industry" (De Bell, 1970:216).

water; it also generates eighty-six percent less air pollutants and fifty-seven percent less mining wastes (*CEQ*, 1973b:200–204). For a variety of reasons, recycling technology has not realized its promise. In spite of all the advantages that might be adduced to justify heavy investment in recycling methods, and in spite of the mounting tide of solid waste (eight hundred million pounds a day on a national basis, due to triple by 1980), "it does not yet appear sufficiently life-threatening and therefore fails to arouse public concern on the scale pollution does. . . . So the solid waste problem is likely to languish, probably until the nation is literally buried in its own refuse" (Rosenbaum, 1973:251).

Land-use planning is an important aspect of natural resource management. With the American population at 210 million, and growing, land is increasingly in short supply. In his 1971 and 1972 environmental messages, President Nixon urged the creation of national land-use policy legislation that would require states to develop and enforce land-use programs protective of the environment. These programs would be subsidized by the federal government. States that fail to participate would lose a substantial portion of their federal funding for highways, airports, and parks. Senator Henry M. Jackson secured Senate passage of a bill authorizing state subsidies to encourage land-use policies, and it is likely that such legislation will be enacted. In a similar vein, the administration proposed in 1971 the passage of a National Resource Land Management Act, which would require the secretary of the interior to protect the environment in the 751 million acres of public domain held in trust by the federal government. Although neither of these two proposed bills has yet passed Congress, they are indicative of heightened national concern (*CEQ*, 1972b:133–134; *CEQ*, 1973b:214).

A major problem in land-use management is how to make more recreational facilities and lands easily available to America's heavily urbanized population (Merriam, 1972). Federal programs have played a major role in helping state and local governments to acquire recreational lands. The Legacy of Parks Program, instituted in 1971, permits the transfer of federal lands to state and local park authorities at a discount of up to one hundred percent of their fair market value. By mid-1972, 144 sites with a total of twenty thousand acres in thirty-nine states and Puerto Rico had been listed by the Property Review Board as available for transfer upon application by state and local authorities.

In 1972, the Department of the Interior's Land and Water Conservation Fund spent 255 million dollars, which was matched by state and local funds, for recreational planning, site acquisition, and the development of facilities. The fund also allocated 101 million dollars to federal agencies to buy lands for parks, recreational areas, historic sites, and wildlife refuges. A similar amount was budgeted for 1973. The Department of Housing and Urban Development (HUD) has an open-space program which also provides financial assistance to state and local governments for the acquisition and development of parks, preservation of historic buildings and sites, and similar improvements. The most recent federal program for the improvement of urban recreational opportunities was the creation of the Gateway National Recreation Area in New York City Harbor, and the Golden Gate Recreation Area in San Francisco Bay (*CEQ*, 1972b:322–325; *CEQ*, 1973b:233).

Population growth and rapid expansion of the economy have gradually reduced wilderness areas to the point where many species are threatened with extinction.* In 1964, Congress passed the Wilderness Act, under which federal lands can be set aside for preservation in a wild state. By 1972, approximately 10.4 million acres were so designated, and another 4.8 million acres have been proposed by the president for inclusion in the program. In 1973, the National Forest Service closed 12 million acres of virgin national forest to lumbering and mining interests in anticipation of their inclusion in the wilderness program. Since most wilderness areas have been established in western forests, parks, and wildlife refuges, the secretaries of agriculture and the interior are identifying areas in the East for possible inclusion in the wilderness system. The designation of federal lands as wilderness areas commonly has been opposed by lumbering, mining, and recreation interests, which argue that resources are being locked up and that the policy is not in accord with the old multiple-use principle (*CEQ*, 1972b:141; *CEQ*, 1973b:227; Rosenbaum, 1973:195).

State governments have also been active in developing programs of land-use management. Many laws have been passed to protect coastal zones and wetlands, regulate power-plant siting and strip mining, and to expand parks, recreational, and wilderness areas, often with the help of federal grants (Haskell and Price, 1973:169–209).

POLLUTION CONTROL

Major federal antipollution legislation has been enacted in the last few years, in response to both public awareness and increased pressure from environmental organizations. The Clean Air Amendments of 1970 called for the EPA to devise national ambient primary and secondary air-quality standards. Drawing on data collected by the National Oceanic and Atmospheric Administration's Environmental Data Service, and its own air-monitoring network, the EPA in 1971 established air quality standards to limit

---

*We can note here what has been aptly called the "Disney Imperative," that is, the destruction of natural environments to make way for artificial ones, like so-called game preserves (Marx, 1969).

particulate matter, sulfur oxides, carbon monoxide, hydrocarbons, nitrogen oxides, and photochemical oxidants in the air. Under the amendments state governments and units under federal jurisdiction, such as the District of Columbia, were required to develop plans that would achieve primary standards for the protection of public health within three years after they had been approved by the EPA. Furthermore, states were to develop plans for secondary standards bearing on aesthetic considerations and vegetation within a reasonable period. Where any state failed to act, the EPA was empowered to draw up a plan for it (*USEPA*, 1972:1–2).

Approximately a year later in May 1972, the EPA approved the plans of fourteen governmental units, and partially approved forty-one other plans. The EPA also granted a two-year extension for primary standards to eighteen states containing major urban areas with heavy pollution from automobiles; however, this action was disallowed by the federal courts, in early 1973, as a violation of the 1970 amendments. In October 1973, the EPA issued final guidelines on restrictions of auto traffic. Another significant court decision, involving the amendments, established that the EPA may not accept any state implementation plan that would allow deterioration of existing air quality, even though it would still be within federal standards (*CEQ*, 1973b:111; *NY Times*, 21 October 1973).

The major source of air pollution in urban areas is the automobile. The federal government began the regulation of automobile emissions with the model year 1968, and the 1970 amendments set stringent emission standards for the 1975 and 1976 model years. In the original law, emissions of carbon monoxide and hydrocarbons by 1975 cars were to be ninety percent below the 1970 levels when there were no controls. The amendments allowed the EPA to grant a one-year extension in meeting the new standards, if it was clearly necessary for the public interest, or if efforts in good faith had failed to produce the necessary technology to meet the standards. An appeal by automobile manufacturers in 1972 for an extension was rejected by Ruckelshaus after three weeks of public hearings. In 1973, however, the EPA allowed a one-year extension for enforcement of the 1975 and 1976 standards, and imposed new interim standards for the intervening years. In December 1973 President Nixon urged another one-year delay in enforcement of the 1975 and 1976 standards because of the energy crisis (*CEQ*, 1972b:110–112; *CEQ*, 1973b:163–164; *NY Times*, 7 November 1973).

A number of other steps are being taken by the federal government to reduce air pollution. In 1972, the EPA issued directives requiring gasoline dealers to provide by July 1, 1974, at least one grade of 91 octane lead-free and phosphorous-free gasoline, the aim being to preclude the fouling of catalytic antipollution devices on cars, as well as to safeguard public health. The EPA and the General Services Administration are supporting several programs for the development of a cleaner automobile engine. The Urban Mass Transit Administration is engaged in similar programs for buses (*CEQ,* 1972b:112–114). Jet aircraft have been another leading source of air pollution in urban areas. In 1970, the air carriers acceded to an agreement with HEW, then in charge of the federal air-pollution-control activities, and the Department of Transportation, to fit over three thousand jet engines with devices that produce more efficient combustion of fuel. By March 31, 1972, in a continuing program, seventy-eight percent of these engines had been retrofitted *(CEQ,* 1972b:114).

The federal government also has moved against stationary sources of air pollution. In late 1971, the EPA defined emission standards for fossil-fuel steam generators, sulfuric and nitric acid plants, portland cement plants, and large incinerators; any newly constructed plants will have to conform, as will existing plants that expand or alter the content of their emissions. The standards cover particulates, sulfur dioxide, nitrogen oxides, sulfuric acid mists, and visible emission. In 1973, EPA standards appeared for asbestos, beryllium, and mercury (*CEQ,* 1972b:114).

The Clean Air Amendments of 1970 impose heavy fines for an assortment of violations. Manufacturers or sellers of autos with engines that exceed emission standards are liable to fines up to ten thousand dollars per vehicle. Owners of fixed emission sources are subject to fines up to twenty-five thousand dollars per day and one-year jail sentences for a violation of standards. A dramatic violation of the 1970 amendments was the manipulation of emission tests by the Ford Motor Company in 1972 to show that pollution-control devices on its 1973 models could function properly for fifty thousand miles.* Ford was hit with a seven-million-dollar fine, but the EPA allowed it to sell 1973 cars if they met modified standards (*NY Times,* 14 February 1973; Edel, 1973).

In summary, it seems fair to say that the federal government, in conjunction with the states, has begun to move effectively in its attack on air pollution. By no means has air pollution been stopped, but real progress in abatement has been made.* Continued watchfulness by environmentalists will be necessary to see that improvement continues, though realities of the fuel crisis may delay timetables (more complete discussion follows in the last section of the chapter).

The Water Quality Act of 1965 is the basic legislation providing for water quality standards and their enforcement on interstate and coastal waters. Standards emanate from state governments and other governmental units under federal jurisdiction, subject to approval (originally by the De-

*A National Academy of Sciences study concludes that pollution-control standards for autos can save 4,000 lives a year (*Environment,* December 1974:22).

*It has been argued forcefully that abatement will not keep pace with the multiplication of air-pollution sources and that bad air is likely to win the day (Brodine, 1972).

partment of the Interior) by the EPA. Plans developed by states and approved by the EPA were to constitute a collective national program for the control and abatement of water pollution. These water quality standards outlined how each waterway was to be used, criteria for measuring water quality appropriate to these selected uses, plans for implementation, and enforcement measures (CEQ, 1970:44; USEPA, 1972:11–12.

The states and local government units had chief responsibility for implementing and enforcing the standards, but once they were approved by the EPA, they became federal standards, and thus subject, if necessary, to federal enforcement. If a state failed to act, the EPA could impose federal standards, but so far the EPA has been successful in negotiating with states to complete them. The standards and antidegradation statements of forty-six states and government units have been fully approved by the EPA, and eight others have had standards partly approved (CEQ, 1972b:165; USEPA, 1972:13–14).

The states are assisted by the EPA in putting their water quality standards into effect through grants for water treatment plant construction. This is the EPA's largest program, with congressional authorization to spend 18 billion dollars in the fiscal years 1973–1975. The waste treatment plants are to prevent discharge of untreated or poorly treated sewage and wastes into waterways. In 1973, the states estimated they would need 60.7 billion for such construction through 1990. The EPA also has authority, under the Water Pollution Control Act of 1956, to give state and interstate agencies funds to establish and maintain adequate water-pollution-control programs. These grants are used for a variety of purposes, including purchase of technical equipment, planning activities, enforcement, and monitoring. The EPA, in conjunction with the states, is developing a national network of water-quality monitoring stations. At present there are nearly six thousand such stations, about five thousand of them operated and funded by state governments (CEQ, 1973b:172–173; USEPA, 1972:13; NY Times, 15 October 1974).

In addition to these programs, the EPA helps state and local governments develop river-basin and regional water-quality-management plans; the Water Pollution Control Comprehensive Basin Planning Grants are intended to encourage their development. Over four hundred have been approved by the EPA (USEPA, 1972:14–16).

The most recent major federal legislation on water pollution came in 1972, when Congress passed, over the veto of President Nixon, an amendment to the Water Pollution Control Act of 1956, which requires plants discharging wastes into waterways to obtain a permit. States can set up their own permit programs under federal guidelines, but the EPA can take over issuance of permits should it judge a state's program ineffectual. Firms and individuals dumping without a permit, or in qualities and quantities beyond permit limits, are subject to a maximum fine of twenty-five thousand dollars and one year in prison. So far over thirty thousand permits have been applied for, but only some five hundred have been issued. The goals established in the amendment are that all industries discharging into waterways will use the "best practicable" technology to control pollution by 1977 and the "best available" by 1983. Under this act in August 1973 the EPA began to set forth effluent-discharge limits for specific industries (*CEQ*, 1973b:168–175).

In addition to air- and water-pollution-control programs outlined above, the federal government is engaged in cleaning up pollution from its own twenty thousand installations. In 1970, President Nixon issued Executive Order 11507, requiring all federal facilities to meet national air and water quality standards. Even larger funds have been budgeted for this purpose: 115.7 million dollars in 1971, 280.4 million in 1972, and 314.6 million in 1973. Along similar lines, a 1973 presidential executive order denied federal contracts, grants, or loans to companies convicted under the Clean Air or Water Pollution Control Acts (*CEQ*, 1972b:123–124).

Under the Federal Insecticide, Fungicide, and Rodenticide Act, the EPA suspended in 1972 the use of DDT for nearly all purposes (although the administration has now requested a partial lifting on the ban), and has banned, or placed restrictions on, the use of other chemical compounds, frequently over the vocal objections of chemical producers (*NY Times*, 28 May, 2 October 1974). A number of states also have passed legislation regulating the use of pesticides. To provide more comprehensive policy direction, Congress enacted in 1972 a Federal Environmental Pesticide Control Act which, among other things, gives the EPA a larger role in the regulation of pesticides. Also under congressional consideration is a proposed Toxic Substance Control Act that would empower the EPA to regulate the use of hazardous materials in commercial products and processes. Another type of chemical pollution is dealt with by the Lead-Based Paint Poisoning Prevention Act of 1971, under which the Bureau of Community Environmental Management of HEW conducts a program—albeit a poorly funded one—to reduce or eliminate lead-based paint poisoning (*CEQ*, 1973b:183–184).

With increased use of radioactive materials, particularly in nuclear power plants, radiation pollution has become a potential hazard. The EPA, in cooperation with HEW, the AEC, and the Department of Defense, recently reviewed all existing federal radiation protection criteria and policies, in line with its responsibility to protect public health and advise federal agencies on possible radiation exposure problems. The AEC recently drew up tougher rules for the dumping of radioactive wastes at sea, and established a program to reduce the amount of radioactive effluent from all AEC-owned facilities. Stricter safety measures to prevent reactor overheating were also ordered in late 1973, with the hope that they would reduce the chance of accidents. State efforts to regulate the emission of radioactive materials have increased significantly, even though the Supreme Court decided in 1972 that a state government cannot impose its own radiation protection standards on activities licensed by the AEC *(CEQ,* 1972b:129–130).

Noise pollution has received considerable attention. The Clean Air Amendments of 1970 established the Office of Noise Abatement in the EPA and required it to report to Congress. The office held an extended series of hearings and made a report in 1972 that thoroughly reviewed the sources and dangers of noise pollution. In 1973, Congress enacted a Noise Control Act that empowers the EPA to set limits on noise emission by construction and transportation equipment. Late in 1974, the EPA issued noise-control standards for trucks using interstate highways *(NY Times,* 23 October 1974). Under this act, the EPA also conducts extensive research into noise pollution.

State and local governments have been active in shaping anti-noise legislation, but enforcement responsibility is often so decentralized among various local agencies as to be ineffectual. The EPA will probably be able to assist local governments in developing better enforcement techniques in the near future. Municipal expenditures for noise abatement have increased markedly in a number of large cities, but as a percentage of the municipal budget, they remain rather small *(CEQ,* 1973b:195–200).

PARTICIPATION IN INTERNATIONAL PROGRAMS

The United States has played an active role recently in the development of international cooperation to protect the environment. It participates, for example, in the United Nations Commission on the Future which was established in 1971 to maintain a constant review and assessment of future trends in scientific and social developments, such as pollution, natural resource consumption, and population growth, and to suggest policies for consideration by the United Nations (Gardner, 1972).

More recently the United States assisted in the planning and conduct of the United Nations Stockholm Conference on the Human Environment. Since the conference, it has joined with fifty-three other nations in the newly created United Nations Governing Council for Environmental Programmes that will oversee such activities as the worldwide Earthwatch on environmental problems, and will administer the Environmental Fund (Johnson, 1972).

Outside the United Nations the United States has entered into a number of bilateral and multilateral agreements on environmental problems. Since the 1950's, the United States has signed several conventions aimed at lessening the damage to the environment from oil spills and dumping at sea. In 1972 the United States, along with some ninety other nations, ratified a convention of the dumping of wastes at sea, which calls for a cessation in the discharge of toxic and noxious substances in the ocean. A year later it joined seventy-nine other nations in a pact that forbids commercial trading in 375 endangered animal species and allows trade in 239 others only by special permission of the nations involved *(UN.* 1971:392; *CEQ,* 1973b:179–180; *NY Times,* 3 March 1973).

The United States, as a member of NATO, participates in its Committee on the Challenges of Modern Society (CCMS), which was established in 1969 at American urging. The CCMS has developed a number of environmental pilot programs, including one on air pollution in which the United States is the pilot nation under study *(CEQ,* 1973b:363).

Along with other industrialized nations, the United States also contributes to the efforts of the Organization for Economic Cooperation and Development (OECD) to combat environmental degradation. The OECD is working to harmonize environmental standards and develop practical methods of financing pollution-control measures. The OECD's environment committee studies technical methods of reducing the emission of pollutants. In 1972, for example, the United States initiated a special meeting of the committee which led to a recommendation that member governments minimize the release of polychlorinated biphenyls *(CEQ,* 1973b:363–364).

In 1972 the United States joined with environmentalists from over a dozen nations, including the USSR and Japan, to create an International Institute of Applied Systems Analysis. The institute will seek out solutions to problems created by industrialization such as overpopulation, urban growth, pollution, and energy shortages. The latter topic will be its first area for study. The institute, which is located in Austria, is led by a Governing Council chaired by a representative from the USSR, whereas its executive director is an American. Other members include Bulgaria, Czechoslovakia, Canada, Japan, West Germany, Italy, Poland, and the United Kingdom *(NY Times,* 4 October 1972).

As part of the rapprochement between the United States and the USSR, a series of steps have been taken on environmental matters. The 1972 Nixon–Brezhnev Summit Conference resulted in the signing of an agreement for the conduct of thirty joint-studies of environmental problems (see Soviet section for details). Other agreements that touch environmental concerns have been signed by private American corporations with the Soviet government. In 1972, Occidental Petroleum signed an agreement with the Soviet government to cooperate in the development and export of fuels, and similar agreements have been reached with other corporations, although their implementation is now in doubt because of the cancellation of the 1972 Soviet–American trade agreement. The Occidental agreement was followed in 1973 by an agreement with General Electric for the joint development of electric power generating technology. Behind these agreements there is an American desire to tap Soviet fuel reserves, and in the long run, to sell pollution-control equipment to the USSR (*NY Times,* 9 January 1972; 13 January 1973).

Bilateral agreements on the environment have been concluded with other nations as well. We have already taken note of the United States–Canadian Great Lakes Water Quality Agreement of 1972. In the same year, the presidents of the United States and Mexico agreed to work out a solution to the high salinity content of the Colorado River and to have lower-level officials hold regular meetings to discuss other common environmental problems (*CEQ,* 1972b:84).

The United States has been less directly involved with developing nations in trying to stop environmental degradation. Most developing nations seem bent upon economic growth regardless of environmental damages, and they tend to interpret suggestions by developed nations that environmental considerations should not be neglected as a device to keep them in a position of economic dependency. The developing nations are concerned that aid to them may have environmental protection strings attached to it by the donor nations that will adversely affect their economic growth, and they fear environmental controls in developed nations may have an adverse impact on the export of certain materials. The tension between developed and developing nations on these issues came out clearly at the Stockholm Conference. The United States and other developed nations unsuccesfully opposed a recommendation adopted at Stockholm that called for increased aid "adequate to meet the additional environmental requirements" of developing nations. The United States also opposed unsuccessfully a recommendation that developed countries should pay compensation to developing nations for any decline in their exports caused by the developed nations' environmental regulations (*NY Times,* 11 June 1972; *Time,* 19 June 1972; Skolnikoff, 1972).

BUDGET ALLOCATIONS

Studies conducted in 1971 by the CEQ, the EPA, and the Department of Commerce on the economic impact of pollution control concluded that adequate pollution controls, while costly, would not permanently damage the economic vitality of most industries. While severe impact will be felt by marginally efficient operations, some of which undoubtedly will be forced to close, the long-term impact on large producers will be marginal (*CEQ*, 1973b:73–117).

Recent surveys by the CEQ and other government agencies have been able to project likely investment and operating outlays by government and private industry for pollution control in the period 1972 to 1981. Using current emission-control standards, and assuming that existing effluent and

Table 7.1   Distribution of Estimated Total Environmental Expenditures in the United States, 1972–1981.

Sector	Water	Air	Solid Wastes	Other	Total
Public expenditures	28.1%	3.1%	5.9%	—	37%
Private expenditures	16.2%	35.6%	10.2%	2%	63%

Source: The Fourth Annual Report of the Council on Environmental Quality, 1973, p. 98.
Note: Total public expenditures for the period were approximately $101,500,000,000; total private expenditures for the period were approximately $172,700,000,000.

emission-control technology is improved, the CEQ offers the following estimates (in constant 1972 dollars): air pollution, 105.6 billion dollars; water pollution, 121.3 billion; noise pollution (aircraft only), 2.7 billion; radiation from nuclear power plants, 1 billion; solid waste management, 41.8 billion; and land reclamation, 4.5 billion. The total projected expenditures will be 274.2 billion dollars. The federal, state, and local governments are to contribute 101.6 billion dollars of the total. Industry will pay 88.3 billion, including 44.4 billion for water-pollution control and 38.4 billion for the control of air pollution from stationary sources. Presumably much of industry's pollution-control costs will be passed on to the consumer, who will pay an estimated 84.3 billion dollars, of which 58.8 billion will go for automobile-pollution controls and 25.5 billion for solid-waste disposal (*CEQ*, 1973b:93; Rosenbaum, 1973:161–164; Kneese and Shultze, 1975: Chapter 6).

Although the total pollution-control cost of 274.2 billion dollars for the period from 1972 to 1981 is large, it represents only 2.5 percent of the estimated total GNP for the period. If present emission and effluent standards have been fully met by 1976 (which seems unlikely), additional costs for pollution control will be incurred only to operate, maintain, and replace existing equipment (*CEQ*, 1973b:116).

Increased commitment of the federal government can be seen from the growth of actual financial outlays over the past few years (McCamy, 1972:227). In 1970, the government spent 751 million dollars on pollution control and abatement; in 1971, this figure reached 1,149 million dollars, and climbed again in 1972 and 1973 to 1,314 million dollars and 1,917 million dollars. In 1974, estimated outlays reached the 3,111 million dollar mark. Of this figure, 1,735 million dollars was financial aid to state and local governments, 590 million was for research and development, 266 million for direct federal abatement and control operations, 345 million for the reduction of pollution from federal facilities, 15 million for manpower development, and the remaining 160 million for a variety of other pollution-control programs *(CEQ,* 1973b:90).

Despite these increased outlays, there are still danger signs on the road ahead. Continued public willingness to accept larger public and private expenditures for the environment is likely to be affected by a number of current developments. Inflation will doubtless cut into the sums appropriated at all levels of government for such "frills" as a cleaner environment, while higher costs will reduce the impact of money actually spent on pollution control. The relatively limited local tax base of many communities will also limit the revenue-collecting power of state and local governments. Perhaps most important, however, in the assessment of future financial commitments is public willingness to accept a higher priority on environmental protection, even in a time of financial pressures and likely energy shortages; without such a commitment, it will be virtually impossible to sustain the political momentum of the environmental movement, which has been a force in the passage and strict enforcement of antipollution measures.

PROGRAM EFFECTIVENESS

An attempt to assess the effectiveness of current environmental programs must be guided by knowledge that five or ten years ago there were few serious efforts at pollution control, waste management, and the like. The distance the United States has come from point zero has been great; today there is a wide gamut of federal, state, and local programs dealing with nearly every type of environmental problem. If, on the other hand, one's goal is a society devoid of environmental corruption, existing programs leave much to be desired.

Despite difficulties, some preliminary judgment must be made. Pollution-control programs already developed, and being improved on the basis of short-lived experience, seem to be reasonably effective. Most environmental legislation has not been around long enough for a thorough test, but early results seem positive. Despite opposition from industry and other anti-environmentalist groups, progress has been toward cleaner skies over major urban areas and better water quality in what have been the nation's worst polluted waterways.* Even the Detroit River and Lake Erie, initially regarded as polluted beyond reclamation, have stirred toward renewed life. The energy crisis, which most environmentalists initially thought was the death knell of the environmental movement, has been a mixed blessing. Certainly it has had its negative effects, but more in weakening the will of the Nixon and Ford administrations to seek stricter environmental safeguards than in turning the general public against the environmental movement. In a recent survey, only two percent of those interviewed placed primary blame for energy shortages on steps taken to protect the environment. At the national level, pressures generated by the energy crisis will, at the very least, postpone the implementation of air quality standards. As we have noted, a number of decisions have already been made concerning the postponement of auto-emission-control standards. Other administration proposals would permit offshore oil drilling in previously prohibited areas, such as the leak-prone Santa Barbara coastline; accept weaker strip-mining controls in the interest of producing coal more inexpensively; go ahead with shale development, despite unsolved environmental problems; oppose previously endorsed land-use legislation; permit the renewed use of DDT in certain areas; suspend secondary air quality standards—that is, those standards relating to things other than health considerations—under some circumstances; allow some electric generating plants to burn coal until 1980; and suspend for as much as ten years certain big-city traffic-management plans aimed at improving air quality. In many cases, these recommendations have emerged only after bitter debate within the administration between pro-industry figures and the EPA and the CEQ. Even under the best circumstances, these proposals will mean long-term delays, especially with respect to air pollution.

But the picture is not totally bleak. While it is premature to judge how many of the administration's recommendations will be accepted by Congress, it is certain that environmental interests will mobilize their now-considerable political talents in opposition. Declining public consciousness of the energy crisis also may work in favor of the environment. Perhaps even more important, however, is the fact that the energy crisis has reminded the nation of its precarious relationship with the environment and the world's finite resources. If anything, the crisis has served to point out what environmentalists and conservationists have been saying for years—that the nation must adjust growth and consumption patterns to correspond with reality, and that a major industrial nation cannot consume finite resources

---

*This judgment should not encourage complacency. There is more than enough cause for worry, as in the case of fouled drinking water across the nation (Crossland and Brodine, 1973).

and pollute the environment with no thought of the future. Environmentalists themselves, when taking the long-range view, have acknowledged that the short-term setbacks may well be an acceptable price to pay for raising more fundamental questions.

THE SOVIET UNION

LEGISLATION

Until recent years, Soviet environmental legislation has tended to be phrased in generalities which set forth often vague and unrealistic policy goals and then has called upon existing state agencies to take appropriate steps for their implementation. The first important set of wide-ranging environmental laws came into being between 1957 and 1963 in the form of general conservation enactments passed by the union republics. The 1960 Russian Republic law was typical, for it contained general directives on air and water pollution and on the conservation of land and other natural resources. But since the enforcement of its provisions was entrusted either to agencies such as the Sanitary Epidemiological Service or to the polluting enterprises or municipalities themselves, it has little impact (*Pravda*, 28 October 1960). While numerous ordinances were passed during the first half of the 1960's, their cumulative impact was diminished by the high priority given economic growth and by a low level of environmental awareness (Goldman, 1972b:293–301; Clawson and Kolarik, 1974:3–22).

By the middle of the 1960's, the deteriorating state of the environment had begun to become apparent to Soviet leaders. The latter half of the decade and the 1970's have been marked by a new outpouring of environmental legislation or the strengthening (or perhaps merely the more stringent enforcement) of existing regulations (Clawson and Kolarik, 1974: 22–45). In addition to the normal flow of legislation and routine policy pronouncements from top Soviet leaders, occasional special enactments were handed down, with considerable publicity, to deal with critical problems like the fate of Lake Baikal. Discussed in detail in subsequent sections, these new laws and regulations came more realistically to grips with specific problems of air and water pollution or resource depletion than had their more vaguely worded predecessors. In addition, other areas of legislation such as land-use control, public health, agricultural policy, and mining began to show the impact of greater environmental awareness.

The 1968 Principles of Land Legislation contained important environmental safeguards. The restoration and recultivation of strip mine areas was ordered within one year, and collective and state farms and other land users were instructed to take steps to prevent erosion and salinization. Industrial users were also instructed to prevent the contamination of land by industrial sewage. Administratively virtually all of the authority for the implementation of these measures was vested in the union-republic governments or the user agencies themselves (*Pravda*, 14 December 1968; Pryde, 1972:184–199).

Other recent legislation has also dealt marginally with protection of the environment. The 1969 Health Law strengthens the hand of health inspectors policing industry, and the new Collective Farm Statutes call upon farm managers to conserve endangered natural resources, especially land (*MG*, 23 December 1969; *Pravda*, 30 November 1969). Other laws were passed concerning the creation of greenbelts around urban areas, timber cutting and log floating, and a number of other environmental issues. New mining legislation is also now under consideration (*Izvestiia*, 18 January 1975). A comprehensive overview of environmental policy was handed down by the USSR Council of Ministers and the Communist Party Central Committee in January 1973, which instructed all planning organs to make yearly long-range conservation and environmental plans an integral part of the economic plan (*Pravda*, 10 January 1973). The resolution instructed the Ministry of Chemical and Petroleum Machine Building to speed the design and construction of pollution-control devices; the State Committee on Science and Technology and the Academy of Sciences were to pool their pollution-research forces in a common scientific-technical council. The Hydrometeorological Service was charged with monitoring overall pollution levels. Existing ministries were told to design and make operational emission-control devices by the end of 1975, and auto emissions were to be reduced to sanitary norms by the same deadline. The resolution also pledged measures to bring open refuse dumps into conformity with sanitary standards and to speed the construction of new sewage treatment plants.

This outpouring of new environmental legislation must be treated with considerable caution, however, since it has done little to alter the basic institutional setup through which day-to-day environmental policy is made and enforced. The January 1973 resolution is typical. While seemingly broad in scope and filled with the best intentions, it offers only a modest tinkering with institutional responsibilities and prerogatives. Responsibility for introducing pollution-control facilities is again laid at the door of the same industrial ministries and municipal governments that repeatedly failed to meet previous deadlines. Little has been done to change the ministerial framework that has proven inhospitable to environmental protection in the past. The same weaknesses also characterize much of the legislation passed from the mid-1960's onward. Sweeping legislative mandates to save the environment have translated quickly into business-as-usual when real problems are dealt with on a piecemeal basis at the ministerial level.

Population Policy

For nonenvironmental reasons, the declining birthrate has confronted Soviet demographers and political leaders with a tough dilemma. On the one hand, they are concerned that any overall decline in population growth will result in an even tighter labor market in coming years. Even more disturbing is the fact that the birthrate has dropped much faster among ethnic Russians than among the central Asian peoples, confronting political leaders with the disquieting prospect that the dominant Russians will become a diminishing minority within the Soviet Union as a whole. Kremlin leaders also view the maintenance of a high birthrate as closely linked to their continued great power status, especially vis-à-vis China. On the other hand, Soviet leaders have been reluctant to divert large sums of capital to necessary improvements in housing and child-care facilities that would encourage a higher birthrate, especially among the more urbanized European sections of the nation.

Officially denying the link between rapid population growth and environmental deterioration, Soviet policy makers have favored virtually unlimited population expansion, although a few demographers have begun to warn of its future impact on the quality of life (Mote, 1971:58; Pryde, 1972: 167–168; VF, February 1973:38; March 1973:46–47; April 1973:64). Specific pronatalist policies have encouraged higher birthrates, although their funding has always been limited. Financial allowances are offered to large families, and day-care facilities are supposedly provided for working mothers, although demand for these services always outstrips supply. Maternity benefits and child support to low-income families have also been offered in recent years. In 1974, the government initiated a new program specifically designed to provide additional funds to larger low-income families; when fully in operation, the program will affect 12.5 million children (*NY Times*, 28 September 1974). Soviet demographers have proposed even greater child support grants, part-time work arrangements for mothers, and preferential housing assignments for larger families as a way of increasing the birthrate (Cohn, 1973:41–55; PRB, 1972a). Negative sanctions also play a role; bachelors and childless couples are taxed more heavily, and social pressures are applied to encourage early marriages and larger families. Soviet media regularly chide bachelors and childless couples for avoiding their duty to society and squandering their income on themselves, while women with ten or more children are awarded the honorific title of "Hero Mother" (PRB, 1972a; LG, 30 August 1972, 27 September 1972, 21 April 1971; SR, 17 September 1970).

Despite these measures, there seems little prospect that the existing decline in the national birthrate or the imbalance between the European and Asian sectors will be altered radically in the near future. Easy access to birth-control facilities will keep the birthrate low among urbanized and better educated parents. Restrictions on abortions were removed in 1955, primarily to avoid the danger of then-frequent illegal abortions, and since that time the ratio of abortions to live births in some cities has risen to three to one. The limited availability of day-care facilities for the high percentage of working mothers has also encouraged smaller families, as has the higher cost of living in urban areas, where one- or two-child families have become the norm. In contrast, few of these restrictions are operative in the central Asian republics, where the proportion of working mothers is far lower, and social and cultural pressures for larger families are felt more strongly. While Soviet demographers point out that the European birthrate could be increased by greater expenditures for child support services and financial incentives to parents, and the central Asian rate reduced by more rapid urbanization of the region, government officials have been unwilling to divert necessary capital for such programs (Cohn, 1973:41–55; PRB, 1972a).

Soviet authorities have made constructive efforts over the last several decades to limit the size of the large urban complexes through an internal visa system which requires that a prospective resident of a crowded urban area already have arranged for employment, or that he be closely related to a present resident. Despite vigorous efforts by the authorities, considerable slippage occurs, especially for short-term laborers or tourists who can arrange to live with friends or relatives (university dormitories are especially closely watched for such transgressions; special passes are required to enter both the university compound and dormitory areas in order to eliminate unauthorized residents). The determination of proper population density is usually based more on the city's ability to provide minimal services than on any desire to preserve a desirable quality of life for the average urbanite. Soviet authorities have attempted to siphon off some of the population pressure through the development of middle-size cities in already settled areas, the creation of new industrial centers in sparsely populated regions, especially Siberia, and the construction of new satellite towns near existing urban centers. But the attraction of the larger cities—especially Moscow—continues, and attempts to secure appointment to this political and cultural hub seemingly remain a favorite sport of educated and upwardly mobile Russians serving out their assignments in the provinces (Listengurt, 1971:121; Sharov et al., 1973:112–118; Strongina, 1974: 132–142).

Resource Management

Until recently Soviet authorities have held that comprehensive resource management was unnecessary in light of the nation's presumably inexhaustible supplies of natural resources. It was assumed that continued exploration would constantly turn up new and adequate storehouses of minerals and fuels to meet all future needs. Only in recent years have Soviet scientists and industrialists acknowledged that the nation may someday feel the resource pinch. Even with this realization, the official view of the resource depletion dilemma holds that a combination of the continued discovery of new deposits and the increased sophistication of extractive and recycling technology, coupled with the greater use of synthetic materials, will provide sufficient supplies of raw materials to permit virtually unlimited future growth.

Given this attitude, it is not surprising that comprehensive resource planning has been largely nonexistent. As of 1972, only the Russian Republic had a plan for resource use that attempted to coordinate the activities of a number of ministries (Kramer, 1973a:73). Recent government enactments have instructed industry to reduce losses in the extraction of ore, improve the efficiency of resource utilization, recycle production wastes more effectively, and improve research on efficient resource use. A new mining law designed in part to curtail waste is now in the drafting stages (*Izvestiia*, 18 January 1975). Western energy shortages have also prompted Soviet leaders to speak out forcefully for more careful utilization of fossil fuels, and for accelerated development of new oil and gas fields. Beginning in 1974, yearly and long-range plans are to be worked out for the rational utilization of natural resources as a part of the economic production plan, with the state planning agencies charged with monitoring the use of potentially scarce raw materials, including fuels (*Pravda*, 10 January 1973; *Izvestiia*, 5 June 1974; Kirillin, 1972; Shelest, 1973). It is likely, however, that the addition of a resource consumption plan to the already complex and incompletely enforced criteria by which production agencies are evaluated will do little to lead to the more rational use of natural resources. As we have noted, the fact that raw materials are given nonscarcity prices to industrial consumers militates against their thoughtful conservation, as does the fact that extractive industries are charged only token rates for their mining sites. (Kramer, 1973b:364–373).

While the OPEC-sponsored oil embargo had little direct impact on the Soviet Union, the specter of some of the world's major industrial powers reeling over the prospects of energy shortages had a sobering effect in Moscow. Although Soviet leaders were quick to point out that their nation was unaffected by energy shortages, steps were taken to conserve existing supplies and to hasten the development of new power sources. A new campaign to conserve energy in industry and commercial establishments was launched, and the media publicly chided wasteful consumers as a lesson to others. Additional oil and gas fields were put into operation on an accelerated timetable, the possibility of offshore drilling off Sakhalin was considered, and shale oil deposits were tapped in Estonia *(NY Times,* 28 November, 26 December 1973; 13, 14 January, 12 April, 13 October, 13, 21 November 1974; Elliot, 1974:243–246). It is probably the case that some portion of this expanded production is destined for export to fuel-poor nations. In an era when expended foreign trade earnings are being counted on to finance the massive influx of Western technology to modernize the Soviet economy, Kremlin leaders have been quick to realize the market potential of their abundant fuel supplies, as well as of other mineral resources. Fuel export agreements have been reached with the United States, several western European powers, and fuel-hungry Japan, and the prices charged the Soviet Union's East European allies have risen dramatically in the last year. Although Soviet leaders have evidently had some second thoughts about new major foreign sales until they are confident that domestic needs can be met, fossil fuels remain the most rapidly expanding segment of foreign trade *(NY Times,* 1 June 1974, 25 January, 25 June 1975; Goldman, 1974; Elliot, 1974:252–258).

Because of possible energy shortages, greater attention has been given to the development of nuclear-power electric generating plants, although the program is still seen more as a long-term answer to energy needs. Having placed the world's first nuclear electric power reactor into operation in June 1954, Russian scientists have maintained their technological lead in a number of critical areas, especially the development of breeder reactors and controlled fusion. At present there are nine major commercial reactors in operation, with more under construction. In 1973, the USSR had an installed nuclear generation capacity of 2,770 megawatts, which represented about 1.4 percent of the nation's total electric generating capacity. By 1980, generating capabilities are expected to reach 30,000 megawatts annually.

Breeder reactors, which generate more fuel than they consume, have also been a special interest of Soviet scientists. Development began in 1949, and the first breeder reactor was recently completed and submitted to testing in November 1972. According to Soviet reports, breakdowns have been frequent. While the reactor, located at Shevchenko, has a generating capacity of 350 megawatts, it is presently working at thirty percent of its rated output because of design problems. A larger reactor in the 600-megawatt range is under construction in Beloiarsk, and future plans call for two more reactors rated at 700 and 1,000 megawatts. Even at present capability levels, the Soviet Union has the world's largest network of breeder reactors and is thought to be years ahead of the other nuclear powers in the development of breeder-reactor technology (Pryde and Pryde, 1974; *NY Times*, 14 June 1974, 26 May 1975).

In addition to the accelerated development of fossil-fuel and nuclear energy sources, the Soviet Union has begun to experiment with more esoteric systems. As we have previously noted, extensive experimentation has been done on tidal-power generating plants. Experimentation has also begun with the use of geothermal energy drawn from the heat of the earth's core. Already one five-thousand-kilowatt power station draws its generating power from steam piped to the surface, and thermal water is used as a natural heating system for several small towns in the Caucasus (Pryde, 1972:131; *Pravda*, 30 March 1973).

The importance of land conservation and reclamation has also become apparent to Soviet authorities in recent years as the per capita amount of productive agricultural land has slowly declined despite the addition of millions of hectares of fertile land through the drainage of wetlands and the irrigation of arid regions. Land-use legislation has grown more cautious in recent years, with both the 1968 land law and the 1969 revisions of the collective farm charter urging more careful use of fertile land and increased efforts to claim unused lands or to increase the fertility of presently cultivated areas. While the new land law asserts the primacy of agricultural usage of land and provides for payments to collective and state farms for the diversion of land to nonagricultural uses, in some areas many problems remain. Although economists have devised a complex land evaluation system, in practice the use of the land is usually determined by the competitive demands of a number of agencies, with the politically influential ministries or construction agencies usually winning out over agricultural or conservation-oriented users (Kramer, 1973b:366–367; Pryde, 1972:26–27; Stebelsky, 1974; *Pravda*, 10 January 1973).

Much land is also lost through strip mining. Although both the 1960 Russian Republic law and the 1968 land law call for the restoration of strip-mining areas, only a small portion of the total area is ever returned to productive use. Even a less ambitious 1966 act designed to prevent losses of fertile agricultural land has been largely ignored. Each year opencut operations lay waste thirty to thirty-five thousand hectares. In the Moscow region, only five hundred hectares of the over eight thousand destroyed have been reclaimed. At the root of the problem are the limited capital allocations provided by the mining industry and the high cost of restoration, which has been estimated at over five thousand rubles per hectare (Goldman, 1974:13–17; Bogdanov, 1970; *LG*, 31 May 1972).

Concern with land management and wildlife conservation has also led Soviet authorities to set aside certain wilderness areas designated as *zapovedniki*, or "forbidden areas," within which no commercial or industrial activity is permitted. There are presently approximately ninety *zapovedniki* in existence covering an area of 4.3 million hectares (the precise number varies from year to year because of the reclassification of existing *zapovedniki* and the creation of new ones). In comparative terms, this represents only .29 percent of the total land area of the USSR, while nature reserves account for 2.9 percent of total land area in the United States and over 4 percent in Japan (but, to be fair, the total land area of these nations must be taken into account). These reserves serve the dual purpose of preserving vast tracts of virgin wilderness and of permitting endangered species to breed without interference. Many reserves were formed with the latter purpose specially in mind. The *zapovedniki* also serve as conservation research stations, with many directly administered by research institutes. Limited tourism is permitted, but only under carefully controlled conditions. It must be noted, however, that Soviet authorities have frequently looked the other way as industry encroached upon the reserves, usually to extract raw materials. In some cases when large mineral reserves were discovered, whole *zapovedniki* have simply been reclassified to permit industrial development (Pryde, 1972:45–67).

The Soviet Union has also had considerable success in the preservation of endangered species. Species which had been critically endangered, such as the beaver, sable, otter, and pine marten, have made a strong recovery. Among the presently endangered and therefore carefully protected species are the European bison, kulan (a kind of steppe donkey), walrus, Ussuri tiger, polar bear, Caspian tiger, wild horse, sika (a kind of deer), wild goat, Persian fallow deer, and fur seal. Other potentially endangered species are under study. Less success has been had in the protection of game birds, which have been killed off in massive numbers primarily by air pollution and deforestation rather than by overhunting. Conservation problems include strict limitations on the commercial hunting of endangered or potentially endangered species and the creation of special protected breeding areas called *zakalniki*, which may be set aside either temporarily for less endangered species or permanently for those under serious threat of extinction. Despite controls over hunting, poaching remains a serious problem. Moreover, Soviet attitudes toward predatory animals permit unlimited killing without any regard for preserving an ecologically sound balance. One hopeful note is that conservation policy makers have now begun to think more in terms of preserving entire interlocked ecosystems than in terms of protecting particular endangered species (Pryde, 1972:68–91; Fisher et al., 1969; Kirillin, 1972; Gerasimov, 1971:217).

Water recycling in industry has developed rapidly in recent years, now accounting for fifty to sixty percent of the water consumed by industry throughout the nation. Given proper technology and capital, however, this could increase into the eighty to ninety percent range for most industries. More extensive recycling would relieve increasing pressure on freshwater supplies, especially in industrial areas. But any large-scale improvement would depend upon massive capital outlays. Such expenditures are unlikely as long as industrial water users are charged nonscarcity prices for fresh-water and are permitted to tap municipal drinking water supplies (Grin and Koronkevich, 1968:45–62; LaMothe, 1971:29; Goldman, 1972b:81–95; Bushtuyeva, 1971; Iandyganov, 1973:83–88).

Sewage recycling through the creation of sewage farms near large urban areas represents another form of waste recycling. Rich in plant nutrients, municipal sewage can, with proper health safeguards, be used to produce bountiful harvests. In 1970, seventy to eighty thousand hectares were fer-tilized in this way, with further development planned (Lvovich, 1969: 115–116; Goldman, 1972b:282).

Industrial recycling of raw materials is also commonplace. About thirty percent of the sulfuric acid used by Soviet industry is obtained from waste gases containing sulfur dioxide. In Irkutsk, organic substances extracted from sewage are used in industry, and in Perm, a cable plant now makes copper cable from materials previously dumped into the Kama River. In 1969, thirty-six percent of the nation's steel output was based on scrap, with half of the recycled metal coming from steel works themselves, twenty-two percent from metal fabricating plants, and the rest from general sources. Twenty-four percent of the tin consumed that year also was ob-tained through recycling. Despite these accomplishments, the fact remains that many valuable resources are lost each year. Only in a few cases do the costs of new raw materials exceed the cost of recycled materials, even including the low labor costs involved, thus making it economically rational for factory directors to divert capital and workers to recycling efforts. In most cases recycling efforts are probably motivated more by the scarce supplies of some raw materials or by the chronic uncertainty of deliveries than by price considerations alone (Kirillin, 1972; Powell, 1971:630–631; USDI, 1969; *Pravda*, 26 January 1975).

The recycling of paper, bottles, and other commodities from the general public is in the hands of the Chief Administration for the Procurement and Processing of Secondary Raw Materials, and much of the practical work of gathering and turning in such items is done by voluntary labor such as the Young Pioneers or by individuals themselves. Despite this high degree of organization, many tons of paper that are collected each year are wasted because the paper factories are unable to process it, and one Leningrad winery has enough recycled bottles in its warehouse for all the city's six wineries for the next three years. The waste collectors themselves face many practical problems, including inadequate and inconvenient collection points, insufficient staff and warehouse space, and the uncooperative responses of factory directors whom they serve (*Izvestiia*, 4 June 1972, 22 May 1975; *KP*, 12 January, 10 April 1974; 25 June 1974).

POLLUTION CONTROL

Any effective pollution-control program must depend for its success upon an adequate network of monitoring stations capable of pinpointing industrial and private offenders. In the Soviet Union, responsibility for monitoring emissions has until recently been solely in the hands of the Sanitary Epidemiological Service of the Ministry of Public Health, which, as of 1967, had 4500 monitoring stations spread throughout the country, 3000 in rural areas and 1500 in towns and cities. In larger industrial centers, measurements of the level of SO_2, CO, formaldehyde, dust, and soot are taken several times daily, with less thorough monitoring in rural areas. These tasks make up only a small part of the sanitary inspectors' work load, however, since they are also saddled with additional responsibilities for supervising the planning and construction of new factories and numerous other health-related tasks. In January 1973 Soviet officials tacitly admitted the inadequacy of the service's performance in calling upon the Hydrometeorological Service also to assume responsibilities for monitoring overall pollution levels (*HEW*, 1970:688–689; Mote, 1971:85; Kramer, 1972:ll; *Pravda*, 10 January 1973).

Pollution abatement work is hampered by the short supply and low technical quality of emission-control devices. Air-pollution-control devices are supplied to industry by the All-Union Gas Purification and Dust Trapping Association, which rarely produces more than thirty to forty percent of its yearly quota because of inadequate factory facilities and capital. As a result, many factories have taken to building their own emission-control devices, usually with amateurish results. The overall national picture concerning the use of any form of emission-control equipment is frightening. As of 1968, of all the factories registered as sources of air pollution, only fourteen percent were fully equipped with control devices, with another twenty-six percent only partially outfitted. Between 1962 and 1965, only 5 factories of the Ministry of the Timber, Paper, and Woodworking Industry received biological purification facilities despite the fact that the ministry had scheduled 134 for such devices. While the regime has recently placed higher priority on the manufacture of purification equipment, the backlog of orders is huge. Even when installed, purification devices usually work far below their potential efficiency because of poor maintenance. Of the 150 water purification devices inspected in one key industrial region in the mid-1960's, twenty-five percent operated normally, thirty percent were below capacity, and forty-five percent were not in operation or were considerably below peak performance. At the factory level, emission-control work is handed over to the chief engineer, who is usually untrained for and unwilling to assume these new duties. Factory directors themselves are often unwilling participants in pollution abatement programs, especially since expenditures in this area are not reflected in the plant's profit calculations (*Izvestiia*, 13 September 1972; 17 November 1973; *KP*, 30 September 1972; *LG*, 30 January 1974; Mote, 1971:86–88, 1974; Kirillin, 1972; Kramer, 1972:8–15).

Pollution control is made even more difficult by the paucity of waste treatment experts in the Soviet Union. By 1970, the Moscow Engineering and Construction Institute, the major training facility for this specialization, had produced only twenty-two graduates in waste treatment management. At the factory level, pollution-control work is treated as a low-status occupation, and its workers are generally paid far below the scale of "productive" laborers. Consequently the level of personnel turnover is high and the skill level low (Powell, 1971:624; Kramer, 1972:8, 1973a:41).

Air quality standards were first established in 1949 at the request of the USSR Ministry of Public Health, whose Sanitary Epidemiological Service was charged with their implementation. Revised in 1963, these standards set maximum permissible short-term and daily concentrations for potential pollutants. The union-republic-level environmental laws passed from 1957 to 1963 instructed existing factories to take steps to meet these standards. A special resolution concerning air pollution in the Moscow area was issued in January 1963, followed by a separate law for the Russian Republic in 1965. Additional regulations on industrial and auto emissions were also handed down in 1963.

To the casual observer, the array of safeguards against air pollution by industry seems impressive. No new factory may begin operations, and no existing factory may introduce new production processes, until local sanitary inspectors certify that purification facilities are adequate and operational and that maximum permissible concentrations of harmful pollutants will not be exceeded. Once operations have begun, the sanitary inspectorate monitors emissions to keep them within acceptable limits, and other inspectors from the All-Union Gas Purification and Dust Trapping Association, which builds most of the nation's emission-control devices, periodically check facilities to assure efficient operation. Industries unable to meet emission standards for technical reasons must be located from six to fifteen kilometers from inhabited areas, depending on the type of industry. Even controlled industries are to be separated from residential areas by air-pollution buffer zones, with the strictest guidelines reserved for high-pollution industries such as metal smelters, petroleum refineries, pulp and paper mills, cement and fertilizer mills, and chemical industries, which must be located two thousand meters from the nearest residential communities. Efforts have also been made to convert many industries and urban areas to low-pollution fuels such as gas or oil, although the scarcity of these fuels in industrial areas has greatly increased the cost of such conversions (Mote, 1971:83–84; Pryde, 1972:151–152).

To the careful observer, however, it is evident that these controls are far from adequate. Despite the apparently wide-ranging powers of the sanitary inspector, his authority is frequently ignored or overridden by higher officials intent upon meeting production goals. Emission-control devices, as I have noted, are frequently inadequate even when operating at peak efficiency, and lax factory personnel seldom operate such facilities at optimal levels either through disinterest or inadequate skills. Even the regulations governing the siting of pollution-prone factories are frequently violated both by central planners, who place enterprises in existing residential areas, and by factory and ministerial personnel themselves, who build residence complexes for their workers within the supposed buffer zone (Mote, 1971:101; LG, 24 May 1972; Kirillin, 1972).

The nation's major nonindustrial sources of air pollution—thermal power stations, domestic boilers, and autos—have also been the targets of abatement programs. To lessen the local impact of thermal power stations, gas and oil have been substituted for low-grade coal, especially in high-priority urban areas. But despite these efforts, coal and peat continue to be used in over half the nation's thermal power stations, and further conversions to oil are likely to be slow-paced, given the relative scarcity of low-sulfur petroleum deposits. The fear of energy shortages has also led to the reconversion of some power stations back to coal. Moreover, these stations are excluded from regulations that govern the siting of industry at a safe distance from residential areas since they are not regarded as productive enterprises (Goldman, 1972b:126—127; Mote, 1971:102–103; NY Times, 13 October 1974; Kirillin, 1975:43–51).

The environmental impact of domestic boilers for heat and hot water has been reduced through the creation of thermal-energy generating plants which serve large segments of densely populated urban areas. While the use of these plants has eliminated scores of small, inefficient boilers, it has frequently created a localized pollution threat of its own, unless carefully controlled. Conversion to these multipurpose units has been most extensive in the larger urban areas—Moscow again leads the nation—but in smaller cities and rural areas domestic furnaces continue to belch forth pollutants (Goldman, 1972b:276).

The need to control auto emissions has been recognized only recently by Soviet environmentalists. Officials have been experimenting with a battery-powered vehicle and with various filtering devices, and high-pollution ethyl gasoline has been banned. However, the most promising corrective actions lie in the recently initiated inspection of individual vehicles and in the continued development of electrically powered urban mass transit. In the former case, Soviet officials have recently established a standard of two percent carbon monoxide in auto exhaust fumes and have begun to establish a network of inspection stations in major cities, where vehicular traffic is heavily concentrated. Given the poor maintenance of the average Soviet auto and the recent birth of the program, effective control is probably years in the future, especially with the projected rapid growth in the total number of vehicles. Of greater short-term impact is the continued development of electrically powered trolleybus, tram, and subway systems. While critics correctly note that the electrical power has to be generated somewhere, it is usually technically easier to control emissions from a limited number of large power stations, hopefully located far from residential areas, than to police the emissions of countless thousands of individual vehicles (Mote, 1971:94; SL, 1972:14; Bush, 1972:22–24; *Izvestiia,* 12 October 1973).

As has typically been the case, Moscow emerges as a showcase of the regime's efforts to cleanse the air. Soviet authorities claim that as a result of the strict application of the control programs outlined above, in the last ten to fifteen years air pollution in the Soviet capital has been reduced to between one-third and one-fourth that of previous levels. A roughly similar assessment is offered by Marshall Goldman, who notes that by 1960, largely as a result of the introduction of pollution-control measures in the 1950's after postwar reconstruction was largely completed, ash emissions had fallen to just over twenty percent of the 1950 level, and sulfur oxides had dropped by one half. Although further progress in cleaning the air was slowed in the 1960's with the development of the chemical industry in and near the capital, by the early 1970's it was possible for both Soviet and Western authorities to agree that emissions had dropped dramatically. But despite this improvement, the skies over Moscow remain less than pure. In 1970, Soviet power engineers candidly admitted to Goldman that concentrations of harmful pollutants often exceeded legally permissible norms, a situation worsened by frequent temperature inversions over the city. Even local authorities guardedly admit to continued violations, noting in a 1973 report on air quality that "as a rule" pollution in the capital does not exceed permissible norms (Promyslov, 1973; Goldman, 1972b:128–129).

The improvement of air quality in Moscow is due in large measure to the preferential treatment received by the city. Moscow was the first Soviet city to build an effective network of monitoring stations. The use of local fuels, high in sulfur and ash content, was restricted, and many factories and domestic boilers were converted to oil or gas far more rapidly than in other regions. Centralized steam plants for heat and hot water also decreased overall pollution levels. By 1971, sixty-five percent of all buildings in Moscow received heat and hot water from such stations, and by 1980 this figure is to top ninety percent. Moscow has also received the lion's share of emission-control devices. Most dramatic has been the regime's decision to close down or to move offending industries from the city and to limit the construction of new factories. While such measures had been long within the power of local officials, they were applied with vigor for the first time in the late 1950's. Within the last decade, nearly three hundred offenders have been moved from the city or compelled to redesign their production facilities to reduce emissions, and the new master plan for the city calls for additional closings. In all fairness, however, it must be noted that these stringent measures have hit hardest against technically obsolete or marginally unimportant installations, and some new factories have appeared within the city (Mote, 1971:103–105; Promyslov, 1973; Kirillin, 1972; Goldman, 1972b:126–129; Bush, 1972:29).

Unfortunately the generally good overall results obtained in Moscow have not been achieved elsewhere. With the concern of Soviet authorities focused primarily on the comparatively more serious problem of water pollution, investments for air-pollution-control facilities have lagged in nonpriority areas. Evidence of continued violations of air-pollution norms and outright evasion of pollution abatement regulations is reported regularly in the Soviet press (Kirillin, 1972; *Pravda*, 21 September 1972; *SE*, 7 July 1972). Unlike the situation with serious instances of water pollution, there is no single case on record in which an *ad hoc* environmental lobby formed to put pressure on the government to deal with a serious air-pollution problem.

The 1960 Russian Republic conservation law was typical of early attempts to limit water pollution (*Pravda*, 28 October 1960). It ordered water users to install purification facilities to cut emissions to legally permissible norms, and the opening of new factories was forbidden until such facilities were operational. Permits to discharge specific amounts of pollutants were to be obtained from state officials and renewed every three years, with the permissible emission levels determined by local officials and all other water users. The discharge of harmful pollutants into drinking-water-supply areas was subsequently forbidden regardless of the level of purification, although this regulation has been poorly enforced.

In December 1970, new Principles of Water Legislation were laid down at the national level with the understanding that union republics would issue new regulations to conform to the national enactment (*Pravda*, 12 December 1970). In many ways, the new water law merely repeated former injuctions against pollution. Water users were again enjoined to take steps to preserve waterways from contamination. The dumping of industrial wastes and refuse without proper treatment was prohibited, and factories and other production organizations were instructed to provide purification facilities. These directives were further strengthened by the January 1973 party and state resolution instructing union republics, in conjunction with the USSR Ministry of Land Reclamation and Water Resources, the USSR Ministry of Public Health, and other relevant agencies, to work out plans for terminating the discharge of untreated or inadequately treated sewage into waterways already heavily polluted or where a depletion of existing freshwater supplies has been predicted. No timetable was established (*Pravda*, 10 January 1973).

Measures have also been written into law to end the dumping of sewage, oil, and bilge water from commercial vessels on inland waterways and on the high seas. Shipping officials have been instructed either to purify or to store sewage wastes onboard, and port cities have been ordered to prepare facilities to transfer and process these wastes. A halt in the dumping of oil, fuel, and bilge water has also been ordered, with uncommonly high fines of up to twenty thousand rubles provided for serious violation (*VVS*, 6 March 1974; LaMothe, 1971:51–74; Goldman, 1972b:293–299).

The regime has also taken steps to control water pollution from agricultural and mining sources. The use of DDT has been banned, and farm officials have been instructed to exercise greater care in the use of other pesticides (Pryde, 1971:20–23; Bushtuyeva, 1971; LG, 4 December 1974). The environmental dangers of chemical fertilizers have also been impressed on agricultural officials, who have been cautioned to exercise greater care in the future. However, the pressing need to increase food yields from the presently cultivated hectarage will undoubtedly limit the effectiveness of these warnings. Mining officials have also been ordered to limit mine runoff, especially from open-pit operations, but the overall effectiveness of such controls will be limited by the extremely high cost of land restoration.

Special resolutions have also been issued in recent years concerning the preservation of specific bodies of water. Lake Baikal has been the subject of several special enactments establishing pollution-control standards for local pulp mills, calling for stricter controls on the dumping of industrial and municipal wastes in the lake's tributaries, and limiting logging operations (*Izvestiia*, 8 February, 1969; *Pravda*, 24 September 1971; 20 November 1974). A special cleanup program was launched in the mid-1960's for the Moscow River, and special regulations were issued in March 1972 for the Volga and Ural river basins (Goldman, 1972b:84–104; *Pravda*, 17 March 1972). The need for such enactments itself testifies to the weakness of existing pollution-control legislation; without such special attention, these important waterways were seen as doomed to unabated contamination.

Despite these wide-ranging safeguards for water quality control, effective pollution-control measures have been limited to a few key waterways (Mote, 1971:66). The Moscow River, where restoration measures have been largely successful, has become a showcase of the regime's antipollution policies. Now officially labeled as "clean," the river has returned since the 1960's from a polluted and lifeless condition. In the mid-sixties, the regime initiated a well-orchestrated program to clean the river, including periodic flushing of the channel by releasing water held in storage upstream, thorough dredging of the river bottom, selective closings or relocation of high-pollution industries, and massive, preferential allocations for industrial purification facilities and sewage treatment centers. One Moscow official notes with pride that the program has led to the installation of over five hundred new purification devices by 1975.

Despite this special attention, problems remain. Both the Moscow party committee and the city soviet have complained of continued violations by industry and acknowledged that "a great deal of work remains to be done." Planned expansion of the city's sewage treatment system has also fallen behind schedule, and little effort has been made to control the discharge of industrial and municipal effluents into the Moscow River's tributaries upstream from the capital, although regional officials have recently worked out long-range plans for the entire watershed (Promyslov, 1973; LaMothe, 1971:4; Goldman, 1972b:101–104; LG, 3 June 1970).

In more recent years, Soviet officials have turned their attention to the intensely polluted Volga and Ural basins. A joint resolution issued by party and government authorities in March 1972 called for the construction of waste-purification facilities in 421 factories and municipal sewage-treatment installations in fifteen cities. In the Soviet republic of Kazakhstan, a program has been initiated to end dumping of untreated municipal wastes into the Ural by 1980, although the funding arrangements, which make both local industry and municipal government jointly bear the costs, will create problems of financial buck-passing. Construction firms in the region have been instructed to give high priority to the completion of industrial and municipal waste-treatment projects, although continued construction delays were reported early in 1974. Commercial vessels on the Volga and the Ural have been ordered to terminate the dumping of effluent and bilge water, and key cities along the two rivers have been instructed to provide facilities to handle these onboard wastes.

While some notable results have been achieved, especially in curtailing emissions from individual factories, the full implementation of this cleanup program has been retarded by the evasive responses and occasional defiance of production-oriented ministries and municipal officials. Soviet environmentalists are quick to point out that some factories and city governments have been slow to construct purification facilities, with a significant portion of budgeted funds remaining unspent (*SR*, 1 July 1972; *Pravda*, 17 March 1972; 5 December 1973; *LG*, 23, 30 January 1974; *Izvestiia*, 9, 22 October 1974; 5 December 1974; 10 April 1975).

For the nation as a whole, Soviet officials admit that serious water pollution remains a problem despite recently accelerated efforts to cope with it. In his report on conservation and the environment before the September 1972 session of the Supreme Soviet Deputy V. A. Kirillin, head of the State Committee on Science and Technology, admitted that many rivers and lakes remained intensely polluted by industrial or municipal sewage, or by fertilizer and pesticide runoff. While he detailed with some pride a number of recently initiated or accelerated abatement programs on an industry-by-industry basis, in virtually all cases he acknowledged the continued existence of "serious shortcomings" (Kirillin, 1972). His conclusions are shared by the chairman of the Russian Republic Soviet's Conservation Committee, T. S. Sushkov, who told the Soviet of numerous instances of freshwater misuse by industry and agriculture and complained of continued emission violations by the metallurgical and chemical industries of the Russian Republic (Sushkov, 1972). Nearly two years later, in December 1974, similar complaints about industry and the slow construction of factory and municipal purification facilities were again voiced before the Supreme Soviet's conservation committee, indicating that violations and delays were continuing (*Izvestiia*, 5 December 1974).

As in the United States, the array of government regulations and unofficial industrial guidelines on uses of nuclear energy and disposal of nuclear wastes evolved slowly as scientists and industrialists experimented with military and peaceful uses of the atom. Effective regulation of the potential environmental dangers of this potent source of energy was limited by the high priority granted to the rapid development of nuclear weaponry, which stressed ever larger stockpiles or more sophisticated warheads rather than adequate environmental safeguards. Environmental safeguards even for the peaceful uses of the atom were hard to implement because of ignorance about the long-term ecological and health hazards of radiation, and because so little was known about the safe disposal of nuclear wastes. The official veil of secrecy that surrounded the military use of nuclear energy further restricted research into its environmental impact and retarded the emergence of effective pressures from the scientific community for stricter controls.

By the mid-1960's, awareness of the environmental dangers of nuclear radiation had risen to a point where regulations governing peaceful uses of atomic energy were tightened. In 1969, new radiation safety standards were enacted which brought maximum permissible exposure levels for the general public and workers in nuclear installations more into accord with the levels suggested by the International Commission on Radiation Protection. Operating procedures for industrial reactors and nuclear power generators were also revised, but not before previously lax standards had resulted in at least one serious instance of radiation exposure in a Moscow installation. New regulations also ordered that any nuclear generating plant had to be located at least ten kilometers from populated areas, and thirty-five kilometers from major urban centers, a sufficient buffer against incidental radiation leaks, but totally inadequate in the event of a failure of the reactor's cooling system—Soviet reactors have no secondary backup cooling system —and subsequent exposure of the fuel core.

The adequacy of Soviet regulations controlling the disposal of nuclear wastes is also questionable. Fuel rods and other radioactive solid wastes are usually dumped untreated into the Black Sea, and there is evidence to indicate a harmful effect on marine life. Even if Soviet officials turn to the burial or partial treatment of such wastes, environmental problems will remain. The treated solid wastes remain so highly radioactive that they require deep burial in cooled underground chambers, which have been plagued by difficulties in Western prototypes. Even the direct burial of unprocessed wastes encounters the long-term environmental threat of poisoning underground water supplies (Pryde and Pryde, 1974; LaMothe, 1971:48; Goldman, 1972b:142–143; USDC, 1970; NY Times, 26 May 1975).

Effective noise-pollution control has proven difficult in the Soviet Union because of the low priority attached to such quality-of-life issues and the lax enforcement of existing standards. The 1969 Public Health Law Principles instructs local soviets and other state agencies, including economic enterprises, to limit noise levels in factories and residential areas, and most cities have passed local ordinances concerning maximum permissible noise levels. Late in 1973, the Council of Ministers issued a stronger resolution concerning noise abatement which called upon industry to reduce noise levels, especially in residential areas. Other ministries concerned with land, air, and sea transportation were instructed to take similar steps (Izvestiia, 23 November 1973).

If Moscow's experience is typical, such regulations will probably prove inadequate. Despite the creation of a special noise-abatement committee by the Moscow city soviet, complaints continue from noise-weary residents. The new regulations have proven especially inadequate to the task of controlling noise in the huge apartment complexes, which comprise most of the residence dwellings in the city, for no preventive steps may be taken against individual offenders before 11:00 P.M. Critics of the Moscow regulations also note that local police officials take a tolerant attitude toward "noise hooligans," although they could, if they wished, fine offenders on the spot. The stiffest fines are reserved for the excessive auto horn use, but they are infrequently applied. Local sanitary inspectors of the Sanitary Epidemiological Service are also empowered to play a role in noise abatement, but they are few in number and more concerned with other environmental and public-health tasks.

New guidelines for apartment construction have also been laid down in recent years to ease noise pollution. Plans for large residential buildings call for improved soundproofing, thicker walls and ceilings, and more careful installation of noisy machinery and elevators. Apparently sanitary inspectors, who are responsible for examining construction plans for possible health or environmental violations, have begun to scrutinize housing construction more carefully; a Moscow official of the inspection service recently disclosed that his office had ordered revisions in roughly forty percent of the plans for new housing because of potential noise abatement violations. Meaningful progress on a nationwide scale will depend, however, not only on the continued vigilance of abatement officials—and probably also on the continued complaints of harassed residents—but also on the economy's ability to supply huge quantities of high-quality construction materials and acoustical insulation, a questionable proposition given the secondary priority attached to housing construction and the shoddy workmanship usually evident in its construction.

Regulations governing the siting of residential areas near noisy factories or major streets and highways have long been in existence, but with the exception of certain high-priority areas, they are little enforced. In the Moscow area, new housing plans take account of these noise abatement regulations, but noise control in already densely populated industrial sectors has proven difficult. Measures have been taken to limit freight traffic on certain arteries, especially in the evening hours, but little can be done during the day. Flights over urban areas have also been prohibited, further reducing city noise levels, and civilian and military airports are located far from urban complexes (Bush, 1972:24–25; Promyslov, 1973; JPRS, 1970b, 1970c; Pryde, 1972:158; LG, 3 December 1972; Vasin, 1975:21).

PARTICIPATION IN INTERNATIONAL PROGRAMS

Increasingly dependent upon oceanic fisheries because of the pollution of her inland waterways, the Soviet Union is a party to a number of international and bilateral agreements concerning high-seas fishing and the protection of spawning and feeding areas. In the Atlantic, it has been a member of the International Commission for Northwest Atlantic Fisheries since 1958, and of the Northeast Atlantic Fisheries Commission since 1959. A number of bilateral treaties governing territorial fishing rights and fish takes have been reached concerning Atlantic fisheries, especially with Norway, but recent attempts to reach an agreement with the United States have snagged on Soviet unwillingness to permit inspection of her fishing vessels and to limit the catch of a species of flounder important to New England fishermen.

In the Pacific, the USSR has reached separate agreements with Japan and the United States. Soviet and Japanese interests first clashed in the mid-1950's, when increased Japanese high-sea takes of pink salmon affected the Soviet catch in her own territorial waters. By mutual agreement reached in 1956, the Sea of Okhotsk and large sections of the Sea of Japan and the Bering Sea were placed off limits to Japanese high-seas salmon fishing. In more recent years the agreement has been enlarged to include other species (Mote, 1971:67; Pryde, 1972:89–91; Mathisen and Bevan, 1968: 23–53).

Since the mid-1950's, a number of agreements have been reached between the United States and the Soviet Union concerning Pacific fisheries. The most recent, reached in February 1973, extends previous agreements to limit the Soviet take of species of special interest to American fishermen in return for greater Soviet docking rights at American ports in the Pacific. The agreement also forbids certain fishing practices such as the use of nets for crab fishing and places certain disputed areas around Kodiak Island off limits to Soviet vessels during the American fishing season. Both nations have agreed to the creation of fisheries claim boards, one each in Moscow and Washington, D.C., to settle disputes between fishing vessels that might interfere with one another in Pacific waters, although the use of the boards will be completely voluntary (*NY Times*, 22 February 1973).

Soviet authorities have been less willing to enter into effective international agreements for the protection of the whale. Sharing with Japan the status of one of the world's most important whaling nations, the USSR has consistently resisted pressures to limit whale harvests, although Soviet authorities did promise in June 1975 to phase out one of the three Antarctic whaling fleets as a gesture to conservationists. While technically a member of the International Whaling Commission, the Soviet Union has regularly exceeded set quotas for different species of whale, quotas which were themselves set by the commission far in excess of the limits suggested by conservationists. Before the 1971 whaling season, in which the United States agreed to stop whaling for one year to protect overhunted species, the USSR, Norway, and Japan agreed to carry international observers to verify kill quotas. Despite this agreement, the Soviet fleet left harbor before the observers could board ship. While subsequent agreements have been reached concerning specific species, both the Soviet Union and the International Whaling Commission continue to resist pressures to limit whale kills, including an outright rejection of the recommendation of the United Nations Conference of the Human Environment for a ten-year ban on all commercial whaling (Bush, 1972:30; Ehrlich and Ehrlich, 1972:130; *NY Times,* 24 June 1975).

The Soviet Union has become a party to a number of international agreements concerning the protection of migratory animals and birds. Soviet conservationists have played an important role in the restoration of the once-endangered European bison and have been particularly strong advocates of international measures to protect the polar bear and the fur seal. The USSR also is a party to a 1964 agreement to preserve natural resources in Antarctica. Soviet scientists and conservationists have been active participants in the International Union for the Conservation of Nature and Natural Resources, which functions to coordinate research on wildlife and resource conservation. It must be noted, however, that the USSR has not become a party to the international treaty which bans the trading of rare or endangered species, undoubtedly because it would severely limit Soviet fur sales to other nations (Pryde, 1972:85–91).

Soviet authorities have been far more reluctant to enter into international agreements concerning pollution abatement. Long unwilling even to admit that the Soviet Union added its share of harmful effluents to the world's seas and oceans, Soviet leaders have approached the question of international controls with jealous regard for their national sovereignty. Soviet representatives to the preparatory conferences for the United Nations Conference of the Human Environment held in Stockholm in 1972 repeatedly stressed their reluctance to enter into any binding multilateral agreements or to envisage the creation of a supranational authority that would implement conference decisions. The USSR subsequently boycotted the Stockholm meeting and abstained on the United Nations resolutions concerning the establishment and financing of the environmental agency set up by the conference, although paradoxically it did vote in favor of locating the agency in Nairobi, Kenya, largely in response to political pressures from the third world nations.

Political considerations have also frequently tainted Soviet cooperation in international pollution-abatement programs. The last-minute refusal to participate in the Stockholm Conference stemmed from the exclusion of the German Democratic Republic, which was barred by a General Assembly resolution which restricted attendance to United Nations members or participants in the work of its functional agencies. Despite concessions that would have permitted East Germany to attend with observer status, Soviet representatives boycotted the meeting. Similar political considerations have also affected the timing, if not necessarily the substance, of other international or bilateral environmental programs. The development of Soviet–American cooperation in the environmental field is in large measure a consequence of their growing *détente* on more fundamental issues, and there is evidence that the pace of the implementation of its provisions is regarded by both nations as a bellwether of current political developments (Bush, 1972:30; Pryde, 1972:135; *NY Times*, 13 February, 22 September, 16 December 1972; 5 February 1973).

Soviet leaders have shown greater willingness to enter into more limited functional or bilateral agreements. In 1972, the USSR, along with ninety other nations, signed a convention controlling the dumping of radioactive wastes and other pollutants into the oceans, and she has entered into a number of multilateral agreements with other riparian states to cleanse the oceans, international waterways, and inland seas which the USSR shares with other nations, including the badly polluted Baltic Sea (*NY Times*, 14 November 1972; Goldman, 1972b:284–285; Pryde, 1972:90; Bush, 1972:30; *LG*, 4 December 1974; *Pravda*, 14 March 1975).

The Soviet–American agreement on joint environmental studies, signed at the 1972 Moscow summit meeting, is a unique departure for Soviet officials since it provides the first opportunity for bilateral cooperation between superpowers on environmental questions. While not an active abatement program in itself—the pact does not commit either side to the application of safeguards against pollution—the agreement does provide for the widespread exchange of environmentalists and conservationists and the initiation of joint study projects on thirty separate environmental topics. These include joint studies of air and water pollution problems on a matched case-by-case basis and coordinated research into fields such as urban environmental problems, earthquake prediction, the development of new urban centers, and wildlife preservation. By mid-1973, the initial exchanges of scientists and environmentalists were already well under way, and experts on both sides predicted that the full implementation of the thirty projects would lead to the exchange of hundreds of environmental specialists (*NY Times*, 22 September 1972; 5 February 1973; CEQ, 1972a, 1973a, 1973c, 1974a, 1974b, 1975).

BUDGET ALLOCATIONS

While Soviet officials note with pride that appropriations for pollution abatement have doubled from 1966 to 1971, the actual sums expended have fallen far short of the need. Soviet authorities place the cost of improving the water supply and sewage treatment facilities at a conservative 17 to 20 billion rubles, although Western authorities predict that the actual figure will be much higher. Expenditures to date fall far short of even the more modest Soviet figures. John Kramer has calculated that between 1967 and 1971, only 1.6 billion rubles were actually spent on such installations. Soviet authorities give a more optimistic assessment, noting that the 1975 budget alone places environmental expenditures at 1.8 billion rubles, although this figure includes all funds for pollution abatement, conservation, and resource-management projects. Even the widely acclaimed special programs for selected rivers and water basins are wide of the mark. Although no projections of future expenditures are available for the nation as a whole, Soviet officials have budgeted over 1 billion rubles to clean up the Volga and Ural drainage basins, 700 million of which will be allocated for purification facilities in over four hundred factories, and 300 million rubles for sewage treatment in fifteen key cities. Moscow alone has allocated 400 million rubles over the next five years for water treatment facilities. But despite the favorable local impact which these allocations will bring, the total expenditures are still far short of the needed amounts for the nation as a whole (Kramer, 1973a:97–98; LaMothe, 1971:5; Bush, 1972:28; Goldman, 1972b:68–69; Kirillin, 1972; Bushtuyeva, 1971:3; *SL*, July 1972:15,22; Levin and Udovenko, 1974:60–70; *Pravda*, 3 April 1975).

Expenditures for air-pollution control have grown even less rapidly, in part because the problem is regarded as less serious by Soviet authorities. In the Russian Republic alone, slightly over 155 million rubles were spent on air-pollution control from 1959 to 1967, excluding the cost of the conversion to cleaner fuels such as natural gas. While these expenditures have brought about an improvement in air quality in some high-priority areas such as Moscow, its nationwide impact has been slight (Sushkov, 1969:6; Mote, 1971:95, 1974:19–21).

Budgetary allocations fail to tell the complete story concerning environmental expenditures. Frequently the large allocations mentioned in well-publicized announcements are expected to come from existing ministerial or local governmental budgets, always hard pressed for funds and little motivated to give high priority to environmental matters. Even when special allocations are provided, they are routinely channeled through existing agencies, which frequently leave these funds unspent or divert them to nonenvironmental purposes. At the factory level, directors frequently shift funds allocated for emission purification equipment to other uses, if in fact they are successful in obtaining these appropriations from their ministries. The low priority attached to sewage treatment and pollution-control projects by construction firms and the long waiting list for emission-control devices also reduce the effectiveness of current budgetary allocations (Mote, 1971:95–97; *KP*, 30 September 1972; *LG*, 30 January 1974; *Pravda*, 24 March 1969; Kramer, 1972:15; *Izvestiia*, 13 September 1972, 17 November 1973, 18 April 1974).

PROGRAM EFFECTIVENESS

Any overall assessment of the success of Soviet environmental policy must distinguish between the routine enforcement of abatement legislation and those exceptional cases in which the regime has launched special programs to clean the air or purify the waterways of high-priority regions such as the nation's capital, Lake Baikal, or the Volga and Ural basins. In such cases, the impact of abatement and restoration projects has been dramatic, although Soviet authorities are still quick to admit that pollution problems remain, especially in the Volga and Ural River areas. While these special projects frequently leave the day-to-day enforcement of abatement regulations to existing control agencies or to the user agencies themselves, they do serve to focus national attention on pressing environmental problems and to cut through the lethargy of frequently complacent local government officials and the opposition of production-oriented ministries and factory directors. This is not to say, of course, that the regime has solved these vexing environmental problems overnight through mere proclamations from top Soviet leaders; in most cases, harmful pollutants still find their way into the air or water, although usually in greatly reduced amounts. And this is not to argue that influential industrial and municipal polluters do not continue to wage a rearguard political action against stricter environmental controls. But it is clear that these special programs and high-level commitments from top political leaders have strengthened the hand of Soviet environmentalists and pollution abatement agencies against offending parties.

Routine enforcement of antipollution measures has been far less successful. As we have noted in earlier sections, mandated pollution-control programs by industry have lagged behind scheduled implementation dates. Technical problems and the limited availability of capital also make effective pollution control difficult. Pollution-control technology and the manufacture of purification equipment are inadequate, as is the training of pollution abatement technicians. Enforcement of pollution-control measures is also made difficult by the small staff and limited powers of state control agencies. The lax legal sanctions which sanitary inspectors may impose against violators have previously been noted, as have the relatively low status and political influence of pollution abatement agencies. The local police and state prosecutors often assign a low priority to those facets of environmental protection which are within their legal power. Local government has also usually proven a willing ally of industrial rather than environmental interests.

While these technical and legal obstacles are formidable, in the long run the primary shortcoming of Soviet authorities in meeting the challenge of the environment can be attributed to *political* factors. It is primarily a failure of the ruling Communist Party elite to accept the political costs of reordering national priorities to initiate adequate abatement programs. We are not speaking essentially of the economic trade-off costs involved in reorienting national priorities; such adjustments would be difficult, as they would for any industrial society. But in the Soviet case, overall pollution levels are notably less intense than in the United States or Japan, and the nation is less likely to feel the constraints imposed by fuel and raw-material shortages. The real political problem is much deeper. Having built a modern industrial nation through a system of authoritarian political and economic institutions which dominated virtually the whole of the society and which placed the highest priority on rapid industrialization, Soviet authorities have been reluctant to surrender these prerogatives and goals —and the implicit legitimacy which accompanies them—through the recognition of new environmental priorities.

JAPAN

Environmental Legislation

To a casual observer, the legal apparatus created to guard Japan's environment must appear exemplary and comprehensive, perhaps the most thorough body of national environmental legislation in the world.

The fundamental document is the 1967 Basic Law for Environmental Pollution Control, which was amended in 1970 to delete an ambiguous phrase to the effect that environmental quality must be harmonized with continued development of the economy. Prior to 1967 no significant government policy existed in the area of environmental protection. This basic law defines pollution, marks off areas of responsibility, comments on control measures and standards, and expatiates on general policy. Environmental pollution is delimited to mean the contamination of air, water, soil, and the presence of noise, vibration, ground subsidence, and offensive odors, as they impinge on human health and the living environment. This definition omits radioactivity. The basic law is most striking in its preoccupation with human health. The conceptual framework does not provide for the deterioration of ecosystems unless such deterioration is "closely related" to loss of life and health. Thus it can be affirmed that Japan's environmental strategy is narrowly anthropocentric and insensitive to the larger context of human dependence on general ecosystem stability (*JEA*, 1971c).

Apart from the basic law, there are some thirty-two laws dealing with various aspects of the environment, eighteen of which were passed by the "pollution Diet" of 1970–1971. The most important of them cover air and water pollution, solid waste disposal, soil pollution, the use of agricultural chemicals, industrial liability, punishment of pollution crimes, and the discharge of harmful substances into air and water. A few deal with the regulation of disputes, pollution control, and aid to victims. Some are marginally environmental in scope, such as the law to protect cultural properties. Two of the laws are unique and bear close watching. One of them, since December 1970, obliges industry to shoulder all or part of the cost of public works initiated to cope with its pollution. The second, supposedly enforced since July 1, 1971, states that discharge of toxic substances as a result of business activities which causes death or injury is punishable by imprisonment or fine (*JEA*, 10 February 1974, Vol. 2, No. 2; *QEJ*, 1972:34–35,192–193).

The Environment Agency does not have centralized enforcement power over these laws, nor does it have regional offices to serve as watchdogs. Strictly speaking, only prefectural governors directly enforce environmental laws, although the agency frequently exerts pressure for more careful implementation. In 1973 the agency empowered thirty mayors of cities with populations of at least 250,000 to enforce the Water Contamination Prevention Law (*JT*, 18 February 1973). However, it has no direct jurisdiction over laws relating to aircraft noise, the discharge of poisonous and deleterious substances, pollution control in specified factories, special government financial measures for pollution control, settlement of pollution disputes, or pollution crimes relating to human health. It has only advisory powers over the regulation of agricultural chemicals, waste disposal, marine pollution, and sewerage. Predominant jurisdiction over the latter group falls to four other ministries: International Trade and Industry, Construction, Health and Welfare, and Agriculture and Fisheries. All four have bad environmental records, and the first two are closely linked to industrial vested interests (*JEA*, 1972a:21–34; *JEA*, 1971c:4–5).

Furthermore, the Environment Agency and its ministerial rivals frequently appear to be working at cross-purposes. The Environment Agency is concerned with the law on soil pollution, but not the one on agricultural chemicals; it handles the law on noise, but not the one on aircraft noise; it advises on the industrial pollution law, but not the one on discharge of poisonous substances; the water-pollution law is under its advisory jurisdiction, but not the one on marine pollution; it handles air pollution, but not the regulation of specific industries. It is also noteworthy that the Environment Agency has no control over the generation, storage, and disposal of nuclear wastes,* even though Japan expects to have fourteen nuclear power stations by 1977. The upshot of not having direct enforcement power is that an elaborate consensus must be worked out, first between the prefectural government and the polluter, and then between the regional administrators and the Environment Agency.

As might be expected, the enforcement of Japan's antipollution laws is weak and indecisive; hence their effectiveness is minimal. The problem can be traced in part to the laws themselves, especially to those passages spelling out emission standards. There is no provision for controlling the total amount of pollutants discharged into the environment, although such a provision is currently being considered. Rather, the government relies on ambient readings not to exceed certain standards over a fixed period of time, and the concentration of pollutants at the point of outlet. With respect to the latter practice, a factory can dilute its waste water prior to discharge and thus meet government standards without making a dent in overall pollution levels. Moreover, ambient standards do almost nothing to lessen the impact of millions of tons of pollutants settling into ecosystems each year. These standards are not adjusted to unique conditions underlying Japanese pollution, most notably the endemic crowding of people and industry into some two percent of the total land area. The prevailing tendency is to imitate American and European quality standards and place reliance on foreign research; as a consequence, Japanese quality standards are often uncritical, and inappropriate.

Although both water- and air-pollution laws provide fines for violations, the amounts are so insignificant that polluters would rather pay fines than make reforms in their pollution-control technology. Fines often come to three hundred or four hundred dollars or less for each offense. In order to monitor properly the industrial establishment of Japan, an army of dedicated inspectors would be needed, and only nine thousand civil servants are now on watch in the provinces. At present the government relies on a law that requires industry to report countermeasures being taken to meet government quality standards, thus permitting thousands of enterprises to evade the law with impunity. Moreover, neither the Environment Agency nor local government authorities have the power to forbid the introduction of high-pollution industries into relatively clean areas or their further concentration in already polluted areas such as the Tokyo-Osaka belt,

---

*The Science and Technology Agency has this responsibility.

although vocal opposition from local environmental *jumin undo* groups has occasionally been successful (*QEJ*, 1973:227; *TMG*, 1971:263-264).

There is strong evidence that local government would be tougher on polluters than the central government, if funds and encouragement were forthcoming. Clearly some of the most vigorous environmental protection activities have taken place at the local level, especially in areas where the *jumin undo* groups are strong and the LDP relatively weak in local government. It is also to local government that most pollution victims have initially turned with their grievances, as in the case of Minamata Bay. However, as a rule local government has traditionally been weak and subservient. While mayors of towns and cities are free in principle to increase the severity of air and water quality standards, there is usually little incentive to do so unless local political pressures from environmentalists are great. National taxes drain off seventy to eighty percent of local tax revenues and return very little to local authorities. Municipalities are normally led by men who see prestige and profit in the greater industrial development of their regions. The established national pattern of coddling industry, and sharp pressure from the ministries of Finance and International Trade and Industry, have a further dampening effect on the initiative of local politicians (Kunimoto, 1972; *TMG*, 1971:48-49; *JEA*, 1972c; *JT*, 31 March 1975).

Under the law, polluters are obliged to pay the cost of public works necessitated by their activities, but industry has not as yet been forced to pay the bill. Although thousands have suffered illness, deformity, and crippling disorders, and hundreds have died, not a single industrialist has been heavily fined or jailed for criminal action, though several suspended sentences have been meted out. For negligence in discharging harmful wastes that cause death or bodily injury, the penalty is no more than three years in jail; for knowingly endangering health and life, it is five years; and for actually causing death or injury, the guilty party can get seven years. It is improbable, however, that anyone will be sent to jail when the offense can be atoned for with a fine. For negligence, the top fine is about ten thousand dollars, as it is for knowingly causing harm. Death and bodily harm can be redeemed for sixteen thousand dollars. While now and then an example is set among the smaller companies, the industrial giants escape effective control. As one staffer of the Environment Agency explained to me, "it is not the custom to send businessmen to jail" (Interview, August 1974).

POPULATION POLICY

At present there is no official view on what would constitute an "optimum" population for Japan, nor is there a clearly defined government policy with respect to future population growth. The demographic fate of the nation has been left to the discretion of individual citizens. There is, however, what might be called a "shadow" policy. Since 1948 the Eugenic Protection Law has sanctioned family planning, abortion for reasons of economic hardship as well as health, and provided for sterilization. After 1952 the government promoted intensive family-planning services and contraception, not primarily as a demographic policy to limit population, but as a countervailing measure to reduce the large number of abortions being sought under the Eugenic Protection Law (*IPP*, 1969).

Like most contemporary peoples, the Japanese tend to associate national power with a large and growing population. Few persons in Japan are likely to agree that the country would be better off with 75 million rather than 110 million citizens. Among some government officials and civilian groups there is firm resistance to the suggestion that population should be stabilized at the present level. Political figures and religious groups have joined to urge repeal of the Eugenic Protection Law, citing an impending labor shortage and Japan's poor image as an abortion paradise. In 1974 a bill to revise the Eugenic Protection Law was narrowly defeated in the Diet; had it succeeded, a woman no longer would have been able to seek an abortion on grounds of economic hardship. In 1969 the Population Problems Council recommended the encouragement of a higher fertility level and the achievement of a stationary population only in the distant future. For a time, there was even discussion of a program to award eighty-three dollars a month to couples for their third child and additional sums for each one thereafter. In spite of a long tradition of enlightened attitudes toward sex and family limitation, the 1969 *Mainichi Shimbun's* Survey on Family Planning showed thirty-five percent of all respondents opposed to family planning.

On the other hand there are straws in the wind indicative of changing attitudes. In July 1974 the *Mainichi Shimbun* released a nationwide poll on population to coincide with World Population Year. Seventy percent of those polled (2,226 persons over age twenty) opted for a two-child family, while fifty-eight percent expressed negative views about further growth of Japan's population (*MDN*, 1 July 1974). The Population Problems Council issued a white paper in April 1974 which expresses disquiet about the prospect of Japan harboring in excess of 140 million people by 2025 A.D. Indeed, the paper declares that "efforts should be made to curb the birth rate so that Japan's population can realize a state of zero population growth" (*AEN*, 18 April 1974). Like all such "white papers," however, this one should be taken with a grain of salt.

It seems probable that demographic policy will remain, at best, in limbo, or at worst, drift toward a policy to stimulate or rationalize further growth. Neither alternative is realistic or rational when one considers the impact of 110 million Japanese on local ecosystems and global energy supplies, or the prospect of Asia's total population topping a desperate 4 billion by the year 2000 (*SAPC*, 1972).

RESOURCE MANAGEMENT

The Ministry of Construction has predicted that by 1982 the nation's economic growth may grind to a halt because of pollution and depleted domestic resources. The ministry also warns that costly investments are urgently needed to transform the economy from a "resources consumption type" to a "resources conservation and recycling type." Even before the energy crisis, similar admonitions came from the Economic Planning Agency and the Industrial Planning Council. Yet the central government is without a comprehensive, long-range resource management policy.

Waste is a fundamental premise of Japan's new industrial order and rising consumerism. The postwar economy has flourished on the tacit assumption that inexhaustible resources exist to bolster every advance of the GNP. Prodigal consumption and waste cannot be slowed or deflected easily when government policy is to double or even triple the size of the economy in less than fifteen years.

Recent energy shortages have compelled the government to try strict energy conservation measures. Early in 1974, oil and electric power consumption by industry was reduced by five to fifteen percent. Ten-percent cuts were experienced by the publishing and broadcasting media, and five-percent cuts were imposed on transportation, food production, pharmaceuticals, and data processing industries. Gasoline consumption was reduced through the Sunday and holiday closing of filling stations. These restrictions were later dropped, but the new realities cannot be escaped. In part because of the oil crisis, Japan's consumer price index rose 25.8 percent for the twelve months before October 1974, the stiffest hike among industrial states. Moreover, in fiscal year 1974 there was a precipitous drop in the growth rate to minus 1.6 percent.

The Japanese have begun to suspect that the apotheosis of their economy may not harmonize with the limits of a politically complex and physically finite world. In 1974–1975, there was a deluge of "white papers" on resources and energy. Many energy-oriented organizations were created, like the New Energy Technology Development Institute, which will ride herd on the Sunshine Project to turn up fresh sources of energy. In general, the emphasis is on producing more energy and finding more resources rather than on conserving either. The Japanese do not want to consume less; they want to consume more and raise their standard of living. But conservation and resource management are recognized, at least on the rhetorical level, as a necessary condition for dealing with the present economic crisis. In its report of July 26, 1974, to the Minister of International Trade and Industry (MITI), the Advisory Committee on Energy asked for greater control over energy by government in the 1980's, and proclaimed conservation, along with supply, to be a twin pillar of energy policy. Another MITI paper, "The Outline of a Resources and Energy Saving Program" (1974b), spelled out all the familiar methods of saving energy and put its finger on a blunt fact—the inefficiency of Japanese energy consumption in relation to growth rate over the past six years (*DY*, 26 April 1974). MITI's Industrial Structure Council has recommended a restructuring of the economy around lower growth rates (6 percent annually to 1980, and 6.5 percent from 1980 to 1985) and less emphasis on resource-hungry industries like steel and petrochemical (*JT*, 14 September 1974). However, talking about a knowledge- and technology-intensive economy to replace the existing resource-intensive one is much easier than actually making changes.*

Nevertheless, there is some evidence of practical moves to save and conserve. MITI has announced definite plans to curb the appetite of industry, which takes sixty percent of the oil used in Japan. At first the restraints will be in the form of nonmandatory "administrative guidance" (see the section on effectiveness), and later will become mandatory (*JT*, 1 November 1974). Many industrial firms have begun tightening their belts as production and sales have fallen off. Fabulous executive expense accounts have been slashed. Where three executives once flew first-class to an overseas appointment, now one goes in tourist class. Many companies have cut out mid-year and year-end bonuses and launched frugality campaigns (*NY Times*, 20 January 1975). A poll in 1974 showed eighty-five percent of Japan's citizens practicing some kind of conservation (electricity, water, stationary goods); eighty percent urged that cars be replaced by public transportation and wanted a new power rate system based on the principle of paying more for consuming more (*JT*, 18 August 1974).

It is very difficult to know what all of this really means. I toured Japan extensively in the summer of 1974. In spite of inflation, energy shortages, economic contraction, and all the rest of it, trains were jammed to capacity, shops and stores thronged with shoppers, and hotels booked up in advance, especially in scenic spots, where room-rates are most expensive, and hordes of people in restaurants (even noodleries) ate as though at their last meal. Statistically, however, consumption seems to be down, though by no means to an austerity level.

In larger perspective, the energy crisis will be both a curse and a potential blessing for the Japanese economy. Less economic growth and consumption mean less pollution. The oil shortage has cut into paper and plastics produc-

---

*A sentiment expressed to me in August 1974 by Masamichi Funago, vice-minister of the Environment Agency.

tion, for example, with the concrete result that Tokyo's garbage volume has dropped. Reductions in steel production, oil refining, and other highly polluting industries will take some pressure off the air and water. On the other hand, announced reductions of the government budget are sure to hurt environmental programs. As government ministries scramble for diminished funds, the less well established Environment Agency is sure to end up with leftovers. Since current environmental appropriations are inadequate, any reduction would be unfortunate. As might be expected, the energy crisis is serving as an excuse to relax existing environmental standards. Leading industrialists have urged the government to dilute controls on the uses of heavy oil and on emissions of sulfur and nitrogen oxides. Oil refiners want the electric power companies to go on a complete diet of heavy oil so that refineries will have at their disposal full supplies of crude oil from which naphtha, gasoline, heating oil, and other petroleum products are made. An increase in the use of coal as a power source will further exacerbate air pollution and further corrupt air quality standards.

One might expect that a nation preoccupied with conservation would inaugurate a full-scale recycling program to recover scarce resources. Such an expedient seems all the more appropriate in a country like Japan, almost wholly bereft of indigenous raw materials. In fact, however, Japan's recovery rate for raw materials is low, and capital investment in recycling technology is not impressive. Thus only forty percent of tires and paper are recovered; for plastics it is eight to ten percent, though this estimate is probably too low. In 1973, some 5.7 million tons of plastics were produced, but only 160,000 tons were collected. Aluminum cans in 1973 amounted to 15,000 tons (600 million units); only a fraction was collected, and the quantity doubled in 1975. Except for scrap metal, industrial waste is not sifted for its recoverable material on a large scale.

However, scattered elements of a true recycling policy are lying about. As of this writing, a bill is before the Diet to recycle six kinds of waste—aluminum cans, plastics, waste paper, tires, cars, home electric appliances—by means of companies jointly managed by government and private agencies. (*JT*, 26 June 1974). A number of special groups have been set up to cope with plastic waste disposal, and special factories are in existance for the reprocessing of discarded plastics. The Tokyo metropolitan government plans to collect plastic waste separately and use it for reclamation work in Tokyo Bay. Some work is being done on the efficient utilization of heat from incineration. Second-phase waste water at the Tokai atomic power station in Ibaraki Prefecture has been sluiced into a seven-thousand-square-meter breeding pond for fish. This unusual fish farm, located on the premises, contains prawns, sea breams, abalone, and eel. The million-dollar five-year pilot project was sponsored by the Japan Fishery Resources

Preservation Association and the Science and Technology Agency to discover if the thermal load of nuclear plants could be put to practical use. Millions have been invested also in "gyosho," or artificial reefs, built with assorted junk, solid refuse, and semisolid trash. Such fish apartments are springing up briskly as alleged "improvements" on marine habitats.

In Tokyo the firm Tezuka Kosan, a refuse processing plant, compresses trash to one-fifth its original volume. One- to two-ton blocks are sheathed in an airtight, wire-mesh, vinyl film and can be used immediately for reclamation work because of their solid, dehydrated state. One hundred tons of blocks can be processed in an eight-hour day, and there are altogether three such plants operating in Japan. Tezuka Kosan drew attention recently with its method for returning junked cars to the resource bin. The company's shredder can process six thousand to ten thousand cars a month into quality scrap, but more interesting and novel is the "carbecue," a technique for "burning" cars and recovering bales of pure iron after nonferrous metals have been sifted out. The carbecue can handle one hundred cars in an eight-hour day and may well be an answer to a monstrous volume of automotive solid waste.

The Environment Agency has budgeted funds to process garbage into fertilizer. A Utility of Biodegradation Research Center was founded in early 1974 to develop the process, and is expected to complete its studies by 1977. It is estimated that Japan's total arable land of six million hectares can absorb up to six hundred million tons of compost arrived at in this manner (*JT*, 11 June 1974). Another example of Japan's potential for environmentally relevant innovation is the marketing of sewage as fertilizer. Tokyo, Osaka, Nagoya, and a dozen other cities are converting sewage sludge into a rich fertilizer ash containing phosphate, nitrogen, and potash by incinerating it in multiple hearth furnaces. In 1972 Tokyo and Nagoya auctioned off fifty thousand metric tons of this ash to commercial fertilizer firms, turning an instant profit while removing a serious pollutant from the environment. In a related development, Tokyo Electric Power's technical institute has successfully developed a method to use coal ash produced in power stations as fly-ash cement, fertilizer, and road base. Another triumph of the institute is the extraction of vanadium, an important "mineral vitamin," from heavy oil ash; the vanadium is then routed back into steel making. The theory and practice of recycling is a fruitful base, along with the development of antipollution methods, for a major shift to the knowledge- and technology-intensive economy so much discussed these days. (The major source here is the Solid Waste Information Retrieval System, U.S. Environmental Protection Agency.)

After twenty years of uninhibited exploitation in the name of progress and regional development, government leadership has taken some steps to control land use and preserve what remains of Japan's natural heritage. The National Environment Preservation Law, which went into effect in April 1973, divides land and seashore into a half-dozen graded categories, each protected by control measures ranging from a prohibition of all human activity to the requirement that changes in environmental conditions by human agents be reported to prefectural governors. Where development is permitted in "nature utilization zones," governors are free to suggest changes in construction plans or to veto them outright. A substantial segment of these protected areas comprises national parks amounting to nearly two million hectares. In a move to preserve the site of Japan's most evocative symbol, the Environment Agency drafted a bill in March 1973 to stop further disruption of Mount Fuji and the surrounding area. The proposed legislation specifies flood control, forestry conservation, restoration of flora and fauna, improved sewerage to maintain the water quality of Mount Fuji's adjacent five lakes, and appropriate monitoring. In principle these laws and designations allow prefectural governors to impose discretionary restrictions on road building, construction of dams and nuclear power plants, felling of timber, collection of gravel, and reclamation of coastal waters. Similar measures are in the offing for other scenic areas. In April 1973 the Environment Agency prohibited further construction of golf courses in national parks and forest preserves. This is a serious matter in a nation where golfing has become a mania with the new middle class. No less than fourteen hundred courses have devoured 144,400 hectares of land, and if eager developers have their way with courses on the drawing board, the figure will top 180,000 hectares (JEA, 1972g; JEA, 1972h).

In 1974, a National Land Utilization Bill was passed, to be administered by a National Land Agency. The ostensible purpose of this legislation was to control rampant land speculation which had driven land prices up since the announcement of Tanaka's remodeling program. The big companies rushed in to gobble up land in hope of windfall profits when regional development and "decentralization" raised the demand for it. As of March 1973, an area slightly larger than Wakayama Prefecture's 470,000 hectares was owned by 3,461 firms capitalized at more than one hundred million yen; of the land at issue, eighty percent was owned by 655 firms capitalized at better than two thousand million yen. Much of the land can be sold at any time, and more than 400,000 hectares are described by the companies as assets for "business activities." Apparently it is too late for the National Land Agency to make a serious difference in how this land is disposed of. In any event, it is commonly agreed that the Land Utilization Bill is identical to the Overall National Land Development Bill that was integral to Tanaka's remodeling scheme. Exploitation of the land is not to be stopped, only regulated with respect to price and pace. It will be instructive to see how well the National Environment Preservation Law can check the momentum of remodeling and the eager greed of business (*JT*, 28 March 1974; *MDN*, 27 June 1974; *JT*, 29 June 1974; *DY*, 5 February 1974).

By mid-1971, Japanese wildlife roamed more than two thousand refuges totaling 1,817,000 hectares; some four hundred of these refuges are protected areas where man's intrusion is rigorously controlled. The hunting of twenty-eight species of birds is forbidden, and in late 1972 the Central Birds and Animal Council asked Prime Minister Tanaka to sanction legal restrictions on their ownership and transfer. There are four special preserves for wild birds as well as eighteen stations across the country for the study of bird ecology. Beginning in 1972, the hunting of birds and animals has been suspended for three years in some two thousand areas. Roughly three thousand special police and wardens have been assigned to the prefectures for law enforcement and the monitoring of wildlife (*JEA*, 1953; *JEA*, 1972f; *JEA*, 10 October 1973, Vol. 1, No. 5:2–3).

POLLUTION CONTROL

Sound environmental policy and meaningful standards imply reasonably precise knowledge of the nature of the pollution threat. The basis for a comprehensive diagnosis of Japan's environmental ills has resulted from a national ecological survey conducted in fiscal year 1973. Under the Natural Environment Protection Law, which obliges the state to mount a geological, topographical, and ecological survey every five years, the entire country was divided into blocks of one thousand square meters for intensive study. Local residents are to be questioned about environmental conditions as part of the inquiry, and all results are to be analyzed by computer to sort out priorities for legislation, funding, and action. As of June 1974, forty-one districts had been designated where government standards must be met in five years; eight more districts will soon be added (*DY*, 5 June 1974).

Since 1972, about ten thousand monitoring operations have been active, especially for air and water pollution. In the latter instance, there is a national survey of water quality each year that includes all forty-seven prefectures and fourteen specially designated cities. Fifteen stations are equipped with automatic monitoring devices to assess air quality from Sapporo to Kitakyushu. Also in use are telemeter systems, mobile air-pollution monitoring units, and computer-regulated pollution-control centers. Qualified personnel are scarce at all levels, so a two-million-dollar national institute was opened in 1974 for the instruction of fifteen hundred to two thousand local officials a year in antipollution techniques. At present, some nine thousand technical personnel are assigned to offices responsible for pollution control in the prefectures and various cities (*QEJ*, 1973:226–229; *GJ*, 1974; *JEA*, 10 November 1973, Vol. 1, No. 6:4–5; *JEA*, 10 January 1974, Vol. 2, No. 1:4–7).

An enlightened change in pollution-control policy is the Environment Agency's recent acknowledgment that control standards based on a parts-per-million formula are deceptive and inadequate. Work is in progress to elaborate the concept of "environmental capacity," or how much waste an ecosystem can handle before its powers of self-purification break down. Ideally this concept will lead to practical measures for assessing the total volume of waste in air and water, thus establishing a basis for environmentally realistic control standards. The first step is to establish ceilings on various pollutants by prefecture and area. The second step is to issue permits to new factories only if their pollution controls keep the load of contaminants below the ceilings. In mid-1973 the Tokyo metropolitan government seized the initiative and pressed for implementation of the new concept. So as to limit the total discharge of pollutants rather than their concentration at the point of origin, preliminary inquiries were made by Tokyo officials from 1973 to 1975 to determine pollution loads in waste water. Factories will be required to install monitoring, water purification, and water recycling equipment. By 1976, it is hoped, tolerance levels for water pollution will be clarified and a rational definition of environmental capacity standards will be in reach. The plan also aims to set a tolerance level for nitrogen oxides by 1981. The Osaka prefectural government has announced similar intentions for contaminated air, and hopes to reduce the entire prefecture's sulfur dioxide level from 374,000 to 54,000 tons a year. It must be kept in mind, however, that the energy crisis has already resulted in pressures from industry and key production-oriented government ministries to ease environmental safeguards to permit the use of lower-quality fuels. Given the relative weakness of the Environment Agency and the localized power base of most *jumin undo* groups, such pressures will undoubtedly be difficult to resist (*JEA*, 10 March 1974, Vol. 2, No. 3).

Two other initiatives bear mention. In March 1973 MITI completed a bill designed to relieve the harmful impact of new industry. The proposed legislation requires new businesses to balance enterprise facilities with green plots, to anticipate conditions that pollute, and to submit plans for pollution prevention measures in advance. Relevant ministries have the power to alter plans or to make counter recommendations should standards be violated. This important bill received Diet approval after the usual "adjustment of views." A unique Japanese development is the pollution-control agreement between local governments and industries that spells out mutually acceptable control measures for noise, odors, and air and water pollution, and defines industry responsibility. By the end of 1972 parties to such agreements included thirty-eight prefectures, 461 municipalities, and 3,202 private firms (*QEJ*, 1973:206–207).

An assortment of controls have been aimed at major forms of pollution. Two general standards affect water quality. The first relates to human health and is uniform for all waters subject to public use. The second relates to environmental conservation and depends on the type of water—river, lake, or coastal. By March 1971 the Environment Agency and prefectural governors had classified 275 bodies of water in fifteen prefectures. The Water Pollution Control Law empowers prefectural governors to adopt tougher standards than the central government, although uniform effluent standards have been spelled out for the entire nation. By 1975, thirty-eight percent of total urban areas will be drained by sewerage systems, predominantly because of a third five-year sewerage construction plan. A four-year plan is trying to cope with heavy metal discharges by some one thousand mines. The Meteorological Agency began in 1972 to examine the seas around Japan against more than fourteen indices of water quality, including pH, heavy metal content, transparency, and chemical oxygen demand. The Maritime Safety Agency has created a Marine Pollution Division in its head office, has acquired a test laboratory, and is due to take on additional personnel, patrol boats, helicopters, and a system for the detection of oil dumping at night. In order to control the growing problem of oil pollution, seventy-nine waste oil treatment plants have been built in fifty ports. The goal for 1976 is not more than five parts per million of oil in discharged effluent. Eight ports are to be renovated by a fifty-million-dollar dredging operaton to remove waste that causes foul odors and water pollution (*JEA*, 1972l; *QEJ*, 1973:118–123; *JEA*, 10 December 1973, Vol. 1, No. 7; *JEA*, 10 August 1973, Vol. 1, No. 3).

Regarding air pollution, standards for sulfur oxides, carbon monoxide, and suspended particulate matter had been promulgated by March 1972. Similar standards are under debate for nitrogen oxides and lead. Eleven areas with heavy air pollution were designated for control of total sulphur oxide emissions from April 1974. As in the case of water, local authorities are free to stiffen air-control standards. By March 1972 eleven prefectures had emission standards better than the national level. If conditions so warrant, emergency reductions can be imposed on five types of emissions. In April 1973, antipollution devices became mandatory for all new cars, trucks, and buses as an interim measure before the Japanese version of the Muskie Act was implemented. Used cars also must be equipped with emission-control devices.* Considerable progress has been made on an

---

*Many cities are taking steps to control the volume of traffic in congested areas. Soon Tokyo will have 132 no-car zones, or "life zones" as they will be called (*JT*, 13 March 1975).

electric car, and market success has crowned a rotary engine antipollution system (Mazda REAPS). Air pollution directly inspired the recent construction of fifteen desulfurization facilities capable of processing 368,000 barrels of oil a day. Three electric power companies in Tokyo, Kansai, and Chiba are setting an example, with MITI support, by constructing test plants to desulfurize exhaust gases (*JT*, 22 November 1974; *QEJ*, 1973:84–107; *JEA*, 1972a).

Industrial waste disposal is to be wrestled with by a joint government-industrial firm, the Japan Industrial Waste Disposal Company, which appeared in 1974 with investment resources of five million dollars. The Science and Technology Agency had announced the creation of a Radioactive Waste Disposal Center, inaugurated in 1974. Much of the center's funding comes from the private sector, notably power companies owning nuclear reactors. In the first year the center conducted surveys for land sites to store wastes. Other problems to be dealt with are sea dumping of nuclear materials, transportation of wastes, and techniques by which their toxicity can be neutralized.

Japan's most sweeping recovery project is to clean up the Inland Sea. Regarded as a precedent-setting example for other such attempts, it was proposed in Feburary 1973 by the Environment Agency, and is watched over by an advisory Council for Preservation of the Seto Inland Sea. Beginning in 1974 the ten-point plan would seek to restore this important waterway over a five-year period. Key provisions of the plan are the suspension of new land-reclamation projects and a reexamination of current ones, strict limitations on the construction of new factories and the expansion of old ones, restrictions on the total volume of waste discharged, tighter control on oil tankers, a pollution-monitoring system, and the protection of fishing grounds. Former Director-General Takeo Miki observed that without local cooperation with the entire plan there was no hope of reversing deterioration of the Inland Sea. Nevertheless governors and mayors of the eleven prefectures bordering the shallow sea have been less than cooperative, for the plan cuts to the heart of cherished ambitions for regional development and economic growth (*JEA*, 10 August 1973, Vol. 1, No. 3:4; *JEA*, 10 October 1973, Vol. 1, No. 5:4).

In May 1971 a set of government criteria specified the noise levels appropriate for various times of the day in areas where medical and residential buildings predominate. The standards applied at once in specially designated neighborhoods, but five years are allowed for compliance in areas next to heavily traveled roads and highways. Aircraft, trains, and construction work are exempt from regulation under this Noise Control Law. Separate regulations have been spelled out for vehicles and apply both to single cars and to heavy traffic in specified places (*JT*, 12 February

1975). It is not clear how these standards are to be monitored or enforced realistically. Aircraft noise is to be mitigated by limiting the time of take-offs and landings at Japan's international airports to the hours between 7:00 A.M. and 11:00 P.M., with the inevitable list of exceptions. Thus far noise-control legislation has avoided the thunderous issue of construction work, though private initiatives have developed masking technology for some types of heavy equipment like pile drivers. Nothing has been done about vibration, on the ground that knowledge of its effects is too primitive *(QEJ,* 1973:258–259; *JEA,* 10 February 1974, Vol. 2, No. 2:4).

PARTICIPATION IN INTERNATIONAL PROGRAMS

After twenty years of quiescence on the world scene, except for trade, Japan has embarked on a peaceful offensive to win a place in international relations commensurate with an undisputed economic stature. Environmental agreements and cooperative environmental programs figure prominently in this new internationalism. Late in 1973 the Economic Planning Agency submitted to the Cabinet a white paper that argues for more intensive cooperation with other nations to resolve world problems of inflation, monetary instability, and pollution. With respect to the last problem, Japan's record of international committee memberships and agreements is difficult to reproach *(QEJ,* 1973:65–68).

These included participation in all meetings of the Preparatory Committee and five Inter-governmental Working Groups at the Stockholm Conference in June 1972. In addition to supporting environment-related activities of United Nations special agencies (World Health Organization (WHO), Food and Agriculture Organization (FAO), and so on), Japan is vice-chairman of the Environment Committee of the Organization for Economic Cooperation and Development, whose subgroups are studying air and water pollution, the use of chemicals, and the urban environment. The air management group held its 1972 meeting in Tokyo so as to profit from first-hand observation of Japan's air-pollution-control system.

In November 1972 Tokyo was host to the second Asian Population Conference, which drew delegates from twenty-four countries. Conference recommendations were forwarded to the World Population Conference in 1974. In late 1972 Tokyo was again the site of an international meeting, this time to discuss problems confronting advanced societies, especially the scourge of pollution. Seventeen experts from various quarters of the globe were invited to attend on the heels of a special report from a team dispatched by the Japan Economic Survey Council to study the United States and eight European countries. In 1974 Japan was active at the World Population and Law of the Sea Conferences.

In March 1972 Japan and the United States concluded a migrant bird protection treaty that shields 189 species of migrant birds and 74 species of wild fowl. Negotiations have resulted in a similar agreement with the Soviet Union, and Australia has been asked to consider such a treaty. In March 1973 Japan also agreed with the United States to set up a joint "high-level" forum of experts to probe means of assuring a stable supply of energy. A Japan–United States Conference on Natural Resources Development is studying air and water pollution, park and forest management, and the conservation of oceanic resources, among other things. It has been agreed that regular "minister-level" meetings will follow the 1970 and 1971 Japan–United States conferences on environmental pollution. The second of these conferences dealt with a wide range of key topics like the economic aspects of pollution control, the legal foundations of environmental protection, and the basis for emission standards. In April 1973 a group of Japanese scientists afforded the public a glimpse of pollution through the eyes of America's Earth Resources Technology Satellite. Designed to survey the earth's natural resources, the satellite system has been able to identify from space the corrosion of Japan's shorelines, the decimation of plant life, and the unwholesome stain of contaminated water (*JT*, 5 April 1973; *JEA*, 10 November 1973, Vol. 1, No. 6:2–3; *AEN*, 32 March 1973).

The cooperative efforts with America are complemented by environmental liaison with several European states, and even with the People's Republic of China. For example, the Toyama Prefectural Research Laboratory of Public Health and the Caroline Institute of Medicine (Karolinska Institutet) in Stockholm are engaged in a joint research venture on cadmium poisoning. Swedish experts have been visiting Toyama each year since 1969 and their Japanese counterparts are collecting data in Sweden. The Chinese have expressed interest in the offer of Japan's paper and pulp industry to provide technical assistance and advice on reforestation and water-purification programs, to "make the Yellow River blue" and "cover the brown earth with green" (Chinese slogans) (*JT*, 4 April 1973; *AEN*, 27 January 1973).

The Environment Agency has undertaken revision of maritime pollution laws in compliance with The Convention on the Dumping of Wastes at Sea, signed by Japan in London in November 1972. This significant international agreement obliges signatories to "individually and collectively promote the effective control of all sources of pollution of the marine environment." Few agreements will test with more rigor Japan's ability to support an international approach to one of the globe's most dangerous forms of pollution.The convention prohibits dumping, except in emergencies and after prior notification of those who might be affected, of just those substances with which the Japanese are having the most trouble: high-level radioactive wastes, crude oil, durable plastics, and pesticides (*SRE*, 1972).

Most of Japan's international agreements and collaborations on environmental matters are of small consequence to vested interests. Perhaps the truest test of good intentions in the global arena is Japan's relationship with the whale. The number of whales in the sea has plummeted dramatically because of overexploitation, so that only the Japanese and the Soviets are still competing to harvest what remains. Japanese whalers are efficient and well-armed, sporting fast boats, sonar, explosive harpoons, and even ship-based helicopters. They roam widely, and the record of their hunt over a ten-year period attests the irrational plundering of a finite resource and a magnificent form of animal life. Smaller, relatively uneconomical species have been sought as the larger ones have given out and fallen under bans of the conservative International Whaling Commission (IWC).

The problem is not a simple one for Japan. Whale meat represents nine percent of all meat produced; the demand is so great that fifteen thousand tons were imported in 1970, much of it from the Soviet Union. It is a staple of school lunch programs. Whale catches provide two or three percent of all income from fishing. Every part of the whale is used for one purpose or another, exonerating the Japanese of wastefulness, unlike the Soviet Union. Officials in government and the whaling industry claim that Japan cooperates scrupulously with quotas set by the IWC and refrains from hunting four types on the endangered list. Yet it is only due to strong pressure that Japan has let up on the scope of whaling operations, and there is stubborn reluctance to admit that a once abundant pelagic resource is being driven to the brink of extinction. Always in search of more "scientific" data to justify severe reductions of the catch, the whaling industry of Japan never seems to find the evidence, and sets out to harpoon as many whales as the sea, the IWC, and public opinion will tolerate (*JT*, 12 April 1974; *MDN*, 24, 27 June 1974).

Near panic resulted when a resolution was presented by the United Nations Secretariat at the Stockholm Conference to begin a ten-year moratorium on whaling to allow the revival of stocks. A flurry of resistance ensued, illustrative of how government and private interests work together. An official of the Fishery Agency announced that whatever the ideals of the conference, Japan did not recognize its competence or authority to ban whaling. The director of the Japan Whaling Association, as the *Japan Quarterly* reports, "made it clear that under no circumstances would Japan consider herself bound by the resolution." Following this dual repudiation, the Fishery Agency and the whaling companies made battle at a meeting of the IWC in London, immediately after the Stockholm Conference. The two *government* representatives were a Fishery Agency official and the director of the Japan Whaling Association, an alliance with instructions to "stop the ten-year moratorium." A not-too-harsh lesson to be drawn from these events is that international responsibility is possible so long as it does not hurt (*JQ*, 1972c:391–394).

BUDGET ALLOCATIONS

The distribution of funds from the state treasury is an instructive barometer of commitment to environmental quality and a solid indicator of priorities in Japan's national life. The fiscal 1974–1975 budget for environmental protection, excluding loans and investments,* was 1.2 billion dollars, or 1.8 percent of the entire government budget, representing a 25 percent gain over environmental funds for 1973.† The share held by the Environment Agency was 51 million. On the other hand, the Ministry of Construction controlled no less than 970 million, nearly the entire budget, and the remainder was parceled out to other ministries and agencies; for reasons that are obscure, the Defense Facility Administration Agency received in excess of 6 million dollars. The enormous share absorbed by the Ministry of Construction was to be spent ostensibly on sewerage projects (627 million), green buffer zones, parks, the preservation of historic sites, and measures against high tides. These expenditures seem legitimate enough, but one cannot help noting that construction is at the heart of former Prime Minister Tanaka's remodeling plan, which is far from defunct, and that construction projects are one of the country's biggest pork barrels. Furthermore, the fiscal decentralization promoted by these budget allocations weakens whatever administrative unity the government has achieved in environmental affairs (*JEA*, 10 April 1974, Vol. 2, No. 4).

How were the figures arrived at and on what principles? Each division of the Environment Agency draws up an estimate of what will be needed for programs and activities under its supervision or surveillance. The estimates are submitted to the agency's General Affairs Division for coordination into the total budget picture. The General Affairs Division sets up environmental priorities, in consultation with other divisions, that will determine the size and distribution of the proposed budget. Negotiations with the Finance Ministry are carried out by the agency's Accounts Division, the outcome of which is governed by factors largely extraneous to the urgent realities of environmental pollution. Ministerial prestige, the relative seniority and imminence of bureaucrats, *batsu* (clique) associations in school or government service, and skill in manipulating the "consensus" between ministries on budgetary priorities determine in the end what is spent on

---

*Government loans and investments for environmental protection in fiscal year 1974 were 1.8 billion dollars, constituting 6.7 of all such government expenditures (26.4 billion). Outlays by prefectural and municipal governments are not included.

†300 yen = 1 dollar. Figures are approximate. Japan's fiscal year runs from April 1 to March 31, designated by the calendar year in which it begins.

pollution control. How much the Environment Agency secures for its programs is partly a function of how much is requested. The amount asked for cannot be "unreasonable," and what actually materializes is heavily conditioned by the relative maturity of the agency (Interview with Masamichi Funago, vice minister of the Environment Agency, August 1974). The ideal rate of materialization has been put at eighty percent of the request, but since that rate is limited by what is asked for, the annual increase is regarded as more fundamental. Real increments of the budget over the past few years have been roughly sixty percent annually. The drop to twenty-five percent in fiscal year 1974 is reputedly because of a tight-money policy to control inflation. However, this reduction in money requested and expected coincides with worsening environmental conditions in Japan (Stunkel, 1974a:78).

If one pulls together all government expenditures, central and local, and adds expenditures by the private sector for pollution control (29.7 billion dollars in 1974), the total is about 1 percent of Japan's GNP in 1974; but this figure does not include management and operation costs, nor enterprises capitalized at less than fifty million yen. If both of the latter are included, the percentage of GNP rises to 2 percent. In 1960 it was only 0.2 percent, so the increments have grown steadily from a base virtually at zero.

Current environmental spending in Japan must be assessed from several perspectives. First, when one considers the billions of dollars lost each year because of damage to health, crops, fisheries, and property, the budget for pollution control and abatement seems pathetically minute. Second, official literature is fond of stressing the husky growth of environmental budgets over the past several years, thus implying eager recognition of the problem. In 1965, however, virtually nothing was being spent on environmental protection in the private or the public sector. It is understandable why large increases in succeeding years seem like quantum leaps when expressed as a percentage of the previous budget. The Environment Agency actually receives miserly financial support in proportion to the real dangers it must wrestle to the ground. The Central Anti-Pollution Council has reported that if all pollution-control investment should stay at the 1972 level from 1973 to 1977, the total amount spent would come to about fifteen billion dollars, but pollution would be four times greater than in 1966. In order to cut pollutants to 1.7 times the 1966 level, it was estimated that nearly forty-two billion dollars would be needed to finance control measures four times greater than those of 1972. If this degree of effort could be sustained beyond 1977 to 1985, pollution would decline to a mere ninety percent of the 1966 level (*JT*, 14 December 1972). A more pessimistic estimate was made in 1974 by the Environment Agency. If one assumes a seven percent economic growth rate through 1977, the public and private sectors would have to spend twenty billion dollars each just to reduce pollution to *one-half* the present level. Moreover, the price tag for a cleanup through 1985 (around seventy-five billion dollars) does not take into account all significant pollutants, such as heavy metals, noise, and land subsidence, nor does it include management and operation costs (Interview with Environment Agency personnel, August 1974; *AEN*, 14 December 1972).

These predictions and recommendations have had no discernible impact on government policy, nor is there evidence that priorities are to be readjusted in light of the energy crisis. The 1974–1975 environmental budget, in the face of all warnings and storm signals, is far below the amount mandated by inexorable realities. Inflation and budgetary "adjustments" prompted by the energy squeeze can only serve to place further limitations on slender appropriations. In late 1972 the central government announced a three-and-a-half-billion-dollar program over the next ten years to reduce pollution in twelve key areas from Tokyo to Kitakyushu. The money will be raised by allowing local governments to float bonds (by means of tax grants), and by tendering low-interest loans to factories, which are expected to contribute some twenty-six billion. Thus, in a ten-year period considerably less money will be absorbed than the Central Anti-Pollution Council had recommended for a four-year period (*IPP*, 1971; *JSTA*, 1971; *PNR*, 1970; *MAF*, 1972; *JEA*, 1972d; *East*, 1971; *Economist*, 1970).

Municipalities will not be able to take up the financial slack. Their revenues are limited, and tax returns from the central government for environmental programs are insufficient. In 1971, for example, Tokyo was slated to receive two million dollars in state funds for antipollution measures, and failed to get all of that token sum. The problem of returning or transferring funds has been exacerbated by the success of socialists and communists in winning mayoral elections in a number of major cities, thus politicizing what should be a public interest matter for the Liberal Democratic Party functionaries in Tokyo.

PROGRAM EFFECTIVENESS

Laws and antipollution programs, abundant as they are, have not stemmed the tide of environmental decay; conditions deteriorate further each year,* though inevitably there are success stories to tell and occasionally some justification for optimism. Apart from inadequate funding and an unwillingness to reorder priorities, all discussed elsewhere, five reasons can be suggested to explain the defectiveness of Japan's struggle against the ravages of pollution.

---

*Various state projects to help "develop" sparsely populated areas, projects which encompass 40 percent of Japan's land, are reputedly debauching nature instead of improving it (*AEN*, 26 June 1974).

One of the most important reasons is the absence of a tradition of public responsibility, a sense of personal obligation to the public weal, or the commitment of groups to the public interest. Where specific personal relationships do not impose restrictions and define obligation, it is every man for himself. A melancholy example of this attitude is the aforementioned reaction of businessmen when Prime Minister Tanaka announced his remodeling program. Instead of exercising public-spirited self-restraint and environmental foresight, which Tanaka had already asked of the business community, hundreds of companies went on a land-buying spree, obviously in anticipation of reaping profits. By April 1973 an area about the size of Saitama Prefecture had been gobbled up by trading companies, many of them representing great *zaikai* like Mitsui, private railways, construction companies, and other enterprises in steel, textiles, and chemicals. The Seibu group of companies alone purchased enough land to accommodate six hundred thousand individual homes. Confronted by a disastrous *fait accompli*, the government pushed belatedly for tough land-management legislation.

A second reason is that laws are being neither enforced nor obeyed. The Administrative Management Agency (AMA) made a study of twenty-four prefectures in early 1973 and concluded that a major cause of environmental disruption is government reluctance on all levels to stop or modify unsound development projects. Out of 200 cases of destructive development, especially in national and prefectural parks, 104 were not followed by punitive or remedial action, in spite of clear legal violations. In 1971, when most antipollution laws were operative, MITI knowingly permitted a mining and chemical company (Ishihara Sahgyo) to release millions of tons of waste sulfuric acid into Yokkaichi harbor. The maritime Safety Agency reported in 1974 that violations of the Anti-Pollution Marine Law in 1973 totaled 1,818 cases, up 645 over the past year. Violations of the Ocean Pollution Prevention Law had doubled. In September 1971 MITI disclosed that forty percent of 872 factories investigated were discharging high concentrations of toxic waste in direct violation of the Water Quality Control Law. Half the metal-plating factories surveyed failed to meet safety standards for heavy metals in waste water, and MITI inferred that some 20,000 factories throughout the country were dumping arsenic, chrome, lead, mercury, and cyanide. The National Police Agency announced in mid-1974 that pollution offenses were up ninety-four percent over the previous year. The waste water of one electric appliance maker contained chromium compounds 1,110 times higher than government standards (*AEN*, 26 March 1973; *JT*, 10 September 1971; *JT*, 31 July 1974; *MDN*, 17 May 1974).

Laws are flouted so widely because, as mentioned above, responsibility and obligations are felt chiefly in connection with clearly defined persons and groups. The motivation to respect individual rights is guided by this obligation, in the absence of which the gyroscope of behavior tends to be power. In the same vein, an industrialist recognizes no obligation to antipollution laws, which are less important than custom, personal obligation (*giri*), and power in questions of conduct. Ideas of public responsibility and ordered relations under law were imposed on Japan from the top during the Occupation, but never have been real competition for the old ideals of loyalty and the personal social nexus. This cultural factor also helps explain why government officials enforce environmental law so selectively and leniently.

On a third level, the effectiveness of antipollution measures is blunted by a persistent tendency to underestimate the severity of environmental problems. Thus the spread of PCB pollution was revealed by a late 1972 survey to be much worse than earlier reports had suggested (Shea, 1973:27–28). Dangerously high concentrations of PCB were detected in the soil of sixty percent of some seventy-five test areas and in water samples from eleven areas. Near some factories PCB pollution climbed to thousands of parts per million (3 ppm is the official government standard). The effects of PCB poisoning are generally known, yet no countermeasures were taken; in lieu of abatement action, additional studies and tests were promised (*AEN*, 22 December 1972).

And here a fourth obstacle to effective action presents itself, the substitution of endless studies for action, a device that postpones or obviates traumatic confrontations or provides lead time for an adjustment of views between industry, government, and other interest groups. I am not talking about the legitimate search for knowledge which must precede intelligent action, but rather the use of inquiry as a delaying tactic. Official boards of inquiry seldom strike to the heart of a controversial environmental problem with dispatch; they dance around it, skirt its edges, evade and minimize it as long as possible. If results submitted by one investigative body should compromise a powerful industrial firm, as in the Minamata case, a second or even third group of authorities may be convened, which usually turns up less injurious evidence and delivers a more "balanced" view. This is precisely what happened in the case of Itai-Itai disease. By 1961 there was more than sufficient evidence from nonofficial studies to warrant caution and countermeasures. Nothing was done. Instead a series of official investigations dragged on until May 1968 when the victims sued Mitsui Mining and Smelting, and the government reluctantly designated Itai-Itai the first pollution-related disease. In September 1966 a Toyama prefectural board of inquiry, in concert with the Ministry of Health and Welfare, had conceded that cadmium is the cause, but no preventive action was taken and the board was dismissed (Ui et al., 1970, passim).

Fifth, the curious dissociation between legal imperatives and actual behavior can be traced to a specific pattern of relations between government and industry known as *gyosei shido*, or administrative guidance. This is an extraordinarily vague device utilized in a highly amorphous and personal way (*Economist*, 27 May 1967). The Environment Agency, no less than MITI and the Ministry of Finance, relies on administrative guidance in its dealings with the industrial sector. The laws are clear but inconvenience to violators seems minimal. Despite a court ruling against them, the five companies that were defendants in the Yokkaichi Asthma case still discharge noxious fumes into the city's air. The government acknowledges more than ten thousand people as victims of pollution, yet no arrests have been made under the 1971 Law for the Punishment of Environmental Pollution Crimes Relating the Human Health. Recently the Hokkaido prefectural and Tomakomai City authorities filed a false environmental impact statement in hopes of winning quick approval from the government for construction of a great petrochemical complex in the southeastern coastal region of Tomakomai (*MDN*, 9 March 1974). Data collection has been deliberately tampered with, as in the case of effluent discharges of the Tsushima Mine of Toho Zinc, whose director confessed ordering the dilution of water samples collected and left temporarily with him by government inspectors surveying rivers near the plant. The explanation given is typical of many such cover-ups:

> I thought it was all for the good of the company and the regional residents because I thought if the mine were closed because of cadmium pollution [the cause of Itai-Itai disease], both the company and its employees would suffer financial difficulties (*MDN*, 9 and 10 March 1974).

How does the Environment Agency handle such cases of misrepresentation, falsification, and illegality? The answer is "administrative guidance," whose details boil down to a ragged phalanx of consultations, exhortations, and "constructive" suggestions, but seldom entails a serious threat of government sanctions or legal prosecution. Indeed, the Toho Zinc director's argument for modifying evidence and breaking the law is one with which most government officials, the general public, and even the law might be very sympathetic; it has an aura of *ninjo*, or human feeling, in the traditional sense.

CHAPTER
8
CONCLUSION

PROSPECTS FOR THE FUTURE

THE UNITED STATES

America's response to the environmental crisis has been shaped by her rapid evolution into one of the world's major industrial powers. Enamored of technology and industrial production, devoted to the style of a consumer-oriented economy, business and government leaders, until recently, have largely ignored pleas of conservationists and environmentalists to weigh costs against advantages of an ever-expanding GNP. Prospects for more effective environmental protection and more judicious consumption of scarce natural resources depend on better awareness of the precarious relationship between a technologically sophisticated, resource-hungry economy and the environment. The political skill and resolve of environmental groups in pressing for pollution abatement and resource-conservation programs are major conditions for change as well.

In the thirty years since the end of World War II, the United States has enjoyed an era of great economic growth. Rich in natural resources, technological skills, and capital, Americans have hoisted their material standard of living to a level unknown in most of the world. Much pride is taken in new houses, automobiles, highways, home appliances, and gadgets like electric toothbrushes and can openers. An expanding GNP came to be regarded not only as a measure of economic growth but also as a symbol of the American way of life and its universal superiority. The Great Depression of the 1930's faded into the past. The fears and doubts it had engendered yielded to a nearly unshakable confidence that the United States had moved into a new era of economic development, in which government intervention could sustain indefinitely a stable pattern of growth. Occasional warnings of dangerous environmental pollution or the depletion of nonrenewable resources were mostly spurned. Americans knew they never had it so good.

Yet by the early 1960's, evidence loomed that all was not well with America. Millions of urban dwellers began to note the polluted, unhealthy air they breathed. Waterways and beaches once suitable for fishing and swimming were closed because of dangerous pollution. Time and again, foodstuffs were found to be contaminated with radioactive materials, pesticides, and industrial wastes. Increased American dependence on foreign resources to maintain economic growth was known to specialists long before the 1973 oil embargo made it painfully evident to the man on the street.

Concern with the environment in the latter half of the 1960's led to an outburst of legislation and administrative decisions aimed at the worst pollution problems. An open political process enabled environmental organizations to press with considerable success for the regulation of air, water, and other forms of pollution. Public opinion polls clearly signaled political leaders that Americans wanted such reform, and environmentalists became adept at using public pressure to beget government action. Heightened media interest in the problem reflected the growing public concern. As they prospered, Americans gradually became willing to pay more for a cleaner environment in the form of taxes and higher product costs for pollution-control measures. Continued progress in controlling pollution is likely if economic prosperity continues for a majority of the electorate, but a serious, long-term setback to the economy may bring a turnabout in pollution-control efforts. If many Americans are faced with a choice between jobs and a pollution-free environment, they are likely to choose the former.

Another reason that Americans have been willing to support pollution-control programs is that such programs largely depend upon the application of improved technology. Probably no other society in the world has more confidence in the ability of scientists and technicians to develop solutions to specific problems such as air and water pollution. Americans have a historic fascination with technology, correctly recognizing it as a major component of their prosperity. Recently they have become aware that misapplied technology has often been the source of major problems, including destruction of the environment, but they retain their basic faith that properly applied technology can greatly improve their lives.

The willingness of Americans to support pollution-control programs may be short-lived even if economic prosperity continues in the years ahead. Continued protection of the environment depends also upon a favorable political climate which permits environmentalists and federal and state environment officials to sustain their efforts against polluters. Legislative approval of such programs was only achieved after protracted struggles in which environmental organizations brought public pressure to bear and fought vigorously against the efforts of polluters to water down proposed legislation. Now that a good deal of the legislation environmentalists wanted has been passed, they are faced with the problem of eroded public interest that will allow polluters to ignore, evade, or delay compliance with the laws.

Reform movements in America have commonly followed a cyclical pattern. The first phase is marked by an outburst of public indignation orchestrated by reformers. The second phase encompasses a political struggle between reformers who seek government action and those opposed to change who try to block such action. The third phase is commonly marked by an erosion of public interest in the reforms, for the public tends to believe that the problems have been corrected if legislation on the subject is passed. The final phase frequently witnesses a counterattack by the opponents of the reform measures designed to vitiate their effectiveness. Many ploys are used, including fighting appropriations to fund the reforms, court suits to test their constitutionality, and outright refusals to obey the reform legislation until forced to do so through court action.

The environmental movement presently appears to be about midway in such a cycle. The public has been aroused; government action has been taken in the passage of the National Environmental Policy Act and other legislation, the establishment of the Council on Environmental Quality and the Environmental Protection Agency, and a good deal of parallel state activity. Whether public interest in environmental matters will wane in the face of continued economic prosperity remains to be seen, but the counterattack by polluters whose activities have been restricted is clearly under way. Automobile manufacturers, petroleum companies, and other industrial concerns have sought to delay implementation of various antipollution legislation and in some instances have simply ignored it, refusing to comply until forced to do so by court action. State and local governments have, in similar fashion, requested delays in the implementation of air- and water-pollution programs.

In the long run, Americans will probably cope with pollution problems without radically altering their life-styles, although short-term dislocations are likely. The solution is largely a matter of adequate funding for technologically sophisticated abatement programs. There is, however, another set of environmental problems not so easily solvable through technological innovation—the problem of resource consumption. The United States is part of a world with a rapidly growing population in which natural resources are finite. With their high standard of living, reflected in a very high level of energy and raw-material consumption, Americans have become increasingly dependent upon imported fuels and other nonrenewable resources. Even though the population of the United States appears to be headed toward stabilization and its economy is moving into a post-industrial phase where more services than goods are consumed, the nation will remain a great consumer of nonrenewable resources, and a major polluter (McCaull, 1972).

Conservationists have warned Americans for years that someday critical resources would run short, but until very recently they were largely ignored. The petroleum embargo imposed by OPEC in the winter of 1973–1974 vividly demonstrated to Americans how dependent their economy and their daily lives had become upon an adequate supply of energy. Intense political pressure built up in a matter of months for increasing domestic energy production through increased offshore drilling for oil, speeding the construction of nuclear power plants, building the Alaskan oil pipeline, clearing the way for extensive strip mining of low-sulfur coal, and increasing the funds for research into more esoteric forms of energy. Such steps will only postpone, often at the price of considerable damage to the environment, the ultimate day of reckoning when depleted resources will impose limits on consumption (Malenbaum, 1973).

It can be argued that the democratic political system that facilitated the enactment of antipollution legislation paradoxically militates against serious consideration of the more fundamental problem of resource depletion. National political leaders could risk taking up pollution control as an issue in anticipation of gaining support from environmentalists and voters at large, since ultimately the quality of American life would be improved by such measures. The only political risks came from the inevitable short-term economic and social dislocations that would occur as abatement programs were first implemented. The problem was seen in terms of limited and short-term sacrifices to be made in the interests of a long-term improvement in the environment. The resource utilization crisis is more far reaching and permanent. The political risks are considerably greater in telling the American public that they must begin immediately to plan for a post-industrial society in which life-styles may have to be radically different, in which economic growth as they have known it will be a thing of the past, and in which centralized governmental social and economic planning and administration will be a necessity (Caudill, 1971). Ironically, the open, democratic political system that has facilitated the attack on pollution problems seems to stand in the way of any immediately successful approach to the more fundamental resource-depletion problem.*

Components of the American ideology also stand in the way of centralized planning and administration that most environmentalists believe will be necessary in the future. The traditional American commitment to the rights of the individual ahead of the good of the community has been weakened in the twentieth century, one of the agents having been antipollution legislation. Nevertheless, this individualistic bent remains an obstacle to the establishment of any concerted national policy that seeks to limit further pollution, resource consumption, or population growth (Utton and Henning, 1973:192). The decentralized system of government in the United States has also been greatly weakened in the twentieth century through the growth of the powers of the federal government, but it still retains enough vitality to be a barrier to the kind of centralized or regional planning that may be necessary in the allocation of limited resources (Kneese and Shultze, 1975:45). Finally, the nation's businesses are operated for the profit of their owners and not for the purpose of the community. The profit and market systems are not self-consciously public spirited.

Americans will probably fail to deal with the resource utilization problem by anticipating potential shortages long before they occur. Solutions to such problems require a kind of sustained and disciplined national effort on the part of both government leaders and the proverbial man in the street which they have rarely been called upon to make (Heilbroner, 1970). Long accustomed to ignoring or diminishing problems until they reach crisis dimensions, Americans will find it nearly impossible, both culturally and politically, to adopt policies necessary to avoid a poorly perceived and understood problem whose full impact will be felt presumably only in the distant future. The American taste for mobilizing massive public efforts to deal with problems only when a crisis point has been reached is a national trait likely to control the way the resource crunch is met when it comes.

THE SOVIET UNION

It is difficult to assess future prospects for more effective protection of the environment in the Soviet Union because the full extent of present

---

*It has been cogently argued that the pluralism of the American political system, which many take to be the essence of "democracy," has come to militate against openness and diversity in the formulation of public policy (Crenson, 1971: Chapter 7).

environmental deterioration and the readiness of Soviet leaders to take meaningful steps are frequently masked by a cover of ritual denial and benevolent rhetoric. Nevertheless some observations can be made about the options realistically open to Soviet leaders.

The first option is simple—do nothing. While Soviet authorities have given grudging recognition to the fact that environmental problems exist, it is clear that the deterioration of the environment has not reached crisis proportions on a nationwide scale. Simply put, the Soviet Union could get away with ignoring the problem far longer than any other industrial nation, both because of the generally lower pollution levels and the vastness of the country.

In the short run, there would be a number of advantages in this approach. Politically and economically it would be the least disruptive. Pressures to strengthen environmental protection agencies would undoubtedly decrease, and there would be little cause to rethink some basic assumptions about economic growth, the value and allocation of natural resources, and the quality of life. There would probably also be some political advantages in the international sphere. The Soviet Union would certainly benefit from economic and social dislocations in the West caused by recurring environmental and resource utilization crisis. The Soviet economy could also forge ahead while Western economies stagnated in a mire of environmental and economic problems. In addition, the relative abundance of fossil fuels and other raw materials would give the USSR considerable political leverage over less well endowed nations. In the long run, however, the dangers of this approach are obvious. Environmental pollution and the consumption of nonrenewable resources are cumulative; they may be ignored for only so long, and then an accounting must be made.

The second option is a middle-of-the-road position in which environmental problems are viewed as manageable within the existing institutional framework. Emphasis is placed on dealing with these difficulties through technological solutions which reduce toxic emissions and supplement the dwindling supply of natural resources through new discoveries or the substitution of other materials. Fundamental commitments to continued growth and the existing political and economic order are maintained, and leaders talk in terms of manageable trade-offs between economic and environmental goals. In the Soviet context, this approach has combined a new outpouring of rhetoric and formal legislation for the protection of the environment with a highly selective *de facto* application of emission-control regulations. While in certain special cases these programs have been reasonably successful—Lake Baikal and the Moscow region come again to mind—they have been less effective for the nation as a whole, largely because of their casual enforcement.

From the perspective of contemporary Soviet leaders, this second option has two distinct advantages. The first is that it entails only limited political costs. The second is that such a program is flexible enough to permit Soviet leaders considerable latitude to tailor concrete abatement programs to the political and institutional needs of the moment. Like all other decisions, environmental policy is a product of the inevitable compromises which emerge from the bargaining of factional and bureaucratic interests within the party and government. As such, it is subject to continuing reevaluable and adjustment. In such a flexible setting, commitments to specific programs can be affirmed or altered without extensive revisions of formal legislation or institutional mandates.

There are also several disadvantages connected with the second option. All too frequently decisions are reached more on political than on environmental grounds. The flexibility inherent in this approach may offer distinct advantages in dealing with the politics of abatement and conservation programs, but it gives no clear objective standards by which the adequacy of environmental programs may be measured.

There is also a potentially disastrous assumption which underlies the second option. What if there is no long-term technological solution to the problem of environmental deterioration? Soviet political leaders have assumed, as have many of their counterparts in other industrial nations, that technology would inevitably come to the rescue. But what if this assumption is incorrect, or, perhaps more accurately, what if technology is only one part of a much larger solution?

The final option is to elevate the protection of the environment to the status of an important national goal. The advantages are obvious. In the Soviet case, a commitment to the environment could be made before the problems of pollution and resource consumption have reached crisis dimensions. While there would inevitably be short-term economic dislocations, Soviet authorities would at least have the advantage of confronting the problem before the development of an economy based upon modern high-pollution technology and the advent of a consumer-oriented society. Strengthened abatement programs and better resource management are certainly possible even within the framework of existing legislation, and there is little to bar the introduction of even sterner measures if a firm commitment were made by party leaders.

What, then, are the prospects for the future? It is probably safe to conclude that despite the potential advantages outlined above, Soviet authorities will continue to try to follow a middle-of-the-road policy as outlined in the second option. In spite of the growing recognition of environmental imperatives by some scientists and intellectuals, there are a number of psychological, economic, and political factors which militate against the emergence of a genuine environmental consciousness or a substantial reordering of national priorities. This is not to say that the USSR, as a highly centralized and disciplined nation, is not capable of dealing with the problem. Rather, the argument is that the prospects for adequate protection of the environment are likely to be limited because of a failure of political will and, in large measure, a failure of comprehension.

In terms of their comprehension of the environmental crisis, Russian leaders and the average man in the street both still view the world from a nonenvironmental frame of reference. Psychologically they have been conditioned both by Marxism and their revolutionary tradition to think of nature as something to be conquered and manipulated. Success and failure are judged in terms of bending nature to man's will, whether it be a Marxist revolutionary responding to an industrially immature society, a factory manager seeking to overfulfill the monthly production quota, or a Soviet diplomat asserting the new-found great power status of his nation. Long concerned with the overriding priorities of developing the economy and protecting the Soviet state from perceived external threat, Soviet leaders now understandably find it difficult to think in terms of environmental priorities.

There has been little to alter this nonenvironmental perspective in recent experience. To be sure, some environmental problems have been recognized and dealt with on a case-by-case basis. But the fact that each of these reasonably successful projects had to be elevated to the status of a crisis program, launched by forceful pronouncements from top Soviet leaders usually only after sustained pressure from environmentalists, demonstrates the inadequacy of routine pollution-abatement procedures. The energy crisis, so sobering for other industrial nations, has had considerably less impact on Soviet thinking, in part because of the relative abundance of fossil fuels and natural resources and the tendency to believe that resource substitution and new discoveries will continue to supply the nation's needs into the indefinite future. The threat of overpopulation is also not likely to be widely recognized as a restraint on further development and an important contributor to worsening pollution. Official policy instead takes exactly the opposite position that the state should encourage further population growth, assuming that the productive capability of the economy will expand to meet human needs.

There are few economic incentives that are likely to foster the development of greater environmental awareness. As we have noted, it is only within the last few years that Soviet leaders have tacitly acknowledged that a socialist system could fall victim to the ravages of environmental deterioration. The priority long given heavy industry, and the subsequent dominance of pro-industry forces in economic, governmental, and, to a lesser degree, in academic and scientific circles further diminish the prospects for a major reversal of national economic priorities. Recently increased investments in the agricultural and consumer-goods sectors of the economy will undoubtedly add to the total burden of effluents and wastes, even though Soviet authorities are now scaling down once optimistic projected growth rates for the latter. Increased consumer-goods production will further endanger the environment through the development of high-pollution production processes, the worsening of a waste disposal problem already acute in some major Soviet cities, and the creation of a consumption-oriented new middle class intent on improving its standard of living through the acquisition of an endless stream of energy-consuming appliances and gadgets with little regard for their environmental impact. These trends can only be worsened by the growing number of automobiles produced in the Soviet Union, most of which are scheduled to go to private consumers rather than government motor pools.

Further limiting the prospects for environmental reform are the nature of the economic accounting system and performance indicators and the chronic lack of adequate investment capital. In the former case, there are virtually no effective economic incentives for Soviet industrialists to perform in an ecologically rational manner. Factory and ministerial success or failure has historically been judged in terms of fulfilling (and hopefully overfulfilling) the production quota, and even recent profit-oriented reforms do not decrease pressures to measure overall performance in terms of the economic, as opposed to the environmental or conservationist, successes of an enterprise. Even the price system conspires against the conservation of resources since the prices set by central planners do not reflect the relative scarcity or abundance of various raw materials. While measures have been taken to try to cope with this problem, their impact has been limited. The more fundamental question of reorienting the whole price and incentive system has been avoided, largely for ideological reasons.

The chronic scarcity of investment capital in the Soviet economy also militates against greater environmental expenditures, especially for costly and "nonproductive" abatement programs. As the world's underdeveloped countries repeatedly point out to the more industrialized states, pollution control and abatement are a rich man's worries, something which becomes a national priority only after the industrial and technological infrastructures are laid and the basic needs of the population satisfied. Until such a point is reached in the USSR, available investment will be channeled largely into the technological modernization of industry (now the major need of the Soviet economy) and, to a lesser extent, consumer-goods production.

Perhaps most critically at the root of the problem is the lack of political will to take effective steps to protect the environment. Leaders bent on industrialization and the assertion of rising eminence on the international stage have little incentive to shift their attention to environmental concerns unless significant pressures are brought to bear to force a rethinking of priorities. The close liaison between the Communist Party elite and the industrial and military elites has further strengthened the tendency to oppose environmental reforms which would shift both economic and *de facto* political power away from the present dominant elite groups. This is not to suggest that an all-pervasive and homogeneous power elite completely controls decision making on all matters of policy. On the contrary, contemporary Soviet political behavior is marked by the frequent feuding of competing government agencies and leadership factions within the party. The important point is that environmentalists have always been excluded from the inner councils on politically sensitive questions. When environmental protection was thought of as merely one of the nuisances of industrialization which could be controlled inexpensively and without extensive dislocations, there was little opposition to a host of environmental and conservation laws passed in the late 1950's and early 1960's. As it became apparent, however, that adequate pollution abatement would require large amounts of capital, challenge the interests of key ministries, and perhaps ultimately impose limits on further development itself, the agreement vanished. It was replaced by a pattern of resistance to and evasion of environmental legislation, sustained by both the political skill and finesse of industrial interests and the willingness of other important segments of the elite to support continued economic development as the primary national priority.

The political impact of pro-environmental lobbies and pollution-control agencies is also unlikely to grow appreciably in the future. Their continuing weakness has been one of the major causes of the generally lax steps taken to protect nature. In contrast, environmental and conservationist lobbies have played an important role in raising the level of environmental awareness in the United States and Japan. It was largely through their efforts that the environment first became a political issue, and their growing political strength and skill have been the sources of some of the most important environmental decisions in recent years. In the Soviet context, lobbies have failed to play this activist role except in a few special cases.

The negative prognosis so far offered does not mean that the Soviet Union does not have potential advantages *if*—and it is a very big *if*—the level of environmental awareness and political commitment were raised. Indeed, there is much in contemporary Soviet culture and the style of political life that would facilitate more effective protection of the environment. The collectivist social ethic, nurtured by both communist ideology and Russian cultural heritage, could easily provide a frame of reference to measure the larger social costs of environmental deterioration and assess the social and economic trade-offs necessary for effective abatement programs. The tendency to think of Soviet society as imbued with a collective historical mission and purpose could also provide added legitimacy for environmental protection to the extent that environmental goals could be linked with other long-term goals concerning social and economic development. The traditional pattern of obedience to formal authority and peer group pressures would ease the task of implementing and enforcing environmental policy.

The presence of an authoritarian and centralized political system would also provide certain advantages if a firm commitment to environmental quality were made. The problem has been that the consensus-oriented decision-making system excluded environmental interests, not that it was based on an elaborate process of consultation and compromise among elite factions that focused national attention on a limited number of high-priority goals. If the environment occupied higher priority, it is probably safe to presume that pro-environmental policy would be implemented as vigorously as present goals. The presence of a highly centralized administrative sytem and nationwide economic planning gives Soviet leaders the ability to affect virtually all aspects of governmental and economic activity. A manipulative and highly effective communications system further provides a mechanism both to educate and mobilize mass support through the media, and an extensive network of Communist Party cells or party representatives within virtually all governmental, economic, and social organizations provides an effective transmission belt for explaining and enforcing policy.

In terms of the future protection of the environment, the Soviet Union has been presented with a unique opportunity. Realizing the problem relatively early, partly as a consequence of more disasterous environmental disruption in more developed states, the USSR now faces pollution and resource utilization problems far less severe than those experienced in the United States and Japan. The pattern of Soviet industrialization has also created an economy only now on the verge of committing itself to high-pollution technology and consumerism. The next decade may well be the critical turning point. If a commitment is made to pursue further technological development and unrestrained economic expansion, especially in the consumer sector, without the simultaneous imposition of adequate environmental safeguards, the USSR will follow the path taken by the other two nations of our study. If, however, Soviet leaders temper their desire for further expansion and greater economic sophistication with steps to anticipate environmental and resource utilization problems, then the nation will be spared extensive future environmental destruction and the need to make up for years of blatant inattention to the needs of the environment. But to have a unique opportunity is not to guarantee that it will be used. Given the overwhelming pressures to modernize the economy and devote greater attention to meeting the consumer demands of the society, to say nothing of the political pressures to preserve the existing dominance of a pro-industrial and pro-growth elite, it is more likely that Kremlin leaders will choose the former course of action and give only passing attention to the environment.

JAPAN

One purpose of this study has been to clarify from the environmental perspective Japan's exceptional vulnerability in the second half of the twentieth century. Although this remarkable nation is a cluster of islands poor in natural resources, short on habitable land for thronging millions, committed to levels of growth and concentrations of industry that have poisoned air, water, and soil, and utterly dependent on others for the raw materials, food, and trade that sustain national life, its gargantuan industrial machine has seemed virtually unstoppable, evoking awed plaudits from eminent observers and critics. Now the euphoria and wonder have been dispersed at one stroke by Arab manipulation of oil supplies. The Japanese economic goliath has been sent reeling on what seem to be feet of clay. Environmental threats have been orchestrated with economic threats to reveal in depth the precariousness of modern Japan's existence, which was never far below the alluring surface (Copper and Stunkel, 1975).

Should the energy crisis cut sufficiently into production and exports to trigger a major recession in Japan, there is good reason to believe that environmental problems, so rapidly accrued as the price for uncritical growth, would be left untended and slip down in the hierarchy of national priorities. Not only would the material fruits of industrial growth dwindle, but the scars and disruptions of the landscape would remain. If the flow of energy is restored before the crisis can modify attitudes and policy, it is reasonable to assume the Japanese establishment will dismiss it as an anomaly and resume the nation's headlong thrust toward continued development (JERC, 1972). More hopefully the Arab oil offensive might force a reluctant awareness of the dangers in growth-fever and excite a sensible reassessment of growth policy. Unfortunately the incentive to do so might be conjured only by massive economic reverses.

But even a deliberate modification of production, consumption, and waste patterns would not end malignant environmental problems.* The politics and economics of overextension in the past twenty years have lessened

---

*The Economic Planning Agency's 1974 white paper, "Beyond Economic Growth," recognizes the problems but is very conservative in its recommendations (DV, 8 October 1974).

the flexibility needed to seek an environmentally sound pattern of national life. An earnest reworking of national priorities, growth expectations, and industrial structure—in the direction, for instance, of a knowledge-intensive rather than a resource-intensive economy—would require substantial sacrifices if realistic environmental programs are to be maintained from diminished state revenues. In short, having proceeded this far down a wrong turn, Japan will have to make its peace with the least unpleasant of several less-than-perfect alternatives.

In the larger context of exponential global increases of population, energy consumption, and polluting wastes, there are two clear options Japan might choose between. The first is to continue with high levels of economic growth (say eight to nine percent a year) within the existing industrial structure, with modest funding for environmental programs and perfunctory enforcement of environmental laws. The general outcome of such a choice is predictable: greater dependence on uncertain foreign resources, prohibitive loads of pollution, political and social unrest, and a steady crumbling of national life. Happily for Japan, this course will not be easy to follow, for the world economy is not likely to yield resources and markets necessary to accommodate a Japanese economic machine two or three times the size of the present one, nor can the environment, judging from conditions now, sustain economic activity of that magnitude. But Japanese planners are very adept at making optimistic assumptions while the storm gathers. Rather than choosing and pursuing a goal as such, they are more likely to let things drift toward as much growth as the world economy and environmental elasticity will permit. Evidence suggests this is precisely what is happening. Month to month, even week to week, readjustments, reevaluations, and revised forecasts are made. The system is being tinkered with, tucked in here, pulled out there, but not seriously altered. Current policy is business as usual peppered with a little caution and prudence. The ship of state has not changed course. It is merely steaming more slowly through much the same waters in much the same direction, with a few more lookouts on deck to spot reefs and other navigation hazards, and hurried meetings in the captain's cabin if there is too much rolling and pitching. As waters become rougher and more dangerous, new officers will surely appear on the bridge, but they are unlikely to be carrying new charts or setting a new course in the balance of the 1970's.

The most environmentally sound course of action would refocus national attention and government policy on the improvement of environmental quality and the welfare of those Japanese still living. Whatever the effects on capital trickling to the poorer nations, selective retrenchment in material production and consumption by the Japanese would not prevent them from sharing knowledge and expertise in technical matters with the developing segment of the world. Indeed, Japan could choose to specialize in the theory and practice of a stabilized, nonpolluting economy and try to become a model in Asia and the world of how to pursue the good life sanely within ecological limits (Gregory, 1971). Such a choice could not be implemented without even slower population growth (preferably negative growth toward a smaller total), and firm restrictions on industrial capitalization in general and on highly polluting industries in particular. While curtailment of all growth is impossible and undesirable, certain kinds of growth should be halted or severely limited (Olson and Landsberg, 1973:3-8). Japan must come to grips with an endemic "technological flaw" (Commoner, 1971: Chapter 9). Energy-intensive, pollution-prone enterprises which flourish from the production of nonbiodegradable merchandise can be scaled down or phased out; plastics, synthetic fibers, and bleached household paper products (which generate ten times the water pollutants of unbleached paper) are typical of such products. The automobile, wholly unsuited in large numbers to a country like Japan, can be subordinated to an energy-efficient, relatively nonpolluting public transportation system, for which the Japanese already have an excellent foundation. The government can provide tax incentives to promote the development and universal adoption of recycling technology, guide the nation into a "materials balance" system of production and consumption (Kneese et al, 1970), and stimulate heavy capitalization of solar, geothermal, and other forms of energy. An ecologically sound land-use policy, the elements of which are in existence, can be enforced with Draconian resolve. The polluter-pays principle (PPP), which is merely under discussion now, can fix responsibility for pollution where it belongs and remove air and water from the category of "common-property resources" once and for all. The PPP would also reduce substantially the regulatory approach of the government to pollution abatement (JT, 22 May 1975). Creative, socially beneficial growth can be defined within the context of net national welfare (NNW) rather than gross national product (AEN, 20 January 1973).

    In the short run, Japan still has an opportunity to embrace orderly change, but it will become less accessible as time slips by and problems mount. In the long run, the prospects for rational change will be dimmed by a world crowded with billions more people, by staggering demands on finite global resources, by vastly more explosive social and political conditions, and by an inevitable upper limit on industrialization (Heilbroner, 1974:50-51). The crucial issue is whether the Japanese with their western-oriented economy and expanded bourgeois culture, which stress material production and acquisitiveness, have the collective will and adaptability to make broad institutional changes before they are forced to do so by debilitating crises and disasters. (IISS, 1972). How well are the Japanese equipped by their historical experience and social patterns to cope with life in an era of tighter environmental limits, endemic shortages, and compulsory downward shifts of national and individual aspirations for an affluent standard of living? There are factors which support the argument that Japan is capable of a swifter, more effective adjustment than many other industrialized states.

The Japanese are a literate and well-informed people whose consciousness of public issues, stimulated by a plethora of books, periodicals, and newspapers, is at least equal to that of any other industrialized state. The average Japanese citizen's well-known political apathy should not be allowed to obscure the significance of this point. An alert, intelligent citizenry will be invaluable when and if a future government presses for change commensurate with global realities, or in direct response to Japan's narrowing options.

Perhaps more important in Japan's case is her long historical experience with relatively authoritarian social and political forms. In time of crisis and general anxiety, commonly provoked by war, rebellion, economic depression, and the like, an observable tendency in all societies is the strengthened position of centralized authority as it acts to promote collective welfare. The foreseeable crises of the near future—global environmental disruption, economic decline or paralysis, and sharper competition between nations for resources—are likely to encourage the spread of authoritarian rather than libertarian styles of government. Thus the traditional attitudes of a people toward authority, more particularly centralized authority, are likely to have distinct utility and survival value. Swift, obedient, collective action in a crisis situation that affords little time for deliberation and few options for the exercise of choice promises to be more adaptive than parliamentary debate and persuasive appeals to the self-interest of individuals. From this perspective, Japan seems better suited to the rigors of the future than the Western democracies, whose value systems tend to focus on the individual rather than the group, personal liberty rather than duty or obligation, and the diffusion of authority rather than its concentration. Authoritarianism runs deep in Japanese life and attitudes, as does the inclination through socialization processes and the pressure of social norms to comply with and respect authority. For the Japanese, authority is not an abstraction; it is a living reality that finds expression at every level of a rigidly hierarchical system of status. Traditional subservience of nearly everyone to somebody else—to parents, teachers, military and government figures, the emperor, the gods—constitutes a still ample reservoir of obedience and conformity that can facilitate efficient, orderly change (Doi, 1973).

Furthermore, the Japanese are heirs to a sturdy tradition of group cooperation, self-discipline, patient endurance of misfortune, and willingness to
repudiate the past when its ways have proved futile. Japan altered her
course radically in 1868 and again in 1945, illustrating an adaptability for
rapid institutional change seldom encountered in world history. These
spectacular precedents, occurring so near in time, augur well for the future
should proper incentive and leadership emerge to support needed change.
Tokyo University's celebrated social anthropologist Professor Nakane, an
expert on Japanese social patterns and psychology, has observed that her
countrymen's aspirations are seldom a result of thought and prudence.
Once powerful circumstances have launched the Japanese people in a given
direction, they proceed with grand inertia unless deflected by a forcible,
contrary set of circumstances. The environmental and energy crises may
be deflecting forces that will set the nation on a new and salutary course.
Once on such a course, the Japanese could become the most environmentally
conscientious people on earth, well short of returning to a preindustrial
stage of civilization.

Also worth mentioning is the close association of business and government in Japan, a cooperative relationship that could accelerate transforma-
tions of industrial structure with a minimum of conflict. In the past, business
circles have been alert and responsive to government advice and pressure.
Thus far government's role has been to smooth the way for industrial
expansion, so one might argue legitimately that passivity is inspired by
a willingness to accept favors and prerogatives, not by a disposition to
acknowledge the wisdom of policies inimical to business. It is possible
that Japanese industry would oppose a government move to restrict growth
or to reduce the existing industrial base to less potent and more manageable
limits, but such opposition, or such unilateral government initiatives, seem
improbable. The Japanese political and economic systems are markedly
symbiotic. Government has drawn strength from the achievements of business, while business has forged ahead under the protective wing of government. Crucial decisions affecting production, resource policy, and industrial
style promise to be as consensual as they have been in the past, and one
virtue of consensus decision making is that it takes the edge off conflict
and confrontation. Paradoxically, a new consensus may be shaped by two
conflicts, one foreign and one domestic: the Arab oil shock and the confrontation tactics of environmentalists.

Unlike most Western business enterprises, those in Japan are singularly
responsive to national image and prestige and are more willing to sacrifice
immediate profits for the sake of nonmaterial values like the national
reputation. Should the nation's reputation, national security, or survival

be perceived as contingent on negative-growth policies, an industrial viewpoint capable of searching beyond company profits would undoubtedly emerge. The company organization of labor in Japan is similarly auspicious for policy shifts that might entail hardship; the ideal of loyalty and devotion to the company rather than to one's own self-interest has versatile possibilities. It is difficult to visualize the employees of Ford Motor Company taking a substantial cut in salary for the sake of the organization, or the company electing to keep everyone on payroll in the face of reduced production and declining profits; yet these reciprocal actions have been observed of late in Japan, where the industrial "family" is a significant force. Labor and management are likely to face economic crises together rather than separately, a generalization which holds for many small businesses as well as the large ones.

A final assessment of the prospects for environmental reform in Japan is extremely difficult. Of all the nations of our study, Japan has developed acute pollution and resource problems the most rapidly and is the most vulnerable to a continued ravaging of the environment and the scarcity of raw materials. Whether the unique cultural and political advantages outlined above will be given a chance to restore a harmonious relationship between a modern industrial Japan and her natural environment will depend largely upon whether effective action is soon taken to deal with present environmental difficulties and to anticipate future problems. As elsewhere, the answer to that critical question will turn upon the skill of the Japanese in comprehending the threat facing them and their political will to take action.

What are the chances of this comprehension and will becoming sufficiently manifest to avert harsh, involuntary "solutions" to the environmental crisis? From the general perspective of this study, the prognosis is not good. The challenge for Japan is stiffened by a phalanx of stubborn circumstances.

First, environmental deterioration, with all its subtle biological ramifications, is already far advanced, and will grow worse even if all existing control measures are enforced to the letter. The problem mounts in complexity and scope as the time interval for workable solutions narrows.

Second, the nation is locked into a pernicious industrial structure resistant to change without deliberate sacrifice and self-inflicted trauma. Sensible measures are discussed and articulated, but authentic change seems remote. Even with some scaling down, the existing structure will still consume immense shares of future resources and generate new burdens of pollution (Trezise et al., 1974). The economic patterns and habits of the 1960's, which built up such prodigious momentum, have a powerful inertial motion in the 1970's.

Third, Japan adds nearly a million people a year to her population, which unavoidably obstructs economic change in the direction of less consumption and waste and makes environmental reform all the more difficult.

Fourth, even if national austerity and negative growth (in the physical sense) were to become immediate policies, there is not, as yet, a consensus about the nature of an environmentally sound economy, nor is there a detailed blueprint of an alternative to the existing scheme of things, one that takes into account Japan's limitations in the larger context of global limitations.

Fifth, Japan will continue to be dependent on foreign resources and foodstuffs no matter what workable changes are made in national life-style. This means continued vulnerability to world disorder, resource scarcity or shutouts, and capricious fluctuations of the global market. In the face of creeping economic hardship and insecurity, it is likely that environmental quality will slip down the scale of priorities.* On the other hand, more antipollution expenditures will mean less export power to pay for needed materials.

Sixth, Japan cannot reasonably hope for presently unknown, unimagined technological breakthroughs to solve all her problems and obviate the need for discipline, sturdy resolve, and adjustment to a lower material standard of living. In spite of status based on GNP, the Japanese already have a standard of living far lower than might be expected from the sheer volume of industrial activity. Worship before the altar of technology is not likely to prevent that standard from sinking still lower.

As though all of this were not enough for a people to cope with, three other problems of a social and political nature obtrude themselves. Few Japanese in authority seem truly aware that a stage has been reached where hard choices must be made. The rhetoric of understanding is frequently to be had, but intrepid words have not been translated into programs and action on a national basis. The Japanese are perceptive and blind at the same time. As someone remarked, they are adept at seeing what is not there and not seeing what is there. With respect to the need for economic reform, a new growth policy, and environmental preservation, there is often great perspicacity on the verbal, theoretical level, but no commensurate inclination to change the way things are. Japanese experts are cognizant that the longer one waits to control pollution, the more expensive and difficult it is to do so. It is well known that a modest investment in antipollution measures from 1960 to 1970 would have restrained environmental disruption by eighty to ninety percent, with only a one percent

---

*Since the advent of the oil crisis, the news media have neglected environmental affairs and featured problems of the economy. Political rhetoric has also shifted from environmental to economic issues.

reduction in the economic growth rate. Yet this knowledge is not expressed in the funding and programs essential to neutralize existing and future loads of pollution (*JEA*, 10 September 1973, Vol. 1, No. 4:4–5). The left and right hands are merrily playing different tunes whose combined effect is discordant. In Japan, knowledge and action have yet to enjoy a harmonious relationship with respect to the environment.

On the political level, there is no authentic leadership, and political activity is seldom keyed to the public interest. The National Diet seems content with its role as debating society and rubber stamp (Ito, 1968). The LDP is content so long as it remains in power. Its notion of "public interest" has been economic growth, a view challenged of late but by no means unseated. Changes of personnel in the LDP are no indication that basic policies have been reworked. Prime Minister Miki's "Mr. Clean" image compared with former Prime Minister Tanaka's shady opportunism symbolizes, at best, a five to ten percent shift in LDP policy and practice, focused on less money in politics and more attention to inflation and energy supply. What is needed is a twenty-five to thirty percent shift in policy to cope with new realities. Instead, the old ministers have been reshuffled, factional tension has been temporarily resolved (until the next "crisis"), and the opposition parties have been held more or less at bay. As in the past, political decision making remains expedient, piecemeal, and unrelated to any larger strategy for Japan's domestic future and role in world affairs.

In the meantime, environmental issues, like virtually everything else, are obscured and distorted in a fog of political suspicion and recrimination. Japanese bureaucrats, businessmen, and politicians tend to view all policy and decision making as politically motivated. Pollution controversies and environmental administration often have politically explosive overtones that drown out the dimension of public interest. Thus a young government lawyer working hard to improve the lot of pollution victims may be viewed by business concerns as a radical in thrall to socialists and communists. No automobile manufacturer is inclined to believe that the Japanese version of the Muskie air-pollution law was contrived merely in the public interest; *political* foes of business, growth, or at least certain industries,* must have been its prime movers! In Japan it is not easy to discuss or pursue controversial issues while remaining politically neutral. Environmental problems have been exploited by leftist parties bent on unseating the LDP. Thus it seems to follow among conservatives that a strong environmentalist is a leftist of some stripe, determined to oust the party of growth and terminate the "economic miracle" (Gresser, 1973:16–17). The Environment Agency, un-

---

*The recalcitrance of auto manufacturers over the air-pollution law in 1974 was motivated in part by a testy conviction that the auto industry is always being singled out and picked on.

derstandably, is on the spot, for it must try to cope with worsening environmental conditions in a highly politicized atmosphere.

Japan is unlikely to sustain high levels (even five to six percent) of economic growth and maintain environmental quality at the same time. Something will have to give. The sacrificial lamb, it seems, will be the environment. The Japanese have great powers of self-deception, and somehow they may convince themselves that cake can be had and eaten too, until irreversible misfortune proves otherwise. Optimism is always soothing and bracing, but tends to blur the hard edges of reality. The year 1975 was the Year of the Rabbit in the Oriental Zodiac, a year suited more to contemplation than determined actions. A bit of allegorizing on this lore, with the help of a fortune teller's book, suggests that the era of high economic growth is over in mid-decade, and that caution, prudence, and humility are the best course.

WHAT'S SO DIFFERENT ABOUT BEING DIFFERENT?

A bold objective of this study has been to seek in the political systems, economic structures, value orientations, and historical patterns of development characteristic of three ostensibly different industrial states some explanation of their environmental troubles, and of the nature of their political and social responses to those troubles. The task has been far more intricate than expected. Obvious differences between the three nations, it turns out, are poor indicators of either proneness to environmental disruption or the likelihood of responsive government action to cope with it. On the other hand, apparently dissimilar factors, such as ideology or cultural values, have played much the same role in fostering industrial development or obstructing policies and programs to safeguard the environment. Clearly such factors are not irrelevant to the distinctive environmental peril confronting each country, or to their individual responses. Rather, what is important is just how three nations with discrepant political, economic, and cultural styles have channeled and adapted to a common array of complex forces associated with industrialization and technological change. The combined impact of these forces has shaped considerably more than economic institutions in these societies.

Forces released by industrialization and modernization have also profoundly affected social structure, political style, and public attitudes. All other differences aside, the USA, USSR, and Japan have become mass societies in which the average man finds his place in the social order defined primarily through association with economic organizations or activities, and his values largely shaped by a mass, frequently manipulated culture. At the political level there are marked similarities, although we shall argue later that differing political institutions and styles of the three nations probably account best for their patterns of response to environmental deterioration. These variations aside, all three have created a political environment increasingly marked by the centralization of political and economic authority (although there are obvious differences of degree), and by a close and symbiotic relationship between government and industry. In each, these facts have nurtured a common orientation toward economic expansion and a tendency to shut out—or at least to resist vigorously—any challenge to the pro-growth policies that have provided skyrocketing GNPs and prestige in the world community.

A comparison of each country's cultural values and ideologies illustrates the point that seemingly divergent belief systems may contribute to a like pattern of environmental deterioration and do little to channel the kindred experience of industrialization along lines least disruptive to the environment. Each has proven easily adaptable to the ethos of economic development and modernization, although some marginal differences of potential future importance may be observed. In the United States, for example, the traditional Protestant ethic, coupled with the notion of an individualistic and laissez-faire society, has resulted in a social ethic which has permitted deemphasis of private economic activities and the concentration of political and economic power into the hands of private corporations and associations. While limited economic controls have been imposed over the last half century, American society remains, nevertheless, far more individualistic than the Soviet Union or Japan.

In the Soviet and Japanese cases, the traditional group-oriented social ethic has been suppressed but not totally destroyed by contemporary value systems stressing industrial growth, consumerism (or potential consumerism, as in the Soviet case), and the assertion of national power. Beginning the process of industrialization much later than their Western counterparts, the USSR and Japan shared the belief that rapid modernization is the key to survival and national independence in the twentieth century. Their rapid development of industry, coupled with suppression of a social ethic traditionally stressing a close, organic relationship between man and nature, has created a perplexing paradox. While the emphasis placed on rapid industrialization displaced the traditional view of man and nature in harmony, the relative success of industrial growth and the quick emergence of serious environmental problems have occurred at a time when at least some consciousness of the preindustrial world remains.

The argument is best seen in the Japanese context, where surviving elements of a collectivist group ethic and a traditional reverence for nature might well be a touchstone for preventing its destruction. In the American situation, the social and intellectual impact of industrialization has been felt for almost two centuries. When the dangers of a ravished environment became apparent, there was less awareness of the preindustrial world, of an organic, congenial man–nature relationship to fall back on as a support for corrective action, except of course among a small group of environmentalists and conservationists. While awareness of this relationship is reemerging, time has been lost because of the need to reconstruct social and intellectual themes whose importance had dwindled in the American consciousness. The Soviet Union falls somewhere between the United States and Japan in this regard. Initially less committed to the notion of a close, symbiotic relationship between man and nature—while the Russian peasant needed and respected the land, it was left to certain elements of the intellectual elite to romanticize the relationship—she found it easier to disrupt emotional and psychological bonds that otherwise would have retarded the emergence of a mechanistic and manipulative view of the world. But Soviet thinking about the man–nature relationship was never coupled, as in the United States, with an individualistic and laissez-faire outlook toward social action and responsibility. Rather the collectivistic ethic remained, because of both its traditional place in Russian culture and its importance to Marxist ideology. Nature was to be used for the benefit of the collective, not the individual. And as in the Japanese case, this surviving emphasis on collective social action may well provide distinct advantages in dealing with environmental problems if a basic political commitment is made to redefine social goals.

Another feature common in the ideological heritage of all three nations is their anthropocentric attitude toward nature. Whether the product of the traditional culture or of the more recent impact of industrialization, this view has been environmentally relevant in two ways. In the first instance, its manipulative aspects have served to insulate man from an awareness of the full impact of his activities on natural ecosystems. But it has also had a subtle and perhaps more lasting influence on man's thinking about the standards by which to judge environmental quality. Placing the welfare of man at the center of a system of values has tended to dull the recognition of the environmental needs of other living organisms. Emission standards and maximum permissible concentrations of pollutants suitable for the survival of *Homo sapiens* may indeed be fatal to more delicate forms, some of which are ultimately linked to the survival of man through their role in more complex ecosystems and food chains.

The basic nature of the economic system is also a poor indicator of a nation's potential to destroy its environment or the likely ways in which it will respond to the problem. It seems to make little difference whether the economic system is communist, capitalist, or some mixture of private enterprise and state regulation. It also appears to be irrelevant whether the economy is highly centralized, either through formal state planning or the informal dominant power of large corporations, or relatively decentralized, although this factor may be important in affecting ability to impose adequate environmental controls at some point in the future. All three economies are characterized by an environmental insensitivity of their economic accounting and success-measuring systems. While the Japanese have recently begun to talk in terms of measuring the net national welfare rather than merely the gross national product, the Soviet Union and the United States still rely on either profit-oriented or production quota systems, each chronically poorly equipped to deal with the larger social and environmental costs of economic activity.

This is not to argue, however, that all economic factors are irrelevant. The size of the GNP can be used as a rough index of pollution potential and resource consumption, although population density and geographic size must be factored into the accounting. Also important are the structure of the economy and the level of technological sophistication. As Barry Commoner points out, a relatively developed and technologically sophisticated economy that has moved beyond the point of laying the basic industrial infrastructure and has begun the process of building a second-generation industrial profile based on the extensive use of petrochemicals and synthetic materials will pollute far more per unit of industrial output than a less technically sophisticated economy. Thus the Soviet Union, which has the least modern and sophisticated technological base of the nations of the study, has the least severe pollution problem (although its relatively low population density and comparatively fewer large urban industrial complexes must be considered as important and contributing factors). This is not to say that relatively primitive technology is necessarily desirable; in certain instances, it can be as destructive environmentally as more modern techniques. The point is that *for industry as a whole*, the quantity, the diversity, and especially the toxic potency of effluents increase per unit of production as the overall level of technical sophistication increases. Both the rapidly deteriorating condition of the environment in the United States after the Second World War and the creation of an incredibly toxic set of environmental problems in Japan during the same period testify to the exponential impact of modern technology.

Consumption patterns also play an important role in explaining the seriousness of the environmental threat in each of the three nations. As a general rule, an economy oriented toward consumer-goods production will create more virulent environmental and resource consumption problems than one intent on channeling the bulk of industrial production into the construction of the economic infrastructure. This pattern is related both to the assortment of goods and services produced by the economy and to the creation of a consumer ethic which stimulates further demand. Both the United States and Japan illustrate the pattern. In the postwar era, the energy and raw-material demands of the average consumer have rapidly increased in both nations, as has the load of effluents and solid wastes he or she casts into the environment. The Soviet Union, which only now is entering the precincts of a consumer society, aptly provides the counter-vailing point, for she is just beginning to face the pollution and resource demand problems long experienced by the United States and Japan.

The three nations evince some striking similarities in dealing with the political dimension of environmental issues. Thus one can observe a marked dissociation between what is said and what is done. National leaders, or their spokesmen, have been saying most of the right things. Official documents, whether spawned domestically or at international conferences, are loaded with solemn phrases about the precious heritage of nature, the critical levels of existing pollution, and the need for immediate remedies. On the rhetorical level, environmental problems receive considerable attention, especially in the United States and Japan. On the level of hard commitment and action, there is much less to show. Ringing affirmations about environmental quality no doubt have several functions. They assuage guilt, and hence are therapeutic. They are a public relations gimmick to reassure the public and maintain a good image in the world community. They are indicative of a common weakness among all peoples—the tendency of words to cloak, distort, or even replace harsh realities difficult to accept or accommodate. They may also be regarded as ideal types we would like to live up to but cannot, at least for the moment. The gap between rhetoric and action in Japan has a precedent in tradition, for harmonious adjustments within the group have always been more important than adjusting behavior to abstract principles of truth or justice. The disparity has more ironies in the United States and the Soviet Union. Pragmatic Americans have normally prided themselves on their objectivity, tough-mindedness, and realism. The Soviets, on the other hand, like to think of themselves as preeminently "scientific" and free of conceptual myths. In all three cases, there is more than a little self-deception.

The three countries also converge in the virtual absence of a *public interest* frame of reference, although the *concept* is surely more developed in the United States. Despite some ideological differences, all three assume that public interest will be defined and emerge *de facto* from the interplay of forces in the political arena. Even in the Soviet context, where contemporary Marxism supposedly equates the general good with the scientific construction of a communist society and a classless (although not "layerless") social order fulfilling the needs and aspirations of the common man, the operational definition of public interest has come to be dictated by dominant political and industrial forces. While newly formed environmental groups in the USA and Japan claim to function as public interest lobbies, it is clear they face an uphill fight to win acceptance of the notion that the public interest may be more than the sum of all the private aspirations of individuals and groups in a laissez-faire economy.

The United States, the Soviet Union, and Japan also continue to think of environmental problems within the nation-state frame of reference. While each has participated in various international agreements to control oceanic pollution and to preserve certain endangered species, it is clear that emphasis is being given to national rather than international aspects of pollution abatement. In part because of a jealous regard for national sovereignty, and in part because of the temptation to exploit common problems such as oil shortages for short-term national benefit, leaders of the countries have established nationalistic priorities that take scant account of their role as major industrial and political superpowers. Although a common realization that all industrial nations will face eventual resource-depletion problems has become manifest in the last few years, even halting attempts to deal with problems, such as increased petroleum prices, have been marked by nationalistic attempts to exploit short-term advantages rather than by genuine efforts to reach cooperative, worldwide solutions.

These three nations have shown a remarkably similar administrative response to environmental deterioration. In each, the effectiveness of pollution-control programs has been reduced by the continued decentralizaton and bureaucratic fragmentation of effective power among a number of agencies. While some attempt has been made to provide centralized direction through the creation of new environment agencies—the Soviet Union is the least advanced in this regard—effective coordination has eluded environmental officials. The relatively low standing and prestige of these newly created agencies have also contributed to their lack of real power. The weakness of the environmental laws themselves, and especially the light civil or criminal sanctions against polluters, frequently limit the effectiveness of even the most ardent enforcement official. With the exception of the United States, where fines can be substantial, the financial penalties for violations have not been an effective deterrent.

At a more fundamental level, however, important differences in the patterns of political responsiveness may be noted as each nation attempts to deal with the threat of environmental destruction. Again, it is not the basic nature of the system—that is, its democratic or authoritarian character, or the presence of a single- or multi-party system—which determines the pattern of response. Rather, the differences seem to be more closely related to both the style of political decision making and the role that interest groups play in the policy-making process. In general terms, it is largely a comparison between two relatively closed and consensus-oriented decision-making systems (the Soviet Union and Japan) on the one hand and a relatively open and conflict-oriented policy-making system (the United States) on the other. The central point of comparison is the ability of each to respond to new issues and policy priorities aggressively pressed by environmental lobbies. In the Soviet Union and Japan, these groups have remained relatively weak, in part because of the formal restrictions on the organization of independent groups as in the Soviet Union, or because of informal pressures not to upset the delicate (and economically profitable) political balance as in Japan. Consequently, environmental groups are primarily *ad hoc* and single-issue oriented in nature, usually centered on some locally significant environmental problem. Only in rare instances such as the Lake Baikal or the Minamata affair do they win national attention. Most important, these *ad hoc* alliances have found it difficult to build a permanent organizational base at the national level.

In terms of impact on policy making, environmental lobbies in the USSR and Japan have few alternative political strategies to challenge the influence of pro-industry lobbies that dominate normal decision-making channels. Existing political parties are unresponsive, and party-dominated legislative bodies have not filled the void. Even when environmental lobbies have built productive relationships with the personnel of environment-related or conservation agencies, their overall effectiveness is severely limited by the agencies' own relative impotence.

The American experience provides a clear example of the response of an open and conflict-oriented system to newly perceived environmental problems. As before, the central point of comparison is the ease with which environmental groups can first raise the question of environmental quality in political form and then build effective organizations to press for pollution abatement. In the United States, environmental lobbies have found it relatively easy to organize; at the national level, over a dozen groups press for stricter environmental policy, and at the state and local levels, the list runs into the thousands. While effective coordination has proved difficult, there is evidence that these groups may act in concert on important issues through the formation of *ad hoc* coalitions. Moreover, the political muscle of environmental groups has also been demonstrated at the polls, and they have made skillful use of the courts.

The open and competitive nature of the policy-making process in the United States works to the tactical advantage of environmental lobbies. Because political and administrative authority is fragmented among a number of legislative bodies and executive agencies, lobbyists enjoy an open field of potential targets for their lobbying activity. Since business and industrial interests are also highly skilled at playing the same game, contention over environmental policy occurs in a series of smaller skirmishes within various legislative and administrative bodies from the local to the national level. The success of the lobbyist is as much dependent on finding a receptive policy-making audience as on the objective merits of the case. This results in a complex system of political gamesmanship in which issues are shifted from one or another branch of government, or from the federal to the state or the local level (or vice versa), to locate the most congenial policy-making forum. While industrial and commercial interests are also skilled competitors equally capable of employing the same tactics, this nonetheless provides great opportunities for environmental groups to bypass hostile policy makers.

The careful reader will note the beginnings of a paradox in this conclusion. We have earlier argued that Japan and the Soviet Union may enjoy long-term advantages in dealing with environmental problems because of their higher degree of political and administrative centralization and a pattern of social and cultural norms which emphasizes deference to authority and a collectivist social ethic; yet we now argue that the United States—the most decentralized and noncollectivist nation—has provided conditions more favorable to the emergence of an effective environmental movement. The seeming paradox is resolved if we bear in mind that it is one task to raise a new political issue and challenge the existing order of priorities and quite another to sustain a long-term commitment to newly formed social goals. The American setting has facilitated the emergence of powerful environmental and conservationist forces primarily because of its open and free-wheeling style; there are few if any formal restrictions preventing environmental groups from taking their case to the public. And after years of public apathy, the issue finally attracted sufficient attention so that a politically viable environmental movement emerged. This does not guarantee, however, that the environment will continue to occupy a high priority. The key to continued power lies in sustaining and institutionalizing this newly found political muscle, either in government agencies such as the EPA or the CEQ or through the creation of firmly rooted lobbies that are capable of continuing battle with industrial and commercial interests intent on reducing the impact of abatement programs once public interest wanes. Therein lies the paradox—today's victors may easily become tomorrow's losers because the battle to define national priorities is never completely won or lost. Policy is more a product of the continuing interaction of conflicting forces than the embodiment of commonly accepted national priorities to which all parties adhere. Since the policy-making process is relatively open and conflict-oriented, there emerges no clear and permanent definition of the complex goals of the society. In short, it is relatively easy to win a battle or two; it is much more difficult to translate individual successes into permanent victory.

Japan and the Soviet Union potentially illustrate the other side of the paradox. It has proven comparatively more difficult to build effective environmental forces and to redefine national priorities because the closed and consensus-oriented decision-making styles of these two nations make it difficult to raise new political issues or to challenge existing priorities. But if such redefinition *were* to occur, then the subsequent implementation of environmentally rational policies would be free of the need to fight a continuing rearguard action against polluters. The all-embracing system would sustain and act out the new priorities with presumably the same drive and single-mindedness as it did the old.

BIBLIOGRAPHY

SUGGESTED READINGS

The best general work on environmental issues is Paul and Anne Ehrlich, *Population, Resources, Environment* (1972). It contains lucid analysis and extensive information and bibliographies. For a careful look into specific pollutants endangering the biosphere, see *Man's Impact on the Global Environment: Assessment and Recommendations* (Wilson and Matthews, 1970). This interdisciplinary study is low key but compelling, with good bibliographies. A recent book everyone should come to terms with is Donella H. Meadows et al., *The Limits to Growth* (1972). For a sensible evaluation of this study, see Robert Heilbroner, "The Limits to Growth" (1972b). For a variety of perspectives on the global environment, see S. F. Singer, ed., *Global Effects of Environmental Pollution* (1970), and Paul Ehrlich and John Holdren, eds., *Global Ecology* (1971a). A convenient and valuable collection of articles is Thomas R. Detwyler, ed., *Man's Impact on Environment* (1971). A now classic treatment of unrestrained growth in a finite world is Garrett Hardin's "Tragedy of the Commons," in G. Hardin, ed., *Population, Evolution, and Birth Control* (1964). There is much additional stimulating material in this book. Georg Borgstrom is especially good on the limits of food production, land and water use. See his *Too Many, An Ecological Overview of Earth's Limitations* (1969). The mathematical biologist La-

Mont Cole attempts an estimate of how much life the earth can support in "The Ecosphere" (1958). On endangered species see James Fisher et al., *Wildlife in Danger* (1969), and the *Red Data Book* (International Union for the Conservation of Nature and Natural Resources, 1966). The latter publication comes in loose-leaf form for easy updating. The impact of pollution on climate is studied in *Inadvertent Climate Modification: Report of the Study of Man's Impact on Climate* (SMIC, 1971) Barry Commoner's *The Closing Circle* (1971) is good on basic ecological principles, but the main point of the book is that certain kinds of technology have caused the environmental crisis. Commoner's theme of "faulty technology" is expounded also in "The Environmental Cost of Economic Growth" (1972), and in "The Causes of Pollution" (Commoner et al., 1970). The relative impact on the environment of population growth, consumption (affluence), and technology is debated by Paul Ehrlich, John Holdren, and Barry Commoner in *Environment* (April 1972). The debate is important for a more precise understanding of the environmental crisis. In connection with this debate, see also Ehrlich and Holdren, "Impact of Population Growth" (1971b). Also relevant is Nathan Keyfitz, "On the Momentum of Population Growth" (1971). Keyfitz argues that an unlikely demographic transition in the UDC's by the year 2000 would still add 2.5 billion to their numbers. On the environmental consequences of a thermonuclear war, see Barry Commoner, *Science and Survival* (1963). On the limits of the oceans, see in general Wesley Marx, *The Frail Ocean* (1967), and *Marine Environmental Quality (NCR, 1972)* which examines five major problems of marine pollution. The limits and vulnerability of oceanic life are explored by John Ryther in "Photosynthesis and Fish Production in the Sea" (1969), and by S. J. Holt in "The Food Resources of the Ocean" (1969).

The environmental crisis, growth patterns in the developed countries, and economic aspirations in the Third World are all closely interconnected. The biological, economic, and political issues are brought together by Barbara Ward and René Dubos in *Only One Earth* (1972), which was published simultaneously in nine other languages as an unofficial report on the Stockholm Conference. In *This Endangered Planet* (1971), Richard Falk sets forth four interrelated threats to the planet (nuclear war, population growth, depletion of resources, and pollution), discusses the kind of world order needed to avert the threats, and enumerates the obstacles standing in the way of meaningful reform. In order to bring the underdeveloped world into the ecological context, see Georg Borgstrom, *The Hungry Planet* (1967), especially chapter 3 on the "protein crisis." French scholars René Dumont and Bernard Rosier discuss the same problems in *The Hungry Future* (1969). A massive compendium of information on feeding the world's billions is *The World Food Problem* (1967). An informative, brief discussion of global living standards is David Simpson, "The Dimensions of World Poverty" (1968). See three other works of Barbara Ward: *Spaceship Earth* (1966), especially chapter 3, "The Balance of Wealth"; *The Rich Nations and the Poor Nations* (1962); and *The Lopsided World* (1968). Overwhelming and frequently depressing is Gunnar Myrdal's *Asian Drama* (1968). See also his earlier *Rich Lands and Poor* (1964). A recent assessment of progress in the underdeveloped world by Myrdal is, "Are the Developing Countries Really Developing?" (1971). On the problems and prospects for development in the UDC's in the 1970's, see Robert Asher, *Development Assistance in the Seventies* (1970), and B. Ward, J. Runnalls, and L. d'Anjou (eds.), *The Widening Gap* (1971). On the attitude of UDC's toward the environmental crisis and the issues of economic growth, see the *Bulletin of the Atomic Scientists* (September 1972), which covers the Stockholm Conference extensively, and Terri Aaronson, "World Priorities" (1972), who comments on the behavior and views of Third World nations at the conference. On the interrelated topics of energy consumption, economic growth, and environmental limits, see Gerald Garvey, *Energy, Ecology, Economy* (1972), D. Berkowitz and A. Squires, eds., *Power Generation and Environmental Change* (1971), and G. J. MacDonald, "Energy and the Environment" (1972). For an overview of global energy consumption, see Joel Darmstadter, "Energy Consumption: Trends and Patterns" (1972), and Darmstadter's more detailed study, *Energy in the World Economy* (1971). Also recommended is *World Energy Supplies* (UN, 1970a). Marion Levy's discussion of energy consumption as a criterion of modernization was part of the Hakone Conference on Modernization in the summer of 1960. The findings of the conference are summarized in J. W. Hall's "Changing Conceptions of the Modernization of Japan" (1965). This discussion of what "modernization" means is of general interest to anyone who wishes to distinguish clearly between developed and underdeveloped countries. On GNP and the environment, see R. Dorfman and N. Dorfman, eds. *Economics of the Environment* (1972) for a useful collection of essays. Yale University's William Nordhaus has devised an interesting Measure of Economic Welfare (MEW) to replace GNP. His proposal is discussed by Julian McCaul in "The Politics of Technology" (1972). See also Edwin Dolan's witty and thought-provoking *TANSTAAFL* (1969). The title is an acronym for "there ain't no such thing as a free lunch," one of Barry Commoner's four principles of ecology. On the role of technology in the environmental crisis, see Kenneth R. Stunkel, "The Technological Solution" (1973). Harold and Margaret Sprout discuss global ecology in relation to global politics in *Toward a Politics of the Planet Earth* (1971). The vulnerabilities of industrial societies are explored by the Sprouts in their recent *Multiple Vulnerabilities* (1974). The polarities of pessimism and optimism can be surveyed respectively in Robert L. Heilbroner, *An Inquiry into the Human Prospect* (1975), and John Ford Maddox, *The Doomsday Syndrome* (1972).

The problems and ambiguities surrounding the notions of zero population growth (ZPG) and zero economic growth (ZEG) are explored in M. Olson and H. Landsberg, *The No-Growth Society* (1973). Highly recommended are recent volumes by team members of the World Order Models Project, notably Rajni Kothari, *Footsteps into the Future* (1974), and R. A. Falk, *A Study of Future Worlds* (1975).

SOURCES

APTIC. Air Pollution Abstracts. Research Triangle Park, N.C.: Air Pollution Technical Information Center.

Aaronson, T. 1972. "World Priorities." *Environment* (July-August).

Ackerman, E. 1953. *Japan's Natural Resources and Their Relation to Japan's Economic Future.* Chicago: University of Chicago Press.

AEN. Asahi Evening News.

Agnew, I. 1972. "Pollution Kills Fish in Caspian Sea." *Science Digest* 71(January):54.

AICE. AICE Survey of USSR Air Pollution Literature. 1969–1972. Vols. 1–14. Silver Spring, Md.: American Institute of Crop Ecology.

AIPO. 1969. "The United States Public Considers Its Environment." *American Institute of Public Opinion* (February).

AIPO. 1970. "United States Sets Top Domestic Priorities." *American Institute of Public Opinion* (May).

Allison, J. 1969–1970. "Japan's Relations With Southeast Asia." *Asia* 17(Winter).

Anderson, F. R. 1973. *NEPA in the Courts, A Legal Analysis of the National Environmental Policy Act.* Baltimore: The Johns Hopkins University Press.

Arabadzhi, V. I. 1965. "Zvuk v prirode i akusticheskii klimat." *Priroda* 11:48–49.

Arieli, Y. 1966. *Individualism and Nationalism in American Ideology.* Baltimore: Penguin Books.

Armand, D. 1966. *Nam i vnukam.* Moscow: mysl.

AS. 1970. "The 21st Century Japan." *Asia Scene* 15(June).

Asher, R. 1970. *Development Assistance in the Seventies.* Washington, D.C.: The Brookings Institution.

Asukata, I. 1972. "Kogai boshi jijitai rengo no koso" (Combination of Public Entities for Environmental Pollution Control). *Jurisuto* (Jurist) 492 (November 10).

Avtorkhanov, A. 1966. *The Communist Party Apparatus.* Chicago: Regnary.

Ayal, E. 1968. "Value Systems and Economic Development in Japan and Thailand." *Journal of Social Issues* 19(January).

Azrael, J. R. 1966. *Managerial Power and Soviet Politics.* Cambridge, Mass.: Harvard University Press.

Ballon, R., ed. 1969. *The Japanese Employee.* Tokyo: The Charles E. Tuttle Company.

Barber, B. 1974. *Water: A View From Japan.* New York/Tokyo: Weatherhill.

Barnett, H. J. and M. Chandler. 1963. *Scarcity and Growth: The Economics of Natural Resource Availability.* Baltimore: The Johns Hopkins University Press.

Barse, J. 1969. "Japan's Food Demand and 1985 Grain Import Prospects." *Foreign Agricultural Economic Report* 53. Washington, D.C.: Government Printing Office.

Bates, J. L. 1957. "Fulfilling American Democracy: The Conservation Movement, 1907 to 1921." *Mississippi Valley Historical Review* 44(June).

Bell, D. 1958. "Ten Theories in Search of Reality: The Prediction of Soviet Behavior in the Social Sciences." *World Politics* 10(April):327–365.

Bellah, R. 1957. *Tokugawa Religion.* Glencoe, Ill.: The Free Press.

Berkowitz, D. and A. Squires, eds. 1971. *Power Generation and Environmental Change.* Cambridge, Mass.: The M.I.T. Press.

BMA. 1971. "Japan's Need for Raw Materials: A Worldwide Search.: *Banker's Magazine of Australasia* 85(September).

Bogatenkov, P. 1970. "Kak pomoch Dnestru." *Pravda* (August 27):6. Translated in *Environment* 12(9)(November):36–37.

Bogdanov, B. 1970. "Okhrana prirody i ekonomika." *Ekonomika Selskogo Khoziaistva* (February):7–11.

Borgstrom, G. 1969. *Too Many: An Ecological Overview of Earth's Limitations.* New York: Collier Books.

Borgstrom, G. 1972. *The Hungry Planet: The Modern World at the Edge of Famine.* New York: Collier Books.

Borodavchenko, I. I. 1974. "Baikal: novaia stranitsa biografii." *Literaturnaia Gazeta* (December 4):11.

Bottomore, T. B., ed. 1964. *Karl Marx: Early Writings.* Trans. T. B. Bottomore. New York: McGraw-Hill.

Boulding, K. 1968. *Beyond Economics.* Ann Arbor: University of Michigan Press.

Brodine, V. 1972. "Running in Place." *Environment* (January-February).

Bronfenbrenner, M. 1971. "A Japanese-American Economic War?" *Quarterly Review of Economics and Business* 11(Autumn).

Brubaker, S. 1972. *To Live on Earth: Man and His Environment in Perspective.* Baltimore: The Johns Hopkins University Press.

Bruk, S. I. 1972. "Ethnodemographic Processes in the USSR." *Soviet Sociology* 10(4):331-374. Translated from *Sovetskaia Ethnografiia* No. 4 (1971).

BS. 1972. *Statistical Handbook of Japan.* Tokyo: Bureau of Statistics, Office of the Prime Minister.

Buiantuev, B. R. 1960. *K narodnokhoziaistvennym problemam Baikala.* Ulan Ude: Buriatskoe knizhnoe izdatelstvo.

Burke, A. E. 1956. "Influence of Man upon Nature—the Russian View: A Case Study," Pp. 1036-1051 in W. L. Thomas, Jr., ed., *Man's Role in Changing the Face of the Earth.* Chicago: University of Chicago Press.

Burton, I. 1968. "The Quality of the Environment: A Review." *Geographical Review* 58(July):472-481.

Bush, K. 1972. "Environmental Problems in the USSR." *Problems of Communism* 11(July-August):21-31.

Bush, K. 1973. "Soviet Economic Growth: Past, Present, and Projected." *Radio Liberty Dispatch* (April 4).

Bushtuyeva, K. A. 1971. "Some Problems in Improving Environmental Sanitation in the U.S.S.R., with Special Reference to Air Pollution." Geneva: World Health Organization.

CACEQ. 1972. *Annual Report to the President and to the Council on Environmental Quality.* Citizen's Advisory Committee on Environmental Quality. Washington, D.C.: Government Printing Office.

CACEQ. 1973. *Citizens Make A Difference: Case Studies of Environmental Action.* Citizen's Advisory Committee on Environmental Quality. Washington, D.C.: Government Printing Office.

CACEQ. 1974. *Community Action for Environmental Quality.* Citizen's Advisory Committee on Environmental Quality. Washington, D.C.: Government Printing Office.

Cahn, R. 1968. *Will Success Spoil the National Parks?* Boston: Christian Science Publishing Society.

Campbell, A. B. 1975. "The Implementation of Water Quality Legislation: A Comparative Study of the United States and Japan." Ph.D. dissertation. New Brunswick, N.J.: Rutgers University.

Campbell, J. 1962. *Oriental Mythology.* New York: The Viking Press.

Campbell, R. W. 1968. *The Economics of Soviet Oil and Gas.* Baltimore: The John Hopkins University Press.

Carey, D. and R. Dockstader. 1972. "The Economic Costs of Environmental Disruption." Paper presented at Fifth National Meeting of the AAASS, Dallas, Texas, March 15-17.

Carr, D. E. 1966. *Death of the Sweet Waters.* New York: W. W. Norton & Company.

Carson, R. 1962. *Silent Spring.* Boston: Houghton Mifflin Company.

Caudill, H. M. 1971. "Are Capitalism and Conservation of a Decent Environment Compatible?" In H. W. Helfrich, Jr., ed., *Agenda for Survival.* New Haven, Conn.: Yale University Press.

CDSP. Current Digest of the Soviet Press.

CDSP. 1971. "Japan Prepares to Reap the Ocean's Riches." *Current Digest of the Soviet Press* 23(8)(March 21).

CEN. Chemical and Engineering News (April 14).

CEP. 1972. Council on Economic Priorities. *Paper Profits: Pollution in the Pulp and Paper Industry.* Cambridge, Mass.: The M.I.T. Press.

CEQ. 1970. *The First Annual Report of the Council on Environmental Quality.* Council on Environmental Quality. Washington, D.C.: Government Printing Office.

CEQ. 1971. *The Second Annual Report of the Council on Environmental Quality.* Council on Environmental Quality. Washington, D.C.: Government Printing Office.

CEQ. 1972a. *Memorandum of Implementation of the Agreement between the United States of America and the Union of Soviet Socialist Republics on Cooperation in the Field of Environmental Protection.* Washington, D.C.: Council on Environmental Quality.

CEQ. 1972b. *The Third Annual Report of the Council on Environmental Quality.* Council on Environmental Quality. Washington, D.C.: Government Printing Office.

CEQ. 1973a. *First Report on the Implementation of the US-USSR Agreement on Cooperation in the Field of Environmental Protection of May 23, 1972* (November 13–16). Washington, D.C.: Council on Environmental Quality.

CEQ. 1973b. *The Fourth Annual Report of the Council on Environmental Quality.* Council on Environmental Quality. Washington, D.C.: Government Printing Office.

CEQ. 1973c. *Memorandum of the Second Meeting of the US-USSR Joint Committee on Co-operation in the Field of Environmental Protection* (November 13–16). Washington, D.C.: Council on Environmental Quality.

CEQ. 1974a. *Memorandum of the Third Meeting of the US-USSR Joint Committee on Cooperation in the Field of Environmental Protection.* Moscow, USSR, December 9–12. Washington, D.C.: Council on Environmental Quality.

CEQ. 1974b. *Summary of Activities Under the USA-USSR Environmental Agreement in 1972–1973.* Washington, D.C.: Council on Environmental Quality.

CEQ. 1975. *Report on the Implementation of the US-USSR Agreement on Cooperation in the Field of Environmental Protection During the Period December 1973 to December 1974.* Adopted in Moscow, December 9–12, 1974. Washington, D.C.: Council on Environmental Quality.

Chernenko, I. M. 1968. "The Aral Sea Problem and Its Solution." *Soviet Geography: Review and Translation* (hereafter cited as *SGRT*) 9(6)(June):489–492. Translated from *Problemy osvoeniia pustyn* No. 1:31–34.

Clark, G. 1971. "Johoka: Key to a Superstate." *Far Eastern Economic Review* 71(March 27).

Clawson, R. W. and W. Kolarik. 1974. "Soviet Resource Management: Political Aspects of Water Pollution Control." Paper presented at the Conference of Soviet Resource Management and the Environment, University of Washington, Seattle, June 7.

Cochran, T. B. et al. 1975. "A Poor Buy." *Environment* (June).

Cohn, H. D. 1973. "Population Policy in the USSR." *Problems of Communism* 22(4)(July-August):41–55.

Cole, L. 1958. "The Ecosphere." *Scientific American* (April).

Commoner, B. 1963. *Science and Survival.* New York: The Viking Press.

Commoner, B. 1971. *The Closing Circle: Nature, Man and Technology.* New York: Alfred A. Knopf.

Commoner, B. 1972. "The Environmental Cost of Economic Growth." *Chemistry in Britian* (February).

Commoner, B., M. Corr, and P. Stamler. 1970. "The Causes of Pollution." *Environment* (April).

Cook, R. C. 1967. "Soviet Population Theory from Marx to Kosygin: A Demographic Turning Point?" *Population Bulletin* 23(4)(October):85–115.

Cooley, R. A. 1970. "Introduction: Politics, Technology, and the Environment." In R. A. Cooley and G. Wandesforde-Smith, eds., *Congress and the Environment*. Seattle: University of Washington Press.

Cooley, R. A. and G. Wandesforde-Smith, eds. 1970. *Congress and the Environment*. Seattle: University of Washington Press.Cooper, J. and K. R. Stunkel. 1975. "Super Power Status: The Elusive Goal." *Japan Interpreter* (Winter).

Cox, G. W. 1969. *Readings in Conservation Ecology.* New York: Appleton-Century-Crofts.

CPGAF. 1972. *Population and the American Future.* Commission on Population Growth and the American Future. New York: The American Library.

Crawcour, S. 1974. "The Tokugawa Period and Japan's Preparation for Modern Economic Groups." *Journal of Japanese Studies* (Autumn).

Crenson, M. A. 1971. *The Un-Politics of Air Pollution.* Baltimore: The John Hopkins University Press.

Cross, W. R. 1953. "WJ McGee and the Idea of Conservation." *Historian* 15(Spring):148–162.

Crossland, J. and V. Brodine. 1973. "Drinking Water." *Environment* (April). CSG. 1970. *Environmental Quality and State Government.* Council of State Governments. Lexington, Ky.: Iron Works Press.

Curti, M. 1964. *The Growth of American Thought.* New York: Harper & Row.

Curtis, G. 1971. "Conservative Dominance in Japanese Politics." *Current History* (April).

Curtis, R. and E. Hogan. 1969. *Perils of the Peaceful Atom.* New York: Ballantine Books.

Dadsiman, Q. 1972. "The Pathology of Lake Erie." *Nation* (April 17):492–496.

Darling, F. F. 1966. *Future Environments of North America.* Garden City, N.Y.: Natural History Press.

Darmstadter, J. 1971. *Energy in the World Economy: A Statistical Review of Trends in Output, Trade, and Consumption Since 1925.* Baltimore: The Johns Hopkins University Press.

Darmstadter, J. 1972. "Energy Consumption: Trends and Patterns." In S. H. Schurr, ed., *Energy, Economic Growth and the Environment.* Baltimore: The Johns Hopkins University Press.

Davis, W. H. 1970. "Overpopulated America." *New Republic* (January 10).

De Bell, G., ed. 1970. *The Environmental Handbook.* New York: Ballantine Books.

De Mente, B. and F. Perry. 1967. *The Japanese as Consumers: Asia's First Great Mass Market.* New York: Walker/Weatherhill.

Detwyler, T. R., ed. 1971. *Man's Impact on Environment.* New York: McGraw-Hill.

Dicks, H. V. 1960. "Some Notes on the Russian National Character." Pp. 636–651 in C. Black, ed., *Transformation of Russian Society.* Cambridge, Mass.: Harvard University Press.

Dodds, C. B. 1965. "The Historiography of American Conservation: Past and Prospects." *Pacific Northwest Quarterly* 56(January):75–81.

Doi, T. 1973. *The Anatomy of Dependence.* Trans. J. Bester. Tokyo: Kodansha International.

Dolan, E. 1969. *TANSTAAFL: The Economic Strategy for Environmental Crisis.* New York: Holt, Rinehart and Winston.

Dolgushin, I. Iu. 1969. "The Effects of Climatic Fluctuations of the Physical Environment and Conditions of Economic Development of the Middle Ob Districts." *SGRT* (June):286–304. Translated from *Izvestiia Akademii Nauk SSSR* No. 5(1968):69–83.

Donaldson, R. H. 1972. "The 1971 Soviet Central Committee: An Assessment of the New Elite." *World Politics* 25(3)(September):382–409.

Dore, R. 1973. *British Factory-Japanese Factory: The Origin of National Diversity in Industrial Relations.* Berkeley: University of California Press.

Dorfman, R. and N. Dorfman, eds. 1972. *Economics of the Environment.* New York: W. W. Norton & Company.

Drachev, S. M. and V. E. Sinelnikov. 1968. "Protection of Small Rivers under Intensive Use: Taking the Moskva River as an Example." *Soviet Hydrology: Selected Papers* No. 3

DSJP. Daily Summary of the Japanese Press.

DSJP. 1972a. "New Development of Foreign Policies Concerning the Resources Problem." *Daily Summary of the Japanese Press* (April 12). Tokyo: United States Embassy.

DSJP. 1972b. "White Paper on Medium and Small Enterprises." *Daily Summary of the Japanese Press* (April 26). Tokyo: United States Embassy.

Dubos, R. 1970. "We Can't Buy Our Way Out." *Psychology Today* (March).

Dumont, R. and B. Rosier. 1969. *The Hungry Future.* Trans. R. Linell and R. Sutcliffe. New York: Praeger Publishers.

DY. Daily Yomiuri.

Earhart, H. 1964. *Japanese Religion: Unity and Diversity.* Belmont, Cal.: Dickenson Publishing Company.

East. 1971. "A Story of Japanese Beef." *East* 7(April).

Eason, W. W. 1968. "Population Changes." Pp. 203–240 in A. Kassof, ed., *Prospects for Soviet Society.* New York: Praeger Publishers.

Ebel, R. E. 1970. *Communist Trade in Oil and Gas.* New York: Praeger Publishers.

Economist, 1967. "Administrative Guidance." *Economist* (May 27).

Economist. 1970. "Where It Comes Down in Chunks." *Economist* (September 5).

Edel, M. 1973. "Autos, Energy, and Pollution." *Environment* (October).

Ehrenfeld, D. 1972. *Conserving Life on Earth.* New York: Oxford University Press.

Ehrlich, P. R. and A. H. Ehrlich. 1972. *Population, Resources, Environment: Issues in Human Ecology.* 2d ed., rev. San Francisco: W. H. Freeman and Company.

Ehrlich, P. R. and J. P. Holdren, eds. 1971a. *Global Ecology.* New York: Harcourt Brace Jovanovich.

Ehrlich. P. R. and J. P. Holdren. 1971b. "Impact of Population Growth." *Science* 171:1212–1217.

Ehrlich, P. R., J. P. Holdren, and B. Commoner. 1972. *Environment* (April).

Ekirch, A. E. 1973. *Man and Nature in America*. Lincoln: University of Nebraska Press.

Ellingsworth, R. 1972. *Japanese Economic Policies and Security*. Adelphi Papers 90. London: International Institute for Strategic Studies.

Elliot, I. F. 1974. *The Soviet Energy Balance: Natural Gas, Other Fossil Fuels, and Alternative Power Sources*. New York: Praeger Publishers.

Emelianov, V. S. 1971. "Nuclear Energy in the Soviet Union." *Bulletin of the Atomic Scientists* 27(November):38–41.

Emmerson, J. 1971. *Arms, Yen and Power: The Japanese Dilemma*. New York: Dunellan.

Engles, F. 1964. *Dialetics of Nature*. Moscow: Progress Publishers.

ENR. 1970. "Japan's Pollution Grows With Population." *Engineering News-Record* 185(December 17).

Environment. 1970. "Spectrum." *Environment* 12(9):S-3.

Environment. 1971. "Spectrum." *Environment* 13(9):28.

EPA. 1968. *Outlook and Basic Policy for the National Economy*.Tokyo: Economic Planning Agency.

EPA. 1970. *New Economic and Social Development Plan, 1970–1975*. Tokyo: Economic Planning Agency.

EPA. 1972a. *The Japanese and Their Society*. Part II of the Report on National Life. Tokyo: Economic Planning Agency.

EPA. 1972b. *New Comprehensive National Development Plan* (October). Rev. ed. (Orig. May 1969). Tokyo: Economic Planning Agency.

EPA. 1973. *White Paper on National Life: 1973*. Tokyo: Economic Planning Agency.

EPA. 1974. *Beyond Economic Growth*. Tokyo: Economic Planning Agency.

EPC. 1974. *Long-Term Prospectus for Preservation of the Environment: An Interim Report*. Tokyo: Planning Committee, Central Council for Environmental Pollution Control.

Esposito, J. C. 1970. *Vanishing Air*. New York: Grossman Publishers.

Ewald, W. R., Jr., ed. 1967. *Environment for Man: The Next Fifty Years*. Bloomington: Indiana University Press.

Fairbank, J. E. Reischauer, and A. Craig. 1965. *East Asia: The Modern Transformation*. Boston: Houghton Mifflin Company.

Falk, R. A. 1971. *This Endangered Planet. Prospects and Proposals for Human Survival*. New York: Random House.

Falk, R. A. 1975. *A Study of Future Worlds*. New York: The Free Press.

FAO. 1971. *Production Yearbook*. New York: United Nations Food and Agriculture Organization.

Farnsworth, L. W. 1973. "Japan 1972: New Faces and New Friends." *Asian Survey* 13(January).

Fedorenko, N. and K. Gofman. 1973. "Problems of the Optimization of Environmental Planning and Management." *Current Digest of the Soviet Press* (hereafter cited as *CDSP*) 25(5):1. Translated from *Voprosi Ekonomiki* (October):38–46.

FEER. *Far Eastern Economic Review*.

FEER. 1972. "Energy: Japan Gears Down." *Far Eastern Economic Review* (July 29).

Feitelman, N. 1968. "Ob ekonomicheskoi otsenke mineralnykh resursov." *Voprosy Ekonomiki* (November).

Fine, S. 1964. *Laissez Faire and the General Welfare State*. Ann Arbor: University of Michigan Press.

Fisher, J., N. Simon, and J. Vincent. 1969. *Wildlife in Danger.* New York: The Viking Press.

Fitch, L. C. 1968. "Eight Goals for an Urbanizing America." *Daedalus* (Fall).

Fleming, D. 1972. "Roots of the New Conservation Movement." *Perspectives in American History* 6:7–91.

Fleron, F. 1968. "Toward a Reconceptualization of Political Change in the Soviet Union." *Comparative Politics* 1(2)(January):228–244.

Fleron, F. 1969. "Cooptations as a Mechanism of Adaptation to Change: The Soviet Political Leadership System." *Polity* 2(2)(Winter):176–201.

Fleron, F. 1970. "Representation of Career Types in the Soviet Political Leadership." Pp. 108–139 in R. B. Farrell, ed., *Political Leadership in Eastern Europe and the Soviet Union.* Chicago: Aldine Publishing Company.

Forrester, J. W. 1971. *World Dynamics.* Cambridge, Mass.: Wright-Allen Press.

Fortune. 1970. "What Business Thinks: Fortune 500-Yankelovich Survey." *Fortune* (February 2).

Fox, I. K., ed. 1971. *Water Resources Law and Policy in the Soviet Union.* Madison: University of Wisconsin Press.

Freeman, A. M. and R. H. Haveman. 1972. "Clean Rhetoric and Dirty Water." *The Public Interest* 28(Summer).

Fujii, T. 1970. "Japanese Economy: Future Outlook." *Asia Scene* 15(September).

Fyodorov, Ye. 1972. "The Threat to the Environment." *Soviet Life* (July):15–18.

Galbraith, J. K. 1958. "How Much Should a Country Consume?" In H. Jarrett, ed., *Perspectives on Conservation.* Baltimore: The Johns Hopkins University Press.

Gardner, R. N. 1972. "UN Think Tank." *Vista* (September-October).

Garvey, G. 1972. *Energy, Ecology, Economy.* New York: W. W. Norton & Company.

Gehlen, M. 1969. *The Communist Party of the Soviet Union.* Bloomington: Indiana University Press.

Gehlen, M. and M. McBride. 1968. "The Soviet Central Committee: An Elite Analysis." *American Political Science Review* 62(4)(December):1232–1241.

Georgiev, A. V. 1972. "On Measures for the Future Improvement and Conservation and the Rational Utilization of Natural Resources." *CDSP* 24(38):8–9. Translated from *Izvestiia* (September 21):4–5.

Gerasimov, I. P. 1963. "Reducing the Dependence of Soviet Agriculture on Natural Elements to a Minimum." *SGRT* 4(2)(February):3–11. Translated from *Izvestiia Akademii Nauk SSSR,* seriia geograficheskaia No. 5 (1962):43–51.

Gerasimov, I. P. 1969. "A Soviet Plan for Nature." *Natural History* 78(10)(December):24.

Gerasimov, I. P. 1971. "Scientific-Technical Progress and Geography." *SGRT* 12(4)(April):205–218. Translated from *Materialy V Sezda Geograficheskogo obshchestva SSSR* (1970), Leningrad.

Gerasimov, I. P., D. L. Armand, and V. S. Preobrazhenskii. 1964. "Natural Resources of the Soviet Union: Their Study and Utilization." Physical Geography Symposium at the Fourth Congress of Geographical Society of the USSR: *SGRT* 5(8)(October):3–15.

Gerasimov, I. P., D. L. Armand, and K. M. Yefrom. 1971. *Natural Resources of the Soviet Union: Their Use and Renewal* (W. A. Jackson, ed.). San Francisco: W. H. Freeman and Company. Translation of *Prirodnye resursy Sovetskogo Soiuza: ikh ispolzovanie i vosproizvodstvo* (1963). Moscow.

Gillette, R. 1971. "Nuclear Power in the USSR: American Visitors Find Surprises." *Science* 173(September 10):1003–1006.

GJ. 1974. *Monitoring of Environmental Pollution in Japan* (February). The Government of Japan.

GJ. n.d. *The Present State of Monitoring and Surveillance of Environmental Pollution.* The Government of Japan.

Goldman, C. R. 1973–1974. "Will Baikal and Tahoe Be Saved?" *Cry California*, published by California Tomorrow (Winter).

Goldman, M. I. 1970. "The Convergence of Environmental Disruption." *Science* 170(October 2):37–42.

Goldman, M. I. 1971. "Our Far-Flung Correspondents." *New Yorker* (June 19).

Goldman, M. I. 1972a. "Externalities and the Race for Economic Growth in the USSR: Will the Environment Ever Win?" *Journal of Political Economy* (March–April):314–327.

Goldman, M. I. 1972b. *The Spoils of Progress: Environmental Pollution in the Soviet Union.* Cambridge, Mass.: The M.I.T. Press.

Goldman, M. I. 1974. "Raw Materials, the Environment, and Foreign Trade in the Soviet Union." Paper presented at the Conference on Soviet Resource Management and the Environment, University of Washington, Seattle, June 6–7.

Gorer, G. and J. Rickman. 1949. *The People of Great Russia: A Psychological Study.* London: The Cresset Press.

Goto, S. 1974. "An Economic Study of Human Exodus from the Agricultural Sector in Japan." Ph.D. dissertation. Honolulu: University of Hawaii.

Graham, F. 1966. *Disaster by Default: Politics and Water Pollution.* New York: Modern Literary Editions Publishing Company.

Green, M. J., J. M. Fallows, and D. R. Zwick. 1972. *Who Runs Congress?* New York: Grossman Publishers; Bantam Books.

Gregory, G. 1971. "The Japanese Model: Prospects for the Future." *Asia Quarterly* 4.

Gresser, J. 1973. *A Japan Center for Human Environmental Problems: The Beginning of International Public Interest Cooperation.* Institute of International Studies. Berkeley: University of California Press.

Grin, A. N. and N. I. Koronkevich. 1969. "Principles of Construction of Long-Term Water-Management Balance." *SGRT* 10(3)(March):118–136. Translated from *Voprosy Geografii* No. 73(1968):45–62.

GS. 1970. *Mercury in the Environment.* Geological Survey. Washington, D.C.: Government Printing Office.

Guillain, R. 1970. *The Japanese Challenge: The Race to the Year 2000.* Philadelphia: J. B. Lippincott Company.

Gwertzman, B. 1970a. "New Russian Movie Discusses Industry Environmental Role." *New York Times* (March 6):6.

Gwertzman, B. 1970b. "Soviet Debates Whether to Expose Sins of Polluters." *New York Times* (December 14):52.

Hall, J. W. 1965. "Changing Conceptions of the Modernization of Japan." In M. B. Jansen, ed., *Changing Japanese Attitudes Toward Modernization.* Princeton, N.J.: Princeton University Press.

Halloran, R. 1969. *Japan: Images and Reality.* New York: Alfred A. Knopf.

Halloway, J. K. 1971. "Dark Satanic Mills and Diplomacy." *Foreign Service Journal* 48(May).

Hardin, G. 1964. "Tragedy of the Commons." In G. Hardin, ed., *Population Evolution, and Birth Control*. San Francisco: W. H. Freeman and Company.

Hardin, G. 1972. *Exploring New Ethics for Survival*. New York: The Viking Press.

Harris, C. D. 1968. "City and Region in the Soviet Union." Pp. 254–276 in R. P. Beckinsale and J. M. Houston, eds., *Urbanization and Its Problems: Essays in Honor of E. W. Gilbert*. New York: Barnes & Noble.

Harte, J. and R. H. Socolow. 1971. *Patient Earth*. New York: Holt, Rinehart and Winston.

Haskell, E. H. and V. S. Price. 1973. *State Environmental Management: Case Studies of Nine States*. New York: Praeger Publishers.

Hay, K. A. 1970. *Canadian Minerals and the Japanese Market*. Ottawa: Canada-Japan Trade Council.

Hays, S. P. 1958. "The Myth of Conservation." In H. Jarrett, ed., *Perspectives on Conservation*. Baltimore: The Johns Hopkins University Press.

Hays, S. P. 1959. *Conservation and the Gospel of Efficiency*. Cambridge, Mass.: Harvard University Press.

Headley, J. C. and J. N. Lewis. 1967. *The Pesticide Problem: An Economic Approach to Public Policy*. Baltimore: The Johns Hopkins University Press.

Heald, M. 1970. *The Social Responsibilities of Business: Company and Community, 1900–1960*. Cleveland: Case Western Reserve.

Heilbroner, R. L. 1970. "Priorities for the Seventies." *Saturday Review* (January 3).

Heilbroner, R. L. 1972a. "Growth and Survival." *Foreign Affairs* 51:139–153.

Heilbroner, R. L. 1972b. "The Limits to Growth." *Foreign Affairs* (October).

Heilbroner, R. L. 1975. *An Inquiry into the Human Prospect*. New York: W. W. Norton & Company.

Hellman, D. C. 1972. *Japan and East Asia: The New International Order*. New York: Praeger Publishers.

Hennessy, J. 1971. "Japan's Need for Raw Materials." *Eastern Economist* 57(August 13).

HEW. 1969. *Report of the Secretary's Commission on Pesticides and Their Relationship to Environmental Health*. Department of Health, Education, and Welfare. Washington, D.C.: Government Printing Office.

HEW. 1970. *Profile Study of Air Pollution Control Activities in Foreign Countries*. Department of Health, Education, and Welfare, Public Health Service, Environmental Health Service. Washington, D.C.: Government Printing Office.

Hibino, K. 1973. "Tokyo: The Overcrowded Megalopolis." *Japan Quarterly* (April-June).

History of Steel in Japan, The. 1974. Nippon Steel Corporation.

Hoag, R. 1971. *Japanese Investment in Alaska*. State of Alaska: Industrial Development Division.

Holdren, J. and P. Herrera. 1971. *Energy*. New York: Sierra Club.

Hollerman, L. 1967. *Japan's Dependence on the World Economy*. Princeton, N.J.: Princeton University Press.

Holt, S. J. 1969. "The Food Resources of the Ocean." *Scientific American* (September).

Hoshino, Y. 1973. "Remodeling the Archipelago." *Japan Quarterly* 18(April-June).

Hough, J. F. 1969. *The Soviet Prefects: Local Party Organs in Industrial Decision-Making*. Cambridge, Mass.: Harvard University Press.

HUD. 1971. "Housing and Urban Development in Japan." *HUD International Brief* (June). U.S. Department of Housing and Urban Development.

HUD. 1972. *HUD International Brief.* Special Supplement No. 7 (July). U.S. Department of Housing and Urban Development.

Huff, R. L. 1973. "Political Decision Making in the Japanese Atomic Energy Program." Ph.D. dissertation. Washington, D.C.: George Washington University.

Hunt, C. A. and R. M. Garrels. 1972. *Water: The Web of Life.* New York: W. W. Norton & Company.

Hutchings, R. 1968. "Declining Prospects of Soviet Population Growth." *The World Today* 24(12)(December):521–530.

Huth, H. 1957. *Nature and the American: Three Centuries of Changing Attitudes.* Berkeley: University of California Press.

Hymans, H. 1974. "Coal: Revival in Japan." *Far Eastern Economic Review* (March).

Iandyganov, Ia. Ia. 1973. "Reserves for Industrial Water Supply in the Urals." *CDSP* 25(40):12. Translated from *Ekonomika i Organizatsiia Promyshlennogo Proizvodstva* (March):83–88.

Iinuma, J. 1974. "The Curious Crisis in Japanese Agriculture." *Japan Quarterly* (October–December).

IISS. 1972. *Study of the World Situation in 1972.* London: International Institute for Strategic Studies.

Ike, N. 1972. *Japanese Politics: Patron-Client Democracy.* New York: Alfred A. Knopf.

Ike, N. 1973. *Japan: The New Superstate.* San Francisco: W. H. Freeman and Company.

Imazu, H. 1974. "Conservative Crisis." *Japan Quarterly* (October–December).

Inkeles, A. and R. A. Bauer. 1959. *The Soviet Citizen.* Cambridge, Mass.: Harvard University Press.

IPP. 1965. *Future Population Estimates by Prefecture, Japan: 1965–1995.* Research Series No. 164 (July 1). Tokyo: Institute of Population Problems.

IPP. 1969. *Eugenic Protection Law in Japan.* English Pamphlet Series No. 68 (March). Tokyo: Institute of Population Problems.

IPP. 1971. *Population and Environmental Problems in Japan.* English Pamphlet Series No. 75 (October). Tokyo: Institute of Population Problems.

IPP. 1972. *Selected Statistics Indicating the Demographic Situation in Japan.* No. 9 (August). Tokyo: Institute of Population Problems.

IRJ. 1975. *Industrial Review of Japan.* Tokyo: Nihon Keizai Shinbunsha.

Irukuyama, K. 1968. "Minamata Disease as a Public Nuisance." In *Minamata Disease.* Kumamoto Medical School.

Irukuyama, K. 1970. "Minamata Disease." For the Assembly of the Formosan Medical Association in Taipei. Taiwan (Formosa), Republic of China (November 21–22).

Ishida, T. 1971. *Japanese Society.* New York: Random House.

Ito, D. 1968. "The Bureaucracy: Its Attitudes and Behavior." *Developing Economies* 6(December).

Iyer, S. G. 1972. "Kogai: Japan's Gross Nuisance Problem." Master's thesis. Cambridge: Massachusetts Institute of Technology.

JAEC. 1972. *Outline of Long-Range Program on Development and Utilization of Atomic Energy* (June). Tokyo: Japan Atomic Energy Commission.

Jackson, W. A. D. 1963. "The Soviet Approach to the Good Earth: Myth and Reality." Pp. 171–185 in R. D. Laird, ed., *Soviet Agriculture and Peasant Affairs.* Lawrence: University of Kansas Press.

Jacobs, J. 1961. *The Death and Life of Great American Cities.* New York: Random House.

JEA. Japan Environment Summary. 1973–1974. Vol. 1, Nos. 1–7; Vol. 2. Nos. 1–5. Japan Environment Agency.

JEA. 1953. *Wildlife Protection and Hunting Law and Related Legislation.* Law. No. 32 of 1918, Cabinet Order No. 254 of 1953, Ordinance of the Ministry of Agriculture and Forestry No. 108 of 1950. Japan Environment Agency.

JEA. 1970a. *Marine Pollution Prevention Law.* Law No. 136 of 1970, amended by Law No. 137 of 1970. Japan Environment Agency.

JEA. 1970b. *Wastes Disposal and Public Cleansing Law.* Law No. 137 of 1970. Japan Environment Agency.

JEA. 1971a. *Administration of Wildlife Protection in Japan.* Tokyo: Japan Environment Agency, Nature Conservation Bureau.

JEA. 1971b. *Agricultural Land Soil Pollution Prevention and Others Law.* Law. No. 139 of 1970, amended by Law No. 88 of 1971. Japan Environment Agency.

JEA. 1971c. *Basic Law for Environmental Pollution Control.* Law No. 132 of 1967, amended by Law No. 132 of 1970 and No. 88 of 1971. Japan Environment Agency.

JEA. 1971d. *List of Endangered Birds in Japan.* Tokyo: Japan Environment Agency.

JEA. 1971e. *Noise Regulation Law.* Law No. 98 of 1968, amended by Law No. 18, No. 108, and No. 135 of 1970, and No. 88 of 1971. Japan Environment Agency.

JEA. 1971f. *Offensive Odor Control Law.* Law No. 91 of 1971. Japan Environment Agency.

JEA. 1972a. *Air Pollution Control in Japan.* Tokyo: Japan Environment Agency.

JEA. 1972b. *Air Pollution Control Law.* Law No. 97 of 1968, amended by Law No. 18, No. 108, and No. 134 of 1970, No. 88 of 1971, and No. 84 of 1972. Japan Environment Agency.

JEA. 1972c. *Enforcement Ordinances of Air Pollution Control Law.* Tokyo: Japan Environment Agency.

JEA. 1972d. *The Human Environment in Japan.* Tokyo: Japan Environment Agency.

JEA. 1972e. *Law for the Punishment of Crimes Relating to Environmental Pollution that Adversely Affects the Health of Persons* (July). Tokyo: Japan Environment Agency.

JEA. 1972f. *Law Relating to the Regulation of Transfer of Special Birds and Related Legislation.* Law No. 49 of 1972, Cabinet Order No. 405 of 1972, Ordinance of the Prime Minister's Office, No. 71 of 1972. Japan Environment Agency.

JEA. 1972g. *Natural Parks Law.* Law No. 161 of 1967, amended by Law No. 140 and No. 161 of 1962, No. 13, No. 61, and No. 140 of 1970, No. 88 of 1971, and No. 52 and No. 85 of 1972. Japan Environment Agency.

JEA. 1972h. *Nature Conservation Law.* Law No. 85 of 1972. Japan Environment Agency.

JEA. 1972i. *Pollution Related Diseases and Relief Measures in Japan.* Tokyo: Japan Environment Agency.

JEA. 1972j. *Quality of the Environment in Japan.* Tokyo: Japan Environment Agency.

JEA. 1972k. *Showa 47 nenban kankyo hakusho, seisaku no atarashii zahyo* (White Paper on the Environment: A New Goal for Environmental Policy). Tokyo: Japan Environment Agency.

JEA. 1972l. *Water Pollution Control in Japan.* Tokyo: Japan Environment Agency.

JEA. 1972m. *Water Pollution Control Law.* Law No. 138 of 1970, amended by Law No. 88 of 1971 and No. 84 of 1972. Japan Environment Agency.

JEA. 1973a. *Environment Agency* (June). Japan Environment Agency.

JEA. 1973b. *Environmental Quality Standards for Aircraft Noise.* Tokyo: Environment Agency Notification No. 154 (December 27).

JEA. 1973c. *Quality of the Environment in Japan.* Tokyo: Japan Environment Agency.

JEA. 1973d. *Report of the Ad Hoc Group on Air Pollution from Fuel Combustion in Stationary Sources.* Tokyo: Japan Environment Agency.

JERC. 1972. *Japan's Economy in 1980 in the Global Context: The Nation's Role in a Polycentric World.* Tokyo: Japan Economic Research Center.

Johnson, B. 1972. "The House that Stockholm Built." *Vista* (September-October).

Johnston, H. 1971. "Reduction of Stratosphere Ozone by Nitrogen Oxide Catalysts from Supersonic Transport Exhaust." *Science* 173:517–522.

JNR. 1971. *Problems of the Human Environment in Japan.* Japan National Report to the Stockholm Conference (March).

JPRS. 1970a. *Commentary on Soviet Periodicals on Environmental Pollution* (April). Washington, D.C.: Joint Publications Research Service.

JPRS. 1970b. *Soviet Research in Sanitation and Noise Measurement* (June 11). Washington, D.C.: Joint Publications Research Service.

JPRS. 1970c. *Soviet Specialists Discuss the Control of Noise.* Washington, D.C.: Joint Publications Research Service.

JQ. 1972a. "Group for the Protection of the Oze Region." *Japan Quarterly* (January-March).

JQ. 1972b. "Tokyo's Garbage War." *Japan Quarterly* (April-June).

JQ. 1972c. "A Whale of a Problem." *Japan Quarterly* (October-December).

JQ. 1973a. "Citizen's Movements." *Japan Quarterly* (October-December).

JQ. 1973b. "Consumerism." *Japan Quarterly* (July-September).

JQ. 1973c. "Fisheries and Industrial Pollution." *Japan Quarterly* (October-December).

JQ. 1973d. "Pollution Case Law." *Japan Quarterly* (July-September).

JSTA. 1971. *The Fundamentals of a Comprehensive Science and Technology Policy for the 1970's.* Tokyo: Japan Science and Technology Agency.

JT. *Japan Times.*

JT. 1972. *Economic Survey of Japan, 1971–1972.* Tokyo: Japan Times.

Kaliuzhnyi, D. N. 1961. *Sanitarnaia okhrana atmosfernogo vozdukha ot vybrosov predpriiatii chernoi metallurgii.* Kiev: Gosmedizdat.

Kawata, T. 1972. "Japan's Responsibility for Economic Cooperation." *Japan Quarterly* 19(October-December).

Kelley, D. R. 1974. "Toward a Model of Soviet Decision Making: A Research Note." *American Political Science Review* 68(2):701–706.

Kelsey, D. P., ed. 1972. *Farming in the New Nation: Interpreting American Agriculture 1790–1840.* Washington, D.C.: Agricultural History Society.

Keyfitz, N. 1971. "On the Momentum of Population Growth." *Demography 8.*

KH. *Kankyo Hakai.*

KH. 1971. "Zenkoku no omona kogai sosho" (Principal Law Suits Against Public Nuisances in Japan). *Kankyo Hakai* (Environmental Disruption) (November 2).

Khody, V. 1974. "A Protective Charter for Baikal." *CDSP* 26(47):24–25. Translated from *Pravda* (November 20):6.

Khotsianov, L. 1973. "The City Needs Quiet Too." *CDSP* 25(13):21. Translated from *Literaturnaia Gazeta* 49(3 December 1972):13.

Khramov, B. 1973. "Pure City Air." *CDSP* 25(2):6. Translated from *Pravda* (January 12):3.

Kinoshita, S. 1969. "How Long Will High Growth Continue?" *Oriental Economist* 37(September).

Kirillin, V. A. 1972. "On Measures for the Further Improvement of Conservation and the Rational Utilization of Natural Resources." Speech to Supreme Soviet. *CDSP* 24(38):4–8. Translated from *Pravda* (September 20):2–3.

Kirillin, V. A. 1972. "On Measures for the Further Improvement of Conservation and the Rational Utilization of Natural Resources." Speech to Supreme Soviet. *CDSP* 24(38):4–8. Translated from *Pravda* (September 20):2–3.

Kirillin, V. A. 1975. "Energetika—problemy i perspectivy." *Kommunist* 1(January): 43–51.

Kiuchi, N. 1971. "Japan Will Have to Slow Down." *Fortune* (February).

Kluckhohn, C. 1961. "Studies of Russian National Character." Pp. 607–619 in A. Inkeles and K. Geiger, eds., *Soviet Society: A Book of Readings*. Boston: Houghton Mifflin Company.

Kneese, A. V. and C. L. Schultze. 1975. *Pollution, Prices, and Public Policy*. Washington, D.C.: The Brookings Institution.

Kneese, A. V. et al. 1970. *Economics and the Environment: A Materials Balance Approach* Baltimore: The Johns Hopkins University Press.

Kobayashi, S. 1970. "Environmental Pollution." *Japan Quarterly* 18(October–December).

Kogai benran. 1972. A Pollution Handbook compiled by Kankyo Kagaku Kenkyu-jo (Research Institute for Environmental Science). Tokyo.

Kogai nenkan. 1971. A Pollution Yearbook published by Kankyo Hozen Kyokai (Environment Preservation Society). Tokyo.

Kolbasov, D. C. 1971. "Okhrana prirody." *Sovetskoe Gosudarstvo i Pravo* 2:12–20.

Kosaka, M. 1972. *100 Million Japanese: The Postwar Experience*. Tokyo/Palo Alto: Kodansha International.

Kothari, R. 1974. *Footsteps into the Future: Diagnosis of the Present World and a Design for an Alternative*. New York: The Free Press.

KP. Komsomolskaia Pravda.

Kramer, J. M. 1972. "Mobilization Systems and Modernization: Environmental Pollution in the Soviet Union." Paper presented at 1972 AAASS Meeting, Dallas, Texas, March 16.

Kramer, J. M. 1973a. "The Politics of Conservation and Pollution in the USSR." Ph.D. dissertation. Charlottesville: University of Virginia.

Kramer, J. M. 1973b. "Prices and the Conservation of Natural Resources in the Soviet Union." *Soviet Studies* 24(3)(January):364–373.

Kramer, J. M. 1974. "Environmental Problems in the USSR: The Divergence of Theory and Practice." *Journal of Politics* 36(4)(November):886–899.

Kreith, F. 1973. "Lack of Impact." *Environment* (January–February).

Kudelin, V. I., V. N. Kunin, M. I. Lvovich, and A. A. Sokolov. 1971. "The Freshwater Supply Problems of Mankind." *SGRT* 12(6)(June):329–345. Translated from *Materialy V sezda Geograficheskogo obshchestva SSSR* (1970), Leningrad.

Kunimoto, Y. 1972. "Pollution and Local Government." *Japan Quarterly* 18(April–June).

Kurihara, K. K. 1971. *The Growth Potential of the Japanese Economy.* Baltimore: The Johns Hopkins University Press.

Kuwata, K. 1974. "Discord Among Conservatives." *Japan Quarterly* (July-September).

Lacey, M. J. 1970. "Man, Nature, and the Ecological Perspective." *American Studies* 8:13–27.

LaMothe, J. 1971. "Water Quality in the Soviet Union: A Review." Medical Intelligence Office, Department of the Army, Office of the Surgeon General (July).

Laird, M. W. 1972. "Natural Resources and International Conflict: A Japanese Case Study." Master's thesis. Cambridge: Massachusetts Institute of Technology.

Lenin, V. I. 1927. *Materialism and Empirio-Criticism.* New York: International Publishers.

Leopold, A. 1966. *A Sand County Almanac: With Essays on Conservation from Round River.* New York: Oxford University Press.

Levin, A. and V. Udovenko. 1974. "Water Resources and Production Efficiency." *CDSP* 26(18):14. Translated from *Voprosy Ekonomiki* 1973 (December):60–70.

Lewis, R. S. 1973. *Citizens vs. the Atomic Industrial Establishment.* New York: The Viking Press.

LG. Literaturnaia Gazeta.

Lichtheim, G. 1965. *Marxism: An Historical and Critical Study.* New York: Praeger Publishers.

Like, I. 1973. "Turning Down the GNP." *Environment* (July-August).

Listengurt, F. M. 1971. "Problems in the Formation of the Population of Cities in the USSR." *SGRT* 12(2)(February):117–123. Translated from *Raionnaia planirovka i problemy rasseleniia* No. 2 (1970):68–73, Kiev.

Litvinov, N. 1961. "Water Pollution in the U.S.S.R. and in Other Eastern European Countries." Pp. 17–63 in *Conference on Water Pollution Problems in Europe.* Vol. 1. Geneva: United Nations Printing Office.

LJ. Look Japan.

LJ. 1974a. "Achievements of Japan's Economic Cooperation in 1973." *Look Japan* (July).

LJ. 1974b. "The Consensus Society." *Look Japan* (October).

LJ. 1974c. "Japanese Labor Unions." *Look Japan* (July).

LJ. 1974d. "Japan's Coal Situation and Mining Techniques (1)." *Look Japan* (October).

LJ. 1974e. "Japan's Coal Situation and Mining Techniques (2)." *Look Japan* (November).

LJ. 1974f. "Restructuring the Japanese Economy." *Look Japan* (October).

LJ. 1974g. "Situation of Japanese Overseas Investments." *Look Japan* (May).

Lockheimer, F. R. 1970. "Japan's New Population Politics." American Universities Field Staff Report Service. *East Asia Series* 17(5). New York.

Lopatina, E. B., A. A. Mints, L. I. Mukhina, O. R. Nazarevskii, and V. S. Preobrazhenskii. 1971. "The Present State and Future Tasks in the Theory and Method of an Evaluation of the Natural Environment and Resources." *SGRT* 12(3)(March):142–151. Translated from *Izvestiia Akademii Nauk SSSR, seriia geograficheskaia* No. 4(1970):45–54.

Lubkin, B. G. 1970. "US-Soviet Collaboration to Measure Pion Charge Radius." *Physics Today* 23(September):18–19.

Luscher, C. W. 1970. "Attitudes Towards Conservation in the Soviet Union." *Living Wilderness* 34(Autumn):13–19.

Lvovich, M. I. 1962. "Complex Utilization and Protection of Water Resources." *SGRT* 3(10)(December):3–11. Translated from *Izvestiia Akademii Nauk,* seriia geograficheskaia No. 2(1961):37–45.

Lvovich, M. I. 1969. "Scientific Principles of the Complex Utilization and Conservation of Water Resources." *SGRT* (March):97–117. Translated from *Voprosy Geografii* No. 73(1968):3–32.

Lydolph, P. E. 1964. *Geography of the USSR.* New York: John Wiley & Sons.

MacDonald, G. J. 1972. "Energy and the Environment." In S. H. Schurr, ed., *Energy, Economic Growth and the Environment.* Baltimore: The Johns Hopkins University Press.

Maddox, J. F. 1972. *The Doomsday Syndrome.* New York: McGraw-Hill.

MAF. 1972. *Fisheries Statistics of Japan, 1972.* Tokyo: Ministry of Agriculture and Forestry.

MAF. 1974a. Annual Report on the Movements of Forestry. Tokyo: Ministry of Agriculture and Forestry.

MAF. 1974b. *Fisheries Production in 1973.* Tokyo: Ministry of Agriculture and Forestry.

Main, J. 1970. "Conservationists at the Barricade." In Editors of *Fortune, The Environment.* New York: Harper & Row.

Malenbaum, W. 1973. "World Resources for the Year 2000." *Annals of the American Academy of Political and Social Science* (July).

Maloney, J. C. and L. Slovonsky. 1971. "The Pollution Issue: A Survey of Editorial Judgments." In L. L. Roos, Jr., ed., *The Politics of Ecosuicide.* New York: Holt, Rinehart and Winston.

Mangushev, K. and N. Prikhodko. 1972. "Put the Earth's Heat to Work." *CDSP* 24(13)(April 26):18. Translated from *Pravda* (March 30):3.

Margolin, M. 1970. "The Habit of Waste." *The Nation* (March 2).

Marine, G. 1969. *America the Raped.* New York: Simon and Schuster.

Marx, K. 1909. *Capital.* Vol. 1. *The Process of Capitalist Production.* Chicago: C. H. Kerr.

Marx, K. 1964. *The Economic and Philosophical Manuscripts of 1844.* New York: International Publishers.

Marx, L. 1967. *The Machine in the Garden: Technology and the Pastoral Ideal in America.* New York: Oxford University Press.

Marx, W. 1967. *The Frail Ocean.* New York: Ballantine Books.

Marx, W. 1969. "The Disney Imperative." *The Nation* (July 28).

Marx, W. 1971. *Man and His Environment: Waste.* New York: Harper & Row.

Mathisen, O. A. and D. E. Bevan. 1968. *Some International Aspects of Soviet Fisheries.* Columbus: Ohio University Press.

Matley, I. M. 1966. "The Marxist Approach to the Geographical Environment." *Annals of the Association of American Geographers* 56(1)(March):97–111.

Matley, I. M. 1970. "The Golodnaia Steppe: A Russian Irrigation Venture in Central Asia." *Geographical Review* 60(3)(July):328–346.

Mazur, D. P. "Reconstruction of Fertility Trends for the Female Population of the USSR." *Population Studies* 21(1)(July):33–52.

MC. 1970. *Urban Land Policy and Taxation in Asia.* Tokyo: Ministry of Construction.

McCamy, J. L. 1972. *The Quality of the Environment.* New York: The Free Press.

McCaul, J. 1972. "The Politics of Technology." *Environment* (March).

McCaull, J. 1972. "The Tide of Industrial Waste." *Environment* (December).

McCloskey, M. 1972. "Wilderness Movement at the Crossroads, 1945–1970." *Pacific Historical Review* (August).

McConnell, G. 1954. "The Conservation Movement: Past and Present." *Western Political Quarterly* 7:463–478.

McKean, M. A. 1974. "The Potentials for Grass-Roots Democracy in Post-War Japan: The Anti-Pollution Movement as a Case Study in Political Activism." Ph.D. dissertation. Berkeley: University of California.

MDN. Mainichi Daily News.

Mead, M. 1951. *Soviet Attitudes Toward Authority.* New York: McGraw-Hill.

Meadows, D. H., D. L. Meadows, J. Randers, and W. W. Behrens, III. 1972. *The Limits to Growth.* New York: Universe Books.

Meier, H. A. 1957. "Technology and Democracy, 1800–1860." *Mississippi Valley Historical Review* 43(March):618–640.

Melosi, M. V. 1973. "Out of Sight, Out of Mind: The Environment and Disposal of Municipal Refuse, 1860–1920." *Historian* 35(August).

Mendel, D. H. 1968. "Japan as a Model for Developing Nations." In E. Skrzypczak, ed., *Japan's Modern Century.* Tokyo.

Merkulov, A. 1965. "Alarm from Baikal." *CDSP* 17(9)(March 24):25–26. Translated from *Pravda* (February 28):4.

Merriam, Jr., L. C. 1972. "The National Parks System: Growth and Outlook." *National Parks and Conservation Magazine* (December).

Metzger, H. P. 1972. *The Atomic Establishment.* New York: Simon and Schuster.

Meyer, A. G. 1965. *Leninism.* New York: Praeger Publishers.

MF. 1974. The Budget in Brief: Japan 1974. Tokyo: Ministry of Finance.

MG. Meditsinskaia Gazeta.

Mickiewicz, E. 1973. *Handbook of Soviet Social Science Data.* New York: The Free Press.

Micklin, P. P. 1967. "The Baykal Controversy: A Resource Use Conflict in the U.S.S.R." *Natural Resources Journal* 7(4)(October):485–498.

Mintz, M. and J. S. Cohen, 1971. *America, Inc.* New York: The Dial Press.

Mishan, E. J. 1970. *Technology and Growth: The Price We Pay.* New York: Praeger Publishers.

Mitchell, J. G., ed. 1971. *Ecotactics: The Sierra Club Handbook for Environmental Activists.* New York: Pocket Books.

MITI. 1974a. *Japan's Sunshine Project* (March). Tokyo: Ministry of International Trade and Industry.

MITI. 1974b. *The Outline of a Resources and Energy Saving Program.* Tokyo: Ministry of International Trade and Industry.

Miwa, Y. 1970. "Policies for Future Economic Growth." *Asia Scene* 15(August).

Mix, S. A. 1966. "Solid Wastes: Every Day, Another 800 Million Pounds." *Today's Health* 44(March).

Miyamoto, K. 1969–1970. "Urban Problems in Japan, With Emphasis Upon the Period of Rapid Economic Growth." *Japan Institute of International Affairs Annual Review* 5.

Miyamoto, K., ed. 1970. *Kogai to Jumin Undo* (Pollution and the Movement of Inhabitants). Tokyo: Jichitai Kenkyushu.

Miyoshi, S. 1971. "Japan's Resources Policy at a Turning Point." *Japan Quarterly* 18(July–September).

Moorcraft, D. 1973. *Must the Seas Die?* Boston: Gambit.

Morley, J. 1970. "Growth for What? The Issue of the Seventies." In G. Curtis, ed., *Japanese-American Relations in the 70's*. Washington, D.C.: Columbia Books.

Morley, J. 1972. *Forecast for Japan: Security in the 70's*. Princeton, N.J.: Princeton University Press.

Morrcrief, L. W. 1970. "The Cultural Basis for Our Environmental Crisis." *Science* 170(October 30):508–512.

Mote, V. L. 1971. "Geography of Air Pollution in the USSR." Ph.D. dissertation. Seattle: University of Washington.

Mote, V. L. 1972. "The Theoretical Roots of Soviet Environmental Problems." Paper presented at 1972 AAASS Meeting, Dallas, Texas.

Mumford, L. 1970. *The Pentagon of Power*. New York: Harcourt Brace Jovanovich.

Murphy, E. F. 1967. *Governing Nation*. Chicago: Quadrangle Books.

Myrdal, G. 1964. *Rich Lands and Poor*. New Haven, Conn.: Yale University Press.

Myrdal, G. 1968. *Asian Drama: An Inquiry into the Poverty of Nations*. 3 Vols. New York: Pantheon.

Myrdal, G. 1971. "Are the Developing Countries Really Developing?" *Bulletin of the Atomic Scientists* (January).

Nagibina, T. 1961. "Organization of Water Pollution Control Measures in the USSR and Eastern European Countries." *Conference on Water Pollution Problems in Europe*. Vols. 1–3. Geneva: United Nations Printing Office.

Nakamura, H. 1964. *Ways of Thinking of Eastern Peoples: India, China, Tibet, and Japan*. Honolulu: East-West Center Press.

Nakamura, K. 1970. "Kogai: Cause for Dismay." *Far Eastern Economic Review* (August 13).

Nakane, C. 1970. *Japanese Society*. Berkeley: University of California Press.

Nakane, C. 1972. *Human Relations in Japan*. Summary translation of "Tateshakai no Ningen Kankei" (Personal Relations in a Vertical Society). Government of Japan, Economic Planning Agency.

Nakayama, I. 1968. "Futurism and the Japanese Economy." *Oriental Economist* 36(January).

Nakayama, I. 1970. "Future of the Economy." *Japan Quarterly* 17(October–December).

Nakayama, I. 1973. "Growth and Inflation." *Japan Quarterly* (October-December).

Nash, R. 1973 *Wilderness and the American Mind*. New Haven, Conn.: Yale University Press.

Novick, S. 1973. "Toward a Nuclear Power Precipice." *Environment* (March).

Novick, S. 1974. "Report Card on Nuclear Power." *Environment* (December).

Novick, S. 1975. "A Troublesome Brew." *Environment* (June).

NRC. 1972. *Marine Environmental Quality*. Ocean Affairs Board of the National Research Council.

NSB. 1971. *National Science Foundation*. National Science Board. Washington, D.C.: Government Printing Office.

NW. Nucleonics Week.

NWC. 1973. *Water Policies for the Future*. Final Report to the president and to the Congress of the United States by the National Water Commission.

NY Times. New York Times.

Odum, H. T. 1971. *Environment, Power, and Society*. New York: Wiley-Interscience.

OE. 1970. "Problems of Public Hazard Prevention." *Oriental Economist* 38(August).

OE. 1972. "Japan Economic Yearbook." *Oriental Economist*.

OECD. 1974. *Major Problems Concerning Air Pollution: The Japanese Experience*. Tokyo: The Organization for Economic Cooperation and Development Publications Center.

OECD. 1975a. *Energy Prospects to 1985: An Assessment of Long Term Energy Developments and Related Policies*. Tokyo: The Organization for Economic Cooperation and Development Publications Center.

OECD. 1975b. *Energy R & D: Problems and Perspectives*. Tokyo: The Organization for Economic Cooperation and Development Publications Center.

OECD. 1975c. *The Industrial Policy of Japan*. Tokyo: The Organization for Economic Cooperation and Development Publications Center.

OECD. 1975d. *Statistics of Energy, 1959–1973*. Tokyo: The Organization for Economic Cooperation and Development Publications Center.

OFR. 1972–1973. *United States Government Organization Manual*. Office of the Federal Register. Washington, D.C.: Government Printing Office.

Ojimi, Y. 1972. "Basic Philosophy and Objectives of Japanese Industrial Policy." In *Industrial Policy in Japan*. Paris: Organization for Economic Cooperation and Development.

Okita, S. 1967. *Causes and Problems of Rapid Economic Growth in Postwar Japan and Their Implications for Newly Developing Economies*. Tokyo.

Okita, S. 1972. "Economic Growth and Environmental Problems." *Area Development in Japan: Japan's Environmental Problems* 5. Tokyo: Japan Center for Area Development Research.

Okunkov, P. S. et al. 1971. "Usilit kontrol za soderzhaniem pestisidov v kormakh." *Veterinariia* 47(7):16–20.

Oldak, P. 1970. "Nature Appeals to Our Generosity." *Current Abstracts of the Soviet Press* 2(6)(June):2. Translation of "Priroda vzyvaet k shchedrosti." *Literaturnaia Gazeta* (June 3):11.

Olson, L. 1970. *Japan in Postwar Asia*. New York: Praeger Publishers.

Olson, M. and H. Landsberg. 1973. *The No-Growth Society*. New York: W. W. Norton & Company.

OMG. 1971. *Environmental Pollution in Osaka City*. Osaka Municipal Government.

Omori, S. 1972. "Two Tasks for Tanaka." *Japan Quarterly* 19(October-December).

Onyx Group, ed. 1974. *Environment U.S.A.: A Guide to Agencies, People and Resources*. New York: R. R. Bowker Company.

O'Riordan, T. 1971. "The Third American Conservation Movement." *Journal of American Studies* (August):155–171.

Owen, L. A. 1937. *The Russian Peasant Movement*. London: King and Son.

Parker, W. H. 1972. *The Superpowers: The United States and the Soviet Union Compared*. London: Macmillan and Co.

PC. 1971. *Country Profiles: Japan*. Washington, D.C.: The Population Council.

PC. 1972. *Reports on Population and Family Planning.* New York: The Population Council.

PCRNB. 1968. *From Sea to Shining Sea: A Report on the American Environment—Our Natural Heritage.* President's Council on Recreation and Natural Beauty. Washington, D.C.: Government Printing Office.

Peffer, E. L. 1951. *The Closing of the Public Domain: Disposal and Reservation Policies, 1900-1950.* Stanford, Cal.: Stanford University Press.

Petrianov, I. 1969. "Vozdushnaia sreda: problemy i perspektivy ee zashchity." *Kommunist* (July):71–80.

Pirages, D. C. 1973. "Global Resources and the Future of Europe." Unpublished paper. Stanford, Cal.: Stanford University.

Pirages, D. C. and P. R. Ehrlich. 1974. *Ark II: Social Response to Environmental Imperatives.* San Francisco: W. H. Freeman and Company.

Pkh. *Planovoe Khoziaistvo.*

Ploss, S. 1965. *Conflict and Decision-Making in Soviet Russia.* Princeton, N.J.: Princeton University Press.

PMPC. 1952. *Resources for Freedom.* President's Materials Policy Commission. Washington, D.C.: Government Printing Office.

PNR. 1970. *United States-Japan Cooperative Program in Natural Resources. Five Year Report, 1964-1969.* Washington, D.C.: Government Printing Office.

Powell, D. E. 1971. "The Social Costs of Modernization: Ecological Problems in the USSR." *World Politics.* 23(4)(July):618–634.

PRB. 1972a. Population Reference Bureau, Inc. "The Soviet People: Population Growth and Policy." *Population Bulletin* 28(5).

PRB. 1972b. World Population Data Sheet. Washington, D.C.: Population Reference Bureau, Inc.

Price, W. 1971. *The Japanese Miracle and Peril.* New York: The John Day Company.

Promyslov, B. 1973. "The World's Large Cities." *CDSP* 25(2):6–7. Translated from *Izvestiia* (January 6):2.

Pryde, P. R. 1970. "Victors Are Not Judged." *Environment* 12(November):30–39.

Pryde, P. R. 1971. "Soviet Pesticides." *Environment* 13(November):16–24.

Pryde, P. R. 1972. *Conservation in the Soviet Union.* New York: Cambridge University Press.

Pryde, P. R. and L. T. Pryde. 1974. "Soviet Nuclear Power." *Environment* 16(3) (April):26–34.

Public Law 91-190 (42 U.S.C. 4321-4347). 1971. United States Code, Vol. 9, 1970 edition. Washington, D.C.: Government Printing Office.

Pusta, B. R. 1971. *The USSR Awakes to Its Environmental Problems.* Institute for the Study of the USSR, Analyses of Current Developments in the Soviet Union.

Rakhmatullaeva, M. D. 1971. "Nauchno-prakticheskaia konferentsiia po voprosam okhrany zdorov za sviazi s shirokim primeneniem pestitsidov v usloviiakh Uzbekistana." *Gigeniia i Sanitariia* 36(4):115–116.

Rathlesberger, J. 1972. *Nixon and the Environment: The Politics of Devastation.* New York: Taurus Communications.

Red Data Book. 1966. International Union for the Conservation of Nature and Natural Resources.

Reitze, Jr., A. W. and G. L. Reitze. 1974 "The Energy Supply Act." *Environment* (December).

Reitze, Jr., A. W. and G. L. Reitze. 1975. "Living With Lead." *Environment* (April-May).

Richardson, E. 1962. *The Politics of Conservation: Crusades and Controversies, 1897–1913.* Berkeley: University of California Press.

Ridgeway, J. 1973. *The Last Play: The Struggle to Monopolize the World's Energy Resources.* New York: E. P. Dutton & Co.

RIEP. 1970. *Environmental Protection in Tokyo.* The Tokyo Metropolitan Research Institute for Environmental Protection.

RIEP. 1972. *Environmental Protection Summary in Tokyo.* The Tokyo Metropolitan Research Institute for Environmental Protection.

Robinson, G. T. 1949. *Rural Russia under the Old Regime.* New York: The Macmillan Company.

Rocks, L. and R. P. Runyon. 1973. *The Energy Crisis.* New York: Crown Publishers.

Rosenbaum, W. A. 1973. *The Politics of Environmental Concern.* New York: Praeger Publishers.

Rosenberg, N. 1972. *Technology and American Economic Growth.* New York: Harper & Row.

Ross, R. D. 1968. *Industrial Waste Disposal.* New York: Van Nostrand Reinhold Company.

Ross, R. D. 1972. *Air Pollution and Industry.* New York: Van Nostrand Reinhold Company.

Rudd, R. L. 1966. *Pesticides and the Living Landscape.* Madison: University of Wisconsin Press.

Rukeyser, W. S. 1972. "Facts and Foam in the Row over Phosphates." *Fortune* 85(January):72–73.

Ryther, J. 1969. "Photosynthesis and Fish Production in the Sea." *Science* 166:72–76.

Sakharov, A. D. 1968. *Progress, Coexistence, and Intellectual Freedom.* New York: W. W. Norton & Company.

Sand, P. H. 1972. *Legal Systems for Environmental Protection: Japan, Sweden, and the United States* 4(May). Rome: FAO Legislative Studies.

Sansom, G. 1958–1964. *A History of Japan.* 3 Vols. London: The Cresset Press. Stanford, Cal.: Stanford University Press, 1958–1963.

SAPC. 1972. *Country Statement of Japan.* Second Asian Population Conference, Tokyo.

Sapozhnikov, N. I. 1970. "Speech to Supreme Soviet June 26." *CDSP* 22(26):4. Translated from *Turkmenskaia Iskra* (June 26):2.

Sarnoff, P. 1971. *The New York Times Encyclopedic Dictionary of the Environment.* New York: Quadrangle Books.

Sasayama, Y. 1969. "Japan's Lagging Standard of Living." *Japan Quarterly* 19(October-December).

Saushkin, Iu. G. 1964. "The Interaction of Nature and Society." *SGRT* 5(10)(December):39–44. Translated from *Geografiia v shkole* No. 4:10–13.

Saushkin, Iu. G. 1966. "Concerning a Certain Controversy." *SGRT* 7(2)(February):9–13. Translated from *Vestnik Moskovskogo Universiteta,* seriia geografiia No. 6(1965):79–82.

Schurr, S. H., ed. 1972. *Energy, Economic Growth and the Environment.* Baltimore: The Johns Hopkins University Press.

Schwartz, J. J. and W. Keech. 1968. "Group Influence and the Policy-Making Process in the Soviet Union." *American Political Science Review* 62(3)(September):840–851.

SE. Sovetskaia Estoniia.

Serova, O. and S. Sarkisian. 1961. *Zhemchuzhina vostochnoi Sibiri.* Ulan Ude: Buriatskoe knizhnoe izdatelstvo.

Seton-Watson, H. 1964. *The Decline of Imperial Russia, 1855–1914.* New York: Praeger Publishers.

SGRT. Soviet Geography: Review and Translation.

Shabad, T. 1969a. *Basic Industrial Resources of the U.S.S.R.* New York: Columbia University Press.

Shabad, T. 1969b. "The Changing Resource Policies of the USSR." *Focus* 19(6) (February):7–8.

Shabad, T. 1973. "Russia Reverses View on Lake Use." *New York Times* (May 20):15.

Shapiro, L. 1971. *The Communist Party of the Soviet Union.* New York: Vintage Books.

Sharov, A., A. Kochetkov, and F. Listengurt. 1973. "The Integrated Organization of Production and Population Distribution." *CDSP* 25(27):15–16. Translated from *Planovoe Khoziaistvo* (February):112–118.

Shea, K. P. 1973. "PCB." *Environment* (November).

Shelest, L. 1973. "Utilization of the USSR's Natural Resources." *CDSP* 25(49):5–6. Translated from *Voprosy Ekonomiki* (September):148–149.

Sherman, J. H. 1969. *The Soviet Economy.* Boston: Little, Brown and Company.

Shirokov, V. 1973. "Harnessed Air: Pneumatic Transport System Serving Sanitation." *CDSP* 25(18):21. Translated from *Pravda* (May 6):6.

Sholokhov, M. A. 1966. Speech to 23rd Party Congress CPSU, 1 April 1966. Pp. 354–362 in *XIII Sezd Kommunisticheskoi Partii Sovetskogo Soiuza, Stenograficheskii otchet.* Vol. 1. Moscow: Izdatelstvo politicheskoi literatury.

Shurcliff, W. A. 1970. *S/S/T and Sonic Boom Handbook.* New York: Ballatine Books.

Simcock, B. L. 1972. "Environmental Pollution and Citizen's Movement: The Social Sources and Significance of Anti-Pollution Protest in Japan." *Area Development in Japan: Japan's Environmental Problems.* Tokyo: Center for Area Development Research.

Simcock, B. L. 1974. "Environment Politics in Japan." Ph.D. dissertation. Cambridge, Mass.: Harvard University.

Simpson, D. 1968. "The Dimensions of World Poverty." *Scientific American* (November).

Singer, S. F., ed. 1970. *Global Effects of Environmental Pollution.* New York: Springer Verlag.

Skilling, H. G. and F. Griffiths, eds. 1971. *Interest Groups in Soviet Politics.* Princeton, N.J.: Princeton University Press.

Skolnikoff, E. B. 1972. A Technological World: Can the UN Meet the Challenge?" *Vista* (September-October).

SL. Soviet Life.

SMIC. 1971. *Inadvertent Climate Modification: Report of the Study of Man's Impact on Climate.* Cambridge, Mass.: The M.I.T. Press.

Smith, H. 1974. "Soviet Sensitive to an Oil Issue." *New York Times* (June 1):35.

Smith, W. E. and A. E. Smith. 1975. *Minamata: Words and Photographs.* New York: Holt, Rinehart and Winston.

Sochava, V. B. 1971. "Geography and Ecology." *SGRT* 12(5):277–291. Translated from *Materialy V sezda Geograficheskogo obshchestva SSSR,* Leningrad, 1970.

Solzhenitsyn, A. I. 1974. *Letter to the Soviet Leaders.* New York: Harper & Row.

Southwick, C. H. 1972. *Ecology and the Quality of Our Environment.* New York: Van Nostrand Reinhold Company.

Sprout, H. 1971. "The Environmental Crisis in the Context of American Politics." In L. L. Roos, Jr., ed., *The Politics of Ecosuicide.* New York: Holt, Rinehart and Winston.

Sprout, H. and M. Sprout. 1971. *Toward a Politics of the Planet Earth.* New York: Van Nostrand Reinhold Company.

Sprout, H. and M. Sprout. 1974. *Multiple Vulnerabilities: The Context of Environmental Repair and Protection.* Research Monograph No. 40. Princeton, N.J.: Center for International Studies.

SR. Sovetskaia Rossiia.

SRE. 1972. *Special Report Ecology* (November 20).

SSD. 1972–1973. *Soviet Statutes and Decisions.* Vol. 9. Entire issue devoted to publication of conservation and environmental legislation.

SSJM. Summaries of Selected Japanese Magazines. Tokyo: United States Embassy.

Stebelsky, I. 1972. "Perspective on the Rural Environmental Deterioration in the Russian Central Black Earth Region." Paper presented at the 1972 AAASS Meeting, Dallas, Texas, March 16.

Stebelsky, I. 1974. "Soviet Agricultural Land Resource Management, Policies, and Future Food Supply." Paper presented at the Conference on Soviet Resource Management and the Environment, University of Washington, Seattle, June 6.

Steinhart, C. E. and J. S. Steinhart. 1974. *Energy: Sources, Use, and Role in Human Affairs.* North Scituate, Mass.: Duxbury Press.

Stone, P. B. 1969. *Japan Surges Ahead: Japan's Economic Rebirth.* London: Weidenfeld and Nicholson.

Strahler, A. N. and A. H. Strahler. 1973. *Environment Geoscience: Interactions between Natural Systems and Man.* Santa Barbara, Cal.: Hamilton.

Strong, K. 1972. "Tanaka Shozo: Pioneer Against Pollution." *Japan Society of London Bulletin* (June).

Strongina, M. 1974. "The Social and Economic Problems of Urbanization." *CDSP* 26(31):13–14. Translated from *Voprosy Ekonomiki* (January):132–142.

Stunkel, K. R. 1973. "The Technological Solution." *Science and Public Affairs: Bulletin of the Atomic Scientists* (September).

Stunkel, K. R. 1974a. "Letter from Tokyo." *Far Eastern Economic Review* (October 18).

Stunkel, K. R. 1974b. "New Hope in Japan." *Environment* (October).

Sushkov, T. S. 1969. "Pravovaia okhrana prirody." *Sovetskoe Gosudarstvo i Pravo* (May).

Sushkov, T. S. 1972. "On the Draft of the Russian Republic Water Code." Speech to RSFSR Supreme Soviet. *CDSP* 24(27):5. Translated from *Sovetskaia Rossiia* (July 1):2.

SZ. Selskaia Zhizn.

Tachi, M. and M. Muramatsu, eds. 1971. Population Problems in the Pacific.

Symposium No. 1, the Eleventh Pacific Science Congress (1966), Tokyo.

Tadashi, S. 1967. "Japan's Economic Growth and Social Welfare." In *Social and Economic Aspects of Japan*. Tokyo.

Taeuber, I. 1951. "Population Growth and Economic Development in Japan." *Journal of Economic History* (Fall).

Taeuber, I. 1958. *The Population of Japan*. Princeton, N.J.: Princeton University Press.

Taeuber, I. 1960. "Japan's Demographic Transition Reexamined." *Population Studies* 14(July).

Taira, K. 1971. "Japan's Economic Relations with Asia." *Current History* 60(April).

Takahashi, K. 1970. "Mining the Riches of the Seabed." *Asia Scene* 15(July).

Tanaka, K. 1972. *Nihon Retto Kaizo-ron*. Tokyo: Nikkan Kogyo Shimbun-sha.

Tanaka, K. 1973. *Building a New Japan: A Plan for Remodeling the Japanese Archipelago*. Simul Press. A translation of Tanaka's book *Nihon Retto Kaizo-ron*.

Tansley, A. G. 1935. "The Use and Abuse of Vegetational Concepts and Terms." *Ecology* 16:284–307.

Taskin, G. A. 1954. "The Falling Level of the Caspian Sea in Relation to the Soviet Economy." *Geographical Review* 44(4)(October):508–527.

Thayer, N. B. 1969. *How the Conservatives Rule Japan*. Princeton, N.J.: Princeton University Press.

Timefeev-Resovskii, N. V. 1973. "Biosphere is 10 Times Richer Than We Think." *UNESCO Courier* 26(January):29–31.

TMG. 1971. *Tokyo Fights Pollution: An Urgent Appeal for Reform*. Tokyo Municipal Government.

TMG. 1972. *Planning of Tokyo, 1971*. Tokyo Metropolitan Government.

TMN. *Tokyo Municipal News.*

TMN. 1972. "White Paper on Small Business." *Tokyo Municipal News* (July).

Trezise, P. H. et al. 1974. *The Impact of Japan's Economic Growth on the World Economy in 1980*. Washington, D.C.: The Brookings Institution.

Trop, C. and L. L. Roos, Jr. 1971. "Public Opinion and the Environment." In L. L. Roos, Jr., ed., *The Politics of Ecosuicide*. New York: Holt, Rinehart and Winston.

Trump, G. G. 1974. "Public Eye on Pollution." *Environment* (December).

Trzyna, T. C., ed. 1973. *Directory of Consumer Protection and Environmental Agencies*. Orange, N.J.: Academic Media.

TsSU. 1971. *Narodnoe Khoziaistvo v 1970 g.: Statisticheskii ezhegodnik*. Moscow: Tsentralnoe staticheskoe upravlenie pri Sovete Ministrov SSSR.

TsSU. *Narodnoe Khoziaistvo v 1973 g.: Statisticheskii ezhegodnik*. Moscow: Tsentralnoe staticheskoe upravlenie pri Sovete Ministrov SSSR.

Tsunoda, R., T. De Bary, and D. Keene. 1958. *Sources of Japanese Tradition*. New York: Columbia University Press.

Udall, S. K. 1963. *The Quiet Crisis*. New York: Avon Books.

Ui, J. 1968. *Kogai no Seijigaku* (The Politics of Pollution). Tokyo: Sanseido.

Ui, J. 1972a. *Polluted Japan*. Reports by members of the Jishu-Koza Citizen's Movement. Tokyo.

Ui, J. 1972b. "The Singularities of Japanese Pollution." *Japan Quarterly* 19(July-September).

Ui, J. et al. 1970. "Environmental Pollution Control and Public Opinion." Unpublished paper. Tokyo.

Ui, J. and S. Kitamura. 1971. "Mercury Pollution of Sea and Fresh Water: Its

Accumulation into Water Biomass." *Journal of the Faculty of Engineering, University of Tokyo* (B)31(1).

UN Stat. Ybk. *United Nations Statistical Yearbook.* Statistical Office of the United Nations, New York, 1970–74.

UN. 1970a. *World Energy Supplies.* United Nations Statistical Papers, Series J. No. 13. New York.

UN. 1970b. *World Population Prospects, 1965–2000, as Assessed in 1968.* New York: United Nations Publication.

UN. 1971. *Everyman's United Nations.* New York: United Nations Publication.

USDC. *U.S.S.R. Literature on Air Pollution and Related Occupational Diseases: A Survey.* 1960–1968. Vols. 1–18. Springfield. Va.: U.S. Department of Commerce.

USDC. 1970. *Radiation Safety Standards, 1969.* Springfield, Va.: U.S. Department of Commerce.

USDI. Mineral Yearbooks. 1969–1972. United States Department of the Interior, Bureau of Mines. Vol. 3. Area Reports: International. Washington, D.C.: Government Printing Office.

USDI. 1970. *The Economics of Clean Water.* U.S. Department of the Interior, Federal Water Pollution Control Administration.

USEPA. Air Pollution Abstracts. Environmental Protection Agency, Office of Air Programs. Washington, D.C.: Government Printing Office.

USEPA. 1971a. *Community Noise.* Environmental Protection Agency. Washington, D.C.: Government Printing Office.

USEPA. 1971b. *The Economics of Clean Air.* Environmental Protection Agency. Washington, D.C.: Government Printing Office.

USEPA. 1972. *A Progress Report: December 1970–June 1972.* Environmental Protection Agency. Washington, D.C.: Government Printing Office.

USEPA. 1973. *The Quality of Life Concept: A Potential Tool for Decision Makers.* Environmental Protection Agency. Washington, D.C.: Grovernment Printing Office.

Utton, A. and D. Henning. 1973. *Environmental Policy: Concepts and International Implications.* New York: Praeger Publishers.

Uyehara, G. E. 1910. *The Political Development of Japan, 1867–1909.* London.

Van Zandt, H. 1970. "Japanese Culture and the Business Boom." *Foreign Affairs* (January).

Vasin, M. 1975. "Combating Noise." *CDSP* 27(10):21. Translated from *Pravda* 12(March).

Vendrov, S. L., G. G. Gangardt, S. Iu. Geller, L. V. Korenistov, and G. L. Sarukhanov. 1964. "The Problem of Transformation and Utilization of the Water Resources of the Volga River and the Caspian Sea." Fourth Congress of the Geographical Society, Physical Geography Symposium; *SGRT* 5(7)(September):23–34.

Venturi, F. 1960. *Roots of the Revolution.* New York: Grosset & Dunlap.

VF. *Voprosy Filosofii.*

Vitt, M. 1970. "Ob ekonomicheskikh stimulakh ratsionalnogo ispolzovaniia prirodnykh resursov." *Planovoe Khoziaiatvo* (July).

Vogel, E. F. 1971. *Japan's New Middle Class.* Berkeley: University of California Press.

Volgyes, I., ed. 1974. *Environmental Deterioration in the Soviet Union and in Eastern Europe.* New York: Praeger Publishers.

Volkov, O. 1966a. "The Days Slip By." *CDSP* 18(23)(June 29):46–47. Translated from *Literaturnaia Gazeta* (June 2):2–3.

Volkov, O. 1966b. "A Trip to Baikal." *CDSP* 18(5)(February 23):14–15. Translated from *Literaturnaia Gazeta* (January 29):1–2.

Volkov, O. 1967. "Lessons of Lake Baikal." *CDSP* 19(48)(December 20):6–8. Translated from *Literaturnaia Gazeta* (October 11):12.

Voltorski, B. 1971. "Ukraine's Nationwide Movement to Protect Its Natural Resources." Interview. *UNESCO Courier* 24:26–29.

Von Laue, T. 1964. *Why Lenin? Why Stalin?* Philadelphia: J. P. Lippincott Company.

VVS. Vestnik Verkhovnogo Soveta.

Wallace, A. F. 1956. "Revitalization Movements." *American Anthropologist* 58.

Ward, B. 1962. *The Rich Nations and the Poor Nations.* New York: W. W. Norton & Company.

Ward, B. 1966. *Spaceship Earth.* New York: Columbia University Press.

Ward, B. 1968. *The Lopsided World.* New York: W. W. Norton & Company.

Ward, B. and R. Dubos. 1972. *Only One Earth: The Care and Maintenance of a Small Planet.* New York: W. W. Norton & Company.

Ward, B., J. Runnalls, and L. d'Anjou, eds. 1971. *The Widening Gap: Development in the 1970's.* New York: Columbia University Press.

Watanabe, M. 1974. "The Conception of Nature in Japanese Culture." *Science* 183(4122)279.

WEIS. 1975. *Economic Information File: Japan.* Tokyo: World Economic Informations Services.

Wideman, B. 1974. "Okinawa: Progress with Conflict." *Far Eastern Economic Review* (April 22).

Wilson, D. L. 1972. "The Charity Profiteers." *Far Eastern Economic Review* (April 15).

Wilson, D. L. and W. H. Matthews, eds. 1970. *Man's Impact on the Global Environment: Assessment and Recommendations.* Cambridge, Mass.: The M.I.T. Press.

World Food Problem, The. 3 Vols. Washington D.C.

Wu. Y. and W. Clemente, II, eds. 1971. *Environment and/or Development in Asia.* Ann Arbor: University of Michigan Press.

Yamamura, K. 1967. *Economic Policy in Postwar Japan.* Berkeley: University of California Press.

Yanaga, C. 1968. *Economic Policy in Postwar Japan.* Berkeley: University of California Press.

Yanaga, C. 1968. *Big Business in Japanese Politics.* New Haven, Conn.: Yale University Press.

Yanagisawa, N. 1972. "Birds in Japan." *Japan Illustrated* 10(4)(Autumn).

Yoshimura, T. 1974. "Characteristics of Diet Operation in Japan." *Japan Times* (October 2).

Zhakov, Z. O. 1964. "The Long-Term Transformation of Nature and Changes in the Atmospheric Moisture Supply of the European Part of the USSR." *SGRT* (March):52–60. Translated from *Vestnik Moskovskogo Universiteta,* seriia geografiia No. 1:37–43.

Zhirkov, K. F. 1964. "Dust Storms in the Steppes of Western Siberia and Kazakhstan." *SGRT* (May):33–41. Translated from *Izvestiia Akademii Nauk SSSR,* seriia geograficheskaia No. 6(1963):50–55.

Zum Brunnen, C. 1973. "The Geography of Water Pollution of the Soviet Union." Ph.D. dissertation, University of California at Berkeley.

Zwick, D. 1971. *Water Wasteland.* New York: Grossman Publishers.

Zykova, A. S., E. L. Telushkina, V. P. Rublevskii, G. P. Efremova, and G. A. Kuznetsova. 1970. "Soderzhanie iskusstvennykh radioaktivnykh izotopov v atmosfernom vozdukhe Moskvy v 1962–1967 gg." *Gigiena i Sanitariia,* No. 4.

MAPS

FIGURE 1. UNITED STATES OF AMERICA: ENVIRONMENTAL TROUBLE SPOTS.

FIGURE 2. UNION OF SOVIET SOCIALIST REPUBLICS: ENVIRONMENTAL TROUBLE SPOTS.

[SOURCES: **Air pollution:** (1) M. Ye. Berlyand, "The Climatological Aspects of Investigation of Atmospheric Contamination with Atmospheric Wastes," in M. Budyko et al., eds., *Modern Problems of Climatology* (Wright-Patterson Air Force Base, Ohio: Foreign Technology Division, 1967), p. 310, cited in Victor L. Mote, "Air Pollution in the USSR," in Ivan Volgyes, ed., *Environmental Deterioration in the Soviet Union and Eastern Europe*, New York: Praeger Publishers, 1974, p. 44. (2) Victor L. Mote, "Geography of Air Pollution in the USSR," Ph.D. dissertation, University of Washington, 1971. **Water pollution:** basic information provided by Philip R. Pryde, *Conservation in the Soviet Union*, New York: Cambridge University Press, 1972, pp. 140–141.]

FIGURES 3 AND 4. JAPAN: ENVIRONMENTAL TROUBLE SPOTS, PAST AND PRESENT.

Pre-World War II: Pre-Meiji (1603–1868): Osaka and Tokyo (Edo); Meiji and post-Meiji (1868–1945): Osaka, Tokyo, Kawasaki, Yokohama, Gifu. Tochigi Pref. (Ashio Copper Mine); Tokushima Pref., northern Shikoku, and Niihama Island (Besshi Mining Co.). *Post-World War II* (1945–present): **Air pollution:** Fukuoka Pref.; Kawasaki; Kobe; Nagoya; Tsushima, Nagasaki Pref.; Yokkaichi, Mie Pref.; Yokohama; Tokyo. **Cadmium:** Jinzu River, Toyama Pref.; Kamioka, Gifu Pref.; Kurobe, Toyama Pref.; Tagonoura Port, Fuji City; Tomakomai, Hokkaido Pref.; Tsushima, Nagasaki moto Pref. **Water Pollution:** Ariake Bay, Kumamoto Pref.; Fukuoka Pref.; Inland Sea; Ise Bay, Mie Pref.; Iyomishima, Ehime Pref.; Lake Biwa, Kyoto Pref.; Shizuoka Pref.; Tagonoura Port, Fuji City; Tomakomani, Hokkaido Pref.; Tsushima, Nagasaki Pref.; Tsushima Island; Yodo River, Kyoto and Osaka prefs.; Tokyo Bay.

[SOURCE: Office of Population Research, Princeton University.]

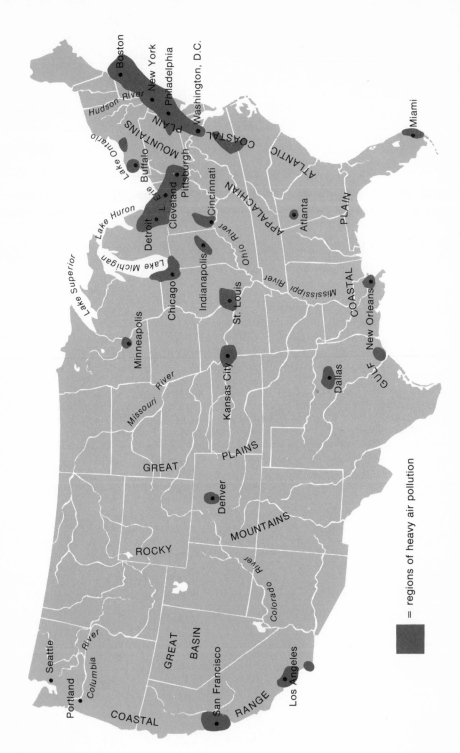

= regions of heavy air pollution

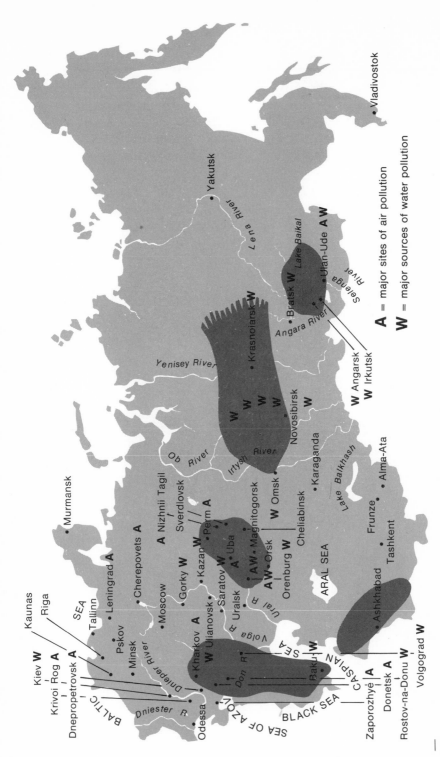

A = major sites of air pollution

W = major sources of water pollution

Vladivostok

Yakutsk

Lena River

Ulan-Ude **A W**

Bratsk **W**   Lake Baikal

Selenga River

Krasnoiarsk **W**

Angara River

W Angarsk
W Irkutsk

Yenisey River

W   **W**   **W**

Novosibirsk

W

Ob River

Irtysh River

Omsk

Karaganda

Lake Balkhash

Murmansk

Cherepovets **A**

Nizhnii Tagil

A   Sverdlovsk

Perm **A**

Magnitogorsk

A W   Uba

Orsk

A   **A W**

Kazan **W**   Saratov **W**   **A W**   Orenburg **W**

Cheliabinsk

Frunze

Alma-Ata

Tashkent

ARAL SEA

Ashkhabad

Leningrad **A**

Gorky **W**

Moscow

Pskov

Kaunas

Riga

Tallinn

SEA

Minsk

Kharkov **A**

Ulianovsk

W Uralsk

Ural R.

Volga R.

Kiev **W**

Krivoi Rog **A**

Dnepropetrovsk **A**

Zaporozhye **A**

Donetsk **A**

Rostov-na-Donu **W**

Volgograd **W**

Baku **W**

Dnieper River

Dniester R.

Odessa

Don R.

SEA OF AZOV

BLACK SEA

CASPIAN SEA

BALTIC

| 325

PREFECTURES

REGIONS AND MAJOR CITIES

HOKKAIDO

Sapporo •
• Tomakomai

• Mutsu

TOHOKU

SEA

JAPAN

SADO

• Sendai

Kurobe
Kamioka
Gifu

• Niigata

Lake Biwa
Kyoto
Osaka
Kobe

• Ashio

Tokyo
Tokyo Bay

HOKURIKU

TOSAN

KANTO

Kawasaki
Yokohama
Sagami Bay

TSUSHIMA
Fukuoka
Kitakyushu

CHUGOKU

Fuji City
Tagonoura Port
Suruga Bay

Hiroshima •

KINKI

TOKAI

Ariake Bay

Nagoya

SHIKOKU

Iyomishima

Ise Bay

Minamata •

Niihama

Yokkaichi

INLAND SEA

KYUSHU

OCEAN

PACIFIC

Shibushi Bay

OSUMI PENINSULA

| 327

INDEX